Triumph III
PHILADELPHIA TERMINAL   1838 - 2000

by David W. Messer

"Books that make a Difference"

COPYRIGHT © 2000 BARNARD, ROBERTS AND CO., INC.
Manufactured in the United States of America

FIRST EDITION September 2000

All Worldwide rights reserved. No part of this book may be produced in any manner without permission in writing, except in the case of critical reviews.

Published by
BARNARD, ROBERTS AND CO., INC.
2606 Willow Avenue
P.O. Box 7344
Baltimore MD 21227
(410) 247-2242

Library of Congress Catalog Card No. 00-091378
ISBN 0-934118-25-6

FRONTISPIECE: The first bridge across the Schuylkill River into Philadelphia exclusively for railroad use is depicted here as it appeared on 18 October 1890. Artist D. J. Kennedy, who made this captivating drawing, would have been standing on the old Market Street Bridge farther south, which was rebuilt in 1850 to carry horse-drawn railroad cars of the Philadelphia & Columbia RR as well as stagecoaches, wagons and pedestrians. The new iron bridge shown here was designed and constructed in 1880 by Wilson Brothers, noted Philadelphia architects and engineers, as part of the Filbert Street Extension into the new Broad Street Station. At left is the old PRR Grain Depot, to the right of that are the stockyard pens and just visible over the bridge to the left of center is the exotic Abattoir. The bridge and connecting viaduct enabled PRR to make a grand re-entrance to its own terminal in the growing business district of Center City Philadelphia. *Ted Xaras Collection*

COVER: If there is one facility that epitomizes PRR's devotion to superb civil engineering and operational excellence, it is ZOO interlocking. We will venture that ZOO is the best-known interlocking in all of railroading, efficiently handling incredible traffic volume. The original photograph of this scene appears on page 90 in black-and-white. We added color to the scene for the cover illustration, deliberately leaving the trackage in black for clarity and contrast.

A NOTE ABOUT CREDITS: Lack of credits indicate that the subject came from the camera or collection of the author, the library of the publisher or from untraceable sources. Some material obviously originated with the railroad (e.g. track charts) so credits were not used in these cases.

Dedication

Almost unique among nations, the United States very early on created capitals separated by over two hundred miles. New York became the commercial and financial center of gravity and Washington DC the political counterpart. The struggle for supremacy began over two centuries ago and continues to this day, probably to the ultimate benefit of the nation and, indeed, the world.

Philadelphia had a brief period of glory but quickly became an also-ran in both categories shortly after the Revolutionary War.

With one glaring exception, however.

Philadelphia became the Citadel of Railroading thanks to PRR. PRR began as a late-starter and nonentity, but by 1874 was supreme and remained so, sometimes rather fitfully, until the breakup of Conrail in 1999. And Philadelphia was its home in every sense of the word.

Ah, Philadelphia. The city that produced several notable expressions imbedded in our language. "The Philadelphia Lawyer," a synonym for slickness and not meant as a compliment. "The Philadelphia Engineering Firm," a euphemism for brutal strikebreaking. And, of course, "The Chinese Wall." The supposed barrier to conflicts of interest. The phrase was taken from the real Wall that formed the approach to Broad Street Station. The real Wall had many holes in it. So does the concept, with as many apertures as Swiss cheese.

And then there was "Broad Street."

In railroading, for well over a century the question always was "'What is Broad Street going to do?"

Father was "in the throne room," as he expressed it, of B&O's Traffic Department, as was his father before him. In the 1950s we were riding home together on a B&O commuter (passing, incidentally, within a hundred yards of the offices of this house) when he said, "Well, Butch, I've ruined my career again." It seems that some big issue was under discussion and someone asked, as usual, "What is Broad Street going to do?" Father blew his cork and said, "To hell with Broad Street. Let them worry about *we're* going to do!"

They all looked at him as if he had lost his mind.

The incident typified the raw power of PRR, exercised with singleminded arrogance and awesome impact whether right or wrong. We remain wryly amused that this monolith was in the City of Brotherly Love awash with Quaker abhorrence of conflict.

So we think it is very appropriate to dedicate this book to the secular temple of railroading, Broad Street.

Not the station. The Icon.

Charles Swann Roberts
30 March 2000

Table of Contents

Chapter 1	PRR Comes Home	8
Chapter 2	Northern Connections	107
Chapter 3	The Golden Arm	160
Chapter 4	The Big Gamble	208
Chapter 5	Tidewater Saga	284
Chapter 6	Southern Conflict and Connections	314
Chapter 7	Decline and Fall and Remembrance	340
Chapter 8	Triumph in Color	353
Chapter 9	Reflections	385

Introduction

It became readily apparent when beginning work on *Triumph II*, the previous volume in this series (covering the PRR Philadelphia Division), that the Philadelphia *Terminal* Division warranted a volume by itself to do it justice. If the Philadelphia Division has a dual personality i.e. separate lines that predominantly handle passenger and freight traffic, the Philadelphia Terminal Division has a personality that is both diverse and complex. It encompasses four-track mains that simultaneously handle through freights, crack passenger trains and local commuter runs – city terminals with a history that could easily become a volume unto itself – numerous yards and short branches serving industrial sidings – in-the-street trackage serving various port facilities – and finally the single-track line that threaded its way up the Schuylkill Valley to iron and steel plants and remote anthracite fields far from the bustle of Philadelphia.

In addressing this diversity we have teased apart various lines into separate chapters to allow closer examination and facilitate a more organized presentation, while at the same time keeping in mind the complex interrelationships among them. Thus Chapter 1 provides a look at the fascinating saga of PRR's lengthy (and ultimately triumphant) efforts to find the ideal locations for its stations and yard facilities serving its home City of Philadelphia. Chapter 2 looks at the short but critical Connecting Railway, which provided a link to enable access to New York City as well as a backbone for several industrial and commuter branches. Chapter 3 examines the remarkable development of *the* Main Line, PRR's legendary crown jewel. Chapter 4 considers the problematic Schuylkill Division (later Branch). Chapter 5 focuses on the West Philadelphia Elevated Line and the Delaware Extension serving the all-important port facilities. Chapter 6 looks at the Junction RR and the complex and sometimes bizarre interrelationships with the Reading, the Philadelphia, Wilmington & Baltimore RR and the Baltimore & Ohio that the line engendered. Finally, Chapter 7 relates a tale of decline and ultimate resurgence, albeit under new dominion.

Unlike the two previous volumes in the *Triumph* series, which deal with primarily *linear* railroad lines, this volume is faced with a series of relatively short sections that either radiate out from Philadelphia itself, or intertwine around it. We have tried to maintain the format of the other volumes, i.e. moving along each section and examining significant developments over time at each point. We have looked at the progression of early (pre-Broad Street Station) Philadelphia depots in chronological order, but interestingly this turns out to be essentially a linear phenomenon, for reasons we will discuss. Dealing with the newer ones by location results in a few aberrations, (i.e. considering Suburban Station before the facility in West Philadelphia as we move westward from Broad Street Station) but the alternative was jumping all around the city just to conform with the complex chronology. Actually we provide an overview near the beginning of the volume that does just that, with a series of maps to make it easier to grasp.

As always, we were forced to omit material in order to focus primarily on the mainline and major branches. Thus we have not dealt with the Octoraro, West Chester, Newtown Square and Philadelphia & Chester Branches extending primarily southwest of the city or many of the short industrial lines branching off the Connecting Railway. Nor have we considered the Delaware River ferries, a fascinating story unto itself. Perhaps these can be presented in a subsequent volume.

These concerns aside, we feel this volume captures the extraordinary richness that both the diversity and complexity bring to PRR's marvelous headquarters domain.

David W. Messer
15 April 1999

Chapter 1
PRR Comes Home

PRR In Philadelphia

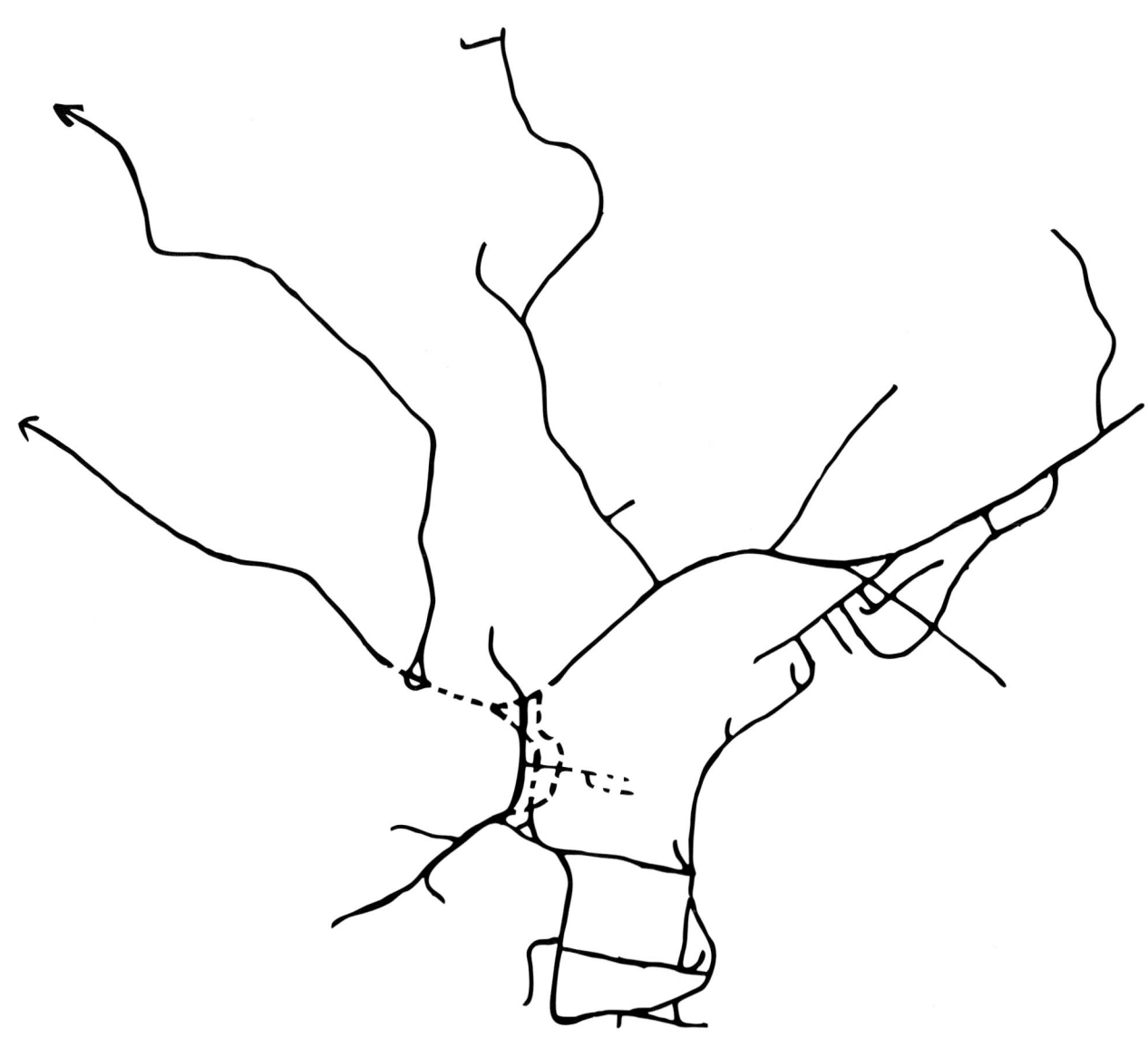

PRR COMES HOME

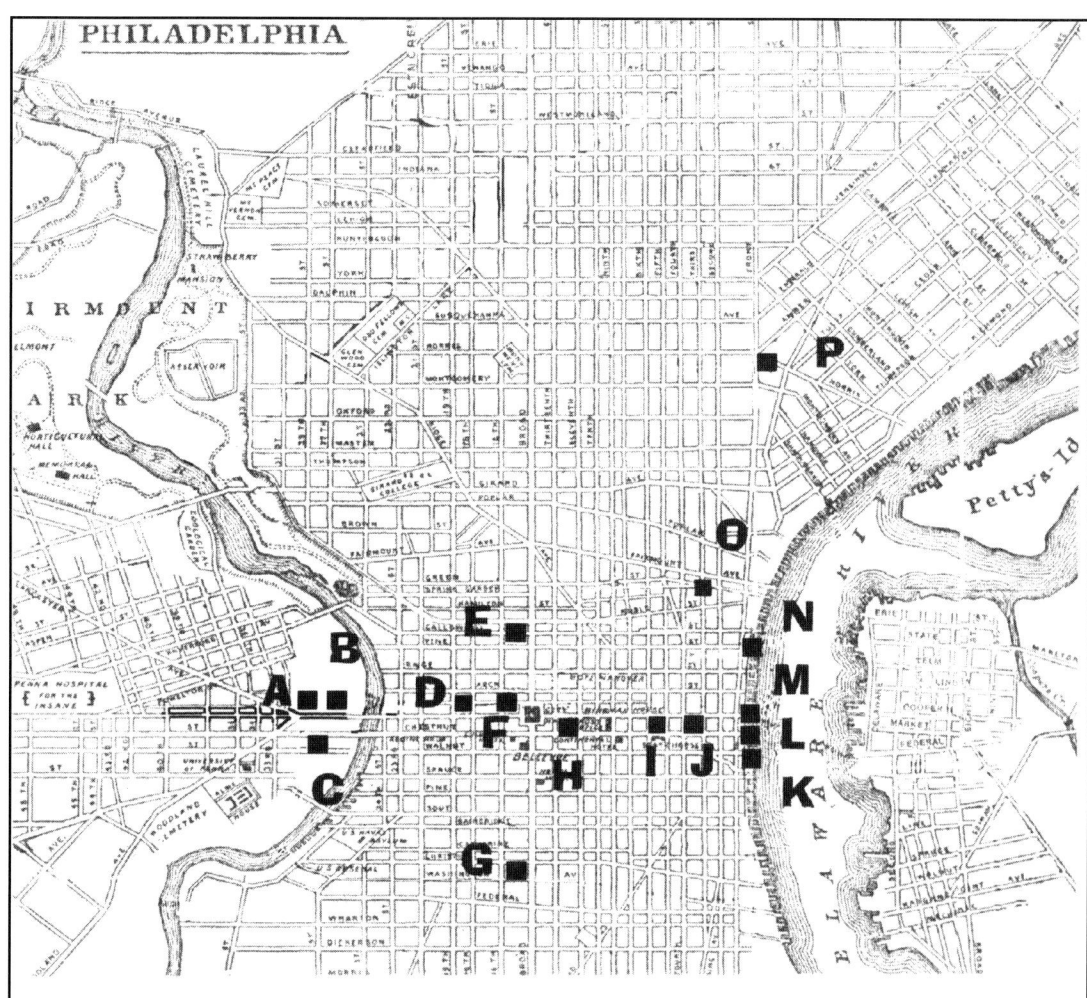

Key	Location	Railroad	Years in Use
A	32nd and Market	Pennsylvania	1876-1881
B	31st and Market	Pennsylvania	1864-1876
C	31st and Chestnut	West Chester & Philadelphia	1866-1881
D	18th & Market	Pennsylvania	circa 1850s
		West Chester & Philadelphia	ca. 1850s-1866
E	Broad and Vine	Philadelphia & Columbia	1834-ca. 1850
F	Broad and Market	Pennsylvania	1881-1952
G	Broad and Washington	Philadelphia Wilmington & Baltimore	1852-1881
H	11th and Market	Phila. Wilm. & Balti.	1843-1852
		Pennsylvania	1853-1864
I	8th and Market	Pennsylvania	ca. 1850-1853
J	368 Market St.	Phila. Wilm. & Balti.	circa 1840s
K	Walnut Street Wharf	Camden & Amboy	circa 1860s
L	Chestnut Street Wharf	Camden & Amboy	ca. 1840s-50s
M	Market Street Wharf	Pennsylvania	ca. 1870s-1952
N	Vine Street Wharf	West Jersey/Camden & Atlantic	ca. 1860s-70s
O	3rd and Willow	Philadelphia & Trenton	ca 1840s-50s
P	Front and Norris	Philadelphia & Trenton	1834-ca. 1920s

John H. Hepp, IV

(Caption for artwork on previous page)

THE SAGA of railroad passenger stations serving PRR's home city of Philadelphia is a fascinating one, and in fact a study in itself. This diagram shows the locations of all main passenger stations used by PRR and its component railroads in Center City from 1832 up to the advent of today's 30th Street and Suburban stations. (The Reading had its own story in Philadelphia, and we will touch on it in passing as it related to PRR, but it is a complex story in its own right, outside the purview of these volumes.) Although there were reasons why the stations were located where they were and when they were by the individual railroads, one can make a case - which is reflected in the railroad's own record from its earliest years - that PRR really couldn't make up its collective mind where the best location(s) were for its passenger facilities in the City. As early as 1852 it debated the best location for a depot, i.e. West Philadelphia vs. "east of the Schuylkill" for both freight and passenger service, weighing the convenience of the Center City location against the inconvenience and delays associated with the conveyance of goods and passengers through the crowded streets. Two points of agreement that seemed to evolve over time: 1) That the Center City area should be approached from the west, and 2) that the station(s) should be located somewhere along the east-west Market Street axis. The problem then became one of finding the optimum solution given these initial constraints (and others, over time). PRR would go on to experiment with various locations - and combinations of locations - for over 100 years, until finally arriving at the right combination by the third decade of the 20th Century. We will examine the chronological sequence as well as some of the myriad of forces determining the station locations as we begin our exploration of this complex story of PRR in its home city.

By 1 November 1855 the Pennsylvania Railroad, heavily financed by Philadelphia interests, was declared "complete" from Harrisburg west to Pittsburgh. This was largely because of the expertise, dedication and total commitment of its Chief Engineer and later President John Edgar Thomson (see *Triumph II* for a biography of this giant of the railroad industry as well as the history of the Philadelphia & Columbia RR). But it didn't enter the City of Brotherly Love on its own rails and was forced to utilize the Harrisburg & Lancaster between these two towns – and worse – the state-owned and poorly-maintained P&C eastward to the banks of the Schuylkill River in West Philadelphia.

Individual transportation companies operated their own freight and passenger cars over the line and maintained their own stations and offices in Philadelphia. Because of a City Ordinance prohibiting steam engines within the business district, cars would be separated from their locomotives in West Philadelphia and pulled by teams of horses or mules across the Market Street Bridge on the tracks of the City-owned railroad. This bridge was an imposing three-arch covered structure, which had been rebuilt in 1850 to accommodate the tracks after the Columbia Railroad sold the original Belmont Plane route and transferred to the West Philadelphia Railroad right of way. The City tracks proceeded eastward on Market Street to Second and Third Streets, and then turned southward to Dock Street and the Delaware River. This line also connected with trackage running south along Broad Street that served warehouses, coal yards and other customers in what was then an industrial district.

An interesting pattern can be discerned regarding the location of the various railroad depots in Philadelphia over time. In the initial years, in the 1830s and 1840s, the early railroad lines generally located their small stations on the edges of the main settled area (refer to figures for details), using carriages and later omnibus service for local transport. Later, in the 1850s through the 70s the depots – now larger, with separate waiting rooms and train sheds – were located a bit farther from the growing business district. This came about largely as a result of increasing property values and the prohibition of steam locomotives; the new locations allowed trains to originate with steam power rather than a time-consuming changeover. The newly developed horse-drawn streetcars (the West Philadelphia Passenger Railway opened on Market Street in 1858), which made these locations practical, were utilized to convey passengers to their final destination within the City. In the latter years of this period, there also began to be a separation of passenger and freight facilities, largely for safety reasons.

Finally, with PRR's acquisition of several competing lines and the construction of Broad Street Station in 1881 and the subsequent building of B&O's station in 1887 and the Reading Terminal in 1893, the three major railroads developed consolidated passenger facilities located within a burgeoning Center City. Thus we have PRR, as it developed and prospered, moving its passenger stations steadily westward along Market Street in the 1850s, jumping to West Philadelphia in 1864 and then swaggering back into Center City with the opening of Broad Street Station in 1881.

Even though PRR initially had no direct track connection it had an early presence in the City. It first used a depot at 8th and Market Streets in 1850, and also utilized the Bingham & Dock facility at 18th and

Market, which PRR shared with the West Chester & Philadelphia. It subsequently leased the former Philadelphia, Wilmington & Baltimore property at 11th and Market and moved its passenger depot there on 20 May 1854. In 1853 PRR purchased property at 13th and Market Streets (in later years the site of another Philadelphia tradition, the wondrous John Wanamaker department store) and opened a freight office. The following year it completed an extensive freight depot there as well, said to be the largest of its kind in the U.S. at the time.

Moving freight and passenger cars over the City railroad to the P & C terminus in West Philadelphia was an arduous process. The tolls were high and the tracks were generally in a bad state of repair, although they were widened in 1858 to allow a 6-ft. clearance from 10th to Broad Street and relaid with wrought iron rails in 1862. Delays were frequent along increasingly congested Market Street - one can easily envision 19th century grid-lock! Not only had PRR arrived at its home port late, but over trackage of three other railroads and under decidedly adverse conditions.

By 1858, with its westward connections established, PRR was, according to the assessment of Burgess and Kennedy,

> "In position to solicit traffic for the city and port of Philadelphia from all over the northern Middle West, except for the fact that the port and terminal facilities were utterly inadequate to handle it. And of course, since the rail-water terminals were inadequate and the land-borne traffic did not come into Philadelphia, neither did the ships. Philadelphia had once led all the cities of the country in the volume of her water-borne commerce, but she had now sunk to a poor second. It could not have been expected that Philadelphia would have outranked New York for long, for the latter had too many natural advantages, and, most importantly, she had the Erie Canal for many years before any other port had comparable access to the interior. Nevertheless, it seems clear that Philadelphia as a port never took full advantage of the potential provided by its wealth of manufactures and its productive hinterland. It seems curious that the State did not promote or provide an adequate outlet to tidewater in connection with its elaborate transportation system for bringing traffic to Philadelphia [i.e. the State Works], but the fact is that it provided very little in the way of terminal facilities of any kind . . . The Pennsylvania Railroad owed great loyalty to Philadelphia, but it could neither pay its debt nor take advantage of its own opportunities till the city had been provided with modern port facilities."

It took a while for PRR to gain direct access to Philadelphia, and longer still to develop an infrastructure of passenger and freight stations, storage and unloading facilities as well as the trackage to serve them, but Thomson and his successors were not about to let this end of the line languish. Thomson's General Superintendent Herman Haupt noted pointedly in 1852 that, "a prime objective in the construction of the Pennsylvania Railroad was the promotion of the mercantile interests of Philadelphia . . . I have never yet been able to perceive that the mercantile interests of Philadelphia, and the pecuniary interests of the stockholders, were incompatible with each other."

Once launched, PRR moved into Philadelphia and steadily increased its presence until by the turn of the century it came to surround and almost literally envelop the city area (As of 1903 it had 450 track miles within the City limits, about the same as the distance from Philadelphia to Pittsburgh). To its customers and rail competitors in the area (primarily Reading and B&O) alike, it became a formidable presence.

Another critical step in the ability of Philadelphia to function as a major East Coast city was the construction of the Junction Railroad. PRR had existing connections with the Philadelphia & Reading and the Philadelphia, Wilmington & Baltimore by means of City-owned trackage in the streets (the PW&B built a passenger and freight station at Broad St. and Washington Ave. in 1852), but as north-south traffic increased this arrangement became increasingly unsatisfactory. Conferences were held among these three roads, and approval was granted by the Legislature for the "Junction Railroad Company," with ownership divided equally among them.

This was a new line on the west bank of the Schuylkill River, running from a connection with the Reading at Belmont (the location of the original P&C route) south along the PRR a short distance to near 35th Street and then continuing southward to a connection with the PW&B near Gray's Ferry. The northern portion, from 35th St. to Belmont, was completed and put in operation 23 November 1863, and the southern portion, from Market Street to Gray's Ferry, was opened 1 July 1866. This latter section included construction of a tunnel under 32nd Street from Market to Walnut Street.

This short (3-mile) but critical link allowed interchange among the three railroads – and a critical north-south route outside of the congested downtown area. The construction of this link was opposed by the City, as it realized a loss of traffic would reduce revenue on its own trackage. Shortly after completion of the Junction RR, it faced the inevitable and decided to remove the tracks along Broad Street between Vine and Market, and in 1868-9 from Market to Washington Avenue, as well as on Market east to the Delaware River.

In later years the stock owned by the other railroads was purchased by PRR, and the Junction Railroad became an integral part of the system (but not before it became an pivotal issue in the colossal struggle over a strategic north-south route between New York and Washington – see Chapter 6).

These improvements, and others to come, still did not allow Philadelphia to overtake New York as an eastern port, but they were a significant advance that allowed PRR to function in its intended role, particularly with the demands of increased Civil War traffic.

During this time PRR made several improvements to station facilities all along the railroad to meet this demand. A major advance in 1864 was the construction of a new passenger station at 30th and Market in West Philadelphia. This was the first of four stations west of the Schuylkill River near the site of the current 30th Street Station.

The 1864 station was typical of the enlarged depots constructed during this period, with the main building or "headhouse" in front and mostly wooden trainsheds extending behind. It consisted of two tracks for east-west trains to Harrisburg and Pittsburgh. To the west was a second, "New York Depot," built in 1867 (also with two tracks) for trains to Trenton and Jersey City, via the Connecting Railway (see Chapter 2). A wooden walkway connected to a single platform for through trains from Jersey City to Washington, DC. This complex also included freight platforms, resulting in a potentially dangerous situation for passengers.

With the building of this station the depot at 11th and Market was abandoned, and horse-drawn passenger cars over the Market Street Bridge (and through city streets) were discontinued. PRR passenger trains did not again operate across the Schuylkill River until Broad Street Station was opened in 1881, and then over an elevated approach (we will explore this later in the chapter).

With the advent of the Connecting Railway to the north (connecting with the Philadelphia & Trenton) and the leasing of the United New Jersey Railways, providing access to New York City (to be discussed in a subsequent volume in this series) – and the approaching Centennial Exposition – PRR undertook a major program to upgrade its right-of-way, facilities and passenger equipment to handle the expected increase in traffic.

As part of the overall expansion project it enlarged the West Philadelphia yards starting in 1873. It also embarked on a long-term program to construct a four-track railroad from West Philadelphia to Paoli, at the end of the Main Line. The initial phase of this monumental undertaking, as far as Overbrook, was completed in 1874, and the section from Overbrook west to Merion was opened in early 1876, not coincidentally just in time for the Centennial Exposition traffic.

To handle this traffic a new West Philadelphia station was constructed at 32nd and Market and opened 6 May 1876, replacing the depots built in 1864-7. Costing nearly a quarter million dollars, it was the largest and most elaborate terminal built by PRR to that date. It boasted two train sheds, each 94 feet wide by 810 feet long spanning twelve tracks, an 80 x 100 ft. "gentlemen's" waiting room, a 50 x 100 ft. "ladies'" waiting room, a 50 x 100 ft. restaurant, "saloons and dressing rooms," ticket and baggage facilities, and company offices. PRR joined with the City in obviously wanting to impress its visitors from across the U.S. and around the world to the greatest extravaganza Philadelphia was to see in its long and colorful history.

It is not often that a railroad has the opportunity to participate in a world-class celebration, but in 1876, the 100th anniversary of the signing of the Declaration of Independence in Philadelphia, the City was host to the world. The Centennial Exposition, almost a city in itself, was located on the southern edge of Philadelphia's huge Fairmount Park, with convenient access (also not coincidental) from PRR's mainline in West Philadelphia.

The Centennial Exposition was held to celebrate the anniversary, to be sure, but its real purpose was to showcase the progress made in various fields of endeavor, particularly the great strides made by this country during the Industrial Revolution. The mighty Corliss Steam Engine, symbolic of U.S. industrial might, held its audience spellbound with its twin walking beams and giant flywheel inside the vast Machinery Hall.

The significance of this event was not lost on PRR. When the only way to get there from any distance overland was by train, the railroad took full advantage of the opportunity to show itself off to the traveling public. Despite depressed economic conditions following the Panic of 1873, PRR undertook several major projects to improve service to the anticipated large crowds. In addition to the expanded passenger station at 32nd and Market in West Philadelphia, a large (but temporary) depot was also built on the Centennial grounds in a confectionery architectural style (known as "stick" style) complementary with the main Exhibition buildings. It was located at the key intersection of Elm and Belmont Avenues. (We should note here that the Reading had to settle for a rather modest affair alongside its river line on the east side of the grounds.) The PRR edifice was served by a novel loop track arrangement allowing trains from either direction to enter the station and then proceed either way or enter a yard alongside the main tracks westward from the city.

These two facilities handled the enormous Centenial crowds. To give some idea of the volume, during the 6-month period between 10 May and 10 November 1876, the two locations handled 42,600 trains, nearly 270,000 cars and close to 5 million passengers, with no reported injuries. In addition, 730,000 pieces of luggage were handled, with only 26 pieces lost.

Clearly, the Centennial Exposition *was the place to be* in 1876, and PRR was *the* way to get there!

After the Exposition closed, the temporary depot was torn down and the area became the site of expanded freight and maintenance yards on property that had earlier been acquired by forward-looking management. In 1887 a freight station was built along Columbia Avenue, just west of the Centennial depot site. This facility was known as "52nd Street Transfer" even though it was located between 49th and 50th Streets, and replaced the earlier depot located farther east at Mantua Junction. This was served by remnants of the depot loop trackage. The vast piece of real estate between Belmont Avenue and 52nd Street was utilized to expand the West Philadelphia freight yards farther westward.

At the same time PRR constructed a small frame enginehouse at 46th Street. This was replaced with a brick roundhouse in 1902 (with a 75-ft turntable) and expanded in 1912 and again in 1918 as locomotives grew ever larger. This engine service facility continued to expand, and in 1930 a new and larger 26-stall roundhouse of brick and concrete construction was built, with a 110-ft. turntable, along with a massive 600-ton coal wharf and other buildings (see photo section for further discussion of these facilities).

Although these two passenger stations served the Centennial traffic well, it soon became apparent that the main depot at 32nd Street was too far from the burgeoning central business district and accompanying hotels. Accordingly, the decision was made in 1879 to embark upon a massive new project, the extension of the passenger line from West Philadelphia into the central business district to a new terminal at Broad and Filbert Streets, opposite the new City Hall at Centre Square. A three-track iron truss bridge on masonry piers was erected to cross the Schuylkill River, carrying trains from the north, west and south. Because the volume of traffic had increased to the point where grade crossings of city streets were no longer safe or acceptable, a high fill with brick retaining walls was constructed from Shock Street to 16th Street, a distance of 2042 feet. North-south streets passed through this structure, known as the Filbert Street Extension, by means of arched tunnel openings. The viaduct consisting of 60 brick arches extended half-way across the City – a full city block in width – to a new Broad Street Station.

The new passenger terminal was an imposing yet dignified brick edifice five stories high, designed by Wilson Brothers, noted Philadelphia architects and engineers, who had been responsible for the two largest buildings at the Centennial Exposition. The first floor was constructed of massive blocks of granite, and the upper floors were made of brick, with imposing Gothic spires symbolizing PRR's pre-eminence and celebrating its return to the Center City area. Ticket offices and baggage room were located on street level, with waiting rooms and dining facilities on the second floor at track level, reached by ascending a 16-ft. wide grand stairway.

A large double-arched train shed behind the station, covering eight passenger tracks with a 20-foot platform between each pair of tracks, extended between 15th and 16th Streets. The remainder of this block was a freight station of unique configuration. It was served by four tracks on the upper level, and hydraulic elevators moved freight between the track level platforms and the freight house along the street level.

The entire project, including property acquisition and the approach fill work from West Philadelphia, was completed and put into operation on 5 December 1881 at a cost of $4,272,000. With the completion of Broad Street Station, which replaced the previous main facility at 32nd and Market, PRR had "arrived," both literally and figuratively, in Center City Philadelphia. Broad Street became the Philadelphia station for PRR, and all trains to and from the city, including through trains, ran into the terminal. Some 200 of them daily coursed in and out of the station – the fastest and most luxurious being the newly-inaugurated all-Pullman *New York and Chicago Limited* (later the legendary *Pennsylvania Limited*), which made the New York-Chicago run in 25 hours, 40 minutes.

The facility was a notable departure from all previous PRR stations in the city, offering distinctive architecture and all the amenities for the traveler in an elegant, comfortable and safe environment, completely separating passenger from freight operations. For its patrons and the citizens of Philadelphia alike, Broad Street Station exemplified both the progressiveness of the growing railroad transportation industry and the solid conservatism of PRR.

It also, as John Hepp has pointed out, "radically altered the fabric of the city when it opened." Not only did it replace the PRR Centennial Station in West Philadelphia, but also the WC&P terminal there along with the PW&B station at Broad and Washington Streets. When it opened in 1881, Broad Street Station was actually at the western edge of the central business district; by 1890 the district had expanded westward to encompass it. Two other factors contributed to this expansion – John Wanamaker's transformation of PRR's old freight station at 13th and Market into his wondrous new retail emporium and the construction of the new Beaux Arts City Hall at Broad and Market. These actions dramatically shifted the city core from the old State House (Independence Hall) to Centre Square, and Broad Street Station was thus at the very heart of Center City Philadelphia at the dawn of the new century.

Interestingly, though, with the opening of Broad Street Station and the closing of Centennial Station, a depot was built in 1882 at Powelton Avenue and 32nd Street, again serving West Philadelphia and offering a small but significant recognition of this general area where the shops were located.

Because of steadily increasing through freight traffic into Philadelphia, the line known as the Trenton Cutoff (see *Triumph II*) was opened in 1892; this allowed through freight trains between New York and the west to bypass the city completely. This 45-mile line ran from a connection with the east-west mainline at Glen Loch (west of Paoli) to Morrisville, just south (west) of the bridge across the Delaware River at Trenton, New Jersey. This significantly reduced congestion in the Philadelphia area, especially in the West Philadelphia yards. Although the line was costly to build, PRR felt that the savings in time and distance for this important traffic were well worth it.

Almost as soon as it was opened, however, Broad Street Station began to experience growing pains. Not only was it in itself an attraction to draw passengers (which was obviously PRR's intent), a substantial increase in traffic occurred because of the transfer of Baltimore and Washington passengers from the PB&W station at Broad and Washington Streets. (PRR had assumed control of the line in March of 1881 – see Chapter 6 and also to be covered in more detail in a subsequent volume in the *Triumph* series) The completion of the Chestnut Hill and Schuylkill Branches to the north and west (see Chapters 2 and 4, respectively) also increased passenger traffic. By the summer of 1886 Broad Street Station was experiencing astounding traffic volumes of 1 million passengers per month – a long way from the horse-drawn commerce of only 40 years before. Memories of the Panic of 1884 were rapidly receding into the past and the resurgent post-Civil War economic boom, along with the crowds revisiting Philadelphia after the Centennial Exposition, were all having their salutary effect.

An interim solution was accomplished in 1889 by moving the freight station west to 17th and Market, widening the elevated portion to Market Street and utilizing the former freight tracks for passenger service. This helped, but it soon became apparent that both the station itself and the track capacity had to be increased still further. In 1892 PRR started promoting itself as "The Standard Railroad of America," and the following year celebrated its new status in its own pavilion at the World's Columbian Exposition in Chicago. It simply would not do to have an overcrowded terminal in its home city.

Thus PRR embarked on construction of a 10-story Victorian addition to Broad Street Station. Designed by noted Philadelphia architect Frank Furness with a massive tower dominating the northwest corner of Broad and Market, it left no doubt as to the identity of *the* predominant railroad in Philadelphia. A huge iron-framed, glass-covered trainshed was erected behind it, spanning the entire 306-foot distance between Market and Filbert Streets and running 595 feet westward. It was the largest single-span trainshed ever constructed in the world!

The new shed, soaring 108 feet high at its peak, was built over the original one (which it dwarfed) to minimize disruption of operations (not a small engineering feat in itself). The shed and accompanying expansion to 16 tracks were completed in November 1893, and the general offices of the railroad were moved from South 4th Street to the new building on 9 July 1894. PRR not only had an expanded station to serve the public ("America's Greatest Railway Terminal," as it was referred to in promotional literature), it had a new symbol of corporate presence in its home city.

The reader should be aware that urban railroad station architecture, particularly during the period of intense city construction in the late 19th Century, was a very visible manifestation of corporate image and rivalry with competitors. In PRR's case in Philadelphia it was of course primarily the Philadelphia & Reading Railroad. The Reading, as it was commonly known, had seen and taken note of the sudden increase in commuter business on PRR, its traditional rival in this endeavor, after the latter road opened Broad Street Station. At that point the Reading was utilizing three separate and increasingly inefficient terminals in the city. To replace them the Reading proposed a Y-shaped viaduct leading to a grand new terminal at 12th and Market. However, the Philadelphia City Council raised several objections to the project. Speculation arose at the time that PRR President George Roberts had a hand in promoting City objections to the project. All was fair in love, war and railroad competition!

After the three-year effort led by his predecessor (and J.P. Morgan ally) Austin Corbin failed, newly appointed president Archibald A. McLeod in 1890 set about to make Philadelphia's conservative citizens stand up and take notice of the Reading. Accordingly, he moved ahead aggressively to counter City objections to the project, and the road completed and opened its handsome Reading Terminal on 29 January 1893, just three blocks away and topping the original Broad Street station in size.

Not to be outdone, when the Reading first announced plans for its eight-story terminal, President Roberts was obligated to enlarge Broad Street Station that would result (not coincidentally) in an edifice even bigger and grander than the new Reading facility, a clear example of what has been called "architectural braggadocio."

In addition to the expansion of Broad Street Station itself, traffic flow on the approach trackage in West Philadelphia was improved by the construction of two tunnels. The first allowed New York trains to pass under the east-west mainline at 36th Street and Girard Avenue; the second allowed similar separation of Philadelphia-Washington traffic. These approaches were revised again in 1903, along with improved connections between the two lines to allow New York-Washington trains to bypass Broad Street Station entirely.

In 1901 a new station was constructed at North Philadelphia (previously known as Germantown Junction) where the Chestnut Hill Branch joined the Connecting Railway (see Chapter 2). A grade separation was made in 1904, known as the "New York-Pittsburgh Subway," to allow through trains from the west to move easily onto this line to New York. These two changes led to the increased use of North Philadelphia Station as the primary stop for New York-Chicago trains and decreased use of Broad Street Station for this purpose.

Likewise, a new West Philadelphia Station was constructed in 1903, replacing the one built for the Centennial, which had been destroyed by a spectacular fire in 1896. The latter depot was no longer used as a station after Broad Street Station opened in 1881. At the time of the fire it was used by Superintendents of the Philadelphia Division and the Delaware Extension, as well as the Kensington Branch. The trainshed was used for storing passenger equipment, resulting in the loss of 28 passenger and two freight cars, with 33 passenger cars damaged. A new three-story brick office building was subsequently erected at Powelton Avenue Yard for the Division offices, and a second small office building was built for car inspectors and Pullman Company personnel. With construction of the West Philadelphia facility, the small station built at Powelton Avenue in 1882 was closed and demolished.

The 1903 track revisions in West Philadelphia, along with the construction of the new station (and many other changes, many of which are discussed in *Triumph II*), were part of A.J. Cassatt's aggressive and visionary program to rebuild the railroad. Specifically, these changes allowed West Philadelphia to serve as the main Philadelphia station for New York-Washington trains, eliminating the time-consuming backup moves into Broad Street Station. To further strengthen its competitive position vs. the B&O it eliminated Philadelphia locomotive changes on this run and implemented crew run-throughs on the route two years later.

In 1903, an additional bridge across the Schuylkill was constructed, allowing further enlargement of the approach trackage to Broad Street Station. It was widened to four tracks in 1910, but even with this latest in the series of improvements it was becoming evident that more fundamental changes would be required. Discussion of electrification of the suburban lines was initiated, along with separation of through and commuter traffic. A Board of Engineers was appointed and directed to review and assess the various proposals for substantially improving PRR passenger facilities in Philadelphia. It should be noted that an early redevelopment plan for the City involving a proposed Parkway would have made it difficult to further expand Broad Street Station, which was one of the proposals.

To improve traffic flow in and out of the station, electrification of the suburban commuter line from Broad Street Station to Paoli was initiated in 1913 and completed in 1915 (see the discussion regarding electrification of the suburban lines in Chapter 3). The recommendations of the Board of Engineers would ultimately lead to what became known as the landmark Philadelphia Improvements (see later in this chapter).

Concurrently, still further improvements were made in 1913-14 between Broad Street Station and West Philadelphia, the Connecting Railway's bridge across the Schuylkill was rebuilt to accommodate five tracks, and the North Philadelphia station was expanded by the addition of four new tracks with high-level platforms. Work was started in 1915 (during the administration of President Samuel Rea) on electrification of the Connecting Railway and the Chestnut Hill Branch. This involved the elimination of a number of grade crossings, but the project was not completed and made operational until 30 March 1918 because of the war and scarcity of labor and materials.

However, by the 1920s the problem of traffic congestion at Broad Street Station had again become acute. The station handled an average of 500 inbound and outbound passenger trains *daily*, carrying some 80,000 passengers. The congestion had been somewhat alleviated by the electrification of the commuter lines; however suburban traffic continued to grow in the post-World War I years. Other problems included the difficulty of moving through New York-Chicago and New York-Washington trains in and out of Broad Street Station, with all the attendant costs and delays. This resulted in these trains stopping at North Philadelphia and West Philadelphia stations, respectively. However as city traffic increased, use of these facilities was becoming increasingly difficult for passengers to and from Center City. In addition, the Filbert Street Extension, or "Chinese Wall," as it had come to be derisively known, was becoming increasingly unpopular with the public and City officials alike.

Philadelphia as originally laid out by William Penn was intended to gradually expand north and westward from the Delaware to the Schuylkill River, which it had indeed done. The elevated approach to Broad Street Station, although solving the problems of rail traffic in congested streets, eventually created new ones for a city bent on still further expansion.

The burning of the Broad Street trainshed in a spectacular fire on 11 June 1923, one of the most serious in the City's history, brought these problems to the forefront of public attention. PRR responded to this disaster with heroic efforts – partial service was resumed the next day using temporary platforms and terminating other trains temporarily at West Philadelphia and North Philadelphia stations. All 16 tracks in Broad Street Station were rebuilt and 70 per cent of all trains were back into the station 5 days after the fire!

But even with plans to rebuild the trainshed (the shed was never rebuilt – umbrella shelters were put up between the tracks instead), the incident emphasized the necessity for new thinking regarding PRR's passenger facilities in Philadelphia. Accordingly, discussions between PRR and the City brought a commitment from the railroad "to properly accommodate the local and through passenger service" and to "reach some mutually satisfactory understanding respecting new passenger facilities and their relation to the present and future transit lines and streets of the City."

These vague political statements notwithstanding, PRR finally decided to locate its main passenger facility on the west side of the Schuylkill River, near where it had been prior to the construction of Broad Street Station. At this location, New York-Washington trains could move directly through the station, and (it was hoped) New York-Chicago trains could be turned via a loop track without the need of the costly and time-consuming back-up moves required in the terminal throat at Broad Street Station. The plans called for the new station to contain about 10 tracks on the lower level, each having 1500-foot platforms for through trains, and six additional tracks on the upper level for suburban commuter trains.

The West Philadelphia location, however, was not convenient for most of the 30,000 daily commuters into the Center City area, so a new "Broad Street Suburban Station" (later just Suburban Station) was planned to serve this clientele. The site chosen was at Pennsylvania Boulevard, between 16th and 17th Streets, in the heart of the downtown area, just north and west of Broad Street Station. Electric propulsion technology made it possible to relocate the tracks below street level for the first time. It was planned to construct a new bridge across the Schuylkill River, south of Arch Street, leading to a subway of at least four tracks beginning near 20th Street and then terminating in an underground station.

These proposals called for elimination of PRR steam trains in downtown Philadelphia, demolition of Broad Street Station and the Chinese Wall, as well as needed downtown redevelopment. The landmark Philadelphia Improvements would not only result in rebuilding PRR's station facilities, but would also unleash a cascade of events that would continue for the next 70 years and radically alter the core of the City. The plans were approved by the PRR Board on 24 June 1925. The program also involved significant financial commitment from the City, and on 13 July the agreement was finalized. The cost was initially estimated at around $60 million, a major undertaking for both parties. New president William Wallace Atterbury made the completion of PRR's new Philadelphia stations one of his priorities, along with substantial investment in new passenger locomotives and cars.

In 1926 the complex excavation work began for the train tunnel connecting Suburban Station with the mainline. Groundbreaking for the station itself was held on 28 July 1927, formally initiating the Philadelphia Improvements. Suburban Station was opened on 28 September 1930, consisting of a concourse 15 feet below street level, with the platforms and tracks below that. When opened, it offered seven station tracks and four platforms each 1130 feet long and 20 feet wide, with provision for expansion to five more tracks and two additional platforms. An extensive network of underground pedestrian passageways allowed passengers to walk several blocks under cover in all directions.

The 20-story office building above the station, with stunning Art Deco trim, was opened on 1 April 1930. It became home to the company's executive offices on 21 July, and on 10 September President W.W. ("General") Atterbury and the directors held their first meeting in the new Boardroom.

At the 30th Street site across the river, PRR was putting together land parcels including the original 1851 Powelton property, on which to build the new station complex.

Work began in mid-July 1926 on enlarging the 32nd Street tunnel to accommodate electrification of the suburban lines to Wilmington and on the West Chester Branch. This was actually the first step of the monumental project to electrify the north-south and east-west lines dramatically announced by Atterbury on 31 October 1928.

The first structure was actually a new 14-story West Philadelphia office building, and PRR general offices were consolidated there in the Fall of 1927 (the executive offices remained in Broad Street Station until the Suburban Station office building was completed). This building was located at 32nd and Market, just west of the planned station.

Negotiations for removal of the elevated rapid transit tracks from Market Street in the vicinity of the new station site were so prolonged that the start of the station itself was delayed for some time. Because of this the north wing of the station was constructed first, for suburban commuter traffic. It was opened at the same time as Suburban Station, looking a bit strange with one finished limestone wall facing the tracks and the back unfinished, looking like a giant stage set.

Finally in 1929 construction began on the train platforms and waiting rooms for the through tracks and a new bridge for Market Street. The project was further delayed by the Depression, but Pennsylvania Station – to be known by the public as 30th Street Station – was finally opened for New York-Washington traffic on 12 March 1933, and the initial portion was fully operational on 15 December of that year.

The new building, designed by Graham, Anderson, Probst and White, was of a stunning design, resembling a classical temple. It was 639 feet long and 327 feet wide, with the long side facing the river and Center City. In the center of the long sides, there were colonnaded porticoes 150 feet wide and 70 feet deep at the entrances to the main concourse. The Main Concourse was 290 feet long and 135 feet wide and rose 95 feet to an ornate coffered ceiling with gold-trimmed colored detailing. Symbolizing the move from Broad Street Station, "Spirit of Transportation," an imposing bas-relief sculpture by Karl Bitter portraying man's triumph in conquering distance, was moved and installed on the north wall of the Main Waiting Room.

Philadelphia had a new transportation center and PRR had another triumph.

Financial difficulties caused by the Depression caused a substantial delay in completing the remainder of the Improvements, although the fact that that much was done is nothing short of miraculous. Although 30th Street Station became PRR's primary through station and regional operating headquarters, Broad Street Station (and the now infamous Chinese Wall) remained – and continued to be used for some 90 trains beginning and terminating in Philadelphia, including New York, Trenton and Atlantic City runs, as well as a terminal for Pennsylvania Greyhound Lines, (which was partially owned by the railroad). In the 1940s the 30th Street Station area was significantly changed by the construction of the Schuylkill Expressway and access ramps along West River Drive, as well as the bridge extending Pennsylvania Boulevard (later renamed John F. Kennedy Boulevard) across the river.

Nothing further was done on the station until after the war, but on 27 April 1952 the last train rolled out of a now-dingy Broad Street Station, with the venerable Philadelphia Orchestra playing in the observation car. The equally venerable old edifice had survived two fires (the second in 1943) and had served PRR well during the golden years, but its time had clearly passed. The station and the viaduct were subsequently demolished, and the remaining elements of the Philadelphia Improvements finally completed, including installation of additional tracks beneath 30th Street Station and revisions to accommodate the radical changes in traffic patterns. Ironically, the loop track – one of the reasons for selecting the site – was never built. In any case, it had taken many years, but PRR had finally achieved consolidation of all through trains serving its home city in one location.

The railroad then embarked on a major program to promote Penn Center Plaza, a massive proposed office building complex on the valuable real estate formerly occupied by Broad Street Station and its approach. This included a hotel and new corporate headquarters relocated to 6 Penn Center Plaza in 1957. Redevelopment of this area touched off a building boom that profoundly changed Philadelphia's skyline.

A serious student of PRR in Philadelphia (or even the casual reader, for that matter) might wonder at this point why it took the railroad so long, and so many tries, to find the right station locations to serve its Philadelphia clientele. Interestingly, as early as 1851 PRR had purchased property west of the Schuylkill for "ample space for the accommodation of the business of the Company at the eastern terminus of the Columbia Railroad." A debate ensued as to the best location for a depot, i.e. West Philadelphia vs. "east of the Schuylkill" – the issue being the convenience of a location in or near the central business district vs. the delays associated with conveyance (via horse) through the city streets from a more distant site. The former location won out, at least initially.

In particular one might ask why Broad Street Station was ever built if such complex switching maneuvers were required to bring trains in and out of a stub terminal, to say nothing of the large support facilities needed to service the attendant motive power. The traditional answer to any such question is that no one could have foreseen the future needs of a growing city. One can excuse the multitude of station sites prior to the construction of Broad Street Station in that light. Yet by the end of the post-Civil War building boom, Philadelphia's growth pattern - at least within the City limits (the City and County of Philadelphia had been consolidated in 1854) - was fairly well defined. PRR had decided to locate a station in the 30th Street area as early as 1864, and we could argue that the advantages of that location (if not the configuration) should have been evident.

A second answer is that Broad Street Station was a necessary prestige symbol at a time when that was considered mandatory in its intense competition with the Reading. It was erected at the beginning of the initial decade of monumental city building in the U.S. What it didn't take into the account was the major impact of traffic from either the acquisition of the PW&B or the rapid growth of the Main Line suburbs approaching the turn of the century, which of course PRR heavily promoted.

Perhaps the most compelling response is that it wasn't until the development of electrified motive power technology, which allowed a smoke-free underground downtown facility, that PRR could achieve the optimum combination of station locations to serve the differing needs of suburban commuters and long-distance travelers alike. The combination of the new 30th Street and Suburban Stations worked together to finally fill the bill.

Returning to our chronology, on 10 August of 1952, 3,000 men and women assembled in the great Main Concourse of 30th Street Station for the unveiling of the bronze Pennsylvania War Memorial sculpted by Walter Hancock. This soaring figure was dedicated to the 1,307 PRR men and women who gave their lives during World War II. It was a significant occasion in more ways than one.

Although passenger traffic during World War II increased substantially and 30th Street Station was crowded with military personnel, it declined sharply after the war despite the introduction of much-heralded new streamlined lightweight trains by PRR and other railroads. With postwar maintenance budgets slashed, 30th Street Station entered a long, slow decline. Its walls, both inside and out, became dingy, its facilities worn and with the 1958 cutback in long-distance trains its concourse largely vacant except for rush hour commuters. Culminating a series of unthinkable events (see Chapter 7) PRR merged with its arch east-west passenger competitor New York Central to form Penn Central in 1968, only to collapse (after a series of even more unthinkable events) into bankruptcy a little over 2 years later.

Out of this debacle the National Railroad Passenger Corporation (better known as Amtrak) was born on 1 May 1971, created by Congress from the remains of the railroads' long-haul passenger business with the charge to become the nation's passenger rail system, and in particular to relieve Penn Central of its intercity passenger burden. Amtrak slowly revitalized this business, particularly on the Northeast Corridor, but 30th Street Station continued to decline.

Finally, in December 1988, after 4 years of planning, the 30th Street Station Rehabilitation Project began. Two and a half years (and $75 million) later, 30th Street Station re-emerged in the Spring of 1991 from the scaffolding and maze of dimly-lit plywood passageways to reassume her rightful place among the crown jewels of PRR's – and the nation's – passenger stations. The exterior masonry shone again and the War Memorial looked out upon a sparkling interior, busy shops and most importantly, a bright future because of increased passenger activity.

Broad Street Station, its former site filled by the modern Penn Center office complex (and joined later by the nearby dazzling Liberty Place cluster across Market Street), is now a distant memory, and Reading Terminal has recently been reincarnated (to the tune of over half a billion dollars) into the adjoining – and thus far successful Philadelphia Convention Center, which gives the City a world-class facility to compete for mega-conventions. The venerable – and famous – Reading Terminal Market underneath the former terminal remains as busy as ever, serving Center City residents, commuters and tourists alike.

In recognition of its historic status, in 1979 30th Street Station was entered on the National Register of Historic Places and on 17 December 1996, the PRR heritage of the station was recognized with the unveiling of a new Pennsylvania Station Historical Marker. A second one was dedicated on 18 May 1999 near the site of Broad Street Station as well, in a belated recognition of its significance in the grand scheme of things in PRR's home city.

PRR fans should be pleased and proud.

TRIUMPH III

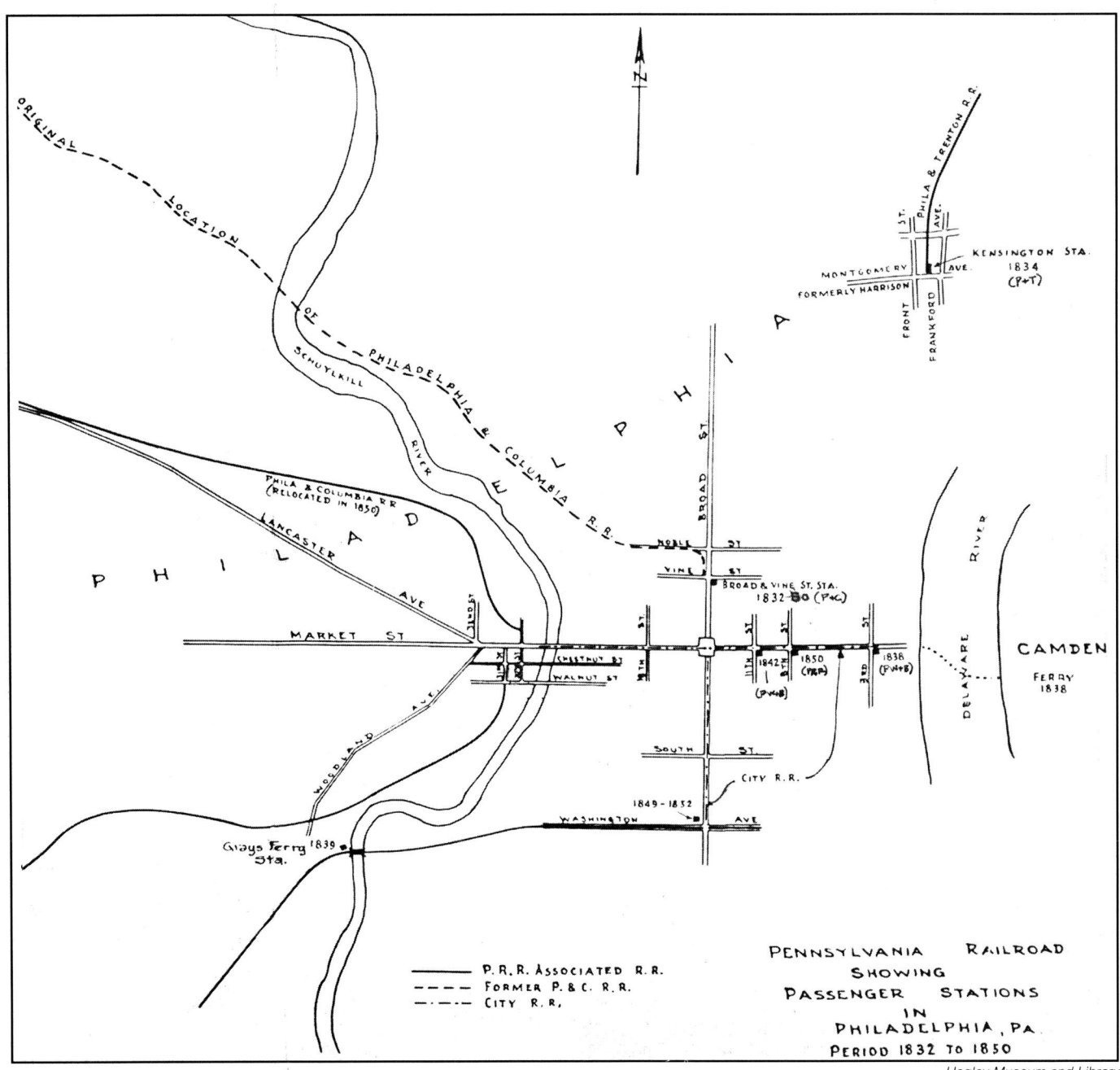

Hagley Museum and Library

THE FIRST RAILROAD into Philadelphia was the State-owned Philadelphia & Columbia, which located its "depot" at Broad and Vine Streets in 1832 (and which it occupied until the terminal was sold to the P&R in 1850). This was followed in 1834 by the Philadelphia & Trenton RR, which approached Philadelphia from the north and whose depot was situated at Montgomery Avenue between Frankford Avenue and Front Street in Kensington. Other than the river ferry terminals, these two early depots and the later Philadelphia, Wilmington and Baltimore station at Broad Street and Washington Avenue were the last "atypical" station locations in the City. Henceforth virtually all of the depots would be situated on or near the Market Street axis, strongly influenced by the rebuilding of the "Permanent Bridge" to accommodate tracks for horse-drawn railcars in 1850, and the laying of the City-owned railroad along this route.

Following the two earliest depots, the PW&B's first station within the city limits was located at 3rd and Market Streets in 1838; passengers were transported by coaches and later omnibus (and ferry across the Schuylkill River) to the terminus of that railroad at Grays Ferry. The following year the PW&B built a station at Grays Ferry and constructed a bridge across the river, allowing horse-drawn railcars to move across to Broad and Washington. In 1842 the Center City station was relocated to 11th and Market, and the cars moved over the City Railroad along Market and Broad Streets to the interchange.

PRR would locate its first station in Philadelphia at 8th and Market, in a building owned by Bingham & Dock, one of the major early passenger and freight contractors. Passenger service (using the relocated P&C) was initiated from this site on 14 October 1850, before PRR had its own trackage into the City. During this period all railroad passengers and freight were loaded and unloaded and hauled in the streets by horse (or mule)-drawn cars along the City-owned trackage.

PRR COMES HOME

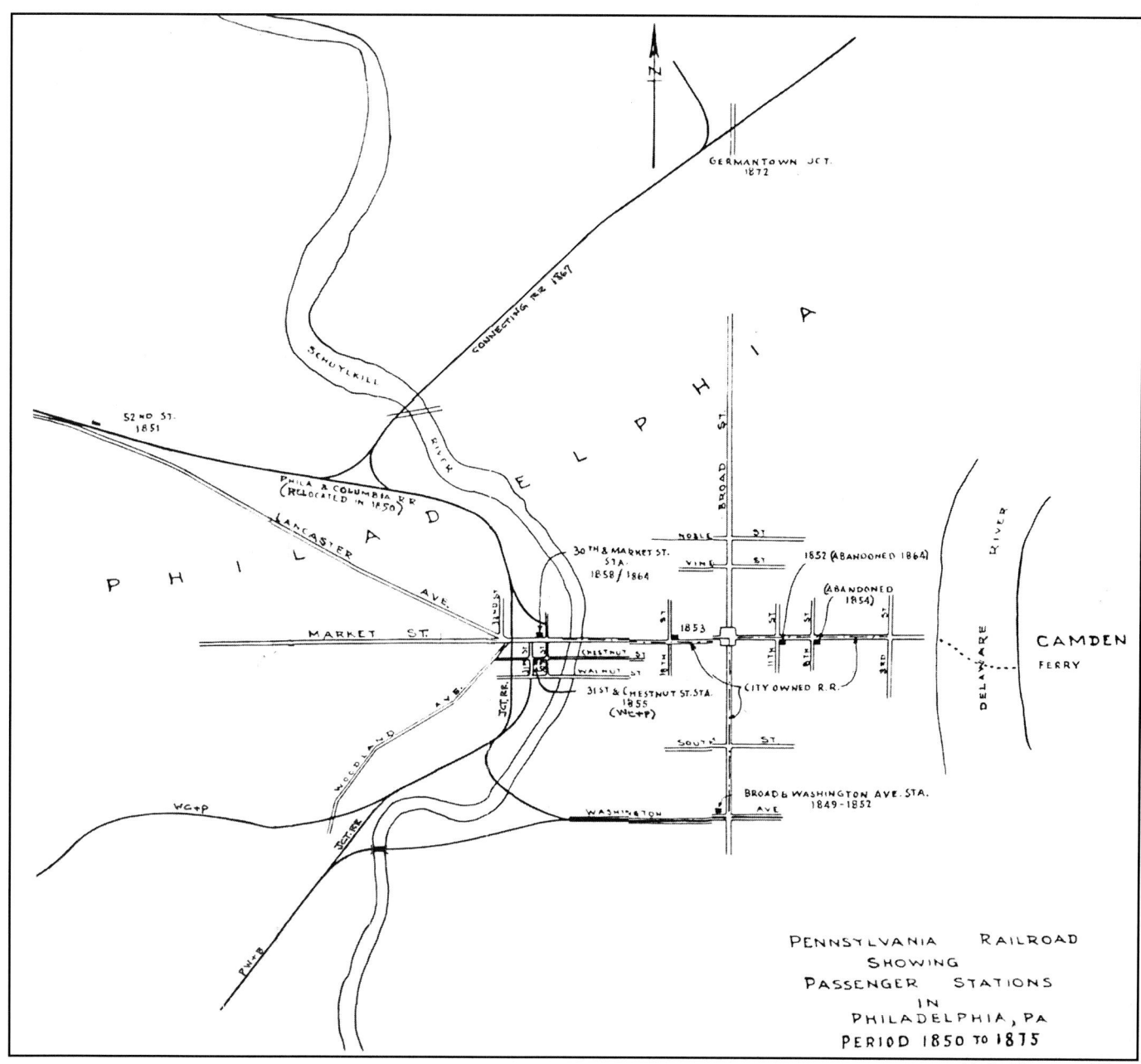

Hagley Museum and Library

WHEN THE PW&B vacated the building at 11th and Market on 2 June 1852 and relocated to a new station at Broad and Prime Street (later Washington Avenue), PRR made temporary use of this facility. In addition, on 3 March 1853, as a result of the landmark agreement with Bingham & Dock "for the purpose of jointly conducting the business of transporting passenger, baggage and mails upon the Philadelphia & Columbia Railroad" PRR acquired a half interest in the expansive passenger station constructed by B&D farther west at 18th and Market Streets, which it used jointly with the West Chester & Philadelphia. On 1 May 1854 PRR leased the facility at 11th and Market Street and later in the month moved to this location; the stations at 8th and Market and 18th and Market were then abandoned.

As early as 1852 Superintendent Herman Haupt advocated that the depot be moved to West Philadelphia (at the terminus of the P&C) to eliminate the delays and costs associated with transfer to the City railroad and moving people and freight through the streets. Property was purchased, but PRR continued to use the city locations. Starting in the late 1850s the railroads concluded that the West Philadelphia location would allow them to use steam power for the entire journey. The WC&P located its terminal at 31st and Chestnut Streets in 1853-5 (Chestnut Street was the locomotive limit), and in 1858 PRR constructed the first station of its own close by. It was a small frame structure located at the terminus of the former P&C (which it had just purchased) on Market Street between 30th and 31st Streets, the first of four stations sites PRR would occupy in this general area. Traffic increased rapidly and on 16 October 1864 PRR consolidated its passenger operation in a new facility at the same location, replacing the frame structure. The station at 11th and Market was closed on this date. If you've been following the pattern thus far, PRR had moved its passenger facilities steadily westward from 1850 on. Thereafter PRR passenger equipment would not operate east of the Schuylkill River until Broad Street Station opened its doors in 1881.

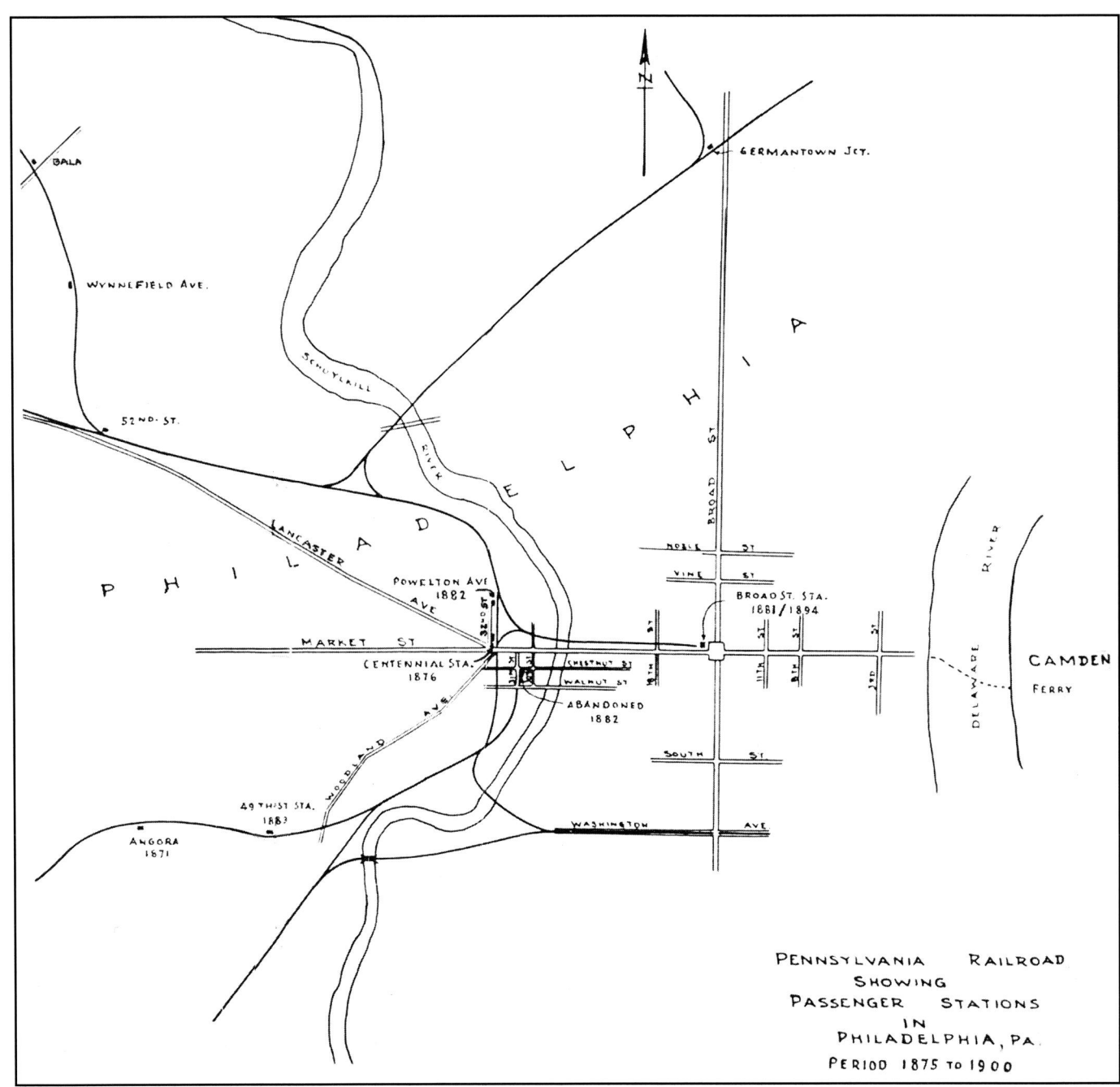

Hagley Museum and Library

BECAUSE OF continued growth in passenger traffic and the further increase anticipated with the Centennial Exposition, a new station was constructed at the intersection of Lancaster Avenue and Market Street, on the east side of 32nd Street (50 years later this site would be used for a PRR Office Building). Centennial Station, as it is often called (although not the same as the temporary station built on the Exposition Grounds, which we'll look at later in this Chapter), was opened on 6 May 1876, just in time for the grand opening of the Exposition. It continued to be PRR's main station in Philadelphia until the Filbert Street Extension and construction of the grand edifice facing Broad Street (and City Hall), which opened on 5 December 1881.

The PW&B had been taken over by PRR in March of that year, and subsequent to the merger with the WC&P abandoned its facility at 31st and Chestnut Streets on 1 January 1882; all trains from this line were then routed into the City, contributing heavily to the growth in traffic into Broad Street Station. Interestingly, a new station was opened at Powelton Avenue at that time to serve north-south trains at West Philadelphia. In 1894 a major expansion of Broad Street Station was carried out, to meet the steadily growing traffic (and increased competition from the opening of Reading Terminal three blocks away). The Connecting Railway had been constructed in 1864-7, providing direct access from Philadelphia and the west to New York City. In 1882 the Chestnut Hill Branch was opened from this line, and a station built at Germantown Junction. After the opening of Broad Street Station, the Centennial station building was utilized for company offices until it was destroyed by a spectacular fire on 18 April 1896.

PRR COMES HOME

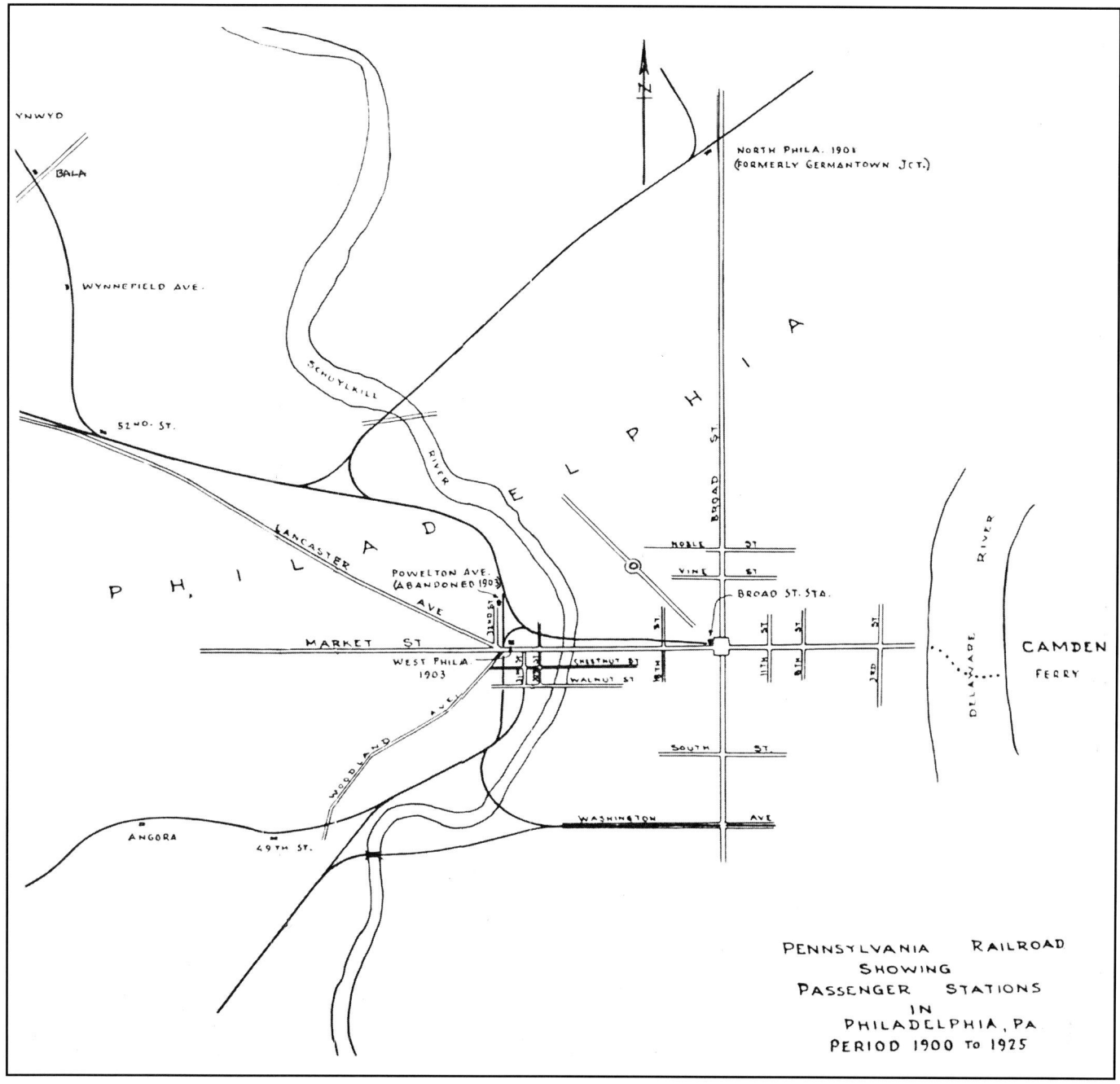

Hagley Museum and Library

DURING THE PERIOD 1900-1925 station building activity in Philadelphia continued, in a prelude to future developments. In what could be termed the first Philadelphia Improvements, new facilities were constructed at North Philadelphia (formerly Germantown Junction) in 1901 serving that area of the city but primarily handling through trains from New York City to the west, and at 32nd and Market in West Philadelphia in 1903, serving through north-south trains. The station at Powelton Avenue was then abandoned. Improved track connections between the PB&W from the south and the mainline and New York Division to the west and north were also made at this time, allowing improved operations not only into Broad Street Station but also allowing through north-south trains to move through West Philadelphia without crossing the river. In the author's judgement construction of these two stations, as well as the revised trackage to serve them, can be viewed as an early acknowledgement that Broad Street Station was not suited to efficiently handle through trains.

TRIUMPH III

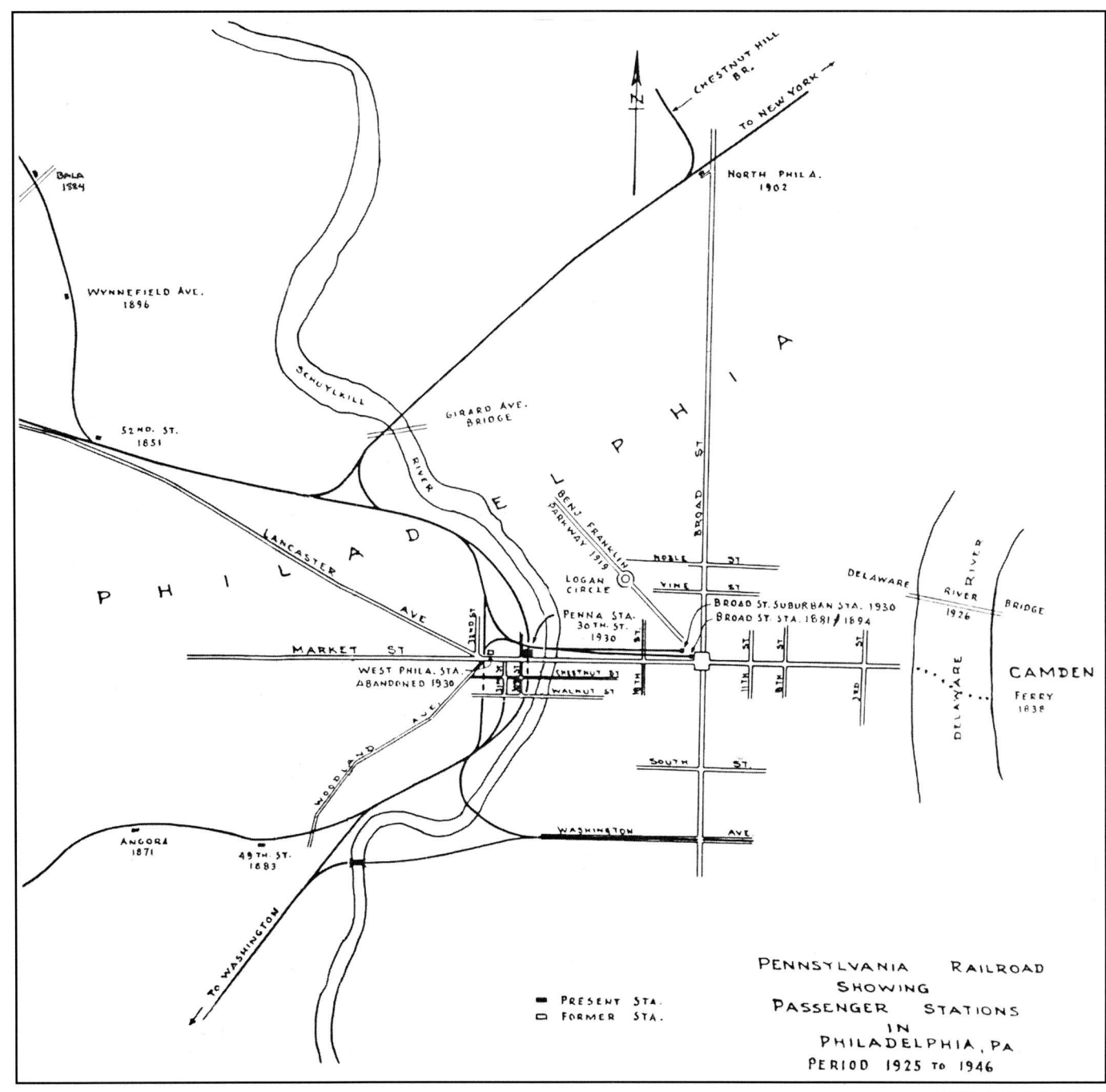

Hagley Museum and Library

THE PENULTIMATE PHASE of PRR passenger station development is shown here, encompassing what are known as the Philadelphia Improvements. Suburban Station and the upper level (Suburban Wing) of 30th Street Station were opened on 28 September 1930 for commuter operations. 30th Street Station was completed and opened for partial through service on 12 March 1933, allowing West Philadelphia Station to be abandoned. The final phase would be the completion of 30th Street Station trackage and the resultant demolition of Broad Street Station in 1952. We will explore the early stations up to the construction of Broad Street Station, and then proceed westward from that edifice across the river to West Philadelphia and on up to and including the 52nd Street Yards, examining the extraordinary array of historical developments in that area.

PRR COMES HOME

PRR USED this expansive "Railroad Depot" owned by Bingham & Dock at 18th and Market Streets briefly for passenger service from 1853 to 1854, when it leased the depot at 11th and Market. The West Chester & Philadelphia used this facility as well, from the early 1850s to 1866. Note that passenger cars are still being moved by horse teams along Market Street in this 1850s drawing.

THIS OLD DRAWING depicts the Bingham House (right) at 11th and Market Streets in the early 1860s. Adjoining that is PRR's first depot of its own, from which cars were hauled to West Philadelphia by teams of mules or horses. PRR occupied the "Mansion House" depot until moving to its new station at 30th and Market in West Philadelphia in 1864, eliminating the need to move cars through the city streets. The Bingham House was named after William Bingham, U.S. Senator from Pennsylvania from 1795-1801 and a wealthy man in his time.

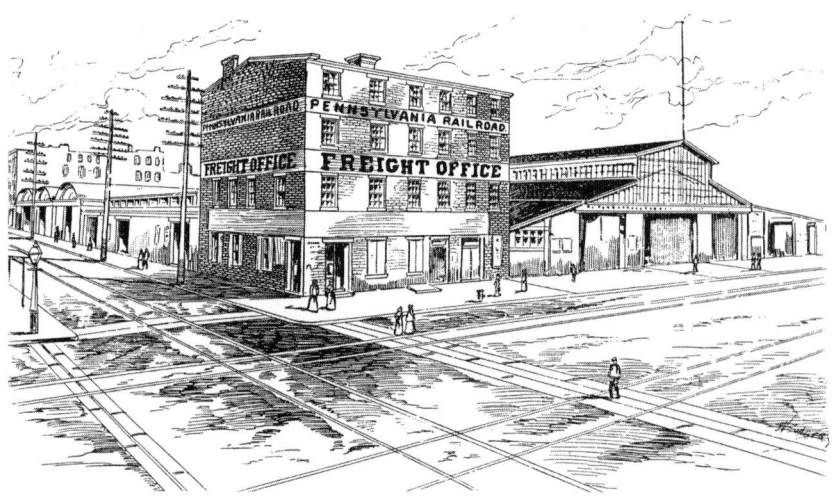

PRR'S THROUGH FREIGHT business in Philadelphia began on 1 January 1851 in the Bingham & Dock building at 8th and Market Streets (local trade was handled by agent Craig & Bellas at Broad and Cherry Streets). The through business outgrew this location and it was moved on 1 January 1853 to the Mansion House Station at 11th and Market. With the subsequent expansion to the 18th and Market Street station for passenger operations, PRR soon realized that its City freight facilities were inadequate for the rapidly growing business. As a result a parcel of land was purchased farther west at the southwest corner of 13th and Market Streets. The freight office shown here was opened on 1 April 1853. In this view the City-owned tracks extend to the right (west) along Market Street, with 13th Street running southward to the left.

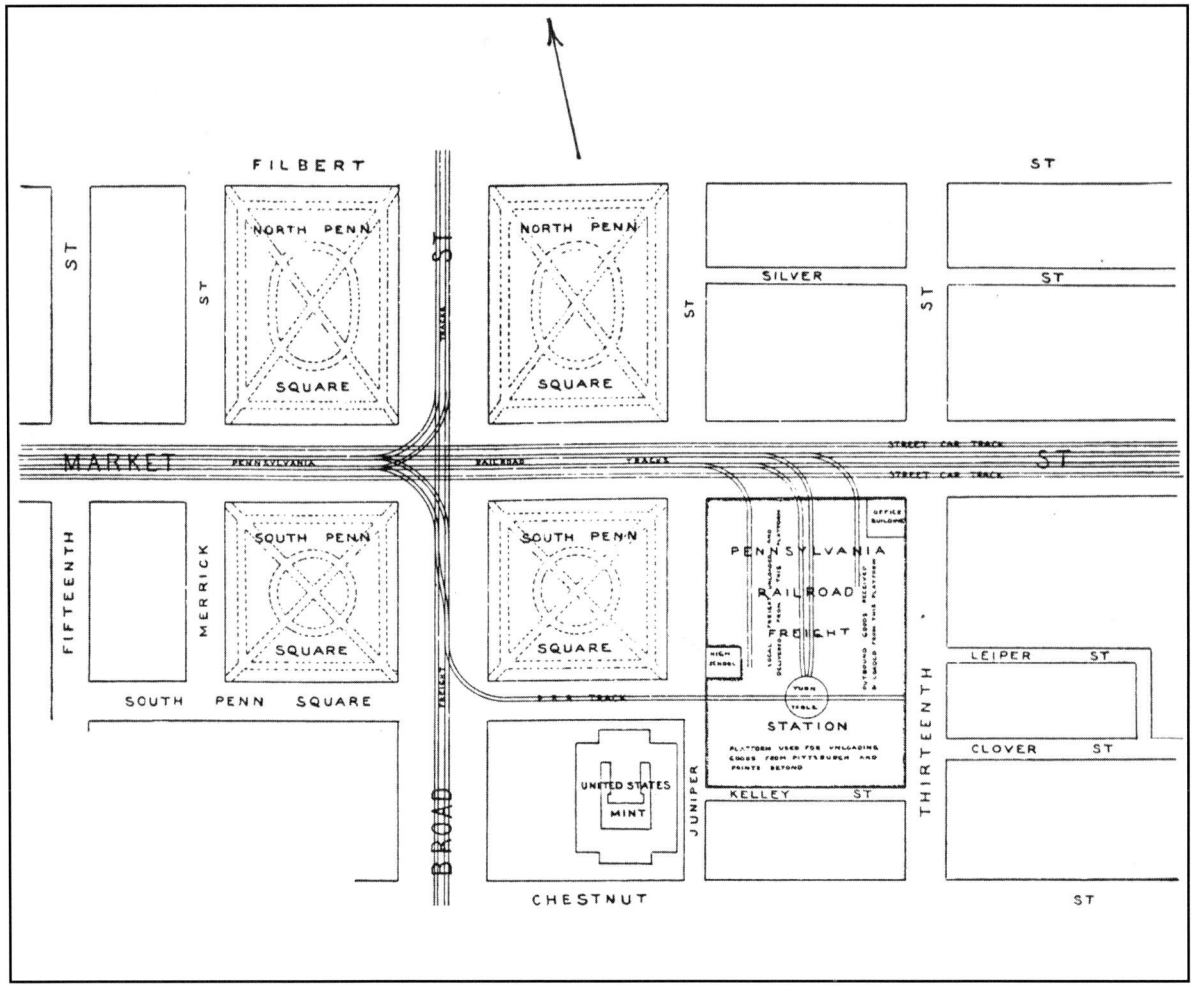

THE FREIGHT WAREHOUSE at 13th and Market Streets was begun 5 July 1854 and the entire facility was opened on 15 December of that year, consolidating freight operations in Center City. This plan view shows the depot ca. 1860, after it was expanded. Cars were moved east on Market Street to Broad, down Broad and into the rear of the station. They were unloaded onto the platform on Kelley Street. They were then turned 90° on the cast iron turntable and moved into the terminal where they were loaded with outgoing merchandise and routed back out onto Market Street to begin their journey westward.

Even at nearly 93,000 sq. ft. – the largest city terminal at the time – it wasn't enough for the burgeoning business. In 1864, just 10 years after it opened, local freight operations had to be moved to a new depot two blocks west at 15th and Market. By 10 August 1874 the through business was moved to the Dock Street Station. The 13th and Market depot was then closed and the property sold in 1875 to Philadelphia merchant John Wanamaker, becoming the site of his famous department store.

PRR COMES HOME

Ted Xaras Collection

THIS OFTEN-PUBLISHED photo shows the intersection of Broad and Market Streets looking northeastward in 1871, after the site was cleared for the construction of City Hall. The large building at the right is the PRR freight shed at 13th and Market. The photo also shows one of the "string teams" of horses (or mules) used to haul freight and passenger cars from West Philadelphia along Market Street on the City Railroad (note the cars along Market Street). Several years prior to the time of this photo, PRR had consolidated its passenger operations in the new station at 30th and Market, eliminating the need to use the declining City Railroad for passenger service. John Wanamaker purchased the old freight depot in 1875, utilizing it as a clothing emporium. In 1877 he transformed it into a cosmopolitan department store, which rapidly became the foremost retail establishment in Philadelphia. The present City Hall now occupies the vacant space in the photo, in 4-1/2-acre Centre Square at the intersection.

WITH THE OPENING of the Junction RR in 1863 PRR made a dramatic move to West Philadelphia by constructing a new consolidated freight and passenger terminal at 30th and Market Streets, the first of four stations to be located in this area. It was a landmark development - with the opening of this facility on 16 October 1864 the earlier small depots on Market Street were closed, and the use of horse-drawn passenger cars on the City RR would be discontinued. The terminal consisted of a wooden train shed covering two tracks for passenger trains, with a brick head house for ticket offices and waiting room, serving east-west trains to and from Harrisburg and Pittsburgh.

In 1867 the completion of the strategic Connecting RR defined a new pattern of north-south traffic. New York trains would no longer run to the P&T facility at Kensington; henceforth they would utilize this "New York Depot," built in 1867 adjacent to the east-west terminal. It was brick building housing "passenger rooms, offices and restaurant, with a commodious car shed attached, and the necessary tracks [two]." This view shows the newly-developed horse-drawn streetcars, complete with rooftop advertising, in front of the latter facility ca. 1870.

Conrail Public Affairs/Penn Central RR Collection/Pennsylvania State Archives

TRIUMPH III

TO HANDLE the immense surge of traffic anticipated for the 1876 Centennial Exposition, PRR constructed this handsome station facing Market Street at the intersection of 32nd and Lancaster Avenue. This station, the second in the area, replaced the first one at 30th and Market and served as PRR's main Philadelphia terminal from its opening on 6 May 1876 until supplanted by Broad Street Station in 1881. The twin train sheds, 94 x 810 ft. long, spanned twelve passenger tracks (three for incoming trains, three for outgoing trains and six for car storage and cleaning). Separate incoming and outgoing baggage rooms were also constructed. This capacity was indeed fortuitous because the station handled an unbelievable 20,231 trains carrying 2,343,500 passengers from 10 May to 10 November during the Exposition. It is shown here while Market Street was being cobblestoned, most likely shortly before the opening (note the retaining wall and top of the tunnel portal for the Junction RR). The depot was destroyed in a spectacular fire on 18 April 1896. The site later became the location of PRR's Office Building constructed in 1926-7 as one of the first parts of the Philadelphia Improvements.

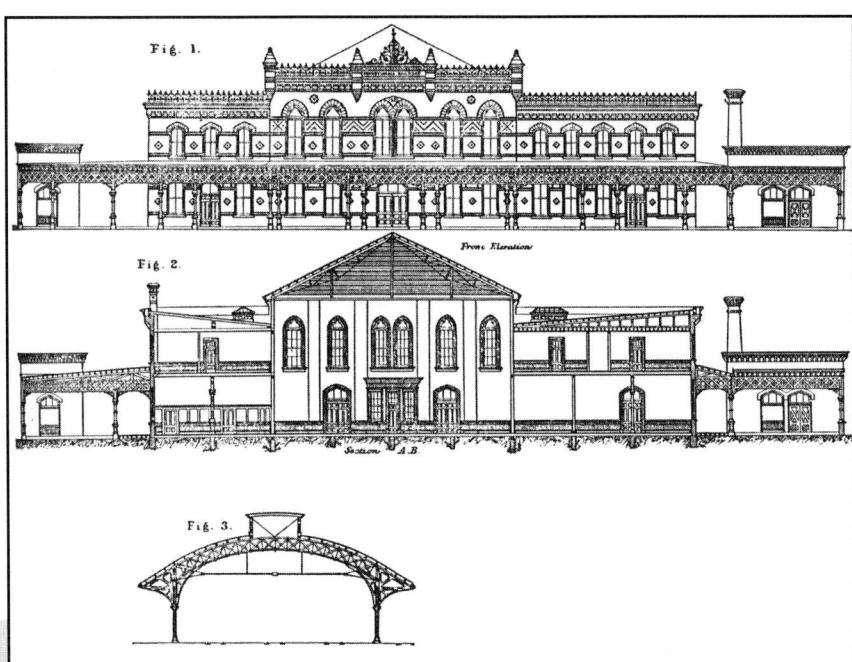

Ted Xaras Collection

Conrail Public Affairs / Penn Central RR Collection / Pennsylvania State Archives

THE CENTENNIAL STATION served the occasion well, but it proved to be too far from the hotels and businesses in Center City. President Thomas A. Scott, at the urging of then First Vice President George Roberts, felt that PRR needed to reassert its presence in the growing business district. Accordingly the firm of Wilson Brothers (responsible for the two largest buildings at the Centennial Exposition and other landmarks in the city) was enlisted to erect an appropriate city terminal, one of the earliest of its genre in the U.S. Located at the head of the elevated Filbert Street Extension, it was a "magnificent" five-story Gothic edifice facing Centre Square and Philadelphia's new City Hall. It was built of granite and brick, with a 176-ft. high, cathedral-like clock tower anchoring the northeast corner, reflecting PRR's solid but conservative management. The head house had a 193-ft. frontage on Broad Street and extended 122 ft. westward along Filbert to 15th Street. The twin trainsheds covering eight passenger tracks extended beyond that.

A freight station was located along Market Street, west of 15th (site of an earlier freight depot built in 1864), and served by four additional tracks. Freight was moved between the track platforms and the freighthouse on street level by means of large hydraulic elevators. The combination of the elevated approach and separation of passenger and freight operations provided a much safer environment for patrons and the general public than any of PRR's previous stations in the city. The overall project including the approach, cost a staggering $4.3 million.

But it was a worthwhile investment. Broad Street Station offered travelers many amenities: separate ticket windows for local and through trains, separate incoming and outgoing baggage areas, cushioned benches, newstand, telegraph office, restaurant and a separate private dining room – all in a genteel elegance of polished wood and leaded glass, hand-carved and inlaid wood ceilings, and bathing and barber services.

Tom Scott did not live to see his efforts fulfilled – he was forced to resign because of failing health on 1 June 1880, as the Filbert Street Extension was being constructed, and died on 21 May 1881. His legacy would reign in Center City for over 70 years from its official opening on 5 December 1881. This view looks from the front façade westward along the Filbert Street side in 1883.

TRIUMPH III

ONCE INSIDE, passengers ascended a grand entrance stairway, 16-ft. wide and flanked by 11-ft. wide side flights. The stairways were lined with "coloured enamelled bricks, artistically set and the ceilings are made entirely of wood . . . handsomely carved." At the top of the stairs was the 51 x 100-ft. main waiting room, with open fireplace. Proceeding forward the doors of the waiting room opened into the train lobby, with ornate cast iron train gates along the western side. These elegant gates, and the equally elegant late nineteenth century attire of the travelers, are depicted in a drawing showing the train shed beyond.

Ted Xaras Collection

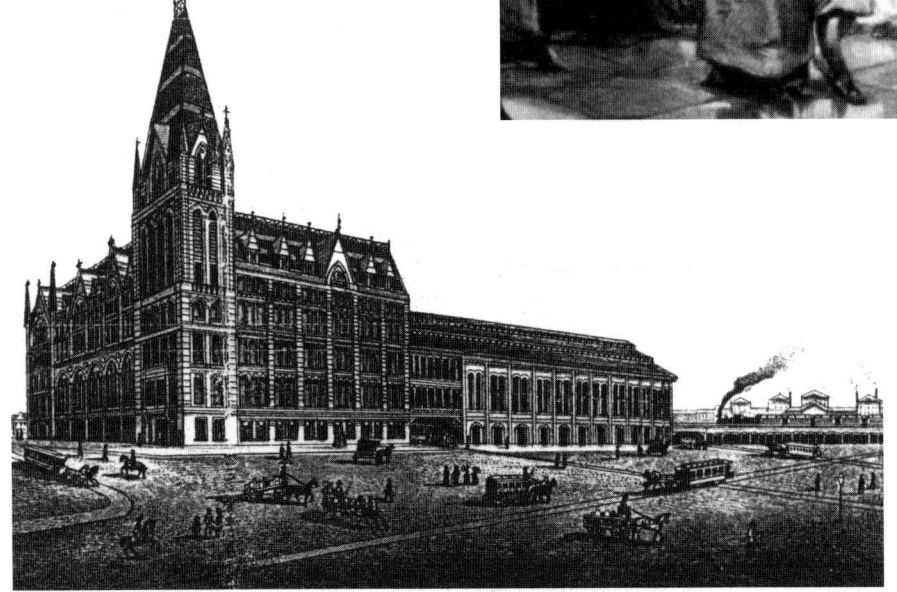

ALTHOUGH the artist has taken quite a bit of license with the expanse of Filbert Street, this drawing from an 1888 "Album of Pennsylvania RR Scenery" gives us an interesting and little-known view of the north side of Broad Street Station. We are looking southwestward as a train approaches the shed on the viaduct. Note the horse-drawn trolleys, including one emerging from the passage through the station, under the shed.

Jim Cassatt, Jr. Collection

PRR COMES HOME

Ted Xaras Collection

THE DELICATE TRACERY of the iron arches over the original trainshed is evident in this photo taken in the Fall of 1881, prior to opening of the station. The twin passenger sheds were near-duplicates of the ones in the Centennial Station, each 85-ft. wide and decorated with ornamental ironwork. The interior walls of the shed were red and buff ornamental brick and terra-cotta, with sill courses and skirting of blue marble. The passenger section shown here had eight tracks, with 24-ft. platforms between each pair. The smaller freight station at left (which actually opened first on 25 April) had four tracks, with 20-ft. platforms between. This photo was taken from the catalog of Wilson Bros., notable Philadelphia architects, who designed and built the station.

TRIUMPH III

IN A SUPERB DISPLAY of late 19th Century motive power, this wonderful photo gives a look at a pair of pristine high-stacked D-Class 4-4-0 locomotives awaiting departure from Broad Street Station in the mid-1880s. This view also shows the original track configuration in the train sheds, with the Adams Express building immediately in front of the freight shed at right center. The Central Market building is at the front right.

Railroad Museum of Pennsylvania (PHMC)

LOOKING EAST toward the back of the 1881 trainshed we see the original 17th Street, or "A" Tower ca. 1889. This classic frame structure, also constructed in 1881, was located near the northern (Filbert Street) side of the elevated viaduct, just east of 17th Street. For maximum visibility of the approach to the terminal, it was three stories high and had a bay on the south side. It contained a PRR-designed 56-lever interlocking machine, possibly the first pneumatically-operated installation, controlling all switches and signals in the throat. This view also shows the small (60-ft.) turntable located right on the edge of the Filbert Street Extension, as the viaduct was commonly known. Note the early iron signal bridge, with six lower-quadrant semaphores.

Ted Xaras Collection

PRR COMES HOME

Ted Xaras Collection

WITH THE pending expansion of Broad Street Station, it became necessary to build a new A Tower right on the edge of the viaduct above Filbert Street, to allow extension of Tracks 14-16. This westward photo is dated 4 November 1893, after the new two-story brick tower was constructed, and before the track expansion and building project were completed at the end of that year. Once the new tower was opened the old tower was demolished and the turntable was moved farther west. Note the trackwork in progress at left and beyond the new tower. Just discernible in the distance is the original wooden B Tower, at the bend in the approach trackage. The Adams Express (later Railway Express) building is at left, constructed in 1892 at this new location farther west.

The interlocking was rebuilt in 1907-8, incorporating single- and double-slip switches, which provided more operating flexibility. In addition new upper-quadrant home signals were installed at A Tower on a test basis; the success of this installation (and others) eventually resulted in the change to upper-quadrant semaphores on the system.

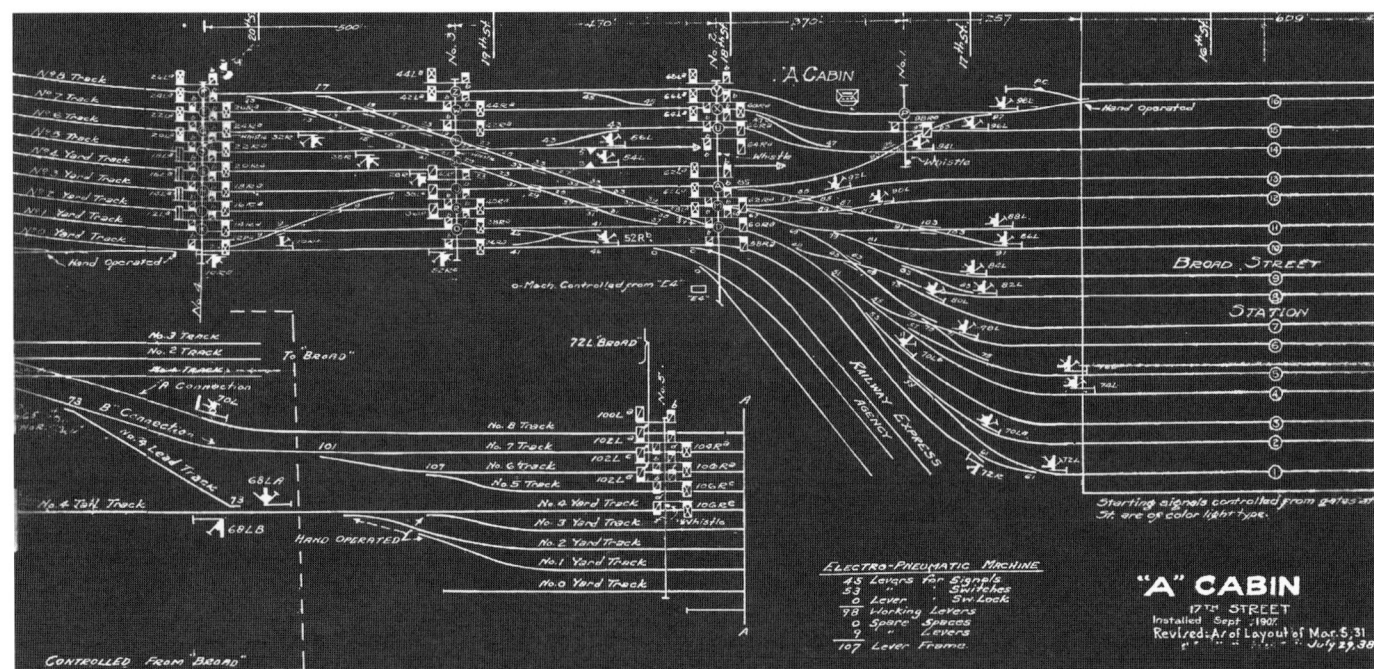

Hagley Museum and Library

A TOWER controlled all the traffic in and out of Broad Street Station – 16 stub-end platform tracks in the new terminal and the Adams Express building tracks plus in later years movements through the "A" and "B" Connections to the Suburban Station approach tracks. Even after 30th Street Station was completed, all trains originating or terminating in Philadelphia did so at Broad Street Station, including the "Clockers" to New York City, the Trenton and Atlantic City trains and an endless multitude of shifting movements, a necessary requirement of a stub-end terminal. At its peak the tower handled a staggering 450 trains a day, in and out. Most of this activity also moved through the upper level of 30th Street Station, so A Tower had to work very closely with BROAD, which handled all of the commuter trains in and out of Suburban Station. The electro-pneumatic machine depicted here, installed in 1907, required five men to operate the 100+ levers.

Railroad Museum of Pennsylvania (PHMC)

B TOWER is shown in this ca. 1900 photo looking eastward toward Broad Street Station in the distance. Seldom photographed because of its distant location from the terminal itself (above Cuthbert Street, between 22nd and 23rd Streets), it was originally the standard ornate wood design located near 20th Street, and then subsequently rebuilt in brick farther west. Note the signals are still lower-quadrant semaphores.

PRR COMES HOME

W.N. Jennings / Ted Xaras Collection

WITH SURGING TRAFFIC reaching a million passengers a month by 1886, the station needed to be expanded. An added impetus was the pending construction of Reading Terminal three blocks to the east. The original station had fulfilled its role of providing PRR with a Center City presence, but it was soon to be dwarfed – and the trainsheds literally engulfed – by the new one.

The first step was to obtain the additional land. The buildings shown here, comprising the Coffee House Block on the corner of Broad and Market, have "For Sale" signs pasted all over them – odd because it is unthinkable that anyone but PRR would have dared to buy them. The eastern end of the freight station is just visible at left in this sloppy 1887 wintertime photo, just before demolition of the block.

Ted Xaras Collection

THIS VIEW taken from City Hall shows the huge, 591-ft. long trainshed being roofed over and the main building about half finished in mid-1893. The freight station at 15th Street was moved two blocks westward (at the left edge of the photo). Incredibly, given the construction methods of the time, erection of the falsework for the shed was begun on 25th January of that year, the first iron truss erected 13 March and the 20th (and last) one put in place on 30 June – certainly a sharp contrast with pace of the City Hall project, which took over 30 years to complete!

TRIUMPH III

Ted Xaras Collection

(*above*) THE GIANT ARCHES spanned 306 ft. and 16 tracks, four more than the old station (which also included the former freight tracks). The station remained in operation during construction, with the old canopy and temporary platform umbrella sheds providing protection to passengers. The completed trainshed is shown in this crisp view taken at exactly 5:03 p.m. by the now-completed City Hall clock. The trackwork has been reworked across the 16 platform tracks. Traffic was unbelievably light, making it most likely a weekend day, ca. mid 1890s. The 26-ton, 36-foot, 8-inch statue of William Penn, one of the largest bronze castings ever made, keeps a watchful eye over the City of Brotherly Love. It was finally hoisted into position in November 1894, 20 years after the cornerstone was laid!

(*right*) THE IMMENSE INTERIOR of the new trainshed is shown in this ca. 1895 view, which makes the trains look almost toylike. The elliptical arches soared to over 104 ft. high at the peak and covered 180,840 sq. ft. - over 4 acres!

Ted Xaras Collection

Ted Xaras Collection

IF THIS PHOTO of the completed Broad Street Station conveys a certain imperiousness it is not by coincidence. In comparison the original station was a rather modest effort to construct a Center City terminal. The expanded version represented President George Roberts' desire to construct the largest passenger station in the U.S. – and have it be an architectural showpiece befitting the "Standard Railroad of America" (later "the World"). Designed by noted Philadelphia architect Frank Furness and opened in November 1893, the "Grandest Railway Terminal in America" was constructed in Beaux Arts style of granite and brick culminating in an ornate tower dominating the corner of Broad and Market.

The terminal boasted marble floors and a 16-ft. wide grand staircase with huge sculptured balustrades leading to a spacious 82 X 120-ft main waiting room (or a smaller ladies' waiting room) on the second floor. Or patrons could take either of two flanking 50-passenger elevators embellished with iron scrollwork. Once there they could dine in style in an elegant 120-table restaurant before proceeding through the gates to the immense trainshed.

The general and executive offices moved from 233 South 4th Street into the new 10-story building on 9 July 1894. This pre-World War I photo shows the two-story addition on the original section, added in 1896 to accommodate the growing staff, the 1905 walkover bridge to the Commercial Trust Building on Market Street and under it the carriage-way to the Headquarters offices. Note the ornate cast-iron lampposts in front of City Hall – and of course the vintage automobiles!

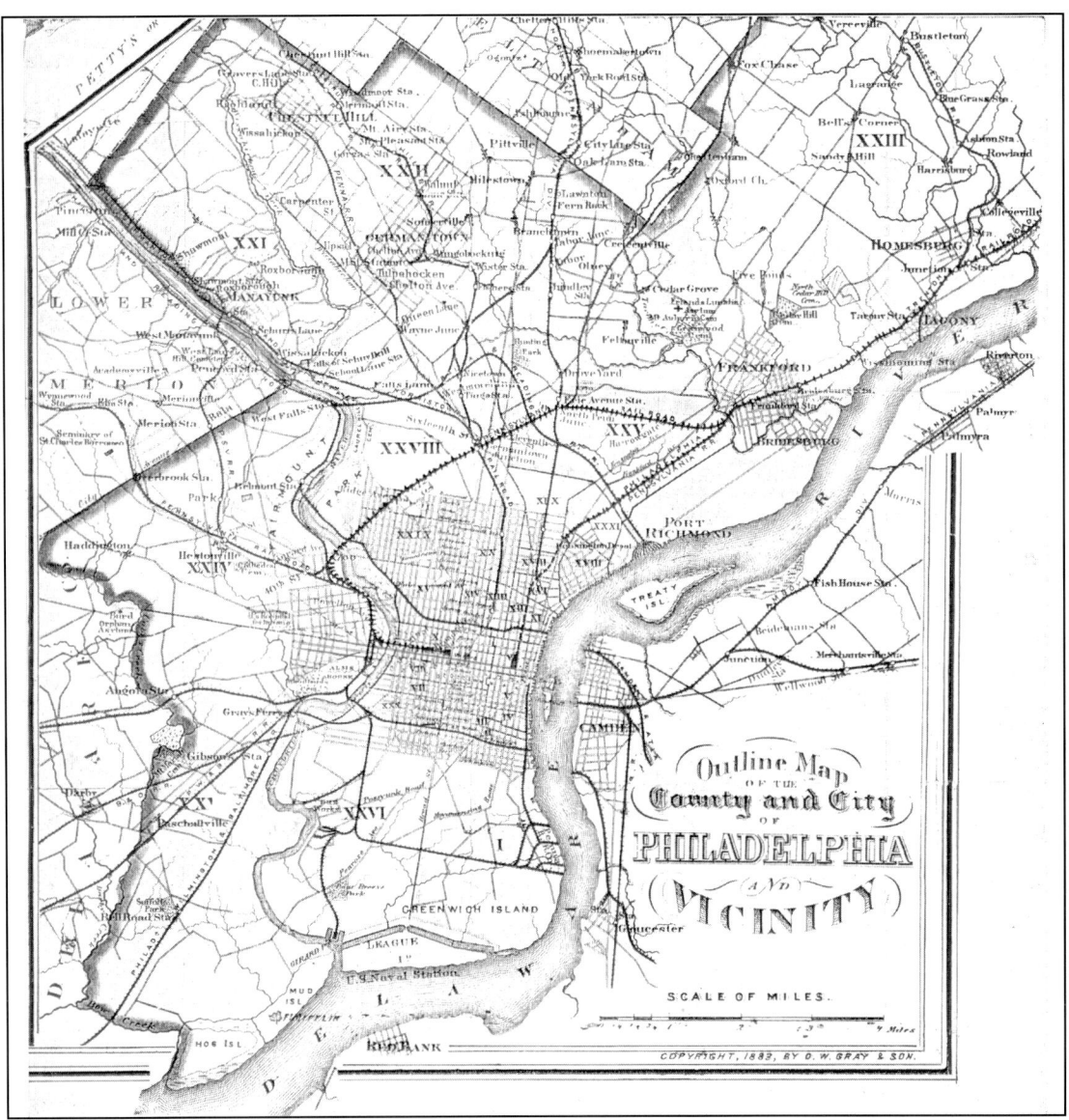

Hagley Museum and Library

THIS MAP accompanied a remarkable report dated 29 October 1888 from Samuel Rea, then Assistant to Second Vice President J.N. DuBarry. The report was remarkable not so much for what it recommended - his specific proposal was ignored - but for the independent thinking and long-range planning that it espoused. It correctly foresaw the construction of Reading Terminal and the increased competition for both intercity and local traffic it would bring. His solution was to build a new PRR station to serve the east side of Philadelphia. It envisioned extending the Philadelphia & Trenton southward to the new facility located at 3rd and Market Streets, offering, he felt, easier travel to New York City than Broad Street Station.

PRR top management chose to expand Broad Street Station instead in 1893 (in another example of corporate one-upmanship to the imminent completion of Reading Terminal three blocks away), but it did eventually heed Rea's point of planning for long-term growth of rail traffic in Philadelphia: "This cannot properly be provided for by the extensions and variations made from time to time, to existing terminals, merely to keep up with the demands of traffic. *We must go beyond this.* [italics added] The unprecedented growth of our cities, with the constantly increasing rail traffic, demands much more gravity in its treatment than formerly. Each city should be taken up separately and a special study made of it in advance; and in doing so the next one-half of a century must be discounted and in a measure prognosticated so that a plan, which may be adopted and carried out in the next decade, will not prove inapplicable in four or five years after completion." We should note that this was written at a time when Broad Street Station was already experiencing severe congestion only 7 years after it was opened.

Rea's fervent plea for long-term planning to meet increasing rail traffic in Philadelphia would wait almost 25 years to take root. He would go on to become Vice President and serve as chairman of the Advisory Committee on Philadelphia Passenger Terminal Improvements. This body made recommendations which began the process which, during his subsequent term as PRR President during the years 1913-25 bore fruit in the form of the Philadelphia Improvements. His other recommendations, notably building a new station at Germantown Junction (North Philadelphia), constructing a railroad bridge across the Delaware River from Frankford Junction and connecting the PRR and Reading terminals with a rapid transit network would all come to pass, some in the near term and others many years later.

COMPARATIVE COSTS OF PROPOSED PHILADELPHIA PASSENGER STATION IMPROVEMENTS

Location	Cost of Main Improvement	Cost of Other Improvements Required	Total Cost
1. West Philadelphia			
A- Small loop station for through trains only; enlarge Broad St. Station	$6,500,000	$12,500,000[1,2]	$19,000,000
B- Large loop station for through and all originating express trains	12,000,000	5,000,000[1]	17,000,000
C- Large station on Darby Creek Route for through and all originating express trains	17,500,000	5,000,000[1]	22,500,000
D- Large station like "C" with Darby Creek line deferred	10,000,000	5,000,000[1]	15,000,000
2. North Philadelphia and Broad Street Subway			
E- Station for through trains; enlarge Broad St. Station, Broad St. Subway built by PRR	12,000,000	14,147,000[1,3,4]	26,147,000
F- Station for through trains; enlarge Broad St. Station, Broad St. Subway built by private capital	4,000,000	14,147,000[1,2,3]	18,147,000
G- Station for through and express trains; Broad St. Subway built by PRR.	15,000,000	6,647,000[1,3,4]	21,647,000
3. Broad Street Station			
H- Kensington Line; enlarge Broad Street Station and build lower-level tracks in open subway from 15th to 18th Streets	20,018,000	2,482,000[3]	22,500,000
I- Enlarge Broad St. Station for upper and lower-level tracks; electrify suburban lines	28,000,000	7,000,000[1,3]	35,000,000
J- Enlarge Broad St. station for upper-level tracks and build "jumpover" at 23rd St.; electrify suburban lines	20,500,000	8,500,000[1,3,5]	29,000,000

1 Includes $5 million for improvements on Connecting Railway, Girard Ave. Bridge, North Philadelphia and Frankford.

2 Includes $7.5 million for widening Broad Street Station to Cuthbert St. and additional yard tracks in West Philadelphia

3 Includes $1.65 million for four-tracking 32nd St. tunnel, and South St. "jumpover," West Philadelphia.

4 Estimates for Plans E and G include $5 million for a Broad St. Subway. If built by private capital this can be deducted. Plans also provide for electrification of the Chestnut Hill Branch.

5 By enlarging Broad Street Station to Cuthbert St. and making other improvements totaling $16 million, without electrifying suburban service, the capacity of Broad Street Station would be extended to 1924.

Hagley Museum and Library

(Caption for artwork previous page)

ALMOST FROM the time it was opened in 1881 Broad Street Station was inadequate for the traffic it was required to handle (this was exacerbated by the seemingly unanticipated inclusion of PW&B trains). Although it was a monument to late 19th century railroading and was the Standard Railroad of the World's very visible "presence" in Center City Philadelphia, it was incapable of efficiently handling through trains, either New York-Washington or New York-Chicago/St.Louis. West Philadelphia handled the former and North Philadelphia the latter, although neither was conveniently located to the Center City area. Broad Street Station was enlarged in 1893-4 (at least in part in reaction to the building of Reading Terminal), but it was not enough.

Serious deliberations for what came to be known as the Philadelphia Improvements began as early as December 1910, when the Board of Directors appointed a Board of Engineers with the directive of "assembling and studying the several plans and suggestions for the improvement of the passenger terminal facilities, and all information bearing on the subject." The Board of Engineers considered an amazing variety of options (shown here based on their report dated 17 May 1911), but interestingly its final recommendation was Plan H, which looked remarkably like Samuel Rea's proposal of almost 25 years earlier- perhaps not too surprising because he was chairman of the Advisory Board to which the Board of Engineers reported.

However, the Kensington line and the lower-level tracks were not to be. The program finally approved by the Board of Directors on 19 December 1911 consisted of expanding the approach to Broad Street Station; adding additional tracks on the Connecting Railway, including widening the Schuylkill bridge and enlarging North Philadelphia Station and approaches by the addition of four new tracks (with high-level platforms); and notably, electrification of the suburban lines (see Chapter 3). These were necessary modifications, but it was not a fundamental re-thinking of the problem of where was the optimum location for Philadelphia's main station. Except perhaps for Plans B-D, which did envision the main station at West Philadelphia, the mindset was still tied to the perceived need for a showcase Center City station, and in particular Broad Street Station. However, the City's proposed Parkway plan (developed as early as this time) made further expansion of that symbol difficult if not impossible.

TLC - The running gear of K4 3731 gets some attention from the engineer under the watchful eye of the conductor in this stunning closeup photo in back of the giant train shed. The original oil headlamp on the locomotive has been electrified in this 1921 view. Note that by this time the glass panes have been removed from the back of the trainshed, presumably to reduce smoke accumulation.

Also note the overhead wires – increasing traffic in and out of the station forced PRR to install electrification in the train shed, on the Filbert Street Extension, the main tracks through West Philadelphia and the Main Line to Paoli in 1915 (see Chapter 3). The intent was to relieve congestion caused by the multiple shifting of steam-powered trains in the stub-end tracks.

Railroad Museum of Pennsylvania (PHMC)

PRR COMES HOME

Conrail Public Affairs/Penn Central RR Collection/Pennsylvania State Archives

AND THEN DISASTER STRUCK – A few minutes before 1 a.m. on 11 June 1923 fire broke out underneath one of the platforms of Broad Street Station. The flames spread rapidly to engulf the entire platform area and the huge trainshed overhead. This spectacular PRR photo captures the raging inferno near its peak at 2 a.m. All available apparatus and virtually the entire City's fire-fighting forces were marshaled to fight the intense blaze. It was finally brought under control by noon that fateful day, although it continued to burn for more than 2 days.

Ted Xaras Collection

THE FIRE is still burning on the next day, but PRR has already begun the repair process. It marshaled an incredible army of 3500 workmen and hauled in 2 million feet of lumber, 200 tons of rail, 300 tons of pipe and fittings and 20 carloads of ties to rebuild the trackwork and platforms. Repair crews worked in shifts around the clock to remove debris and rebuild the platforms and tracks, as well as restore communication circuits and the overhead catenary. Floodlights were set up to allow work to continue through the night hours. The overall loss was estimated at $1.5 million. Note the new office building rising on Market Street across from the gutted trainshed.

PRR COMES HOME

Ted Xaras Collection

THE TRAINSHED was doomed – its members twisted from the intense heat. But the platforms were replaced with wooden planking, perhaps a questionable expedient given what was to transpire later. In typical PRR fashion, the day following the fire all 530 scheduled trains were accommodated, either on temporary platforms at the west end of the trainshed (and using wooden stairways to the street) or terminating them at West or North Philadelphia. Unbelievably, within a week of the fire, all 16 tracks and their platforms and overhead for a distance of 600 ft. were rebuilt and restored to service, including the lighting and signal systems. Here an MU train unloads its passengers – complete with summer straw hats - a short time after the fire.

AND THEN IT BEGAN — the dismantling of the great trainshed, one arch at a time in the reverse of the process 60 years before, until only one was left, shown here later in 1923. Erecting the steelwork to support the crane and wooden cribbing under each arch prior to dismantling must have been a project in itself.

Ted Xaras Collection

BROAD STREET STATION – what's left of it – looks considerably diminished in this early 1924 photo, somehow aware of its impending fate. Umbrella sheds have been erected over each platform to shelter passengers from the weather. This view gives us a look at the 1893 power plant at 16th and Filbert Streets, with its stack soaring over 100 ft. above the platforms. Note the vintage automobiles and trolleys on Market Street.

Ted Xaras Collection

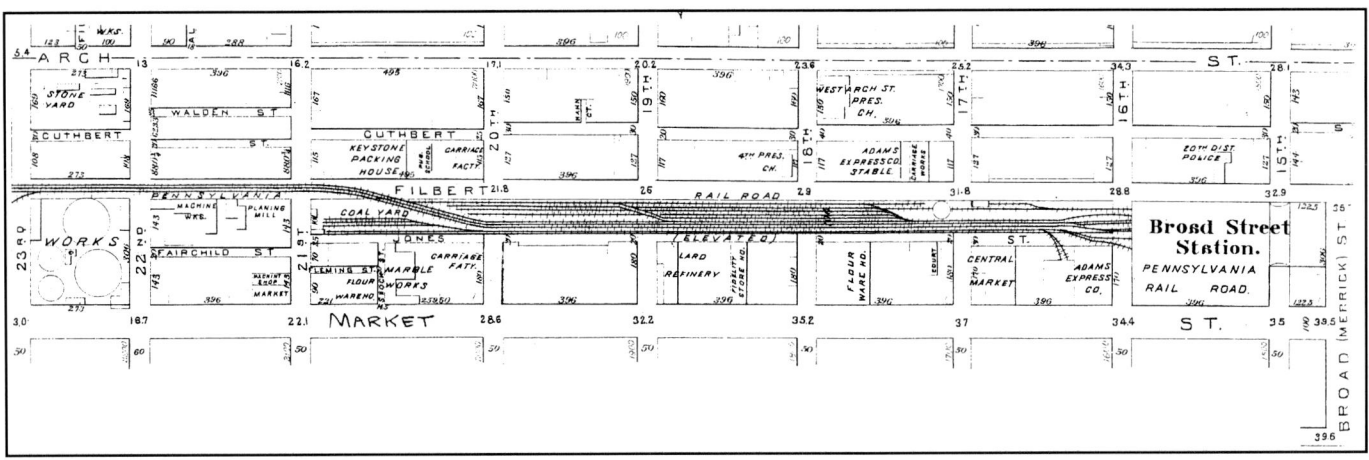

Ted Xaras Collection

WHEN PRR first elected to build a new terminal conveniently located in Center City in the latter part of the 19th Century, it obviously had to get the trains there. Not only did it have to construct a new rail bridge across the Schuylkill River, it had to move trains eastward from 20th Street to railhead on the west side of 15th Street. Undoubtedly remembering the horrors of moving trains through congested streets earlier in the century, PRR constructed the Filbert Street Extension, a 2042-ft. long brick viaduct. This massive structure filled the blocks between Filbert and Market Streets and required the demolition of 200 buildings. It was made up of 60 individual arches - 48 were 26 ft. in diameter, eight were 24-ft. and four spanned 50 ft. across 19th to 16th Streets. The final bridge across 15th Street was made of cast-iron plates to the station building as part of the passenger concourse; it was 106 ft. wide and held nine tracks. The viaduct was first used for freight on 25 April 1881 and for passenger service on 5 December of that year - the official opening of the station. It was an engineering triumph, moving passengers and freight quickly to and from Broad Street Station without interference from the mere mortals in city traffic below. This diagram from the 1888 City Atlas shows the original configuration, including the turntable just west of "A" Tower and the leads to the Adams Express Company facility.

PRR COMES HOME

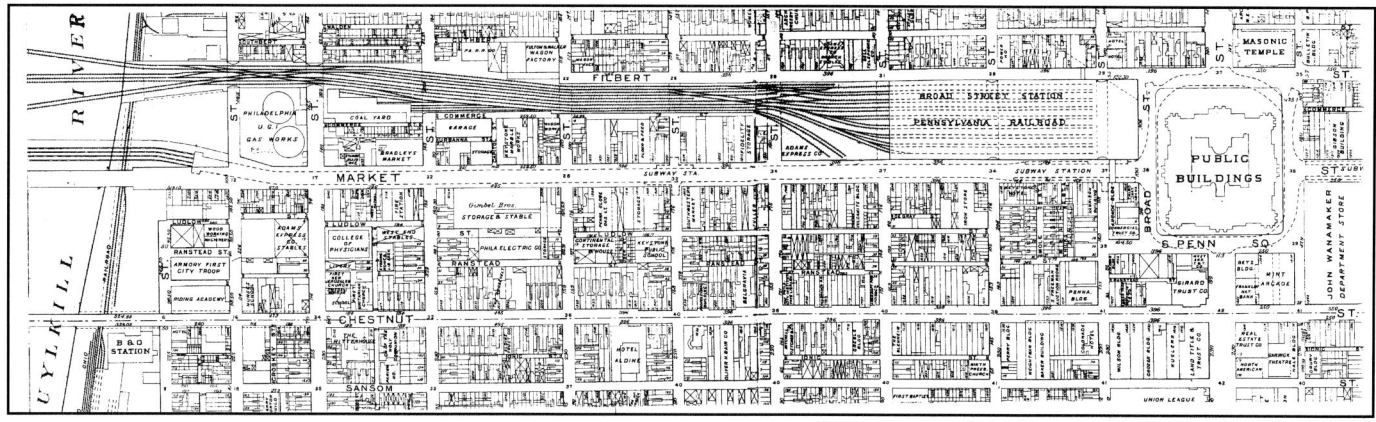

Ted Xaras Collection

HERE WE SEE the configuration for the full 16-track expanded station, from the City Atlas of 1910. Note how the Adams Express facility was moved westward to 18th Street to make room for the terminal throat enlargement, as well as the two new bridges and major expansion of the approach trackwork. Note also the B&O station at 22nd and Chestnut Streets. Interestingly, when it was constructed the viaduct reinforced the role of Market Street as the social boundary between the traditional Quaker population to the north and the more glamorous Episcopalian and Presbyterian social elite residing in the high society neighborhoods to the south.

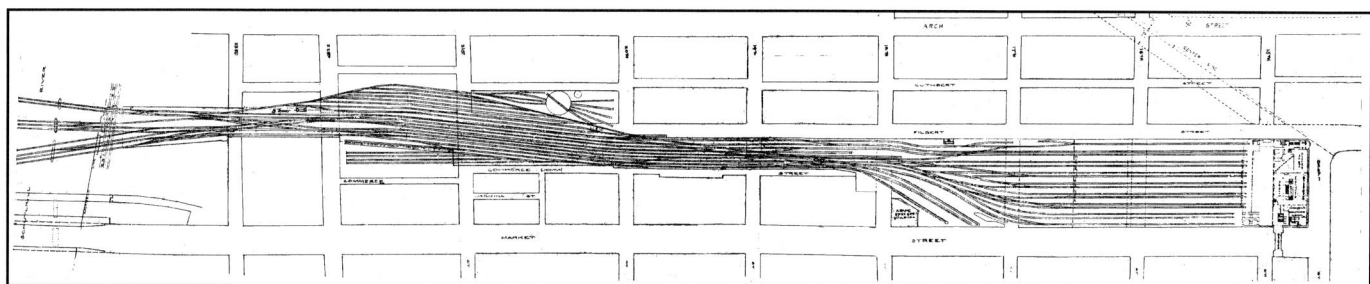

Ted Xaras Collection

IN AN EFFORT to improve traffic flow in and out of the station Bridge B (the bottom one, for trains to and from the west and north) was widened to four tracks in 1910, and the approach trackage expanded to Cuthbert Street near the west end. This ca. 1915 diagram shows the extent of the trackage at the time of electrification, and essentially the configuration up until the Improvements in the late 20s. Note the location of B Tower above Cuthbert Street between 22nd and 23rd and the turntable between 20th and 21st.

H.P. Albrecht / Ted Xaras Collection

AS THE YEARS went by, the viaduct masonry became grimy and stained, and the low arches increasingly formed an obstacle to north-south vehicle traffic flow. PRR's once great triumph was given the derogatory moniker "Chinese Wall" that effectively blocked development to the north as well as westward along its path. Here we see a Class H9 2-8-0 moving express cars above 19th and Market Streets in 1949.

SOME IDEA of the complexity of the approach trackage is shown in this 1920s photo looking west under the massive signal bridge located near the Adams Express building - the first of a tunnel-like array of such structures, which also supported the catenary wires. A steam switcher and a variety of P70 coaches and MU equipment, both moving and in storage, are visible in this photo.

Ted Xaras Collection

(caption for artwork on next page)

AND TRAFFIC continued to increase. As it turned out, the fire was the catalyst that forced PRR and City officials to face the need for a joint effort to solve their mutual problems - Broad Street Station was no longer an efficient operation for the railroad, and the City considered the elevated "Chinese Wall" as an eyesore and an impediment to north-south traffic flow and business expansion west of City Hall.

By 1925 a staggering total of 510 trains operated in and out of Broad Street Station each weekday. In addition 77 trains stopped at North Philadelphia, 47 of which also stopped in West Philadelphia. Of the unbelievable total of 587 trains utilizing the three stations, all but the 30 trains from New York City to the west stopped at West Philadelphia, as inconvenient as it was to Center City. This in no small measure led to the eventual conclusion that West Philadelphia was the optimum location for the main facility to handle through trains for the City of Philadelphia. A station on this historic site would not require the costly stub-end terminal movements of Broad Street Station. Coupled with the West Philadelphia location was the concept of separating through and suburban traffic, thus requiring a new facility convenient to the downtown area to handle this operation. Electric propulsion technology and the success of the suburban electrification program in reality made an underground commuter station possible.

Thus a new main station and a separate Center City commuter station emerged as key components of the plan to finally implement what became known as the Philadelphia Improvements. The plan envisioned the new main station at 30th Street in West Philadelphia (the fourth at this general location, replacing the 1903 facility) to handle both through trains and a stop for suburban trains, a new underground Suburban Station (and office building) in Center City and the eventual elimination of Broad Street Station and its elevated approach. It also called for a new general PRR office building west of 30th Street Station, a new Post Office building across Market Street from the station and a relocated freight terminal and Railway Express facility south of that. It further allowed the City of Philadelphia to proceed with its long-planned Parkway development program, extension of Pennsylvania Boulevard across the river to access the new 30th Street Station and continuation of West River Drive along the river.

Key elements of the track design included greatly expanded north-south tracks through the 30th Street Station area, connecting to a new four-track River Line, and two loop tracks south of the station that would allow all through trains from New York City and the west to enter the station from either end and then move in a continuous route either north or west. The entire plan was approved by the PRR Board on 24 June 1925, by City Council ordinance on 2 July, and the landmark 19-page agreement was signed by PRR and the City on 13 July of that year.

It was a grand and noble plan that would eventually change the face of Philadelphia. Implementing the plan to completion would take a monumental effort, a huge infusion of funds ($85 million) - and time, well beyond the stipulated 5 years.

Hagley Museum and Library

ONCE it was decided the Filbert Street Extension was to be removed, proposals old and new emerged for development of the prize real estate underneath. This one developed by PRR in 1924 encompasses the City's plan to extend the Parkway (right) from the Art Museum in to City Hall and envisions massive blocks of buildings between Market and Arch Streets. In the foreground a modified Broad Street Station building remains. A new Pennsylvania Boulevard stretches to an imposing new "Pennsylvania Station," which shows a Market Street subway wing on the south side. The concept was noble, but it would turn out somewhat differently, although embodying the same general ideas, and taking three decades to be fully completed.

Hagley Museum and Library

Ted Xaras Collection

BECAUSE of its scope and complexity, implementation of the Philadelphia Improvements required close cooperation – and financial support – from the City. A few smaller projects were initiated in 1925, including the PRR West Philadelphia Office Building, but the major work did not begin for 2 years.

The first task on the east side of the river was construction of a subway tunnel for the approach tracks to the new "Broad Street Suburban Station," or just Suburban Station as it came to be known. This required destruction of all the buildings between Filbert and Cuthbert Streets in a swath from 15th Street west to the river. Demolition actually began on 16 March 1927; the groundbreaking ceremony took place on 28 July 1927 at 20th and Cuthbert Streets, with Mayor W. Freeland Kendrick and President W. W. Atterbury doing the honors. This marked the formal initiation of the Philadelphia Improvements, although major construction did not move forward until December.

This PRR photo taken from the Suburban Station Office Building looking westward on 3 September 1930 shows the result of the initial effort, under the executive direction of PRR Vice President Elisha Lee. The PRR Office building, the first section of the new 30th Street Station, Suburban Station and the Steam Generating Plant have all been constructed. (We will examine the projects on the west side of the river shortly) Note the temporary crossover track connecting the Broad Street Station throat to the Suburban Station approach trackage. There were grand plans to demolish Broad Street Station and develop the area along the Filbert Street viaduct as well, but first the Great Depression and then World War II put further construction on hold in this area.

PRR COMES HOME

BROAD STREET STATION lingered on, its demise postponed first by the Great Depression and then World War II. In addition, the B&O's and the Reading's decision to back out of a move to the new 30th Street facility as a union station left PRR reluctant to shift the New York "Clockers" and New Jersey Seashore trains out of Broad Street. In an interesting development, PRR purchased shares of Motor Transport Corporation and in 1931 formed Pennsylvania Greyhound Lines. The north end of the Broad Street Station ticket office was utilized as Greyhound ticket offices, and busses arrived and departed from the canopied sidewalks in front of the station. North-south electrification and the arrival of the GG1's reduced the time between Broad Street Station and New York to a little more than 1-1/2 hours. During this period the number of trains was reduced to 120 per day.

In this 1939 photo a B5 switcher shuttles cars between Broad Street Station and the coach yard in West Philadelphia. In the background is Philadelphia City Hall, which reigned as the world's tallest building from 1901 to 1908, soaring nearly 585 ft. to the top of William Penn's hat. It is still the largest and tallest masonry building in the world – and the largest public structure in the U.S. – even taller than the U.S. Capitol building.

Dave Cope/Ted Xaras Collection

AND THEN it happened again! At approximately 9:30 on Sunday morning 12 September 1943 fire again broke out at Broad Street Station, this time in a washroom located in the power house on the Pennsylvania Boulevard (north) side. An exploding kerosene tank spread the fire over the oil-soaked wooden platforms (installed after the first fire 20 years earlier) and it spread rapidly, fanned by a stiff north wind. It advanced toward the 10 a.m. Clocker for New York, loading on track 14, burning the air hoses connecting the five rear cars and locking the brakes. A steam engine rescued the forward six cars (the overhead had been turned off), but the remaining cars were badly damaged in the ensuing blaze. The fire was under control 4 hours after it began; there was no trainshed to burn this time, but damage to the platform area was extensive. The blaze leveled all of the canopies and platforms, the tracks were twisted and the timber shoring was destroyed. Many of the steel support beams were twisted as well. It was *déjà vu* all over again! This photo looks east toward the back of the head house as firemen battle the stubborn blaze. Note one platform has already collapsed.

Charles Horan Collection

IN TYPICAL PRR FASHION 1,200 men were rapidly mobilized and the rebuilding work began Monday morning, even as train service was being gradually restored. By Monday evening over 200 carloads of equipment and materials for reconstruction of the platform superstructure were moved into staging areas. This photo at mid-week shows a few tracks have been put back into operation as a small army works on rebuilding the platforms at left center; full service was restored by the end of the week. Note the Suburban Station building at right.

In an ironic footnote to the Broad Street Station fires, sprinklers were installed in the main building in 1945!

Charles Horan Collection

(caption for artwork on next page)

THIS SUPERB PHOTO, taken from City Hall tower, looks down on Broad Street Station (we hesitate to use that phrase, even though "Old Broad" was on borrowed time in this ca. 1950 photo). It was a time after the initial phases of the Philadelphia Improvements had been completed, but Broad Street Station is still in use in what must have been an expensive operation of four city stations (including North Philadelphia), and undoubtedly causing confusion to the traveling public.

We are looking westward: Broad Street Station is directly below us, with the nearly full platforms extending outward; Suburban Station and office building is to the right, with cars parked on the lots over the subway tracks below; the triangular Railway Express building is in the center of the photo, with A Tower in between, on the northern edge of the Chinese Wall. Beyond Broad Street Station the approach tracks connect to the Suburban Station trackage. B Tower and the temporary crossover have been removed. Across the river the east façade of 30th Street Station faces the city; to the left (south) of the station is the Post Office building. Behind the station is the PRR West Philadelphia Office Building; the High Line extends left to right between them. Dominating the West Philadelphia skyline to the right is the heating and auxiliary power steam plant, with its 425-ft. high stack. This facility, put in operation in November 1929, supplies steam and backup power to all PRR facilities in the terminal area. Market Street extends westward at the left (note the trolleys still in operation).

PRR COMES HOME

Railroad Museum of Pennsylvania (PHMC)

SUBURBAN STATION office building was completed in 1929. It was 22 stories high and occupied a full city block. PRR utilized the upper floors for its executive offices and Board Room and leased the rest as office space. The two-level station portion, below ground level, was opened with minimal fanfare on 28 September 1930. The exterior of the building is faced in black granite on the first two floors and Alabama limestone and sandstone above that, with ornamental cast iron and bronze trim. An example of some of the superb Art Deco adornments on the façade of the station building is shown in this 1974 photo. The contrast between the golden bronze metalwork and the polished black granite facing on the street level is still stunning today, making the station one of the finest examples of the Art Deco genre.

Herbert H. Harwood, Jr.

Fred W. Schneider, III

THE STATION ITSELF – with marble wainscoting and terrazzo floors in the waiting room and offices – was located 15 ft. below street level, with the platforms 20 ft. below that. The platform area was designed for 12 tracks, but initially only seven were installed because of interference with the Filbert Street viaduct foundation. An eighth track was added later. These were served by four 20 x 1130-ft. high-level platforms. An extensive underground concourse was constructed that connected with subways, Broad Street Station and City Hall. It was the first underground complex of its type in a major U.S. city.

Two years into Penn Central the PRR keystone still glows on remarkably clean MP54 569. Fred Schneider captured the contrast of light and dark within Suburban Station on 6 April 1970. The time is 9 p.m., and the equipment – old and new – is laying over awaiting the morning rush.

PRR COMES HOME

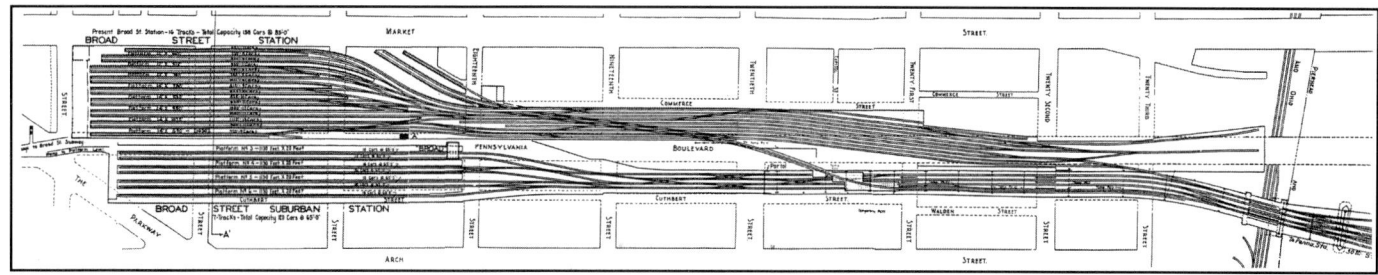

Ted Xaras Collection

WE TEND to think of Suburban Station as being located significantly west of Broad Street Station, but as this 1935 diagram reveals, the building was only 1 1/2 blocks west (between 16th and 17th Streets) and the platform tracks extended almost as far east as its elder sibling. This close proximity undoubtedly led PRR to use the initial designation, "Broad Street Suburban Station," because it was in function the Suburban portion of the older facility. The public adopted the shorter name, which prevailed, and PRR went along.

The platforms are numbered 3 through 6 - two more were planned (plus five more tracks) - but these had to wait because of interference with the foundations of the Filbert Street Extension. Note the stub remnant of the old approach tracks at right; the temporary crossover tracks allowed access from the full range of Broad Street Station platform tracks to the new bridge. Note also that this diagram is "upside down," i.e., east is to the left.

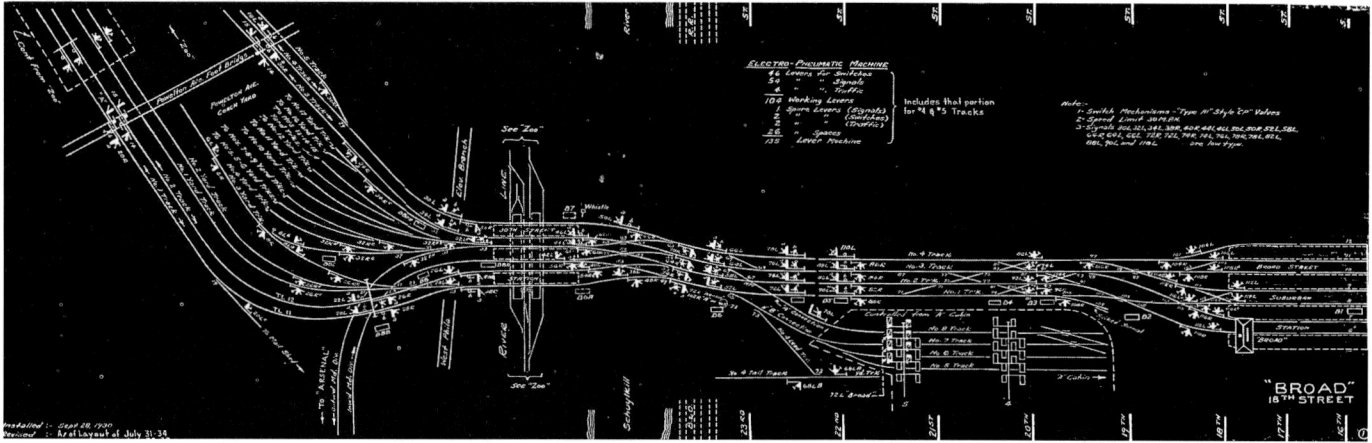

Hagley Museum and Library

BROAD Tower is located within the Suburban Station building, below the street level. It was one of four new interlockings installed during the Improvements – BROAD, PENN, ZOO and ARSENAL replaced 16 plants previously required in the area. Installed in 1930, PENN controls all movements in and out of the station, extending through the six-track upper level of 30th Street Station. As indicated on this 1938 diagram (before all the tracks were installed) the 135-lever electro-pneumatic machine controlled 48 single switches, 8 double-slip switches and movable-point frogs, 22 high signals and 69 dwarf signals. It initially worked closely with A Tower at Broad Street Station, and interacted with ZOO and ARSENAL Towers (north and south, respectively), as well as the Yardmaster in Powelton Avenue Coach Yard, where the MU equipment is stored awaiting the next rush hour.

Richard S. Short/Fred W. Schneider, III Collection

(*left*) A LONG STRING of MP54's heads west up the 2.2% grade out of Suburban Station toward 30th Street Station in September 1968. Note the low clearance of the overhead out of the subway tunnel, compressing all the pantographs. The last unit has already been repainted in Penn Central commuter green.

53

TRIUMPH III

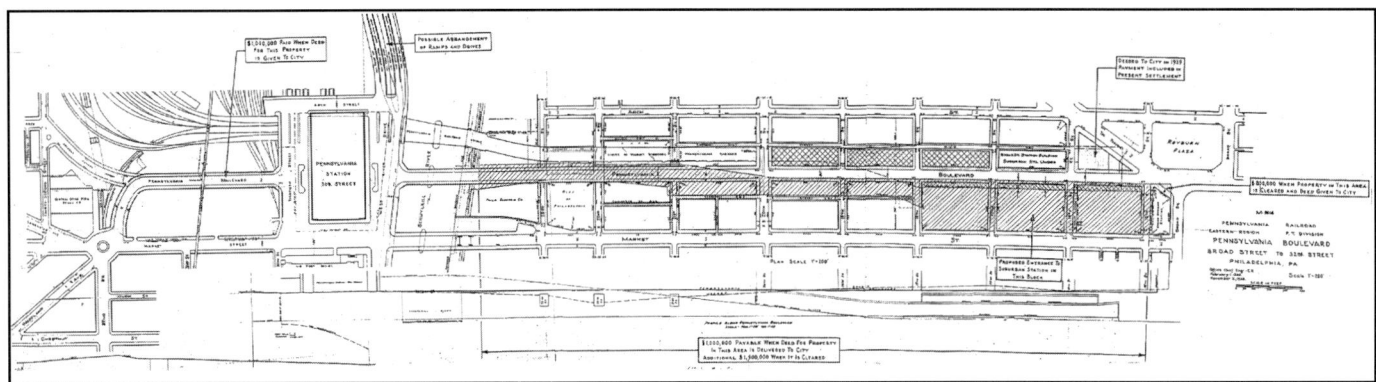

Hagley Museum and Library

AFTER WORLD WAR II, PRR and the City resumed discussions on implementation of the remaining Philadelphia Improvements, which would be mutually beneficial to both parties. The City had long wished to develop the area along West Market Street with new office buildings and retail stores. The key to proceeding was demolition of Broad Street Station and the area west of the station, totaling 18 acres. This included the property under the elevated station approach (diagonal lines on this 1946 diagram - the crosshatched areas represent air rights only), plus other parcels to be sold to the City. As PRR owned the land it would prove to be a lucrative real estate venture for the railroad in the postwar building boom. It would also allow completion of Pennsylvania Boulevard (later John F. Kennedy Boulevard) to provide grand access to 30th Street Station. A major obstacle to completing the Improvements was the Market Street Subway Elevated Line, which was originally designed to pass through an elevated enclosure on the south side of 30th Street Station.

A new Improvements Agreement was drawn up that addressed all the remaining issues. The problem with the Market Street Elevated Line was eventually resolved - after protracted negotiations with the Philadelphia Rapid Transit Co. This agreement called for the Department of City Transit to replace the elevated line by extending the Market Street Subway west from 20th Street to 46th Street, including a tunnel under the Schuylkill River, replacing the Market Street bridge. PRR in turn agreed to complete the remaining lower-level platforms and tracks in 30th Street Station to allow that facility to assume the additional traffic still utilizing Broad Street Station. Completion of this project would allow PRR to finally begin demolition of the venerable station.

ECONOMICS - the lure of badly needed income from the planned new Plaza project and the increasing cost of maintaining Broad Street Station - finally led to the fateful announcement by President James M. Symes in early 1952. Venerable Broad Street Station, 71 years after opening its grand doors to Philadelphia travelers, and having lived for 22 years on borrowed time, would finally close on 27 April. Train 231, the last inbound, arrived just before midnight on 26 April; Train 431 was scheduled to be the last outbound train at 1:10 a.m. on the 27th. Here we see the last train, after a platform concert by the equally venerable Philadelphia Orchestra and a tearful singing of "Auld Lang Syne," departing the station. Orchestra conductor Eugene Ormandy is at the center of the observation platform. The 18-car train was led, appropriately, by motor No. 4800, "Old Rivets" - the first GG1.

R.J. Long/Ted Xaras Collection

PRR COMES HOME

A CEREMONIAL SWING of a sledge hammer the next morning (which failed to break away any of the solid granite) signaled the beginning of the demolition process. Broad Street Station's walls finally yielded to power equipment and, piece by piece, the debris was loaded and hauled to Greenwich Point in South Philadelphia, where it was unceremoniously dumped into the Delaware River as fill for a new ore import pier. But it took several years to complete the job of redeveloping the area. In this ca. 1954 photo looking westward we see the result of the demolition process, with the foundations of the station in the foreground and Suburban Station at right ... 30th Street Station across the river is just visible behind the Fidelity Storage Building.

On 30 June 1954 the Suburban Station Office Building was sold for $7 million – becoming One Penn Center – with the railroad retaining rights to the station itself, below ground level. Construction of a new Railway Express facility across the river (to replace the old one shown here in front of the Fidelity Storage Building) allowed complete demolition of the Filbert Street Extension, finally making all the Penn Center properties available for development.

Ted Xaras Collection

Conrail Public Affairs/Penn Central RR Collection/Pennsylvania State Archives

ONCE the demolition was complete, the development of the $35 million Penn Center complex finally got underway. Six Penn Center, part of the first group of buildings, was constructed by PRR itself and became its new corporate headquarters in 1957, replacing space occupied in both Suburban and Broad Street Stations. Two (1958) and Three (1956) Penn Center were erected in the area previously occupied by Old Broad. A Sheraton hotel (1957) was constructed above the subway tracks between 17th and 18th Streets, along with an ice rink at 17th Street and JFK Boulevard. Four, Five and Seven Penn Center were built in the early Sixties, apartment buildings occupied the next two blocks toward the river and Eight Penn Center replaced the rink in the Seventies. With this undertaking, the grandiose plans first envisioned in the Twenties were finally complete - over 30 years later and markedly different in appearance. This aerial view looking northwestward shows the complex in 1957, with Three Penn Center in the foreground, Six to the west and the hotel north of that behind Suburban Station (now One Penn Center). Note the Parkway has been extended from the Art Museum in to City Hall.

WE NOW MOVE westward to the Schuylkill River and an examination of the bridges that carried PRR and its predecessor into the city. The first one – and in fact the first covered bridge in the U.S. – known as the Market Street Bridge (previously the Permanent Bridge),

was originally constructed by Timothy Palmer and opened 1 January 1805, replacing temporary float bridges in use since Revolutionary War days. It was rebuilt in 1850 by Daniel Stone to carry the Philadelphia & Columbia in its revised routing into the city (see *Triumph II*). The tracks occupied the north side and carriages and wagons used the south side; pedestrian walkways were located on the outside. The P&C had its terminus just west of the bridge and cars were moved into the city by teams of mules or horses onto the City-owned RR, as previously discussed. Like so many other wooden bridges, this 550-ft., three-span Howe truss with arches was destroyed by fire, in this case on 20 November 1875; it was rebuilt by PRR in a little more than a month. This marvelous undated but very early view looks northward, showing the lumber unloading dock in West Philadelphia.

Ted Xaras Collection

Ted Xaras Collection

THE FIRST PRR BRIDGE exclusively for railroad use was constructed north of Market Street in 1880, as part of the Filbert Street Extension project to serve the new Broad Street Station. It was an iron structure erected by Wilson Brothers, noted Philadelphia architects and engineers. (The three Wilson brothers, John A., Joseph M. and Henry A. were grandsons of Major John Wilson, who laid out the original route of the P&C. They were all graduates of Rensselaer Polytechnic Institute in Troy, New York, *alma mater* of the author). The approach cuts across the West Philadelphia Yards on a fill leading to elevated deck plate girders and then over the river on a three-span Howe deck truss shown here. This view looks eastward ca. 1890, with the southern extension trackage along the river in the foreground that served as an early freight bypass of the Junction RR.

PRR COMES HOME

Ted Xaras Collection

A SUPERB 1890s photo looking southeastward shows the mainline tracks sweeping toward the bridge. To the left is the southern end of an extensive stockyard complex in the West Philadelphia Yards, and south of the bridge approach is the large grain elevator. This slate-roofed wooden structure, completed in 1869, was 125-ft. wide and 555-ft. long. It contained 600 bins, each holding one carload. Just to the right of the elevator the B&O passenger station is visible across the river. To the right of the dual signal mast is the PRR West Philadelphia freight station on Market Street. We'll look more closely at all of these facilities shortly.

TWENTY YEARS have elapsed, and we have quite a few changes evident in a similar view looking toward Center City. The grain elevator has given way to an additional mainline bridge south of the first one, and a third bridge, north of the original one, for Maryland Division (former PB&W) trains from the south. C tower has been rebuilt, upper-quadrant semaphores have been installed and of course we have the overhead catenary, recently erected at the time this photo was taken on 24 June 1915. The Philadelphia Gas Works tanks across the river rise above the three bridges.

Ted Xaras Collection

THE NORTHERNMOST of the three "second generation" railroad bridges across the Schuylkill River to Broad Street Station was known as Bridge A, the PB&W connection for trains from the south (Maryland Division). This was a double-track, three-span through steel truss structure - two 156-ft. end spans and one 150-ft. center span over the river itself - constructed in 1902. This line also involved a new 65-ft. deck plate girder span over the B&O tracks on the east side of the river, and on the west side a 69-ft. half-through girder bridge over 30th Street and a 68-ft. half-through girder span to the Market Street Freight Yard, all built in 1902. The western approach to this bridge was by a large curved tunnel, which carried the tracks under the southern end of West Philadelphia Yards. It allowed a separation of traffic from the south and the mainline and New York Division tracks to the west and north. An improved connection between the PB&W and the New York Division was also made at this time, allowing passage of through New York-Washington trains without entering Broad Street Station. This 1920 view looks eastward across the river.

National Archives

BRIDGE C was the middle bridge of the three. It was a 455-ft., three-span steel deck truss built in 1911, replacing the original 1880 bridge, plus a 141-ft. deck plate girder span constructed in 1891. This bridge carried the Filbert Street Extension trackage into West Philadelphia Yard; once the two other bridges were completed in 1902-3 this bridge was used primarily to move empty trains between Broad Street Station and the yards. The 1920 photo shows a train headed inbound to the station.

National Archives

THE THIRD BRIDGE was built as a two-track, three-span steel deck truss plus deck plate girder structure, totaling 607 feet. Bridge B was completed in 1903 as part of a new passenger mainline running from the tunnel at the eastern leg of the wye at Mantua Junction (later ZOO) to join with the Filbert Street Extension into Broad Street Station. It became the primary bridge to carry mainline trains from the north and west into Broad Street. It was widened to four tracks in 1910 as part of the program to expand the approach and thus further improve traffic flow into the station. A 730-ft. steel viaduct on the west end carried the mainline tracks over the southern end of the West Philadelphia yards. This 1920 view also looks eastward.

National Archives

PRR COMES HOME

WE NOW MOVE across the river to look at the succession of stations near 30th and Market Streets in West Philadelphia. We have already seen the first station at this site, built in 1864 and expanded in 1867, as well as the Centennial Depot at 32nd and Market, constructed (of course) in 1876. Here we see the ivy-covered two-story West Philadelphia Freight Office, opened 6 November 1889. It was located on the north side of cobblestoned Market Street at 30th, replacing an earlier facility constructed at 31st and Market in 1878. This photo looking north is from the 1890s. We're not sure what the white-coated gentlemen is carrying in the cart, unless it represents an early coffee wagon!

Ted Xaras Collection

Ted Xaras Collection

NOW WE COME to the station in West Philadelphia whose function (and even existence) is arguably least understood of all major PRR depots in the Philadelphia area. It was opened in 1903 at 32nd and Market Streets, strategically located at the crossing of two lines. Constructed of granite with terra cotta trim and a red Spanish tile roof (not unlike North Philadelphia, built at about the same time), it was 112 ft. long and cost a very reasonable $125,000. It was built to relieve Broad Street Station of certain groups of trains. To do this it was configured with platforms on two levels – the two upper level ones, shown here in a view looking west on Market Street, served trains headed into Broad Street Station from New York City and the West. Note the trolleys and horse-drawn wagons on Market Street in this photo taken shortly after the station opened. The front area later became a cab stand.

59

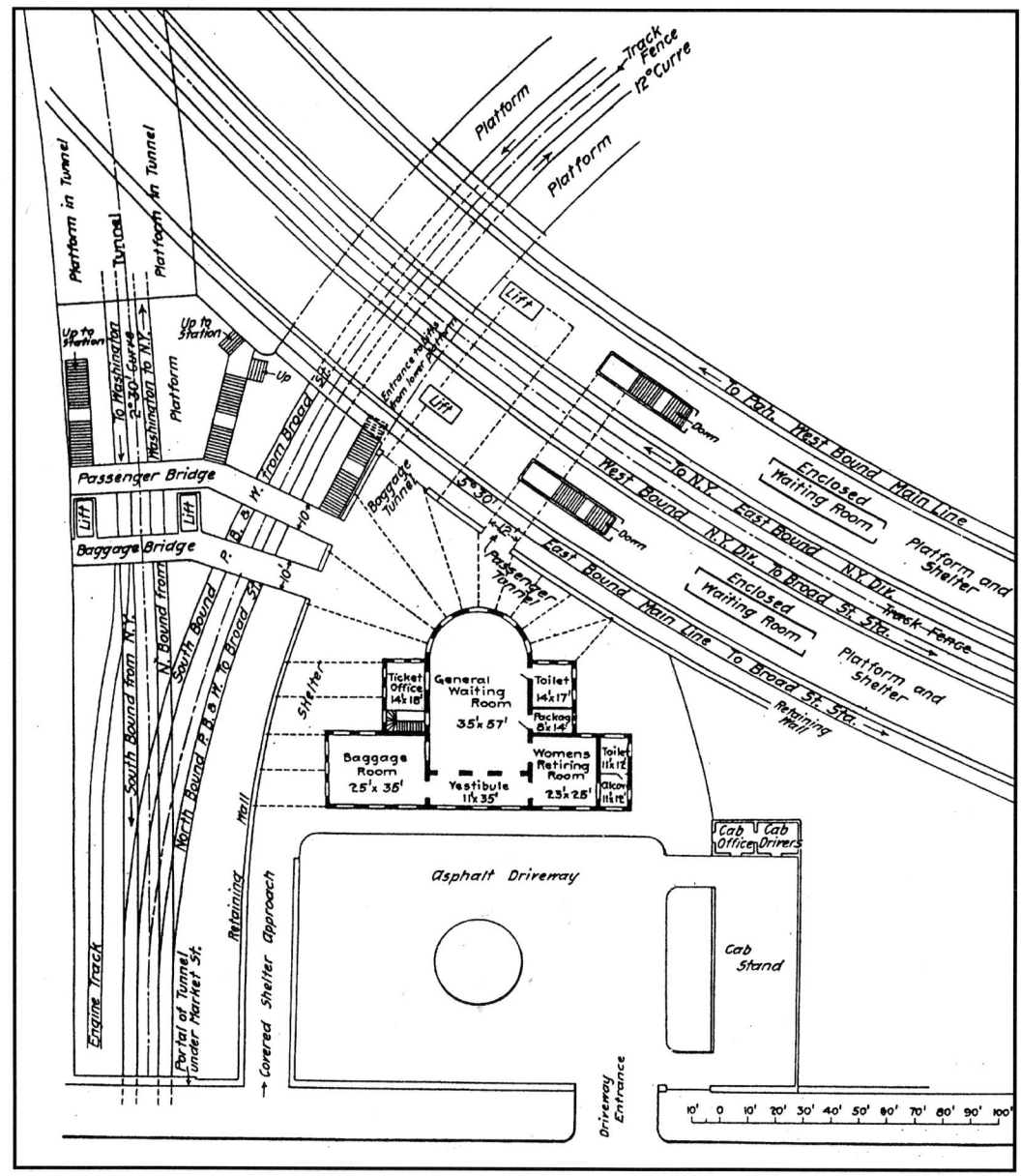

Ted Xaras Collection

THE COMPLEX LAYOUT of West Philadelphia Station is evident in this diagram. The two upper level platforms on the curve served trains to and from the west and New York City into Broad Street Station. The four lower ones served the PB&W tracks in and out of Broad Street Station as well as PRR New York-Washington trains. Thus the station could serve a total of eight trains at once. Even though it might be argued that this was the most flexible station of any to date in terms of the lines it served (it handled north-south traffic far better than Broad Street Station) to this author its construction 10 years after the expansion of that facility represented at best PRR's continuing indecision as to the best location for its main Philadelphia terminal and at worst an early recognition that Broad Street Station was not at the optimum site. Locating a station on the west side of the river to serve all but suburban commuter traffic was seemingly the best solution, but this configuration fell short of the mark and the facility lacked adequate capacity to do the job. It would be eliminated in the Improvements and abandoned on 12 March 1933 when 30th Street Station was operational for through trains.

PRR COMES HOME

Ted Xaras Collection

THIS GLOOMY Winter view of West Philadelphia Station looking northward ca. 1910 gives us a look at the lower level platforms serving the Maryland Division (ex-PB&W) tracks from the south, which swing under the upper level right-of-way and across the river into Broad Street Station. They also served through New York-Washington trains, which passed through the tunnel in the background at left center of the photo. This latter role was probably its most valuable one, illustrating the value of this location for what would later come to be known as Northeast Corridor trains. The Powelton Avenue footbridge passes from its namesake street into the maelstrom of the West Philadelphia Shops, obscured in the smoke. This photo also shows the brick interlocking towers constructed in 1896 at 32nd Street (D – left center) and Powelton Avenue (G – center background).

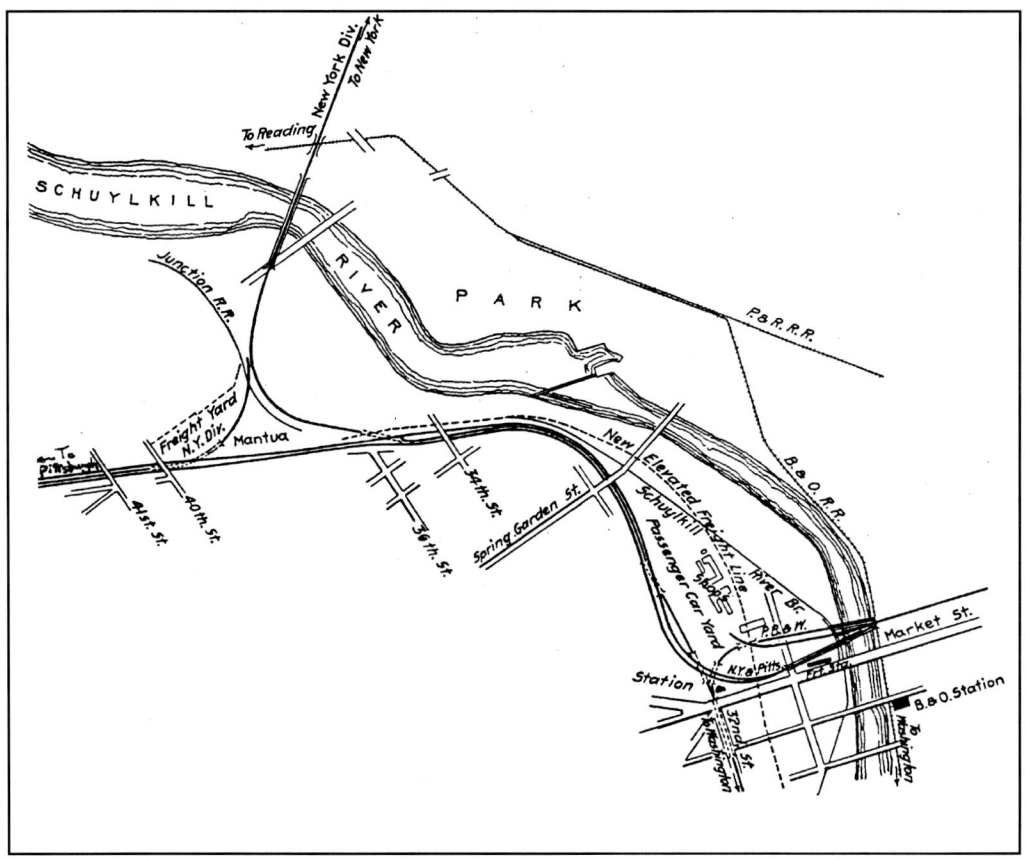

Ted Xaras Collection

WE WILL LOOK AT several more-detailed maps of the complex West Philadelphia area shortly, but this one shows the general layout of trackage at the time of construction of the station at 32nd and Market in 1903. It clearly indicates how the station, although not convenient for Center City commuters, was ideally suited to serve through New York-Washington trains, as well as trains from Broad Street Station to the north, south or west. Note the West Philadelphia Elevated Line (High Line), as well as the B&O tracks connecting to the Reading (more on these in Chapters 5 and 6).

The map will allow us to follow the mainline trackage out of Broad Street Station, as of 1903 (each line represents double track). The four mainline tracks emerging from the station and crossing the river on Bridge B (the southern one) are made up of the Philadelphia Division (to Pittsburgh) and also the Schuylkill Division (to Pottsville) on the outside, with the two New York Division tracks between them. From West Philadelphia Station the tracks run parallel to 34th Street, where the outer (Philadelphia Division) tracks separate and the New York Division tracks descend through a 500-ft. long walled cut and pass under the outbound track of the Philadelphia Division through a 550-ft. tunnel. From there they curve to the right on the wye at Mantua Junction and extend across the Schuylkill River again on the Connecting Railway toward New York City.

For through trains operating between New York and Washington, connecting tracks diverge from the New York Division main, descend into a 1750-ft. long walled cut and pass under the outbound main via a 400-ft. tunnel. They continue in a 785-ft. cut and then through a second, 305-ft tunnel at West Philadelphia Station, connecting with the PB&W tracks southward. These tracks also connect with the Philadelphia Division so that through Washington-Pittsburgh trains can avoid Broad Street Station. The wye at Mantua Junction also allows through New York-Pittsburgh trains to move directly west, utilizing North Philadelphia instead of Broad Street Station. Trains from New York pass under the east-west tracks via a 485-ft. tunnel to move southward into West Philadelphia. We will examine the operations at Mantua Junction more closely later in this chapter.

Trains between Philadelphia and Washington can, of course, depart Broad Street Station and cross the river on Bridge A and then utilize the PB&W connection to proceed southward. It was the beginning of a complex trackwork pattern on the west side of the river, allowing trains to move just about anywhere. The map also shows the Schuylkill River Branch, which was built in 1880 to provide a through north-south freight route independent of the Junction RR. It was obliterated in the construction of 30th Street Station. (If you got through all of this, congratulations, but don't let it go to your head, as PRR would continue to change and further add to the track complexity in this area.)

PRR COMES HOME

Ted Xaras Collection

THIS HIGH-LEVEL VIEW, a PRR photo taken 3 September 1930 from the West Philadelphia Office Building looking eastward, shows a lot going on. At lower right are the high-level platforms of West Philadelphia Station. The tracks continue across the river on Bridge B. To the right of that is the infamous Market Street Elevated trackage, with its twin arch truss spanning the river, and then Market Street itself. Between them is the 30th Street interlocking tower, constructed in 1896. To the left of Bridge B is Bridge C, on the original right-of-way into the city. At lower left, curving past the West Philadelphia Substation and crowded engine terminal, are the tracks of the Maryland Division (PB&W), which sweep in the cut up to the three truss spans of Bridge A. The 32nd Street tunnel carrying this line was enlarged and electrified in 1926, one of the initial projects related to (but not funded by) the Improvements program. The High Line extends north-south across it all, dramatically illustrating the purpose of its construction.

But on the left, next to the remains of the stockpens and abattoir, something else is happening . . .

Ted Xaras Collection

WHAT WAS HAPPENING was the new railroad bridge over the Schuylkill River, which would eventually replace the other three, and more significantly the beginnings of 30th Street Station. The attractive stone-faced concrete arch bridge carries the suburban tracks through the upper level of the station. Interestingly, during construction of this bridge the concrete forms were suspended from a heavy steel truss overhead to prevent interference with river traffic below. Because of protracted negotiations over the disposition of the Market Street Elevated line, which delayed construction of the main portions of 30th Street Station, the six-track suburban (north) wing was completed by itself, which was a strange sight. It was opened on 28 September 1930, at the same time as Suburban Station across the river. As odd as it looked (it was likened to a movie set) it was a beginning! This westward PRR photo dated 10 September 1930 shows the new bridge and station in a frenzy of activity only a short time before opening. Note Bridge A at left, the PRR West Philadelphia Office Building in the smoke at left rear, and the girders for the station plaza at right, taking away more of the stockpens. The bridge girders in the left foreground carry the tracks over the B&O right-of-way below.

PRR COMES HOME

Herbert H. Harwood, Jr.

30TH STREET STATION, constructed of steel and concrete faced with gleaming Alabama limestone, presents the majestic appearance of a classic temple. The west façade, shown here in a 1974 view, stretches 639 ft. along 30th Street and 327 ft. on Market Street (right). The massive Corinthian columns, 71 ft. high and 11 ft. in diameter, dominate the porticoes at each end of the main concourse, which reaches 116 ft. in height. This design, prepared by Graham, Anderson, Probst and White, was selected over more than 130 others. The facility was opened for partial service on two tracks (for north-south through trains) on 12 March 1933, and West Philadelphia Station was then closed. The 60 x 145-ft. main waiting room and 135 x 290-ft. main concourse finally opened on 15 December of that year. It was PRR's fourth station in this historic area of the city. Note the upper level commuter platform just visible at left.

THE ISSUE of where to put the Market Street Elevated line produced lengthy discussions. Originally it was planned for the line to pass through an extended south wing of the station, making it symmetrical with the suburban north wing, but PRR objected to the appearance of the elevated and its twin bridges over the river, feeling that they would detract from the appearance of the new facility. Once a supplemental agreement was made with the City in 1927 to remove the elevated structure and bridges and locate the line in a tunnel passing under both the lower-level tracks and the river and connecting with the subway in Center City, construction of the remainder of 30th Street Station could begin. Thus the station was built without the south wing extension.

Although construction of the new Market Street Bridge and subway was begun, the Depression hit City finances hard. With World War II then intervening, both projects were further delayed and would not be completed for 25 years.

PRR fortunately had made sufficient financial arrangements to proceed with construction, although this effort was plagued with the discovery of a 17th Century Quaker burial ground (the coffins were relocated), a fire in the partially-completed structure in 1932 and a strike the following year. Problems were also encountered with obtaining a secure foundation in the soft silt where the river had previously been located. This required driving 5,000 steel piles to bedrock and then filling them with concrete. A post-World War II view looking west along Market Street shows the line curving in front of the south façade of the completed station (PRR was right about the Elevated!). A freight rumbles along the High Line in the background as trolleys stop in the station plaza.

H. Albrecht/Ted Xaras Collection

TRIUMPH III

Ted Xaras Collection

FINALLY FREE of all external encumbrances, 30th Street Station emerges in all its intended glory in the sunlight, in a stunning aerial photo ca. 1957. This view shows the station with wide plazas and the remaining through tracks completed. The Schuylkill Expressway has been extended along the riverfront, taking over from West River Drive. The old bridges- including the Market Street Elevated structure - are all gone and the new railroad bridge, along with new bridges for Pennsylvania (later JFK) Boulevard and Market Street, closely tie the station to the Center City area. Across the river the initial buildings have been completed in the Penn Center development program. To the right of the station is the large Post Office building, completed in 1935, and the B&O Station above it, across the river. At the bottom of the picture, below the High Line, are the Steam Plant and the 14-story PRR Office Building, opened in 1927. Between them are the MU storage yard and two tunnels, the upper one for the West Chester Branch and the lower one for the Grays Ferry Branch - a remnant of the Junction RR (see Chapter 6). All through trains enter the lower level of the station via the River Line, and all commuter trains move across through the upper level. It had taken PRR over a century to find the right locations for its Philadelphia stations, but 30th Street (for through trains), in combination with Suburban Station (for Center City Commuters) was the triumphant conclusion. We especially like this photo, not only for its illustrative value, but also for its superb composition and dramatic lighting.

PRR COMES HOME

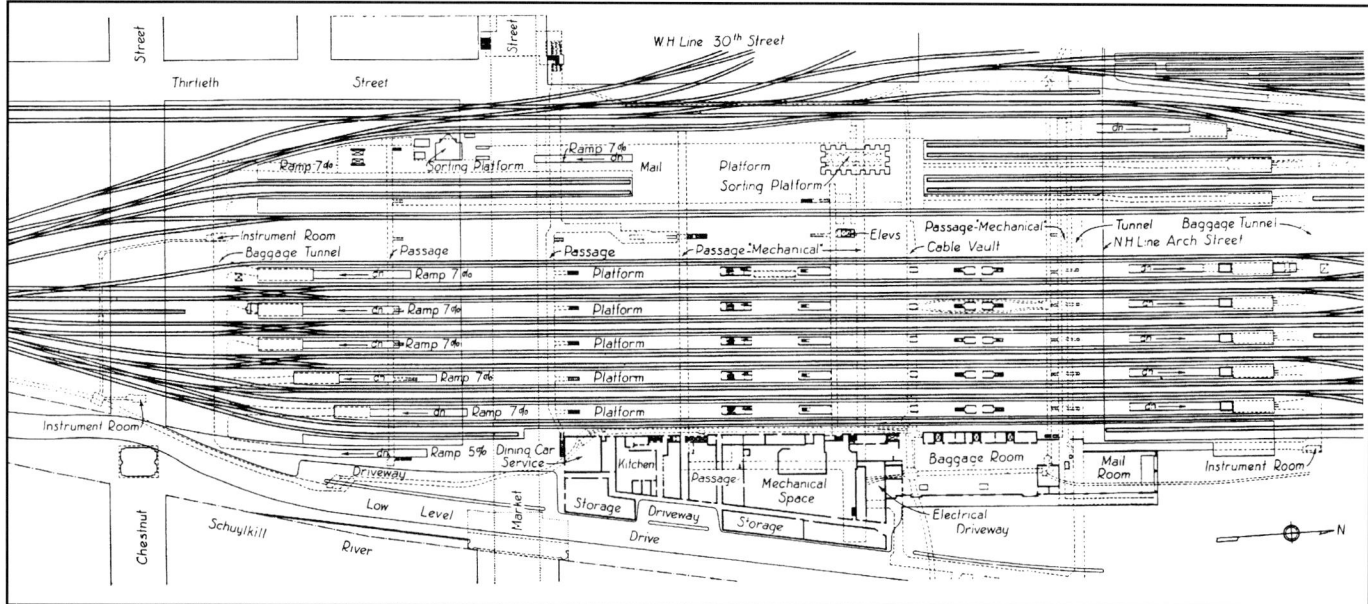

THIS DIAGRAM shows the original plan for the lower-level tracks and platforms at 30th Street Station. The platforms are nearly 25 ft. wide and 1500 ft. long; ramps at either end connect via tunnels to the track-level baggage and mail rooms. When the facility was initially opened for through service on 12 March 1933, only two of the 10 tracks were placed in operation for through north-south trains. Additional platforms and tracks were added in 1937, but the major expansion came in 1950 when construction finally began for the remaining trackage and the last three platforms and baggage ramps. The cost of this 3-year program was nearly $11.5 million, along with another $3.25 million to complete the final platforms at Suburban Station.

In addition to passenger and baggage handling capability, the station was closely linked to the new $10 million Post Office complex, which opened directly across Market Street on 24 June 1935. There were two through and six stub-end tracks exclusively for handling of mail – on 2-1/4 miles of conveyor belts! The mail-handling facilities were further improved in 1956.

ONCE DEMOLITION of Broad Street Station began in April 1952, all remaining trains, including the New York "Clockers" and steam-powered PRSL Shore trains, were transferred to the enlarged facilities at 30th Street Station (the Greyhound Bus Terminal was also relocated to the north side of the station). PRR had considered transferring these trains (with electric power) to an expanded Suburban Station back in the 30s, but the cost was deemed prohibitive, and they continued to operate from Broad Street. Interestingly, because operation of steam locomotives under 30th Street was prohibited, outbound PRSL trains were set up at the north end, with the locomotive coupling to the train outside the station. Inbound trains used the upper level platforms. In an uncommon photo ca. 1955, we see a Shore run about to depart behind veteran K4 No. 3882. This arrangement was not to last long (steam had only a 2-year lease on life on PRR) but we can enjoy it here.

Ted Xaras Collection

67

TRIUMPH III

Fred W. Schneider, III

GENERAL OF THE ARMY Omar Bradley delivered the dedication address at the unveiling of the War Memorial in 30th Street Station on Sunday 10 August 1952, The statue, towering 36 ft. 7 inches and weighing 10-1/2 tons, is located in the main concourse. One of the largest cast bronze statues made, it suggests the archangel Michael, Angel of the Resurrection, holding the figure of an uplifted soldier in his arms. It was sculpted by Walker Hancock and dedicated in honor of the 1307 PRR employees who gave their lives during World War II. Over 54,000 PRR employees served in the conflict. This dramatic photo shows the statue silhouetted against the east entrance at precisely 12:23 p.m. on 12 December 1970. The 18-ft. long light fixtures hang from a colorful coffered ceiling 95 ft. above the broad expanse of the Tennessee marble floor. The stairways and escalators on either side of the information booth descend to the mainline tracks below.

PRR COMES HOME

WITH STYLE – Here's a closeup of the information booth in the center of the Main Concourse. There aren't many interior shots in the *Triumph* series, but we happen to like this one. It captures the information clerk posting train arrivals, carefully and in precise handwriting, on the pre-electronic board on 10 October 1969. Thanks, Fred.

Fred W. Schneider, III

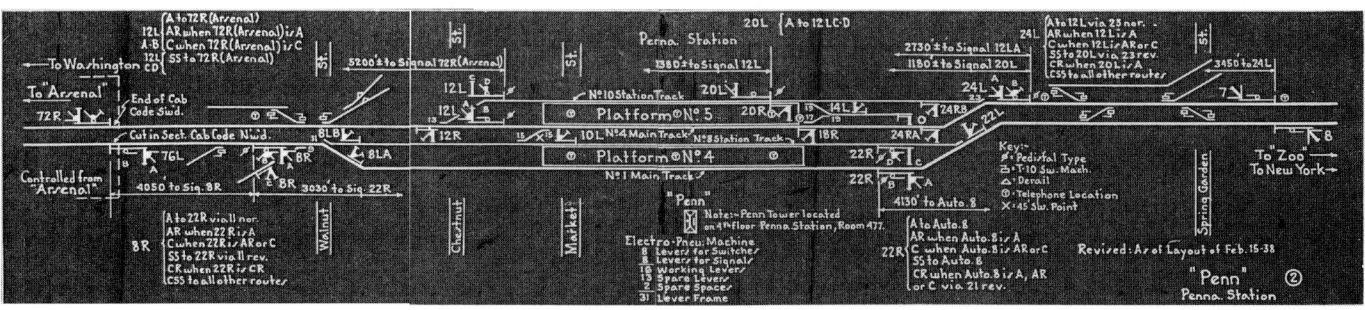

Hagley Museum and Library

ANOTHER EXAMPLE of a tower within a station, PENN Tower is located on the fourth floor of 30th Street Station. The 31-lever, electro-pneumatic machine initially handled only limited north-south (lower level) traffic through the station, but when Broad Street Station was finally abandoned its role and capacity increased dramatically to over 250 levers. The changeover took place on Sunday (fortunately) 27 April 1952, with seven men handling the problems related to the change in traffic routing; it subsequently became a two-man operation. This diagram shows its configuration as of 15 February 1938.

The Philadelphia Terminal Dispatcher's office, known as "S" Office, was also located on the fourth floor. This operation took three dispatchers to handle the traffic: The "A" Dispatcher covered the main from BRILL to 30th Street, plus the High Line, Delaware Extension and the West Chester Branch; "B" Dispatcher handled 30th Street to HOLMES, including the Chestnut Hill Branch; and the "C" Dispatcher covered Suburban Station to PAOLI, including the Schuylkill Valley Branch.

69

THE TWO PRR PRESIDENTS most closely associated with developments in the City of Philadelphia are George Brooke Roberts and William Wallace Atterbury. Samuel Rea, although instrumental in formulating many of the early plans for the Philadelphia Improvements, is better known for his work implementing A.J. Cassatt's vision for entrance into New York City and he will be profiled (along with Cassatt) in a subsequent volume in the *Triumph* series covering that monumental undertaking.

George Brooke Roberts was born on 15 January 1833 at "Pencoyd," his Welsh family's ancestral home for five generations (John Roberts had first emigrated from Bala in Wales in 1683 and purchased a 150-acre tract, in what became known as the Bala section of Philadelphia). Young George graduated from Rensselaer Polytechnic Institute in Troy, New York, completing the 3-year course in 2 years (Class of 1849). He then followed, literally, in John Edgar Thomson's footsteps, working for the master as a rodman in locating the PRR's Mountain Division. He subsequently left PRR and worked in several engineering positions of increasing responsibility, locating and overseeing the construction of future components of both the PRR and Reading systems.

His experience and expertise were rewarded when Thomson named him as Assistant to the President on 28 May 1862. His initial responsibility was the Philadelphia & Erie, but he soon took on other tasks, resulting in his appointment as Fourth Vice President and a Director on 3 May 1869. He jumped to Second Vice President in 1873 and to First Vice President under Tom Scott in 1874. He was perhaps known less for his vision than for his sheer hard work.

Conrail Public Affairs/Penn Central RR Collection/Pennsylvania State Archives

George Roberts was named president upon the retirement of Scott on 1 June 1880. His tenure as President was marked by modest but operationally significant improvements, including the Trenton Cutoff bypass of Philadelphia and new yards, connections and track upgrades in the Pittsburgh area, all resulting in faster and more efficient freight traffic flow, which had tripled over his years at the throttle. In 1879 he recommended the construction of a new passenger terminal in Center City Philadelphia. This subsequently led to the building of the Filbert Street Extension in 1880 and the opening of Broad Street Station in 1881.

He was known by his PRR colleagues for his modesty and gentleness of manner. Another side of his persona, however, seems to have come into play when it came to dealing with the Reading, PRR's – and singularly George Roberts' – bitter rival in Philadelphia. Incensed at the Reading's outflanking of PRR in gaining access to New York City, Roberts launched a competitive and openly adversarial series of moves. These included the takeover of the PW&B in 1881 (thwarting the Reading-B&O forces – see Chapter 6), invasion of heretofore sacrosanct Reading territory with the construction of the Chestnut Hill Branch in 1882-4 and the Schuylkill Division in 1881-6 (see Chapters 2 and 4, respectively), the dramatic expansion of Broad Street Station in 1893 (in part because of the opening of Reading Terminal earlier that year, which Roberts reportedly tried to block), and finally the construction of the aforementioned Trenton Cutoff in 1890-92 (see *Triumph II*).

While on a vacation trip in August 1896, he suffered a heart attack and subsequently died at his home on 30 January 1897. Mild-mannered George Roberts would leave his own marks on PRR – not all of them ultimately triumphant – but the Reading surely knew he had been there!

PRR COMES HOME

Conrail Public Affairs/Penn Central RR Collection/Pennsylvania State Archives

WILLIAM WALLACE ATTERBURY was born 31 January 1866 in New Albany, IN. After graduating from Yale University, he joined PRR on 11 October 1886 as an apprentice in the Altoona Shops. He advanced rapidly, in just 3 years becoming Assistant Road Foreman of Engines on the Philadelphia Division. After assignments on several other divisions he was named Assistant Engineer of Motive Power on the Pennsylvania Company's (Lines West) Northwest System in 1892. The following year he became Master Mechanic for the Pennsylvania Co. in Ft. Wayne, IN. In 1896 he advanced to Superintendent of Motive Power of Pennsylvania Lines East, headquartered in Altoona, and in 1901 he was promoted to General Superintendent of Motive Power.

His talents were recognized by President Cassatt and he was brought to Philadelphia, becoming General Manager of Lines East on 1 January 1903. In this role he significantly reduced congestion in this territory. On 24 March 1909 he was appointed Fifth Vice President, responsible for Transportation. Two years later he became Fourth Vice President and was elected a Director of the railroad. On 8 May 1912, with the number designations abolished, Atterbury was named Vice President of Operations.

With the entry of the U.S. into World War I, he was selected by the Secretary of War as the "ablest man in the country" to become Director General of Transportation for the American Expeditionary Forces. He sailed for France in August 1917 and on 5 October was commissioned Brigadier General. General Atterbury (the name stuck even after he returned to civilian life on 31 May 1919) was decorated by the U.S. and several Allied nations for his outstanding work in directing transportation operations in France under extremely difficult circumstances.

Upon his return to PRR he set about rebuilding the railroad after federal control was relinquished. He was also responsible for development and implementation of the regional operational structure for the consolidated Lines East and Lines West, allowing PRR to be run effectively and efficiently for the first time as an integrated railroad. It was the most sweeping change in the operating structure since Thomson's original line and staff system was introduced in 1857. He was named to the newly-created position of Vice President on 15 November 1924 as heir apparent and became President upon the retirement of Samuel Rea on 1 October 1925. He not only effectively ran PRR, but he also demonstrated an enlightened view of the need for coordination within the industry, leading to the formation of the Association of American Railroads in 1934.

As president Atterbury presided over the implementation of the Philadelphia Improvements, beginning with the West Philadelphia Office Building in 1925, the opening of Suburban Station and the upper level of 30th Street Station in 1930 and finally the completion of the main portion of the facility in 1933. He also oversaw the final phase of suburban electrification in Philadelphia during 1930 and the dramatic extension of the overhead on the mainline from New York to Washington on 10 February 1935. These projects involved heavy demands on his engineering, finance, management and diplomatic skills, and proved physically demanding as well. Shortly after completion of the monumental electrification project Atterbury announced his well-deserved retirement on 24 April of that year. His health had been poor for some time, and he died on 20 September. With his organizational changes, major terminal improvements in Philadelphia and Cincinnati and the north-south electrification project, Atterbury can be remembered for having brought PRR into the 20th Century.

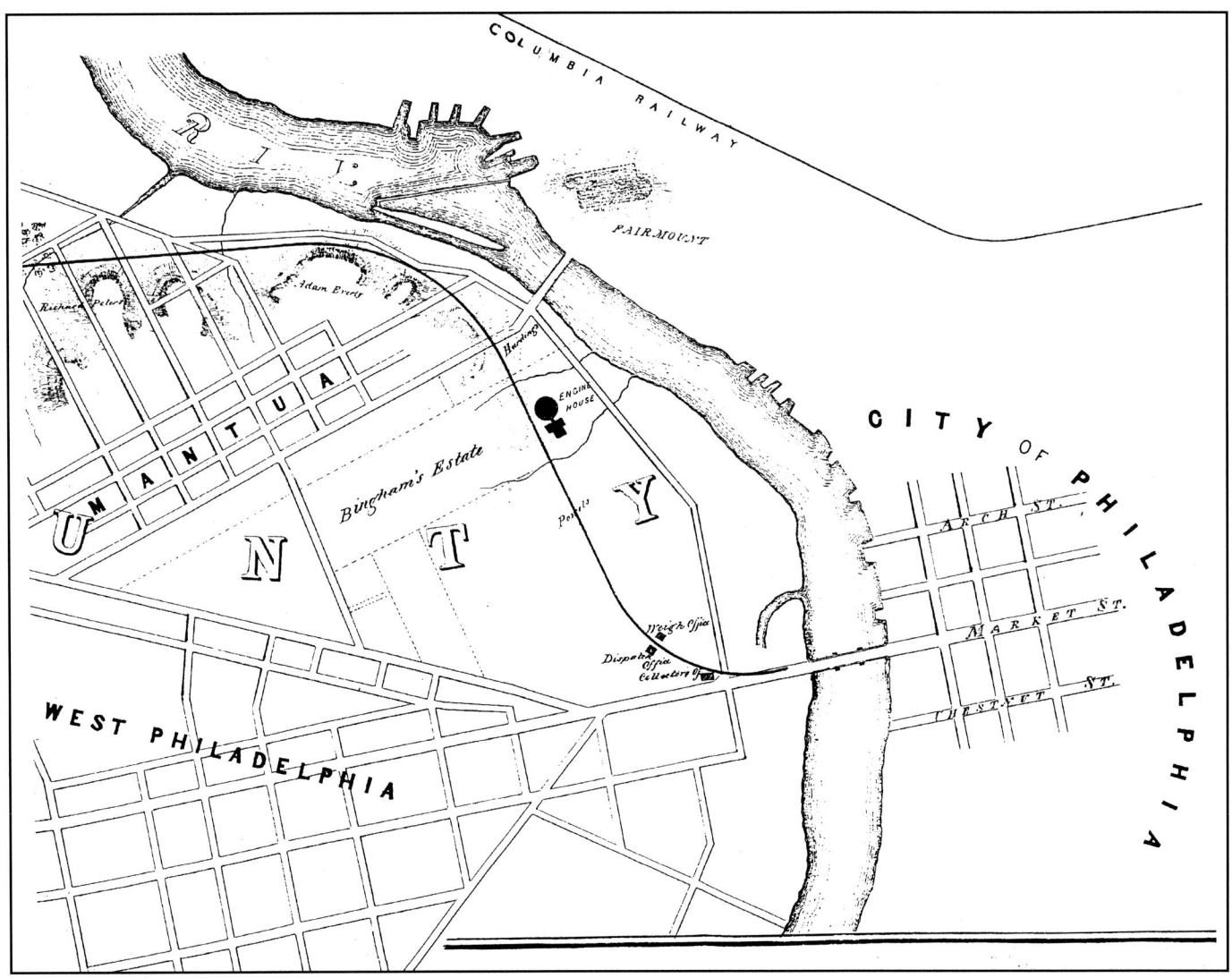

Ted Xaras Collection

AS PROMISED we now move to a study of the West Philadelphia Yard area. We will examine this rich stretch of railroad real estate along the Schuylkill River at several points in time, and examine the facilities and changes that occurred in them. It should be noted that early PRR records, including the Annual Reports, were often vague as to exactly what area in "West Philadelphia" was being referred to. For convenience and precision we will divide the area into three parts: First, the yard area opposite Center City and running north of the historic station area at 30th and Market Streets along the river; second, the wye junction of the mainline with the Connecting Railway at Mantua; and lastly, the extensive yard areas between that junction and the beginning of the Main Line at Overbrook, which also encompassed the junction with the Schuylkill Division.

In the Beginning – well almost, this 1851 map predates the PRR purchase – we see the relocated P&C approach through West Philadelphia to the newly rebuilt Market Street Bridge. The line swings through Mantua, through the Peters and Bingham estates, and past an enginehouse to a Weigh Office, Dispatcher's Office and Collector's Office at the terminus on the west end of the bridge. On 16 May 1853 the State Canal Commissioners authorized PRR to build a siding for its own use – the beginning of the West Philadelphia Yards! Note the original P&C route at the top, now the Philadelphia & Reading's route into the City.

PRR COMES HOME

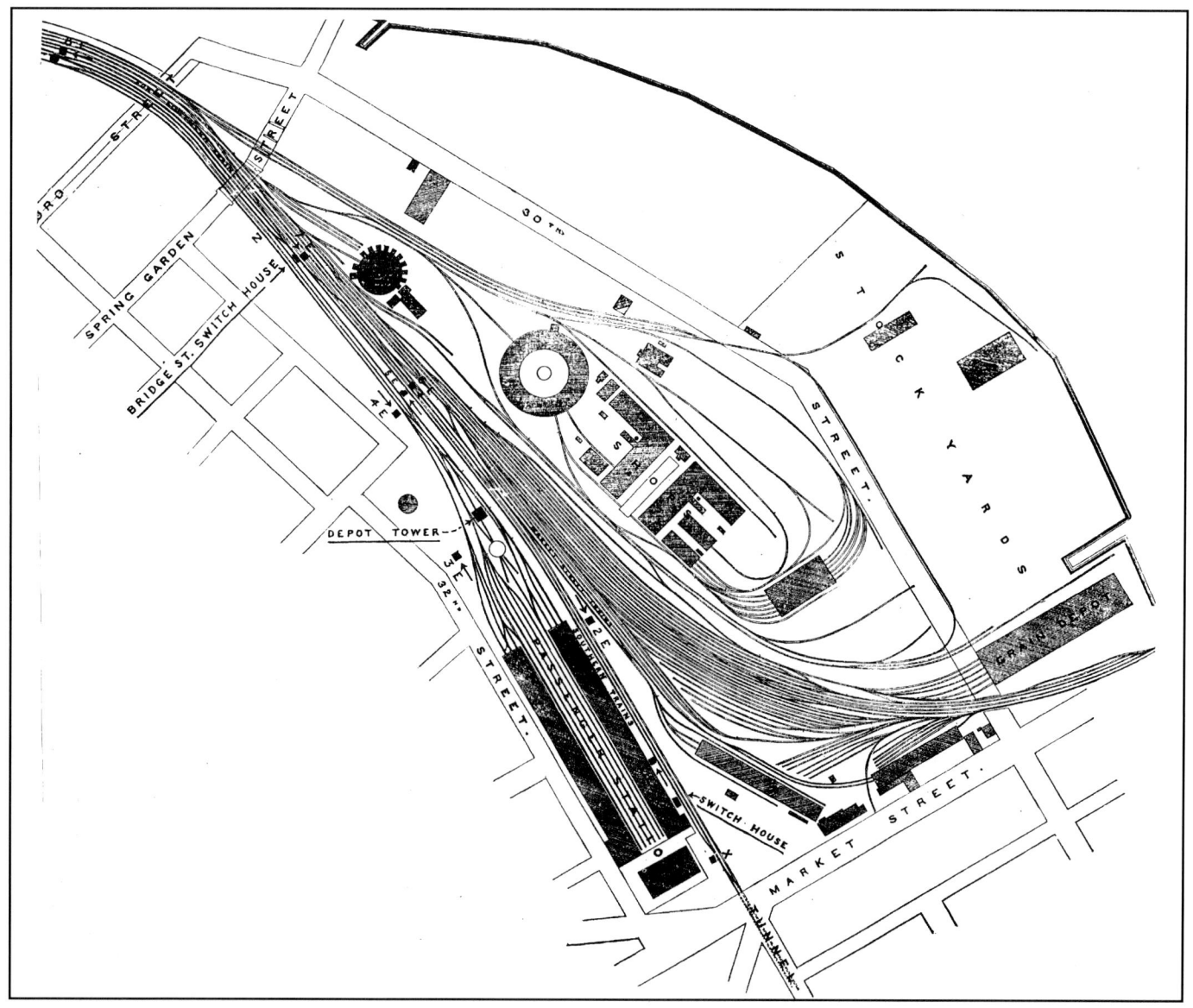

Ted Xaras Collection

TWENTY-FIVE YEARS have passed, PRR has purchased the P&C and there have been momentous changes in West Philadelphia. This 1876 map captures several of them: At bottom center is the Centennial Depot with its trainsheds. To the right of the depot, labeled "Southern Trains," are the Junction RR tracks connecting through the tunnel to the PW&B. At the right are the tracks leading past the previous 1867 New York Depot and the 1864 station for trains to the west, and then onto the Market Street Bridge (which was rebuilt after a fire in 1875). Above that is the original grain depot and north of that the large stockyard area, opened that year. Between the stockyards and the depot tracks are the West Philadelphia Shops, including the large Enginehouse No. 2 and beyond it the smaller Enginehouse No. 1. We will look more closely at all of these facilities, the extent of which is truly amazing given that PRR had purchased the P&C barely 20 years previously, followed by the tumult of the Civil War and then the Panic of 1873!

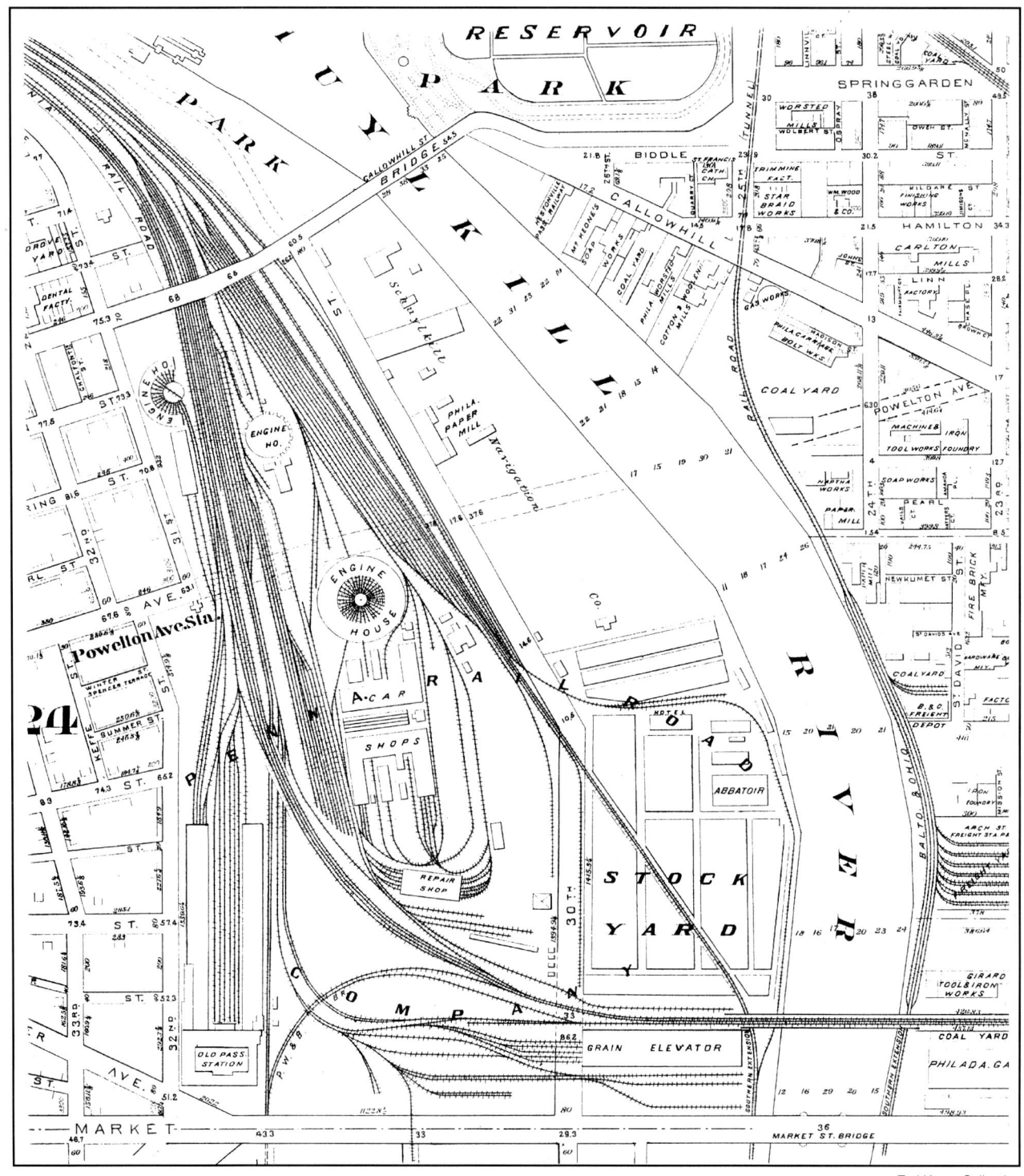

Ted Xaras Collection

THIS MAP from the 1888 City Atlas shows us a few changes. The new (1880) bridge now carries the realigned PRR main across the river toward Broad Street Station. With the construction of the new terminal across the river the Centennial Depot is now the "Old Passenger Station." The connecting loop for PW&B trains to enter Broad Street Station has been added, along with the track for through New York City-Washington trains. The stockyards have been greatly expanded, complete with abattoir and, interestingly, a hotel – which must have been delightful on hot summer nights! A new 18-stall enginehouse and 60-ft. turntable were constructed at 31st and Spring Garden Streets (upper left) in 1880. With the opening of Broad Street Station the Powelton Avenue Station (left) was built in 1882 to serve West Philadelphia; it was rebuilt in 1885 after a fire. Note the B&O and Reading trackage on the east bank of the river.

PRR COMES HOME

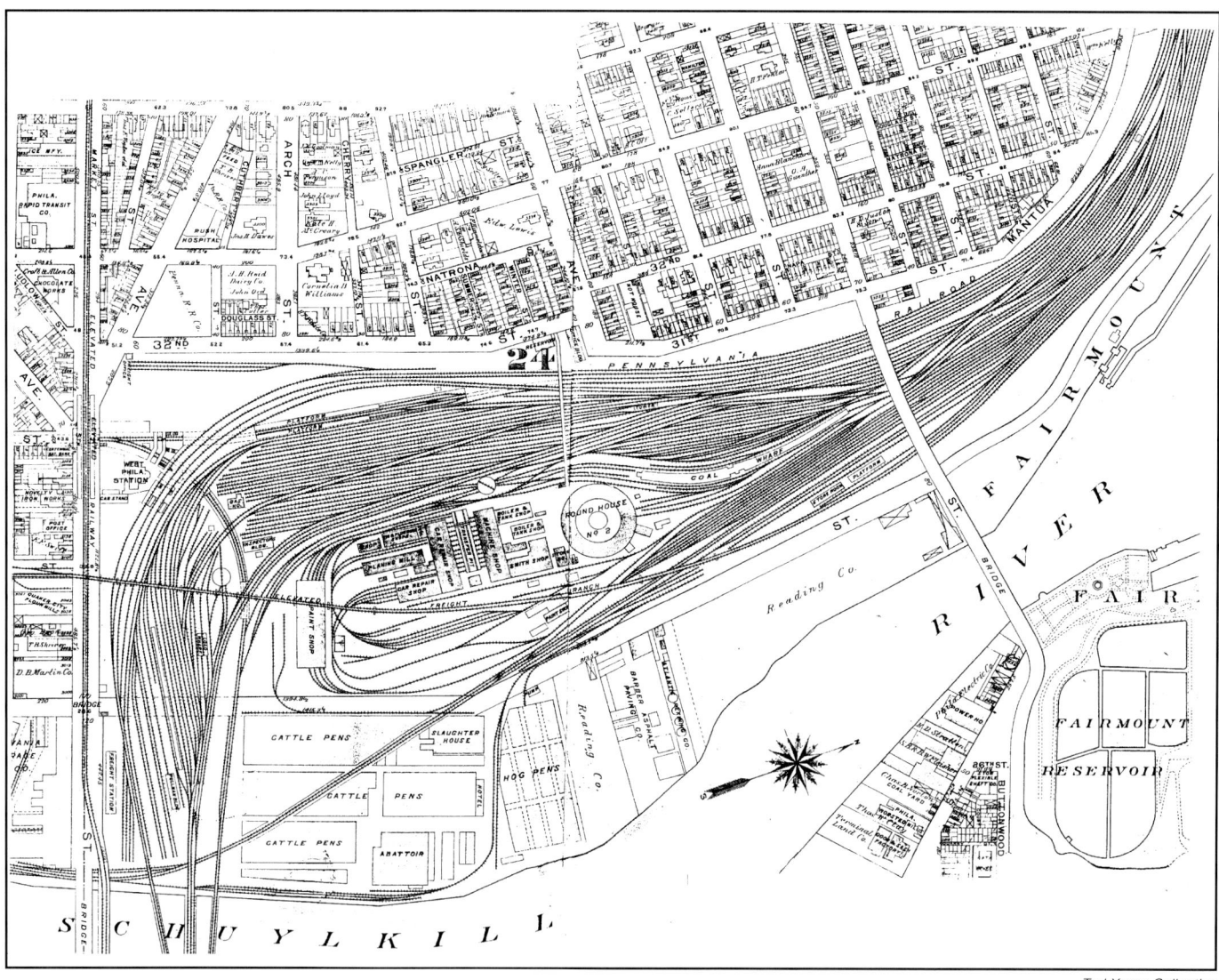

Ted Xaras Collection

BY 1910 many more changes had taken place. The Grain Elevator and Centennial Station have both gone (the latter destroyed by fire in 1896), and the West Philadelphia Station has been strategically located on Market Street at the apex of the two north-south lines. The West Philadelphia Freight Terminal (1902) has also been constructed along Market Street; note also the Market Street Elevated Railway (transit line).

Two additional bridges across the river into Broad Street Station have also been added. The mainline to and from New York City has been realigned to Bridge B (the southernmost one), while Bridge C (the middle, original one) is now relegated to the movement of trains in and out of the passenger yards. Bridge A handles trains to and from Washington, D.C.

After the late 1880s, engine terminal facilities were gradually shifted to the 46th Street area, and the Powelton Avenue passenger yards were enlarged and used primarily to serve the terminals on both sides of the river. The two smaller roundhouses have been eliminated, and a long coal wharf has been constructed north of recently-rebuilt Roundhouse No. 2. Two separate new turntables have also been added, one adjacent to the Machine Shop and the other just northeast of West Philadelphia Station. The Elevated Freight Branch (High Line) crosses over it all. Our hotel remains near the slaughterhouse in the stockyard area (pun intended).

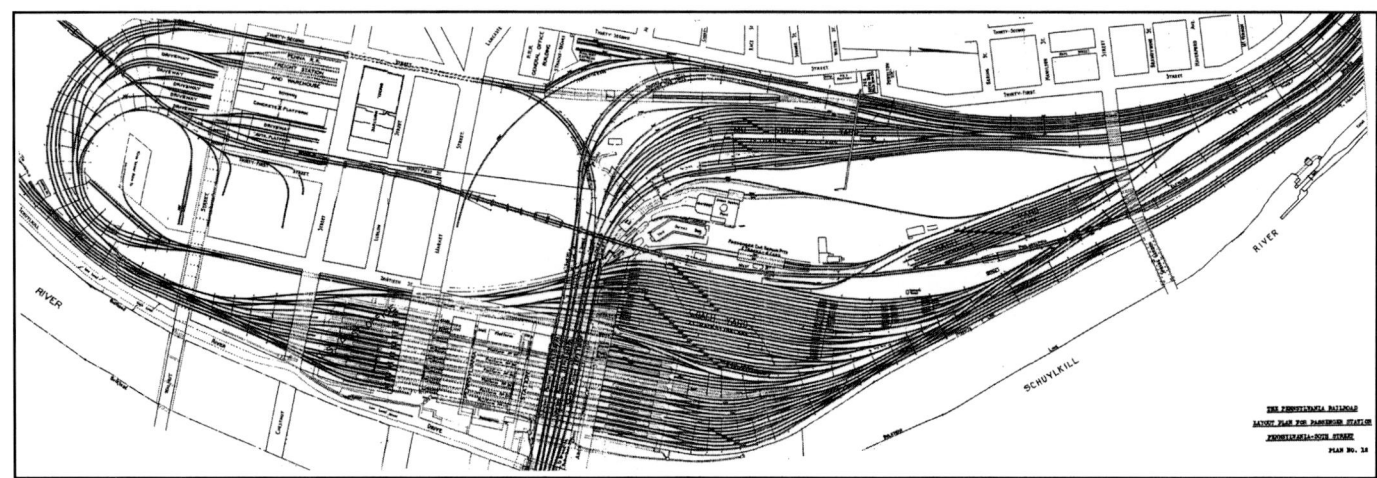

Ted Xaras Collection

THIS DIAGRAM, part of a comprehensive series prepared in 1935 for possible consolidation of railroad lines in Philadelphia, shows the near-final configuration of 30th Street Station trackage and the associated yards in West Philadelphia. "Pennsylvania Station" is located at bottom left of center, with suburban tracks crossing on the upper level and the through tracks underneath. To the right (north) are the approach tracks and above them the coach yard for through equipment. Above that is the storage yard for MU cars. South of the station is the newly-completed Post Office, as well as the Freight Station and Warehouse, opened in 1929, replacing the one at 30th and Market, which was displaced by the new passenger facility. The Elevated Freight Line spans above it all.

At far left – and here we need to be careful with this diagram – are the planned loop tracks. Pennsylvania Station was initially envisioned as a "union" facility to handle not only PRR but also B&O and Reading trains, some of which would use the loop for turning. The other two roads lost interest (if they ever really had it), and a recommendation was made in July 1948 not to build the loop because of cost (upwards of $2 million), tight curves on a grade and interference with the freight holding yard south of Walnut Street. The decision was finally made on 15 February 1951 to cancel plans for the loop. We should also point out that the Railway Express facility was ultimately located farther south, at South Street.

It took almost 20 years from the date of this diagram to fulfill the plan for 30th Street Station, but when it was PRR had finally found the answer to its passenger station needs in Philadelphia.

PRR COMES HOME

Ted Xaras Collection

WE WILL NOW go back and take a closer look at the evolution of the West Philadelphia Yard area. It is ca. 1890 and we are looking westward at the approach to the 1880 bridge. To the right are the stockyard buildings, with the edge of the Repair Shop just visible at the edge of the photo. To the left is the slate-roofed grain elevator, with the freight yards beyond. The double track to the right is the main that curves across 30th Street (in the cut) and through the yards. The single track on the left leads straight ahead into the freight yards, but notice the track that diverges and curves just in front of the tower - this is the PW&B inbound connection, which then swings around to the south. The outbound track branches off the main, just visible to the right of C Tower. In the background is the station building and long trainsheds of the Centennial Station, which served the Exposition traffic well but which has been displaced by Broad Street Station and is being used for car storage by the time this photo was taken. It would be destroyed by a spectacular fire before the turn of the new century. Note the lower-quadrant signals on the mast at right.

Ted Xaras Collection

IN THIS very early view ca. 1875, we are standing on unpaved 30th Street looking south. In front of us is the graceful 63-ft. arch bridge carrying six tracks into the Grain Depot on the left. The attractive iron and masonry structure was another Wilson Brothers creation; both the bridge and grain depot were constructed in 1869. Beyond are the mainline tracks approaching the Market Street Bridge.

Ted Xaras Collection

AS THE CIVIL WAR was drawing to a close PRR built a large car shop complex in West Philadelphia. A view of this facility ca. 1903 shows the southern end of the shops, with an interesting collection of varnish lined up alongside. Note the detailed brickwork, remarkable for shop buildings. This complex would remain until gradually displaced by the Philadelphia Improvements beginning in the late 1920s. The main approaching the river crossing is in the foreground.

PRR COMES HOME

Conrail Public Affairs/Penn Central RR Collection/Pennsylvania State Archives

JUST NORTH of the shops PRR also erected this rather impressive Enginehouse No. 2, shown here in the 1880s, in a winter view dominated incongruously by a single large tree. Like the shop buildings, this structure carries elegant brick arcade trim; also note the series of spired cupolas at the roof peak.

E.P. Alexander Archive/Ted Xaras Collection

THE FREIGHT YARDS along the river are shown in this ca. 1890 photo looking south. On the right are the two roundhouses: the domed Enginehouse No. 1 and beyond – in the smoke – is Enginehouse No. 2, at the north end of the shops. The yards contain an interesting collection of two- and four-wheeled wooden coal cars and on the left, a string of stock cars serving the stockyards in the distance.

79

Ted Xaras Collection

THIS PANORAMA of West Philadelphia Yards looking north ca. 1920 shows the now-electrified main tracks on the left, curving toward Broad Street Station across the river. To the right of that is the cut carrying through New York-Washington trains into the lower level of West Philadelphia Station. Note D Tower perched on the edge of the cut in front of the tunnel portal, and G Tower behind the Powelton Avenue Footbridge, which extends across through the smoke to Roundhouse No. 2. This 44-stall, 340-ft. diameter fortress-like structure was constructed in 1903, replacing the earlier enginehouse at that location. The area was soon to be altered by the first of the Philadelphia Improvements, with a new steam plant to be built in the area occupied by the nearest cluster of shop buildings. The High Line arches above it all at right and into the distance; across the river the Art Museum is just visible through the smoke.

Ted Xaras Collection

THE POWELTON AVENUE station was constructed in 1882 to serve West Philadelphia after Broad Street Station was opened on the east side of the river and the Centennial Station was closed. This rare photo shows the front of the brick station as it appeared on 27 October 1896. It was demolished in 1903 after the West Philadelphia station at 32nd and Market was opened.

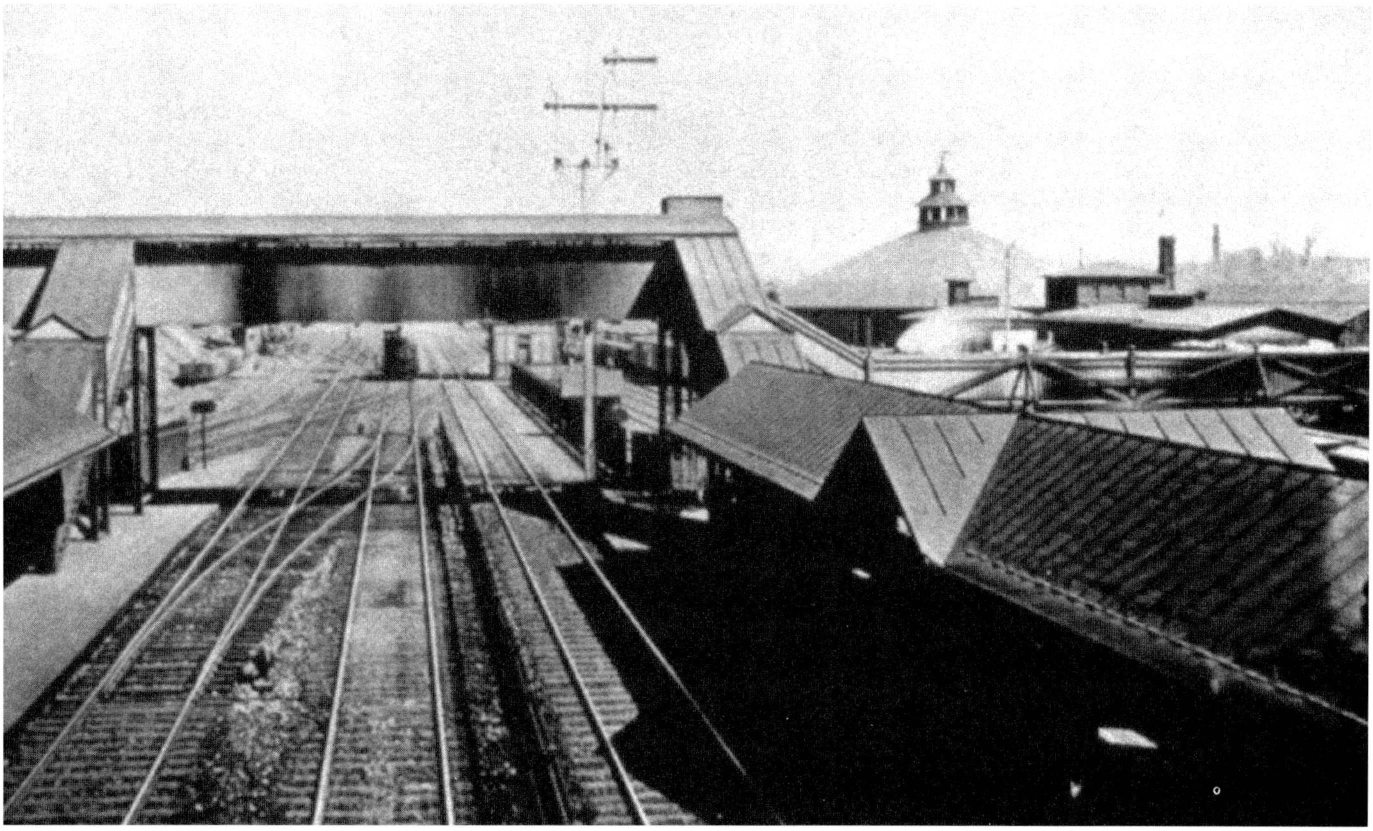

Ted Xaras Collection

HERE WE HAVE an earlier view of the Powelton Avenue facility looking northward ca. 1890. This excellent photo shows us the inbound and outbound platform shelters. Extending over the tracks is the Powelton Avenue footbridge, which serves both as a walkway for the station and as access to the West Philadelphia shops, located behind the station at right. Behind the shops is the clearest photo we have of the distinctive domed Enginehouse No. 1 and just visible under the footbridge is the base of G Tower.

Ted Xaras Collection

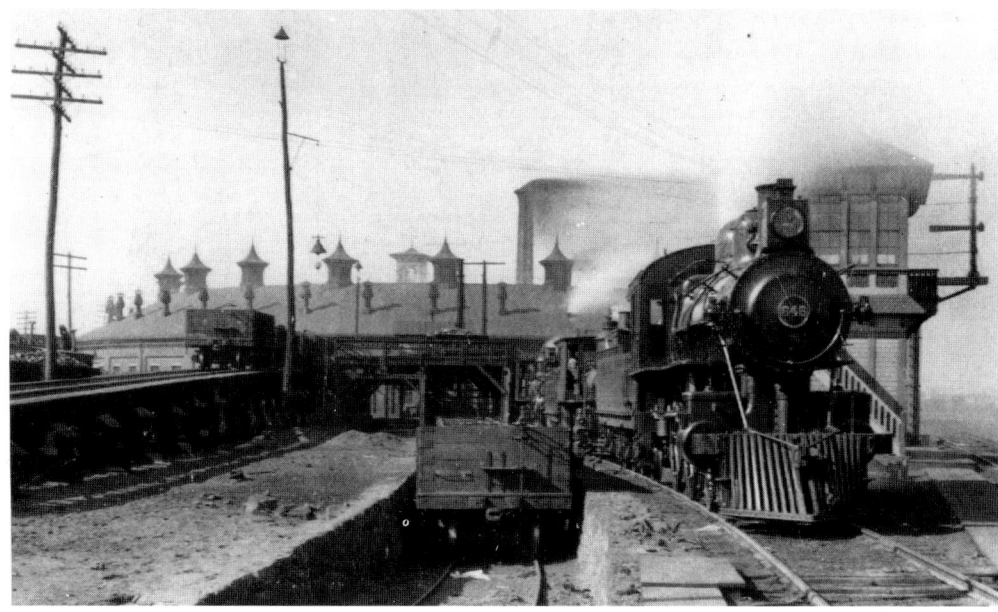

D16 NO. 646 – equipped with knuckle couplers – sits at the service facilities in front of Enginehouse No. 2 in this southward view ca. 1900. The coal-fired power plant adds its contribution to the yard smoke. Note the early coal trestle.

WE ARE STANDING on the Powelton Avenue footbridge ca. 1910, affording us a relatively clear view of the shops and rebuilt passenger yards from the north, as a D-Class 4-4-0 moves a passenger train through the area. Note the abundance of P70 steel coaches, coming into common usage at this time.

Railroad Museum of Pennsylvania (PHMC)

Ted Xaras Collection

POISED – The herd of iron horses looks ready to stampede in this ca. 1905 view looking south from the Spring Garden Street bridge at the engine terminal yards. They are standing in the area formerly occupied by the "tent" Enginehouse No. 1, demolished in 1902. To the left is the ramp to the coal trestle. Note the early electric lamp fixtures.

PRR COMES HOME

R.L. Long / Ted Xaras Collection

STATEMENT– With a spectacular smoke plume that dwarfs the GG1 a K4s leads one of the last regular steam runs out of 30th Street Station in 1952. The train is headed through the West Philadelphia yards, past the High Line and on towards the Connecting Railway to its destination on the Jersey Shore. Like the train, we will move out of the yard area along the river and on toward Mantua Junction, where the Connecting Railway joined the east-west main.

ANOTHER very early photo ca. the early 1870s looks westward across the north end of the West Philadelphia Yards. A Roebling (another notable RPI graduate) suspension bridge is under construction to carry Spring Garden Street across the narrow neck of the Schuylkill River and over the yard trackage. The sign on the fence advertises Gem Stove Polish and Merchant's Gargling Oil.

Ted Xaras Collection

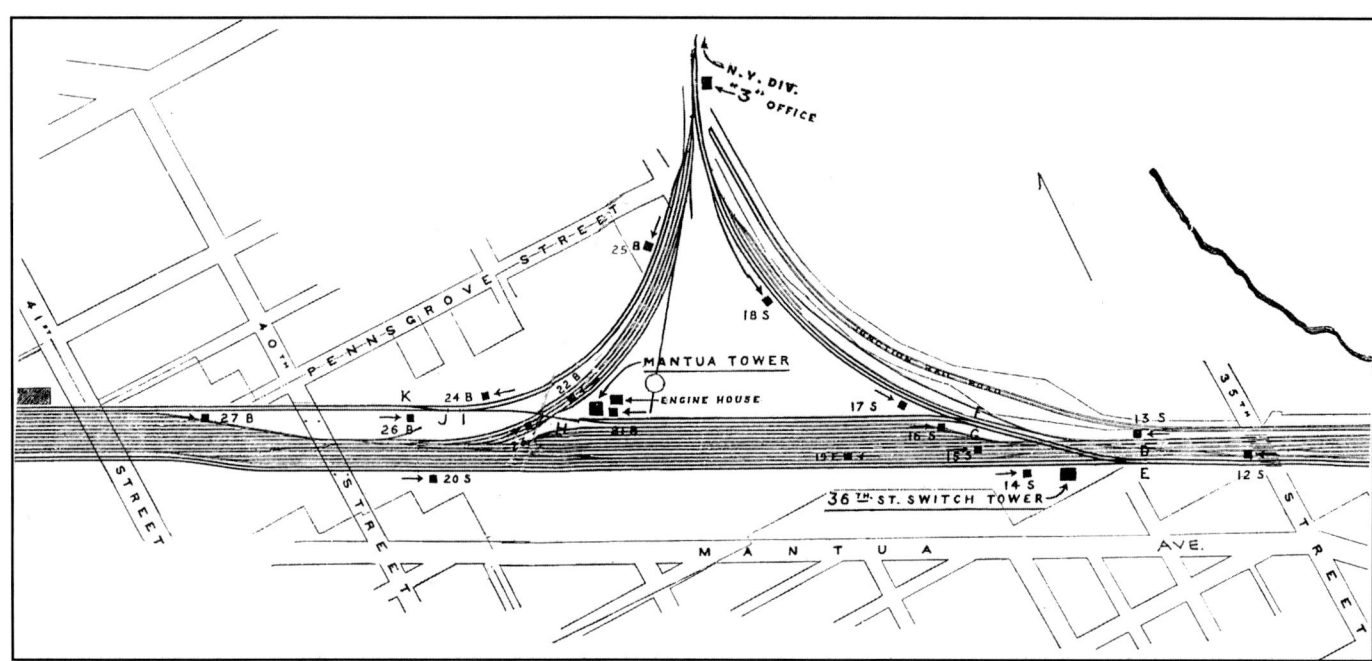

Ted Xaras Collection

WE NOW MOVE to a critical area originally known as Mantua, or New York Junction, where the Connecting Railway began. A freight transfer station measuring 57 x 278 ft. was opened on 1 February 1883 northeast of 40th Street, opposite 39th. This facility was later replaced by a larger one farther west. This 1876 map shows the configuration of Mantua Junction as of that date. Note the location of the towers, enginehouse and turntable, and the Junction RR, before it ducks under the New York main on the northern tail of the wye and connects with the Reading main. This area was to undergo significant change as traffic increased and the yard area farther south was filled up.

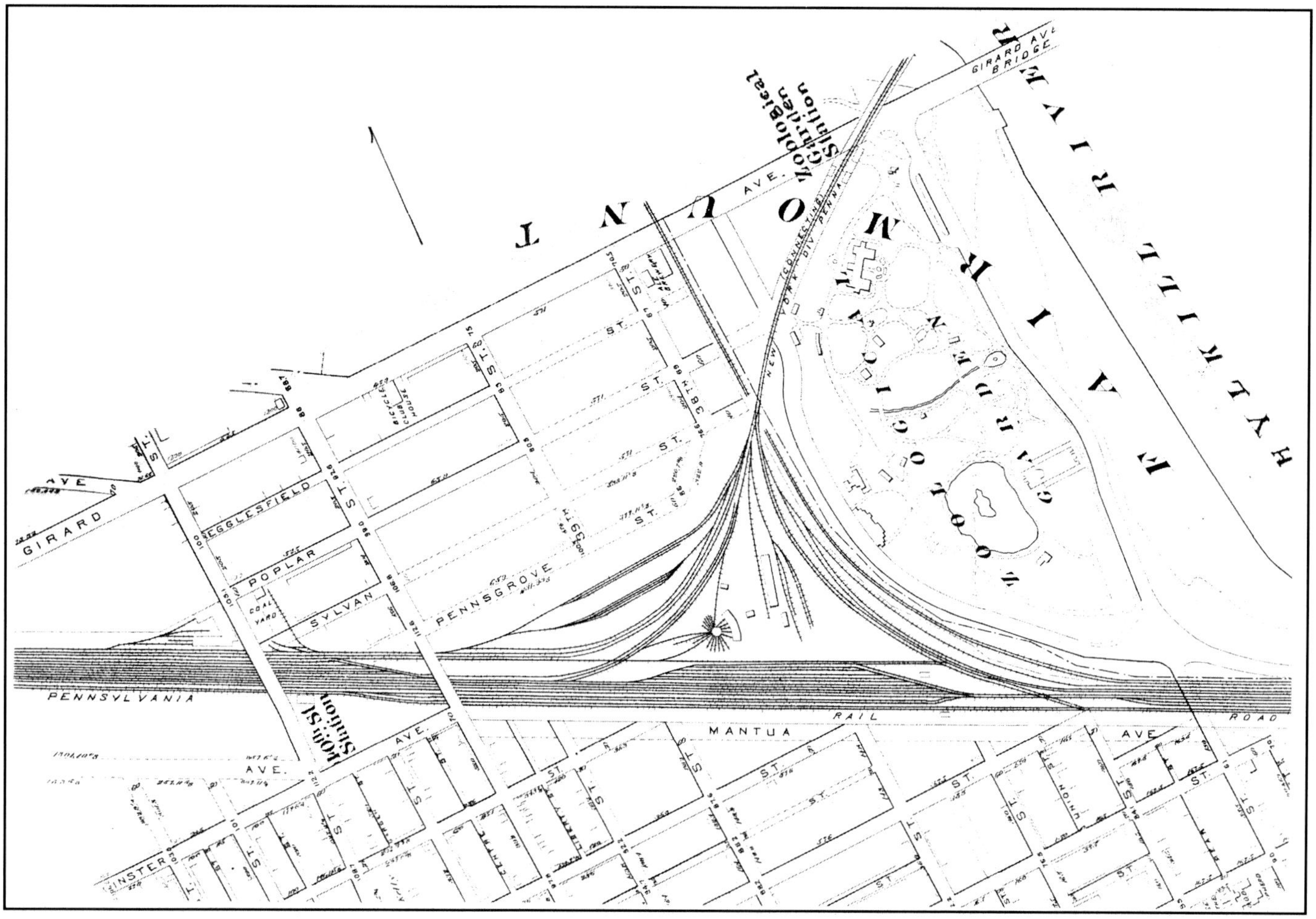

PRR COMES HOME

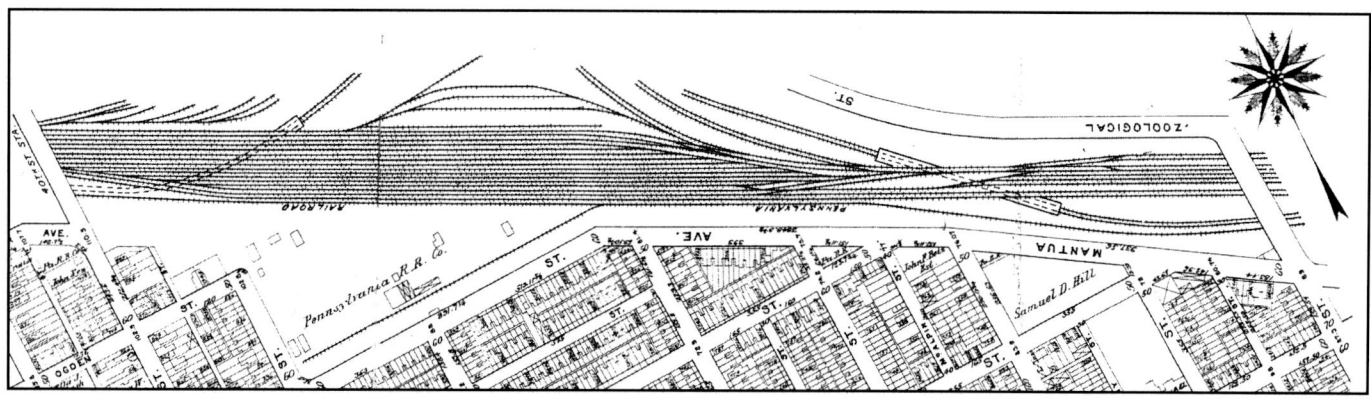

Ted Xaras Collection

BY 1888 the trackage has expanded somewhat, both within the wye and to the west in the beginnings of Mantua Freight Yards. The 40th Street Station was constructed in 1868 and enlarged the following year. Note the Zoological Gardens nestled within the curve of the wye, at the southern end of Fairmount Park, and the short-lived station built in 1886 serving the site.

Ted Xaras Collection

THE 1910 DIAGRAM shows two important changes – the New York and Pittsburgh Subway tunnels, which allow trains to pass under the east-west main without interference. These were the first of the tunnels to improve traffic flow at the junction. We should note that the diagram is incomplete because the Atlas page showing the upper portion of the wye is poorly drawn.

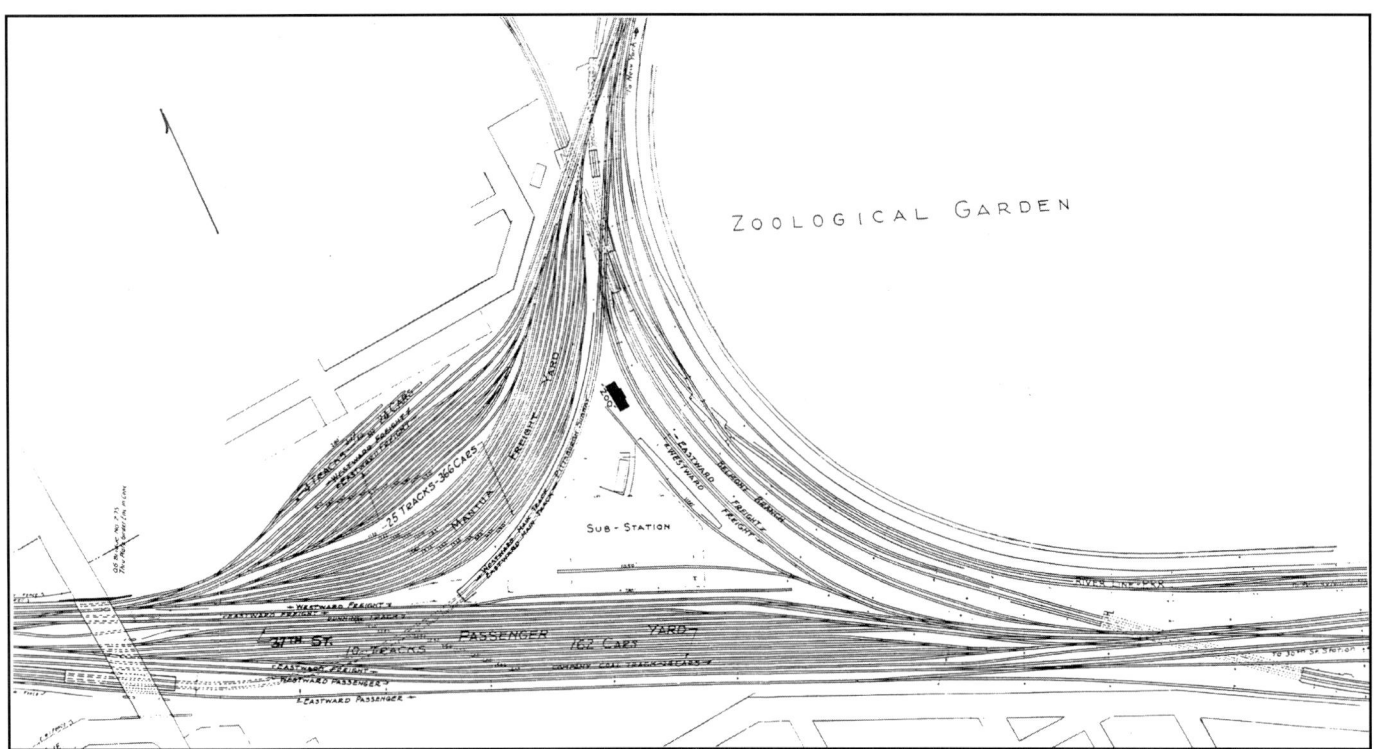
Ted Xaras Collection

FINALLY, by 1935 the changes at "ZOO" Junction, as it was known by that time, were truly profound. Mantua Freight Yards have expanded considerably, as have the 37th Street Passenger Yards. But the most important feature of this complex area is the complete series of tunnels that facilitate train movements without interference with other lines. Starting at the left is the Pittsburgh Subway, which allows westbound New York City trains to move to the westward main. At the top, in addition to the Belmont Branch (formerly Junction RR) tunnel, the New York Inbound Tunnel allows those trains to pass under the main, around the wye and under the east-west main into Philadelphia. We can say without fear of argument that ZOO was an engineering and functional triumph! ZOO Tower itself was constructed within the wye to control it all. It became the most complex and critical interlocking on the entire PRR system (see endpaper for diagram). Let's take a closer look at the evolution of this important area.

HERE'S WHAT "New York Junction" looked like in the 1880s. We are looking west from the 34th Street bridge. The New York Division tracks diverge from the east-west main, cut across the freight tracks and curve off to the right, a situation that clearly became unacceptable to PRR for a main-line junction. To the right of that, on the lower level, is the Junction RR, and at the far right are the excavations for the pioneering Philadelphia Zoological Gardens in Fairmount Park. Beyond the junction to the left of the early lower-quadrant signal mast is 36th Street (H) Tower, and in the center distance is 37th Street Yard.

Ted Xaras Collection

PRR COMES HOME

A FEW YEARS have gone by and we are looking west from the 34th Street bridge again, but something profoundly significant has happened. We see a southbound train emerging from the newly-constructed New York Tunnel, a stone and brick arched passageway opened 28 August 1892. To enter this the inbound main from New York swings outward and under the westbound tracks in the first of two tunnels, curves around the wye and into the second tunnel shown here as it passes under the freight trackage and the westbound main. It then runs southward through the West Philadelphia passenger yards. This was a major improvement – indeed a triumph – to eliminate the dangerous crossing of multiple tracks at grade and allow New York City trains to duck under the east-west mainline without interference. No. 1 (inbound) track is at left and the ornate 40th Street bridge is just visible in the distance. Note the fresh fill excavated from the cut.

Ted Xaras Collection

Ted Xaras Collection

THIS STUNNING PHOTO looks the other way, showing the New York tracks in action in 1904. At the right is a southbound train from New York City that has emerged from the cut and is ascending to grade level as it approaches "K" Tower toward Philadelphia. On the left is Train No. 1, the *Mainline Express*, headed by new Class E3a 4-4-0 No. 744 (Juniata 1904) on the westbound main toward Pittsburgh (the eastbound main is not visible, to the right of the southbound train). At left are the freight yards and Mantua Avenue is at the far right. Note the manicured lawn and razor-sharp ballast on both mains – nary a stone out of place! Do we like this photo? You bet, both for its historical value as well as its superb photographic composition and triumphant depiction of turn-of-the-century railroading!

THIS SUPERB PHOTO is labeled "PRR New York and Washington tunnels, Girard Avenue Philadelphia." When we first encountered it we were fairly certain that this was the first tunnel (at the west end of the Connecting RR), but we were not sure. The lighting is not conclusive; however, the building in the background at the upper left labeled "Smiths Ale" offers a lead. If we look at the 1888 Atlas map (before the tunnel was built), lo and behold, there's the brewery north of the wye, on the corner of Girard Avenue and 38th Street; it was this landmark that confirmed it.

In any case we offer this construction photo to show how it was done. This view ca. 1892 looks north over the inbound track in the foreground, and the westbound leg of the wye, on a temporary timber trestle, behind that. Note the steam winch powering the crane at center left, the cut stone walls and the heavy timber cribbing supporting the earth cut and tunnel arch.

Conrail Public Affairs/Penn Central RR Collection/Pennsylvania State Archives

Ted Xaras Collection

PROFUSION – We are standing at the northern end of the wye, looking southwest through the maze of tracks and wires at ZOO Tower ca. 1950. Replacing four others, the tower and the junction acquired this name during the Philadelphia Improvements. The east- and westbound mains extend to the right onto the western leg of the wye, descending into the Pittsburgh Subway beyond the tower. The tracks continue on the eastern leg around in front of the tower. The northbound New York tracks are on the left, with the southbound tracks out of sight in the cut (under the girder bridge). The ZOO substation is to the left (southeast) of the tower. Zoological Street and the Gardens (the nation's oldest) are at left, giving the tower its name.

ZOO is the single most critical tower on the entire PRR system, coordinating all traffic from three directions (north, west and south). In its heyday the 227-lever machine controlled an unbelievable 88 single switches, 14 double-slip switches and movable-point frogs, 75 high signals and 52 dwarf signals (see endpapers for interlocking diagram)! It interacted with five other towers (BROAD, A, ARSENAL, PENN and NORTH PHILADELPHIA), as well as 46th Street Enginehouse and Penn Coach Yard. It took five operators to keep up with everything – there was a Train Director, an Assistant Train Director, and Assistant *to* the Train Director and two levermen. The Director called (shouted) the routes to the levermen, the Assistant Director communicated with the Dispatcher and the Assistant to the Director interacted with the five other towers on train movements.

PRR COMES HOME

CONFUSION? – What looks like a confused array of tracks is actually ZOO Junction functioning as it was intended. It is an ingenious and triumphant example of PRR's use of the "flying junction," where key lines meet and cross without interference. Perhaps we can make some sense out of this superb photo of multiple trains running through the marvelous three-dimensional maze. We are looking northward from ZOO Tower in the late 50s, in the opposite direction from the previous photo. The freight is headed southward, most likely onto the High Line; PRR's lightweight, *The Keystone*, is also headed south, on the Inward Track toward 30th Street Station; and the string of MP54's is moving northward on the Outward Track. The westward main tracks are to the left of the freight, about to descend into the Pittsburgh Subway, and the northern end of Mantua Freight Yards is above that. Buildings of the Philadelphia Zoo are just visible above the MU train.

Ted Xaras Collection

THESE TWO superb mid-50s aerial views will help us to better understand the layout at the marvelous creation known as ZOO. The first looks westward along Mantua Avenue and the east-west mainline. The southbound freight demonstrates the duckunder under the main. To the right of it is the River Line curving around Zoological Street and the Gardens on the right. To the left, descending northward into a tunnel is the Belmont Branch (former Junction RR). ZOO Tower and the Substation occupy the center of the wye, with the 37th Street Yard half filled with loaded coal hoppers. The 40th and 41st Street bridges cross beyond the yards.

Jesse E. Hartman/Ted Xaras Collection

LOOKING EASTWARD from above those bridges gives us a panorama of the Schuylkill River, with the New York tracks at upper left and the Girard Avenue Bridge to the right of that. The tunnel entrance for the southbound tracks to duck under the northbound main is visible to the right of the tower. Below that, in the center of the photo, we can see the Pittsburgh Subway for New York trains to move onto the east-west main and proceed westward. These trains move through a 600-ft. walled cut, pass through a 1,000-ft. tunnel under the yards and then ascend to grade through a 1,670-ft. cut between the east-west tracks. At left is the Mantua Yards, being used here for a variety of work equipment, including several wire cars. The entire complex is a triumph of track engineering!

Jesse E. Hartman/Ted Xaras Collection

MOVING TO the western end of the wye, we are standing on the 40th Street bridge looking eastward ca. 1890. At the left is the Mantua Freight Yard and the Mantua Tower, which controlled the west leg of the wye at the point where the New York tracks joined the main westward. The Pittsburgh Subway, constructed in 1901 at a cost of nearly $300,000, eliminated this junction, similar to its eastern counterpart. At the right is the eastbound main and the 37th Street Yards, with an assortment of early wooden coal and high-sided coke cars. The original engine terminal at this location is to the right of the tower, inside the wye.

Ted Xaras Collection

PRR COMES HOME

Ted Xaras Collection

WEST OF Mantua Junction PRR constructed an evolving series of freight yards along the east-west mainline. This view looking eastward ca. 1890 shows the precisely-ballasted main tracks on the right and the 40th Street Yards filling the rest of the photo. Crossing over the tracks in the distance are the bridges for 41st Street and, barely visible beyond that, 40th Street.

Ted Xaras Collection

THIS DRAWING shows the little-known 40th Street (Mantua) Station, a three-story brick structure located on the south (eastbound) side of the main, just east of 40th Street. Like several others in less densely settled areas it was a combination passenger station, telegraph office and agent's quarters. Constructed in 1868 and expanded the following year, it remained in service until 1901, was closed until 1909 when it reopened and was finally closed in 1918.

PHILADELPHIA had an abundance of bridges associated with PRR, both carrying the tracks and carrying roadways over the right-of-way. Two of the latter that especially capture the eye are the bridges over the yards at 40th and 41st Streets. The distinctive – and almost fantasylike – 40th Street structure is shown here, a striking 232-ft., three-span suspension bridge erected in 1876 to provide easier access to the Centennial grounds. The towers reflect the styling of the nearby Centennial buildings. This view looks eastward ca. 1880, with the western tail of the wye just visible at the left.

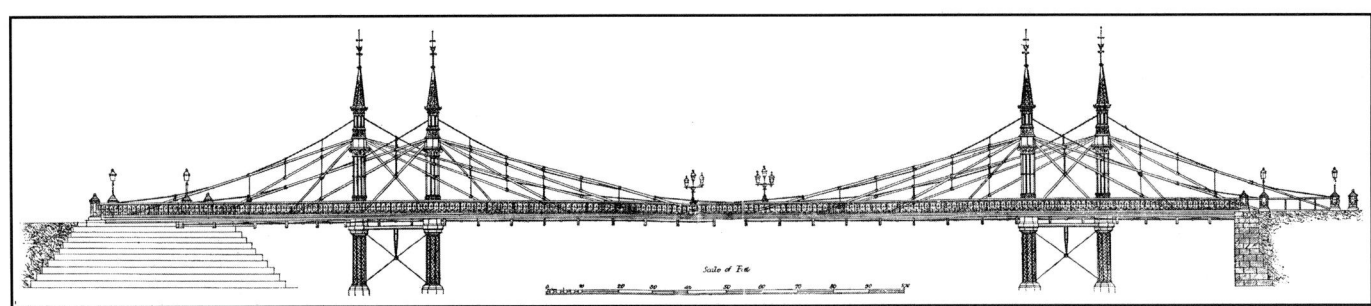

EVEN THOUGH these were roadway bridges, they are distinctive enough to warrant a second look, in drawings from James Dredge's superb 1879 engineering study of PRR. The 40th Street structure shown above was a stiffened Whipple suspension bridge, using pin-connected iron bars instead of the more familiar cables for the suspension members. It was fabricated of wrought iron except for the cast iron pedestals.

PRR COMES HOME

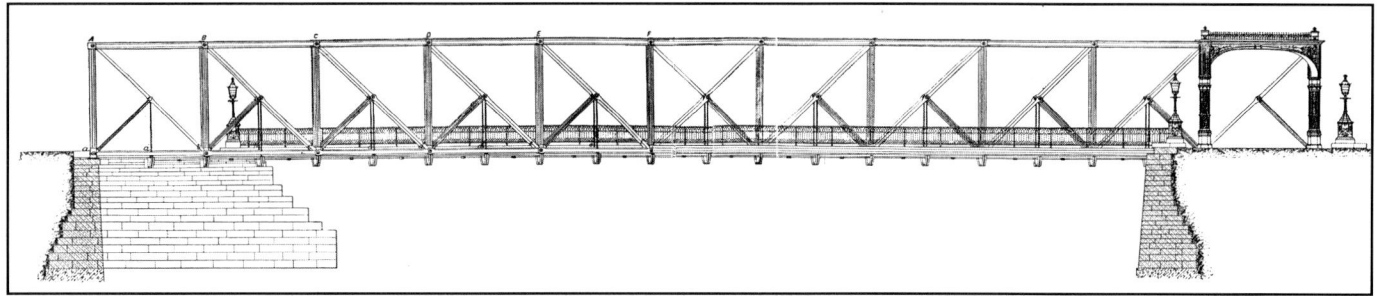

THE 41ST STREET BRIDGE was totally different from its counterpart a block away. It was a stiffened through Baltimore truss, 213-ft. long and 22-ft. high, skewed about 30°. It was also wrought iron, with highly detailed cast iron end framing.

Ted Xaras Collection

THE BRIDGE at 41st Street, although not as well known as its distinctive 40th Street counterpart, nevertheless demonstrates a refined elegance in its detailing and delicate laciness and cast iron detailing. The exquisite bridge frames the Centennial buildings beyond, which provides a convenient segue to that most grand and notable of Philadelphia celebrations.

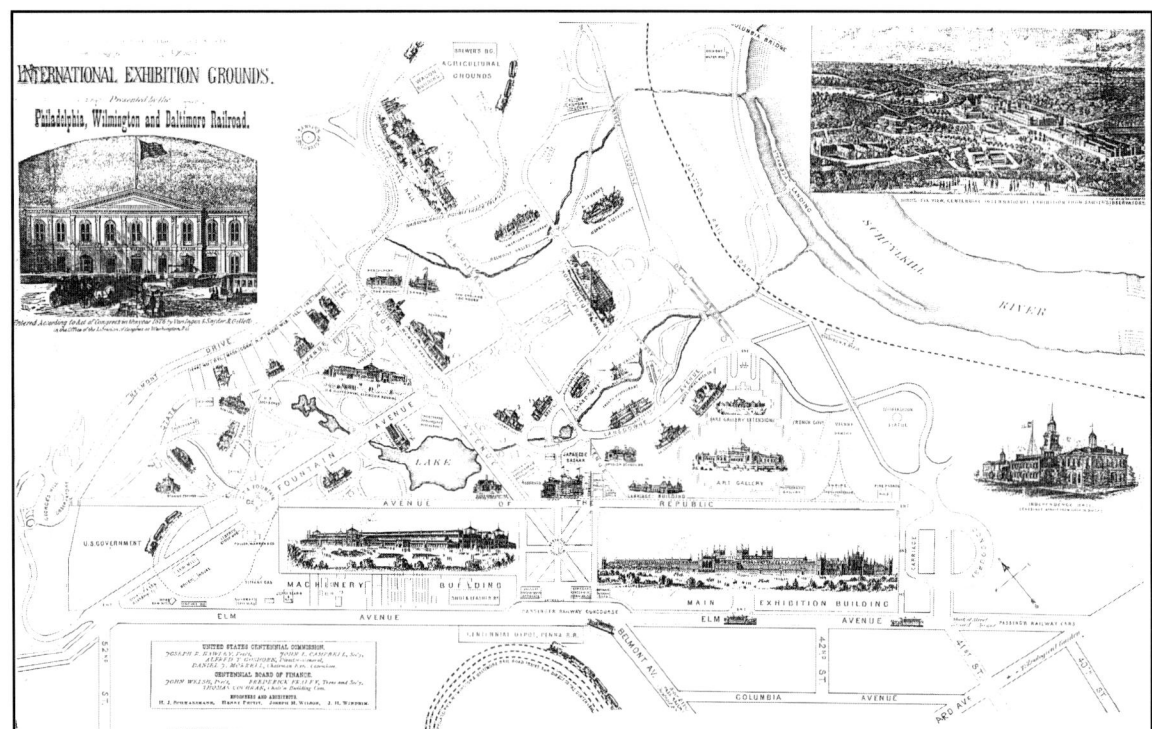

Pennsylvania State Archives

IN 1876 the U.S. celebrated its 100th birthday and the grand observance was held, most appropriately, in Philadelphia, where the nation was born. It was a celebration not just of the Centennial, but a showcase of the surging industrial powerhouse that the country had become. This fascinating map, prepared by the PW&B, "The only route via the National Capital," shows the layout of the grounds. The main depot, used by PRR and PW&B trains "direct to the Centennial Grounds," is located at bottom, in front of the main gate. The Reading had to settle for a lesser station on the Junction RR (right of center). The main PB&W depot at Broad and Washington Streets in Philadelphia is shown in the inset at upper left. Note the narrow gauge, double-track "Palace Car Railway" that wound around the Exposition grounds.

A CLOSER LOOK at some of the Exposition buildings that were located on the spacious grounds in Fairmount Park is shown here, including the commodious (but temporary) PRR depot located at the southern edge of the property. It was constructed in a Victorian style similar to the other buildings and opened on 10 May 1876.

Charles Denlinger Collection

PRR COMES HOME

IN ADDITION to accommodations for passengers, PRR made special provision for the estimated 40,000 tons of exhibits. Special platforms were installed to handle the load. Freight was moved in loaded cars directly to the Exposition buildings via these platforms. This drawing shows freight being unloaded and transferred – seemingly with considerable dispatch – to the mammoth Main Building at left. Beyond is Machinery Hall and at right is the Judges Pavilion and the narrow gauge passenger railroad that ran through the grounds.

Charles Denlinger Collection

PRR ACCOMMODATED not only passengers and freight for the Centennial, but also the Exposition staff. Here we see a view of the special excursion train "tendered" by the railroad to the Commissioners and judges. We are not sure of the location, but the eight-car train includes a variety of Civil War era and postwar equipment. The distinguished passengers gathered for this photo sport a wide variety of hats – some on their head, some in hand – but *everyone* has one, including the tower operator.

Ted Xaras Collection

TRIUMPH III

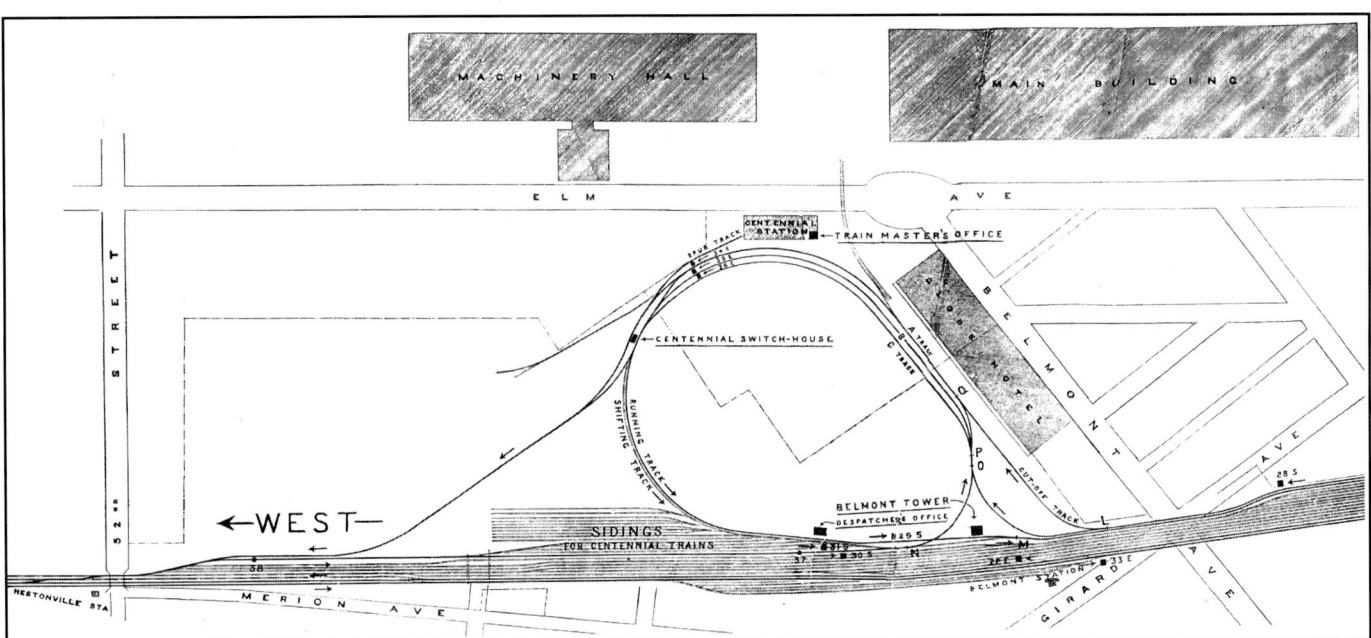

THIS DIAGRAM shows the track layout for the station on the Exposition grounds. The interesting loop arrangement allowed for movement of trains in and out of the station from either direction. Although the Reading had a depot on the other side of the grounds PRR obviously provided *the* entrance to the Exposition.

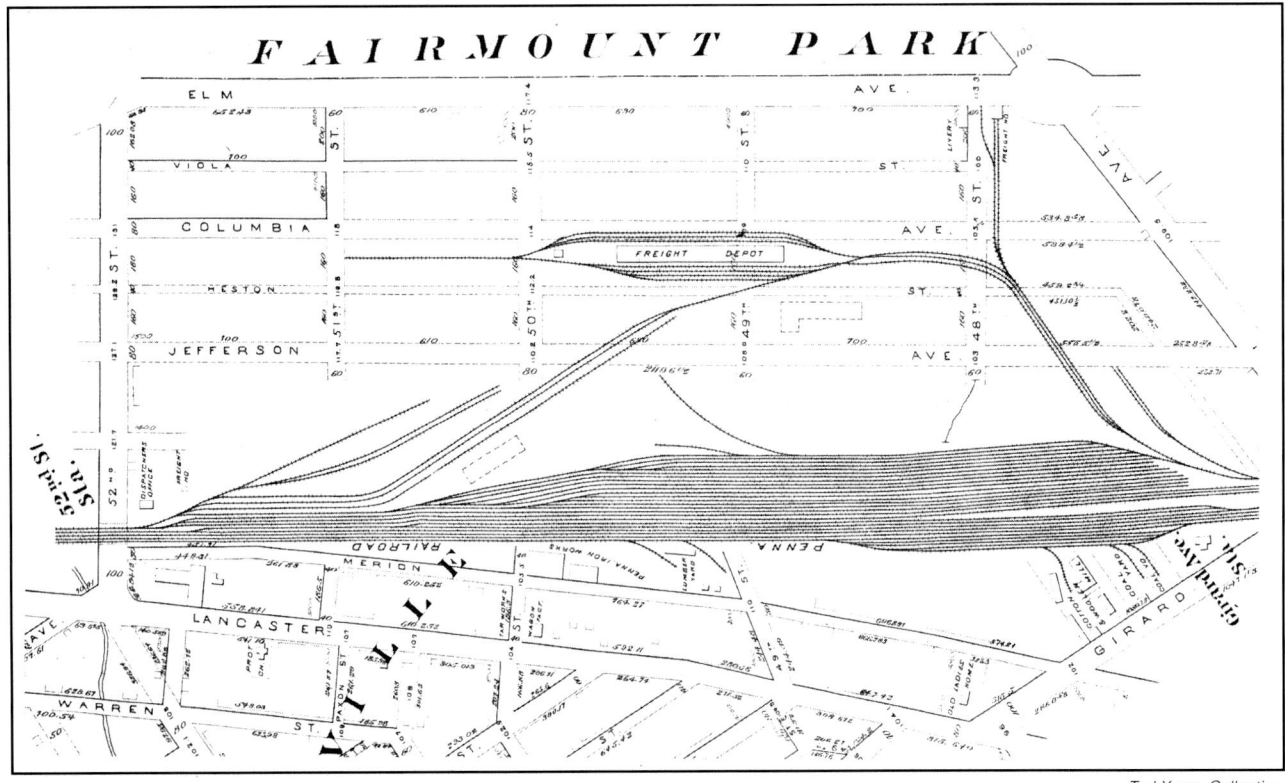

AFTER THE EXPOSITION closed, the station and a portion of the loop were removed and the large tract of real estate that PRR had been buying between Belmont Avenue and 52nd Street was used to expand the freight yards westward from Mantua Junction. This 1888 Atlas map shows the area, including a freight transfer station constructed along Columbia Avenue in 1887, replacing the earlier one at Mantua. The 70 x 700-ft. facility, with a two-story office, became known as "52nd Street Transfer," even though it was located between 48th and 50th Streets. It was served by the remaining portion of the loop tracks.

PRR COMES HOME

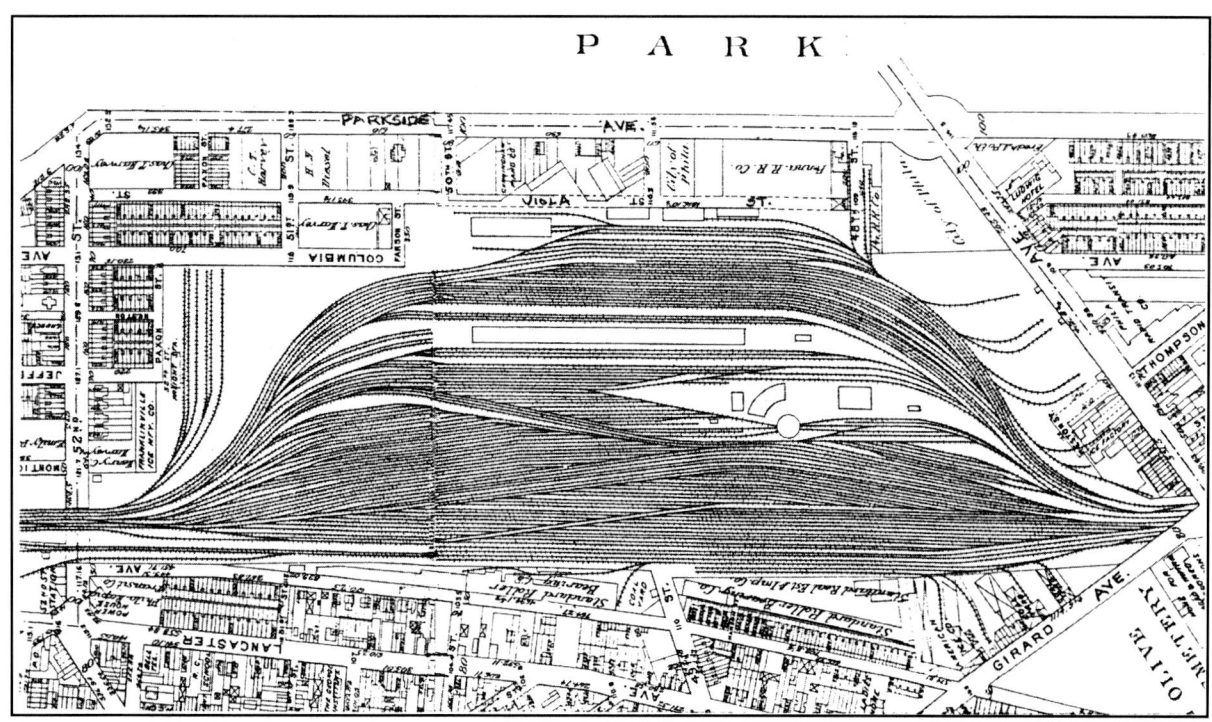

Ted Xaras Collection

BY 1910 the yards had burgeoned to virtually fill the entire space, 4,000 ft. long and 1,200 ft. wide – about 85 acres – between Mantua Avenue and Viola Street (note Elm Avenue has been renamed Parkside Avenue). A freight station and team tracks have been added at the 52nd Street (west) end. We also see an enginehouse and turntable incorporated within the yards.

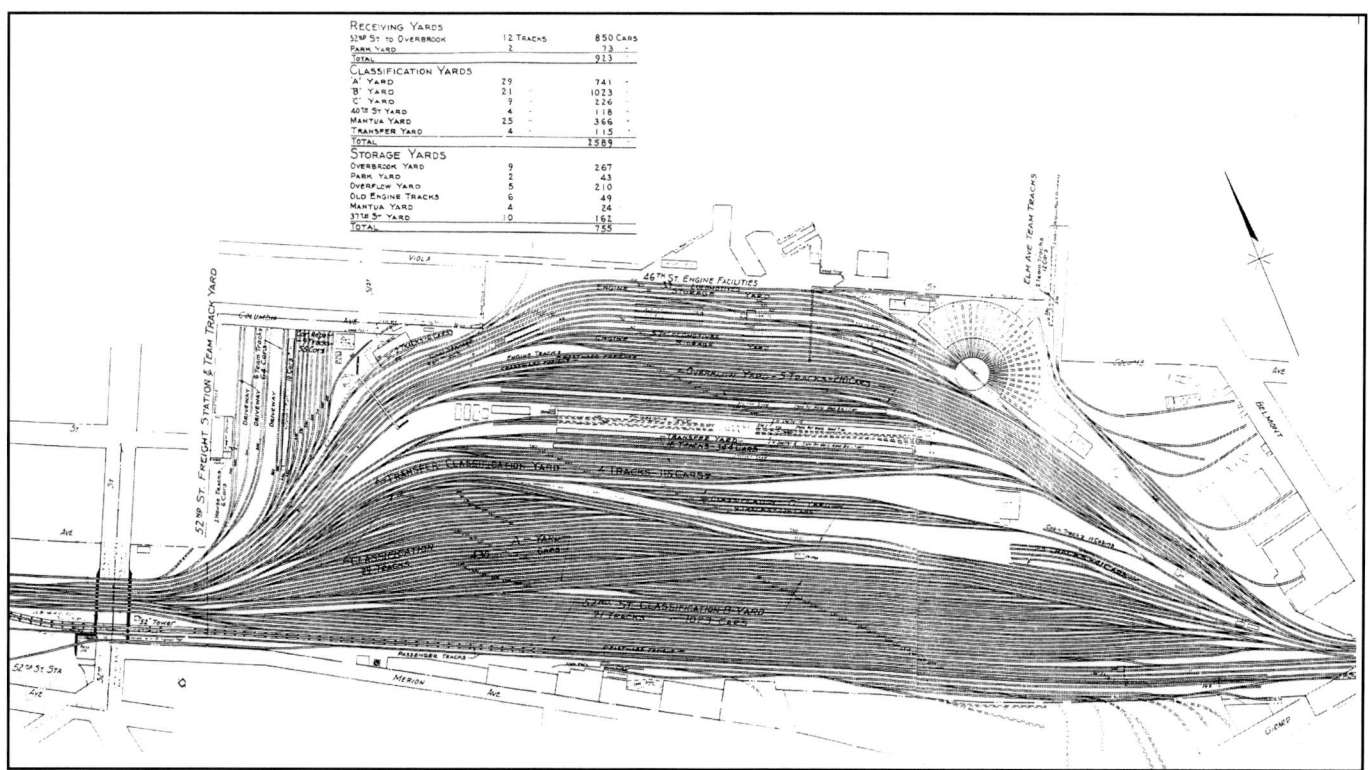

Ted Xaras Collection

THE 1935 MAP shows only a few refinements to the yard itself, but a car repair yard has been added at the 52nd Street end and a new roundhouse and engine terminal have been constructed at the 46th Street end. We will look at these latter facilities in a moment. The major yard areas (from top to bottom) are the Engine Storage Yard, Overflow Yard, Transfer Yard, Transfer Classification Yards and Classification Yards "C," "A" and "B," the largest, holding 1023 cars.

IN 1887-8 PRR constructed an eight-stall frame and corrugated iron enginehouse plus a car repair shop toward the eastern end of the yard. This was the first enginehouse complex at 46th Street, although like the freight facility it was initially referred to as "52nd Street." A second eight-stall building was built in 1902, replacing the earlier one. This was constructed of brick, with a temporary end wall to allow for expansion to 16 stalls (this was completed some time after 1912). The facility utilized a 75-ft. turntable,

Ted Xaras Collection

which accommodated steam engines of the time. Adjacent buildings in the expanding complex, known as the Park Shops, included a machine shop, power plant and coaling wharf. The entire enginehouse was lengthened in 1918 to accommodate longer locomotives, and a toolroom and office were added to the rear, along with a new smith shop and carpenter shop.

This view looking northwest at the 1902 enginehouse shows the temporary wall on the eastern end to allow for expansion. At right are the 52nd Street Transfer buildings.

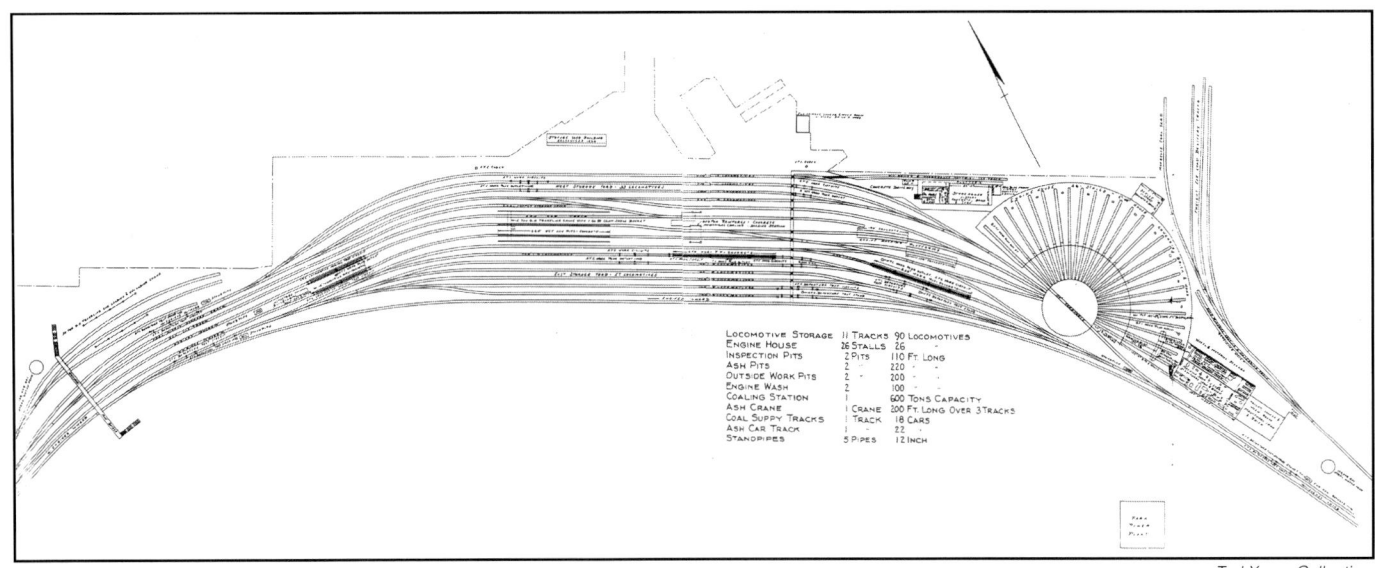

Ted Xaras Collection

WITH MOTIVE POWER steadily increasing in size over the next several years, both the enginehouse and turntable became inadequate. In 1930 a new 26-stall brick, concrete and wood-framed facility was constructed north and east of the 1902/18 structure (which was subsequently demolished), alongside the outer curve of the yard trackage. Known as the "micrometer" because of its configuration, this $1.5 million complex included a semicircular roundhouse with machine and smith shops and crew locker facility forming the "handle." A 110-ft. turntable, a massive four-track, 600-ton coaling wharf and sanding facility, two 100,000-gal. steel water tanks and a two-track, 220-ft. long concrete ash pit with traveling overhead crane were also constructed to service PRR's steam power fleet.

All of these facilities were built as part of the Philadelphia Improvements. The new roundhouse replaced the 1903 No. 2 roundhouse in West Philadelphia - engine service operations at the Powelton Avenue yards were transferred to 46th Street, allowing expansion of the passenger car storage and service function at that location serving the new Center City stations. Freight classification and storage were increased by further expansion of the 46th Street yards. This program, although prolonged by the Great Depression, provided jobs to thousands of workers during hard times. The new complex served PRR well during the heyday of steam, although its usefulness diminished with traffic declines and the advent of dieselization.

PRR COMES HOME

E6S NO. 5222 and colleagues sit in the locomotive storage yard just west of the 1930 roundhouse at 46th Street Engine Terminal ca. 1932. The brick and concrete oil and storehouse building is visible at left, between the locomotives.

E.P. Alexander/Ted Xaras Collection

THE MASSIVE 600-ton concrete coal wharf was located west of the roundhouse, between the East and West Locomotive Storage Yards. It was designed with three compartments to hold 200 tons each of passenger, freight and low-volatile coal. It also held 60 tons of wet sand and heaters to dry 15 tons of material. The wharf served four tracks in its heyday, but is shown here past that time ca. 1959. K4s No. 830 is also past her prime, in storage with her stack capped - and having suffered the ultimate indignity – missing the keystone number plate. She is destined for the scrapper's torch.

Bruce G. Saylor/Ted Xaras Collection

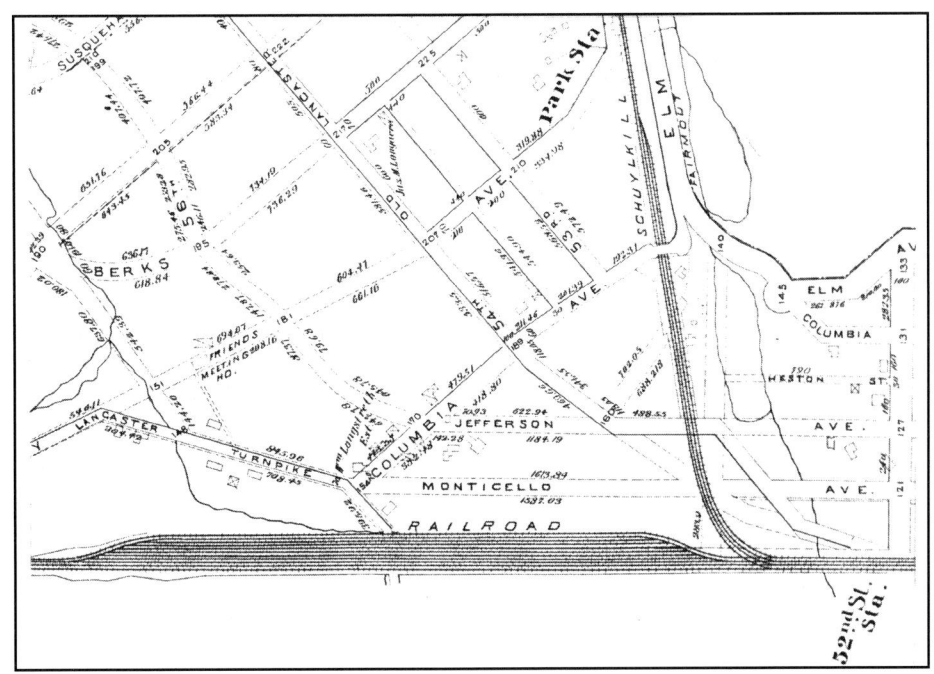

WE NOW MOVE westward to the 52nd Street area, originally known as Hestonville. The original PRR depot, a three-story stone station and dwelling, was built in 1869. When the Schuylkill Division was initially constructed in 1883 the junction with the east-west mainline at 52nd Street looked like the original ones at Mantua Junction to the east, that is a multiple-track crossing at grade. This 1888 Atlas map shows how the intersection looked at that point in time.

Ted Xaras Collection

TRIUMPH III

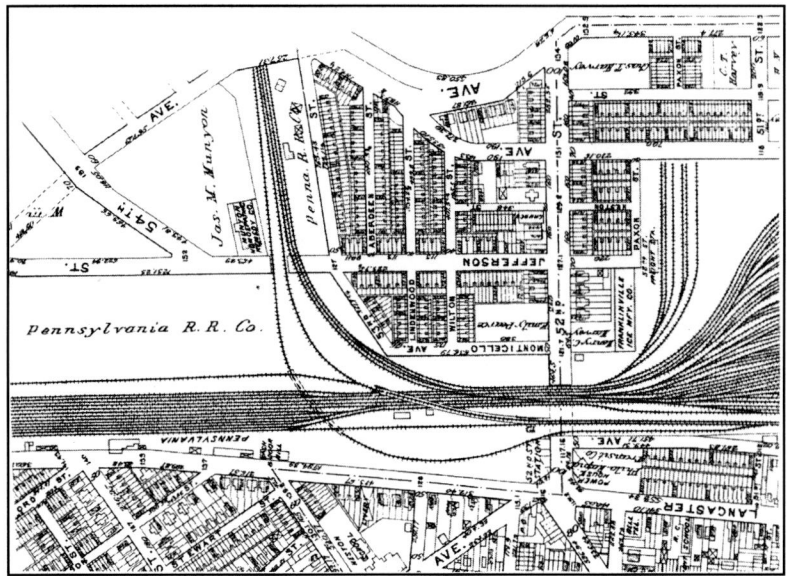

PRR REBUILT the entire junction in 1902, constructing a massive jumpover bridge west of 52nd Street for the westbound passenger main as well as the Schuylkill Division track, which diverged at the western end of the bridge. A tunnel was built farther west to carry the eastbound Schuylkill Division passenger track under the eastbound main and yards, and joining the main east of 52nd Street. This Atlas map shows how the junction looked in 1910.

Ted Xaras Collection

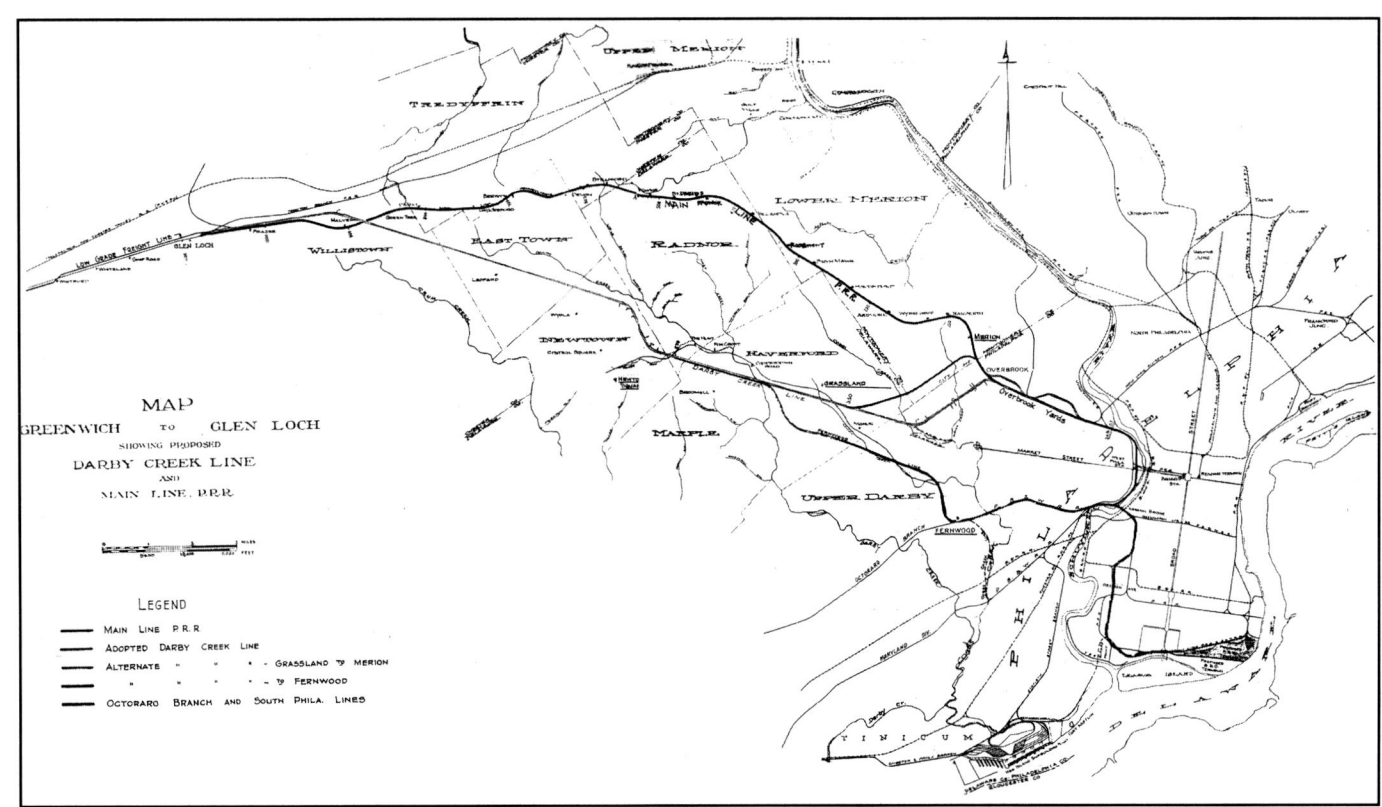

Hagley Museum and Library

AS THE Low-Grade freight line between Glen Loch and Enola Yard was being completed (see *Triumph II*), PRR in 1905 proposed an eastward extension into Philadelphia. Three routes were considered, and the Darby Creek Line (shown as a shaded line on the map) was selected as the favored choice. As traffic analyses for this line were carried out it was determined that the existing yard at 52nd Street would be inadequate. Accordingly PRR developed a plan for a major expansion of the yard, including extending it westward to Woodbine Ave., just west of Overbrook, at the beginning of the suburban Main Line communities. The alternate routes involved proposed new yards at Grassland, outside the City limits, or South Philadelphia. Both of these sites (and their corresponding routes) were rejected because of the added cost and delay of moving freight from these locations to their final destinations in the city.

On 23 November 1905 a City Council ordinance was approved authorizing PRR to construct the extension, including a 2,500-ft. approach tunnel under Malvern Ave. in Overbrook, to join with the mainline at or near 56th St. as proposed by the railroad. It set a time limit of 10 years to complete the project. However the cost

(continued from previous page)
of the entire program and growing neighborhood opposition to both the extension and the yard expansion delayed the start of construction. In 1907 the PRR Board voted not to authorize funds for the extension (although moribund it was not completely dead). However, plans to expand the 52nd St. Yard continued.

For a variety of reasons the project languished until the spring of 1914 when PRR realized it could not complete it before the 10 years was up in November 1915. It therefore had a new ordinance introduced. This was similar to the 1905 one, with additional provisions for civic improvements including grading and paving of city streets, building sewers and constructing bridges across the tracks from 54th to 63rd St. PRR was required to complete the yard project within 2 1/2 years of approval of the plans, except 7 years were allowed for the widening of the bridge over Woodbine Avenue. Work on the still-proposed Low Grade extension was to be completed within 5 years.

However, when the residents of the Overbrook area became aware of the plan for the expanded yard, they formed the Overbrook Association, which lobbied strongly against the proposal based on the potential for residential property destruction, as well as smoke, noise and resultant property devaluation. Based on these objections the ordinance was withdrawn. After months of negotiations it was reintroduced the following year, with amendments in which PRR agreed to electrify the Malvern Ave. tunnel, not to place the yard in operation for 4 years after approval and not construct any roundhouse or coaling tower, or store any steam locomotive, west of 54th St. to City Avenue. It also agreed to submit the eventual choice of motive power used within the yard to an arbitration panel. With these amendments the ordinance was finally approved on 8 July 1915.

These concessions represented a remarkable precedent for PRR, indicative of the importance of the project. However, one should remember that this agreement was within the same time frame as the general suburban electrification program in Philadelphia, which would reduce the need for steam motive power.

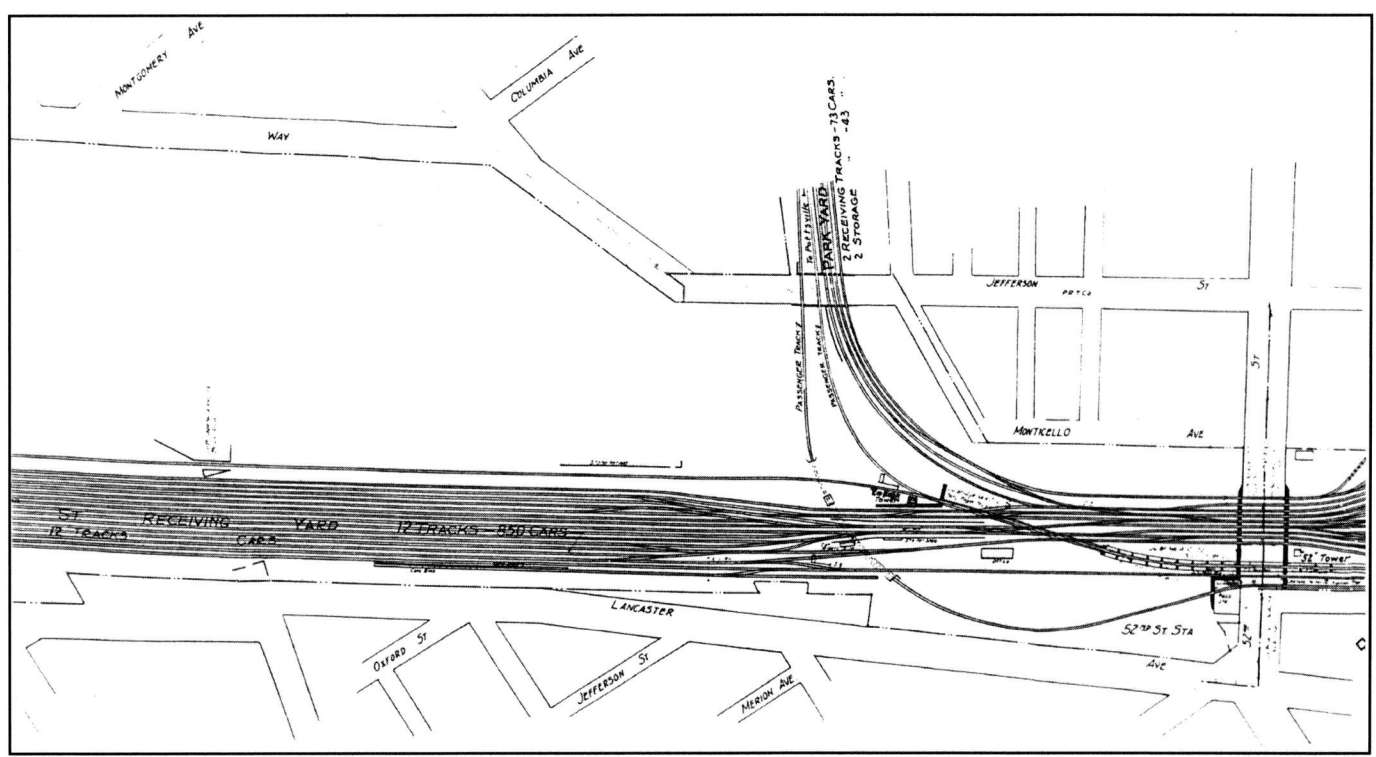

Ted Xaras Collection

GRADING for the new yard and streets was begun in the Fall of 1916, but stopped on 22 February 1919 because of the war. Even after all the opposition from local residents to the proposed design, consideration was given during this period toward moving the connection with the still-proposed Darby Creek Line west of Overbrook Station, allowing longer tracks in the yard. This was rejected because of the cost and difficulty of property acquisition and concern over public reaction. Grading was resumed in 1920, and the new yard was eventually completed, but at a considerably reduced scale. This was perhaps fortuitous, because of a number of factors including mainline electrification and then dieselization, traffic declines and the expansion of yard facilities in South Philadelphia, the grand design originally envisioned in the 52nd Street area would not be needed. The 1935 map shows the junction fundamentally unchanged, although some modifications were made west of 52nd Street (see also the corresponding map of the yards east of 52nd Street). Additional freight yard facilities (known as Park Yard) were added near the beginning of the Schuylkill Division.

The last mention of the Darby Creek Line we have found in the PRR record is dated 28 November 1921 –16 years after it was proposed – indicating its cost at $14.5 million (of which nearly $1.5 million was for property already acquired). It was not to be – although it had precipitated major yard expansion in West Philadelphia.

A REMARKABLE VIEW from 52nd Street shows the yards to the east ca 1890. At the far left in the background is 52nd Street Transfer, with its two-story office building in the center. Farther to the right is the original (1887) frame enginehouse. The yards stretch into the smoky distance, with the east-west main on the far right, and Lancaster Avenue beyond that. Close examination reveals some track gangs at work in the center of the photo.

E.P. Alexander Archive/Ted Xaras Collection

LOOKING WESTWARD ca. 1890 we see the original junction with the Schuylkill Division tracks, which intersect the east-west main at grade and then diverge northward to the right. At left are the 52nd Street passenger station and the tower (constructed in 1884) controlling the junction. There's more trackwork going on at left. In 1901 a tunnel and connecting track were constructed, at a cost of $460,000, under the mainline to allow eastbound passenger trains on the Schuylkill Division to avoid running across the main and freight trackage at grade. This track descends a 3.5 % grade and curves under the east-west main and freight tracks through the 325-ft. tunnel, swings sharply to the left and passes through the second level of 52nd Street Station and then joins the eastbound main east of the station. This was the first phase of rebuilding this junction, to improve safety and traffic flow.

Ted Xaras Collection

PRR COMES HOME

THE SECOND PHASE involved rebuilding 52nd Street Station. This view shows the station during construction in 1903, looking northwest at the building and track superstructure. It was a three-story facility – the first floor contains the waiting room and ticket office at street level, the second floor platform served the inbound mainline and Schuylkill Division trains, and the third floor platform was for the outbound trains for both lines. Stairways, passenger elevators and baggage lifts connected all three floors.

Ted Xaras Collection

FROM THE Belmont Avenue crossing the westbound track ascends a 1.5 % grade so that when the station is reached it is on the third level, 35 ft. above street grade. This undated view looks westward through the station at the jumpover bridge allowing the westbound track to cross over the freight tracks.

Railroad Museum of Pennsylvania (PHMC)

THE JUMPOVER bridge at 52nd Street in West Philadelphia was completed in 1902 by the American Bridge Co. (formerly Pencoyd Steel). This allowed westbound passenger trains from either New York or Philadelphia to cross over the freight trackage without interfering with either passenger or freight operations. At the west end of the bridge the westbound Schuylkill Division passenger track diverted from the westbound mainline track. This massive structure was an imposing 388-ft. Pennsylvania Truss center span, shown here in an early 1930s view looking eastward, with Canadian grain cars moving underneath.

E.P. Alexander /Ted Xaras Collection

THIS VIEW looks eastward from VALLEY Tower through the bridge in the 1920s. 52nd Street Station is framed in the massive bridge members in the background. In the foreground the Schuylkill Division track diverges to the left. Note the eastern approach to the bridge in the background at left, a 2170-ft. embankment between masonry walls leading to a plate girder viaduct. Just visible to the left of the jumpover bridge are the tops of several plate girder bridges - part of a series of nine (seven freight, two passenger) 106-ft. spans over 52nd Street built in 1902.

Ted Xaras Collection

AN EASTBOUND MU train moves through the second level of 52nd Street Station, alongside the approach viaduct carrying the westbound main, 24.5 ft. above. The viaduct is formidable in itself, made up of 47 steel deck girder spans totaling 1668 feet, plus a 106-ft. steel deck truss over 52nd Street, all on masonry piers. It was also constructed by American Bridge Co. in 1902. The eastbound main is supported on a 700-ft. embankment supported by the masonry retaining wall shown here. The photographer is standing on Merion Avenue looking westward in 1948.

Ted Xaras Collection

PRR COMES HOME

Fred W. Schneider, III

AN EASTBOUND PAOLI LOCAL with Silverliner IV No. 355 leading the way heads into 52nd Street Station on 23 June 1978. The train is nicely framed between the station and the viaduct. Note the Penn Central and early SEPTA logos.

Fred W. Schneider, III

THE WASHINGTON SECTION of the Amtrak *Broadway Limited*, with two heavyweight cars on the rear, moves eastward past the 52nd Street jumpover bridge into the station on the same day in June 1978. The 59th Street Yard is in the background.

E.P. Alexander/Ted Xaras Collection

WE ARE LOOKING eastward at the 59th Street Yards, toward the 52nd Street jumpover bridge in the distance at left. In the foreground is the westbound main on the long fill. And in front of us we have a strange beast: Class L5 was PRR's final jackshaft electric design. Not living up to mainline expectations, the 80"-drivered monsters were assigned to terminal areas, mostly in New York City. No. 3930, shown here in a 1940s view, was fitted with a second pantograph (becoming Class L5faw) and used in Philadelphia-area freight service.

105

TRIUMPH III

MORE CONVENTIONAL POWER is shown at work in the 59th Street Yards in this view. An unidentified Consolidation performs mundane chores in a ca. 1948 photo looking eastward.

E.P. Alexander/Ted Xaras Collection

Ted Xaras Collection

WOODBINE TOWER was located west of the yards, near Woodbine Avenue. It is shown here in an eastward view ca. 1890, showing a pall of smoke in the direction of the yard area. Behind us, to the west, is Overbrook, the City line and the Main Line, to be discussed in Chapter 3. With this shot we come to the end of our tour of West Philadelphia.

Chapter 2
Northern Connections

The Connecting Railway and Branches

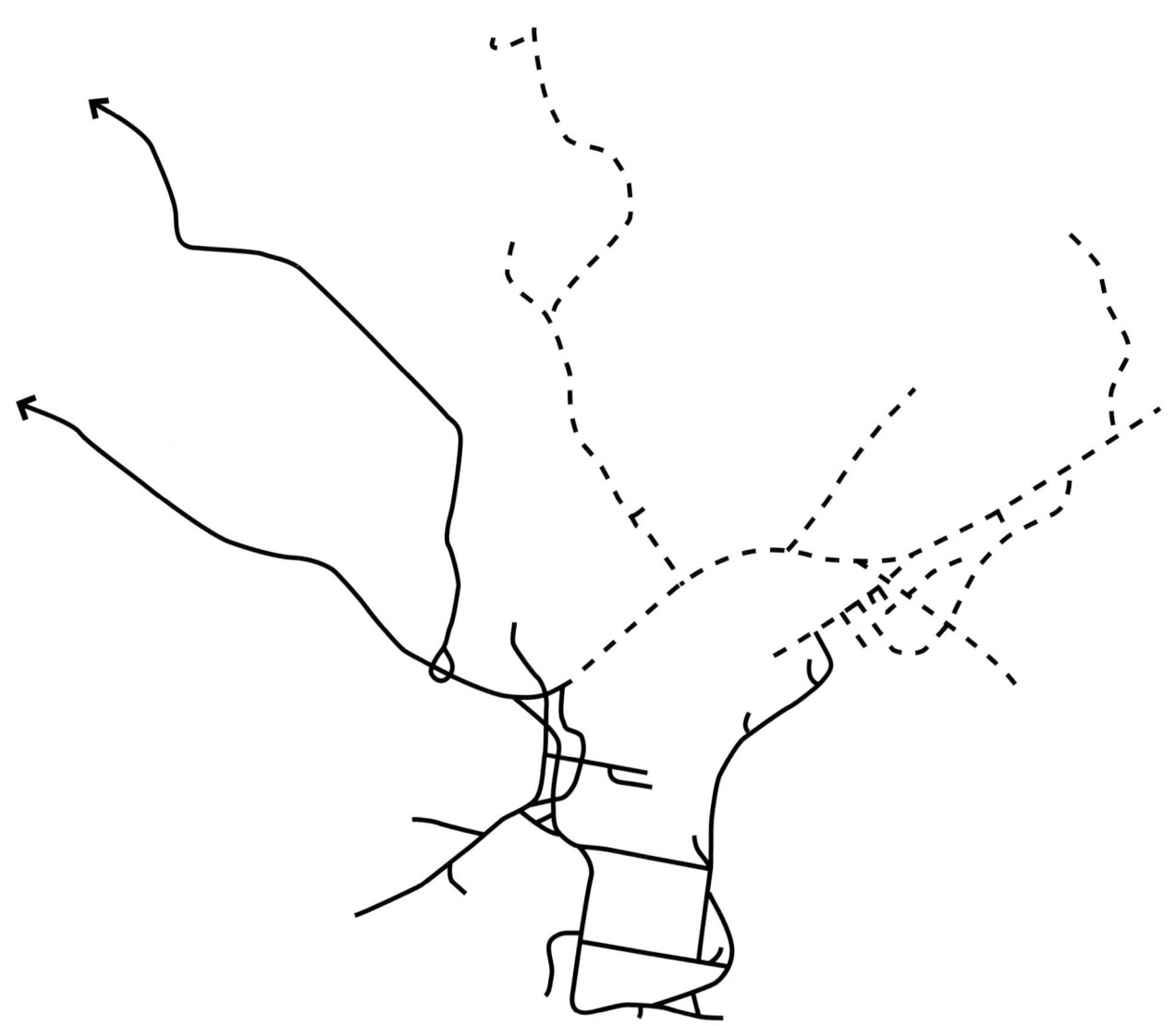

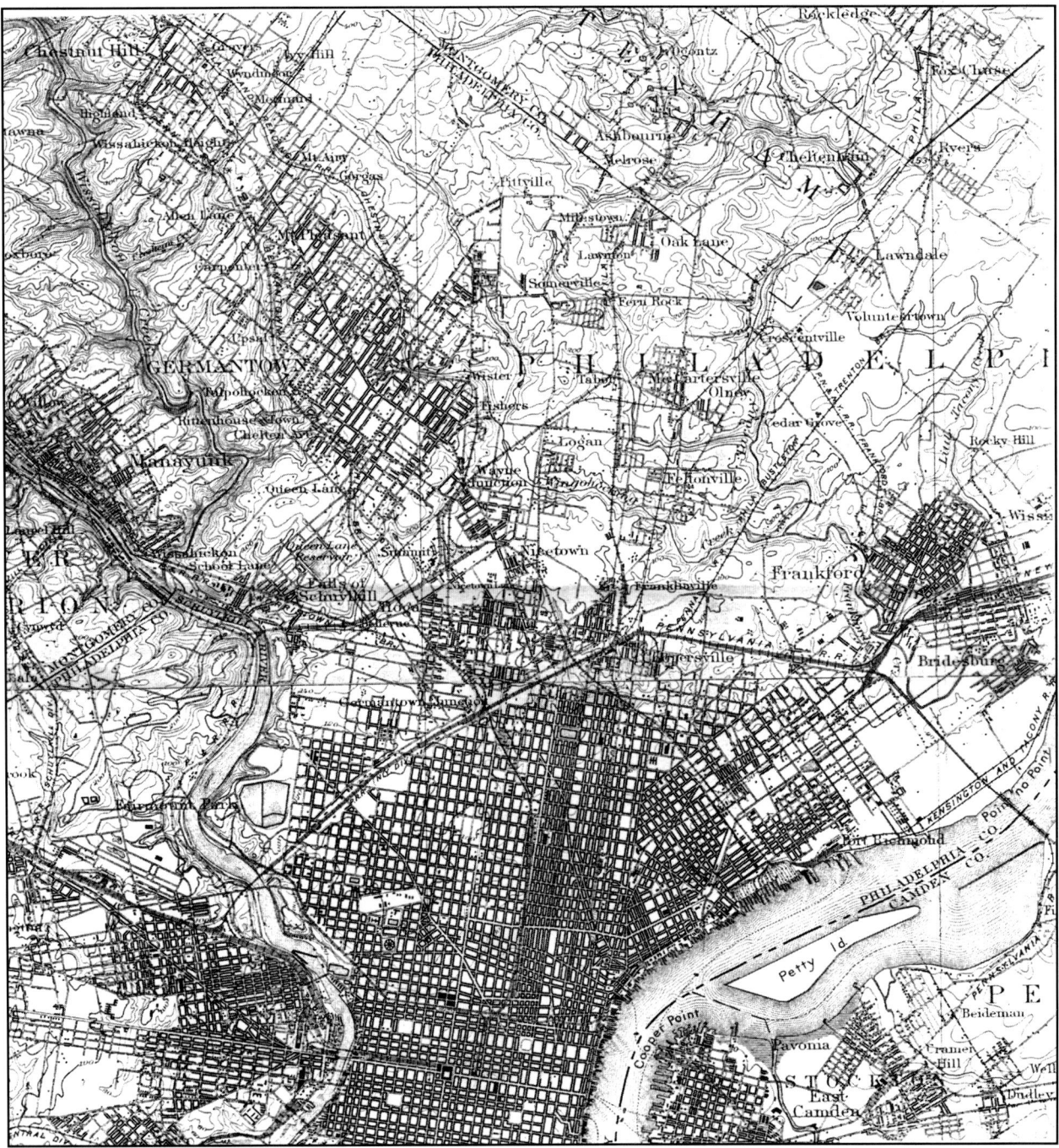

THE CONNECTING RAILWAY, as originally built from Mantua Junction (now ZOO) to Frankford Junction, is shown in this 1898 USGS map. It is a critical 6 1/2-mile link between the original Philadelphia Terminal Division and the Philadelphia & Trenton RR, subsequently the New York Division. This link allowed PRR to access the P&T to New York City and ultimately to achieve its triumphant New York-Washington and New York-Chicago/St. Louis system.

The Connecting Railway crosses over a series of north-south Reading lines and also provides a "backbone" for several PRR branches and yards serving local industries. Left to right, starting at the wye at ZOO, is the Belmont Branch (formerly the northern portion of the Junction Railroad) on the west bank of the river; on the east bank it crosses over the Reading Schuylkill main; at North Philadelphia (Germantown Junction) is the PRR Chestnut Hill Branch to the northwest, and crossing over the Reading Chestnut Hill and Norristown Branches; at North Penn Junction it crosses over the Reading Port Richmond and North Penn Branches, followed by the PRR Oxford Road Branch (Philadelphia, Bustleton & Trenton). At Frankford Junction the Delaware River RR & Bridge Co. extends across the river to New Jersey. This line crosses over the Frankford freight yards. The P&T then curves to the northeast. Note the extensive Reading facilities at Port Richmond, its main export gateway for anthracite.

An examination of railroad development in Philadelphia reveals a number of interesting patterns. We have discussed in Chapter 1 the progression of multiple small depots from the edges of the settled area to locations outside of the central business district in the 1840s through the 70s and finally a return by the three surviving railroads to the heart of Center City with major terminals in the 80s and 90s.

The approach of these three roads (B&O, PRR and P&R) was primarily from the south, west and northwest, respectively, in order to enter the business district. The exception to the pattern was the Philadelphia & Trenton Railroad, which entered the city from the northeast and built a station at Montgomery Avenue and Front Street in the Kensington section in 1834. This required passengers and freight from New York City to the west and south having to be transported across the City to West Philadelphia, resulting in considerable delay, expense and inconvenience. In fact there was no direct north-south rail route through the City at all, which was of primary concern to the Union Army at the outset of the Civil War. (Initially, Federal troops from New York City and New England moved via the Camden & Amboy RR, were ferried across the river to the foot of Washington Avenue and then marched to the PW&B depot). Something clearly had to be done.

The first step was the formation of the Junction RR (see Chapter 6) to link PRR, the Reading and the PB&W; the second was a 6-1/2-mile connecting line known appropriately as the Connecting Railway, which was chartered on 14 April 1863. In 1862 PRR entered into negotiation with the group of railroads known as the "Joint Companies" (Philadelphia & Trenton RR, Camden & Amboy RR and Delaware & Raritan Canal Co.) with the objective of forming a through north-south route to the New York City area. This route ran from the PRR mainline at Mantua Junction (1-1/2 miles north of the new West Philadelphia station) eastward across the Schuylkill River to Frankford Junction with the P&T.

Under the terms of the agreement, approved by the PRR Board on 17 February 1863, PRR gained operating access to New York City, and the P&T was given trackage rights into West Philadelphia Station and access southward via the Junction RR and the PB&W. PRR was to construct the line and guarantee $1 million of the bonds.

Construction began in 1864 and it was completed and opened for freight traffic in July 1867 and for passenger service in October of that year, at a cost of nearly $2.3 million. The line was leased to the P&T for 999 years on 1 January 1868; this lease was transferred to PRR on 1 December 1871 when that road in turn leased the P&T and the United Railways of New Jersey. The Connecting Railway thus provided the critical link for President Thomson's strategic expansion in 1871 toward the New York City area.

The line opened up a new east-west through routing, eliminating the need for the "Allentown Route" for freight via the P&R and CRR of NJ through Allentown and Harrisburg. It also allowed New York City trains to connect directly with PRR's east-west main to the midwest, and subsequently the north-south main to Washington, DC. In so doing it reinforced the pattern of access to the City from the west (we will discuss the role of North Philadelphia Station shortly).

The Connecting Railway was initially double track. In 1882 it was four-tracked from the Schuylkill River bridge to Germantown Junction (later North Philadelphia). Work was begun in that year to extend additional tracks to Frankford Junction and elevate the right-of-way, eliminating existing and future grade crossings north of the business district; this work was completed by 1889. A fifth (No. 0) and sixth (No. 5) tracks were added between 1887 and 1918.

In addition to its role as a critical mainline connection, this line also served extensive industrial areas by means of nine branches and several yards of varying sizes. Traffic over the line was heavy almost from the beginning, and grew steadily once the New York-Washington connection was completed. It consisted of all passenger and freight trains between those two cities, all through east-west trains to New York and local service between Philadelphia and Atlantic City, North Philadelphia, Chestnut Hill and Fort Washington, as well as Frankford, Bristol and Bustleton. The average traffic in 1918 was about 1175 passenger cars and 2750 freight cars per day.

Although there are some cuts the majority of the line is on a fill composed of stiff clay and gravel, with very little rock. There are five grades eastbound with a rise of 42 ft. in 2.6 miles and four westbound grades totaling 96 ft. in 3.5 miles. There are five curves totaling 1.5 miles, the maximum being 4°, at the tight curve between Frankford Junction and Frankford.

The line begins at the junction with the east-west main at the western end (initially known as Mantua, or New York Junction, and later as ZOO after the Philadelphia Zoo that was laid out between the eastern leg of the wye and the river) that evolved into perhaps the most critical junction on the system. The mainline curves through the complex, multi-tracked (and multi-level) wye and over the Schuylkill River on a massive stone arch bridge and then over the Reading Schuylkill main into Philadelphia on the east side of the river. Continuing eastward (railroad north) across the City the line intersects with the short Engleside (to the south) and Stifftown (to the north) branches, several small yards and then the Chestnut Hill Branch at North Philadelphia (originally Germantown Junction), which curves off to the northwest.

The Philadelphia, Germantown & Chestnut Hill Railroad was organized on 27 December 1882 to construct a line from Germantown Junction on the Connecting Railway to Chestnut Hill, a distance of 6.5 miles. Originally proposed in 1879 as a line to tap the coal fields of the Lehigh and Wyoming Valleys, it instead became PRR's double-tracked Chestnut Hill Branch to a growing upscale residential area of Philadelphia when it opened on 11 June 1884. The branch represented not only a business investment into an exclusive northern suburb but also a blatant invasion of rival Reading turf, another salvo in retaliation for that line's success in 1879 in gaining access to New York City.

As an example of the close interweaving of PRR and the communities it served, the case of Henry H. Houston is illuminating. Mr. Houston was General Freight Agent from 1852 to 1867, organizer and manager of the Empire and Union Fast Freight Lines and eventually a Director of PRR from 1881 to 1895. In true PRR form he was, "ever alert and watchful in promoting the interests of the Pennsylvania Railroad Company." He was also a real estate entrepreneur who played a major role in Chestnut Hill becoming the most desirable residential area within the City limits of Philadelphia, and facilitated the construction of the PRR-guaranteed road (in direct competition with the Reading line to this community) to serve the area's well-heeled clientele. This development paralleled the development along the Main Line, although into an area that otherwise might be considered exclusive Reading territory.

In January 1892 work began on an extension of the Chestnut Hill Branch 6.2 miles from Cresheim Junction, near Allen Lane Station to Fort Hill (later Fort Washington) on the Trenton Cutoff. This was initially called the Cresheim Branch, later known as the Fort Washington Branch, and opened on 30 July 1893.

As part of a program to improve traffic flow in and around the City, work was started in 1915 during the administration of President Samuel Rea on electrification of the Connecting Railway and the Chestnut Hill Branch. This involved the elimination of a large number of grade crossings, but work was not completed and the line made operational until 30 March 1918 because of the war and scarcity of labor and materials. Multiple-unit (MU) trains then began carrying commuters on these lines, which thus became the second link in PRR's eventual north-south electrification.

Immediately to the east on the Connecting Railway is North Philadelphia Station, which not only serves that portion of the city, but also became the primary stop for New York-Chicago trains to avoid the delays associated with the moves in and out of Broad Street Station. This station opened in 1901, replacing the original depot at Germantown Junction constructed in 1884.

Passing underneath this complex is the Reading Norristown Branch (originally the Philadelphia, Germantown & Norristown) and that road's Chestnut Hill Branch, which roughly parallels the PRR line to that suburb. These two lines join and continue south to Reading Terminal.

From North Philadelphia the line continues eastward to North Penn Junction where it crosses over Reading trackage again, this time a combination of the Port Richmond Branch and the North Penn line to the Bethlehem area. Just to the east the PRR Oxford Road Branch (originally the Philadelphia, Bustleton & Trenton RR) runs to the northeast.

The Connecting Railway continues eastward, passing under the Frankford Elevated line and then curves sharply to the northeast at Frankford Junction, where it follows the original P&T route parallel to the Delaware River. The Delaware River RR and Bridge Co. line extends eastward across the Delair Bridge into New Jersey. There are two branches off of the Connecting Railway in this area – the first is the short Kensington & Tacony Railroad (completed in 1892), which loops to the south into the southern end of Frankford Yard, and the Bustleton Railroad (completed in 1896) to the north at Holmesburg Junction.

Both lines served industrial and warehouse areas along the Delaware River and north of the business district. There are numerous yards and smaller branches along the entire stretch serving the northern industrial areas of this sprawling city.

On 1 January 1902 the Philadelphia, Germantown & Chestnut Hill Railroad, Engleside Railroad, Kensington & Tacony Railroad, Fairhill Railroad, Bustleton Railroad, and the Philadelphia, Bustleton & Trenton Railroad companies were consolidated into the Connecting Railway, unifying operations of these local railroads between the mainline and the P&T. In 1916 the Connecting Railway and branches, the Philadelphia & Trenton Railway as far as Liddonfield and the Delaware River Railroad & Bridge Co. to the east end of the Delair Bridge were transferred from the New York Division to the Philadelphia Terminal Division, further simplifying operations in this short but complex segment of the system.

The line continues to the division post with the New York Division at Liddonfield, just north of Pennypack Creek.

Let us now take a closer look at this short but critical segment of mainline trackage.

THE ELEGANT ELITE of Philadelphia Society, in full plumage commensurate with their social - and economic - status, partake of refreshment and conversation on the latest happenings while at Belmont Mansion in Philadelphia's famed Fairmount Park. This marvelous view looks southward down the Schuylkill River toward the City, with the Reading Columbia Bridge (formerly used by the P&C) on the left and the recently constructed Connecting Railway bridge in the center. Note the equally elegant tied-arch truss center span, with arched masonry piers on either side. The Civil War is over and sunlight breaks through the clouds and bestows its promise of a bright future for Philadelphia and PRR. All is well with the world!

TRIUMPH III

PRR'S OWN ELITE, the *Broadway Limited*, thunders eastward on the Connecting Railway near Girard Avenue behind K4 5396. Note the interesting pilot on the locomotive and that electrification and early upper-quadrant signals have been installed on the line in this 1920s view.

Railroad Museum of Pennsylvania (PHMC)

Ted Xaras Collection

THE ORIGINAL Connecting Railway bridge over the Schuylkill River is shown in this stunning ca. 1870 photo looking westward. The photo documents the beautiful stonework, the cast iron railing and lampposts as well as the tied-arch truss over the river. The photographer's train (most likely Frederick Gutekunst) and a host of dapper individuals are gathered for the occasion. Girard Avenue is just visible at the left as it passes under the railroad bridge on the west bank.

NORTHERN CONNECTIONS

Ted Xaras Collection

BY THE MID-80'S the arch had been removed and additional tension members and masonry supports added to reinforce the cast iron structure as tonnage increased. This view looks northeastward as a southbound "flyer" from New York City passes over the bridge. Note the brackets carrying telegraph wires.

Ted Xaras Collection

TRAFFIC CONTINUED to increase and by the 1890s the cast iron bridge was no longer adequate. The old structure was replaced with a new steel Pratt truss completed in October 1897. PRR accomplished the replacement with minimal disruption of traffic, as matter-of-factly related in the 1897 Annual Report: "In placing this span in position the old span was moved out and the new one moved twenty-seven feet to replace it in two minutes and twenty-eight seconds, the actual time elapsed between the passing of trains over the old span before moving and over the new span after being placed in position being only 13 minutes." This valuable, but unfortunately murky, photo shows how the task was accomplished.

Ted Xaras Collection

TRAFFIC WAS HEAVY on the Connecting Railway on this day ca. 1908 as a stalwart H-Class Consolidation moves an eastbound freight across the new bridge over the Schuylkill River. The double-tracked steel Pratt truss was 235 1/2 ft. long and weighed 660 tons. Note the brakemen atop the fascinating string of wooden freight cars in this westward view.

NORTHERN CONNECTIONS

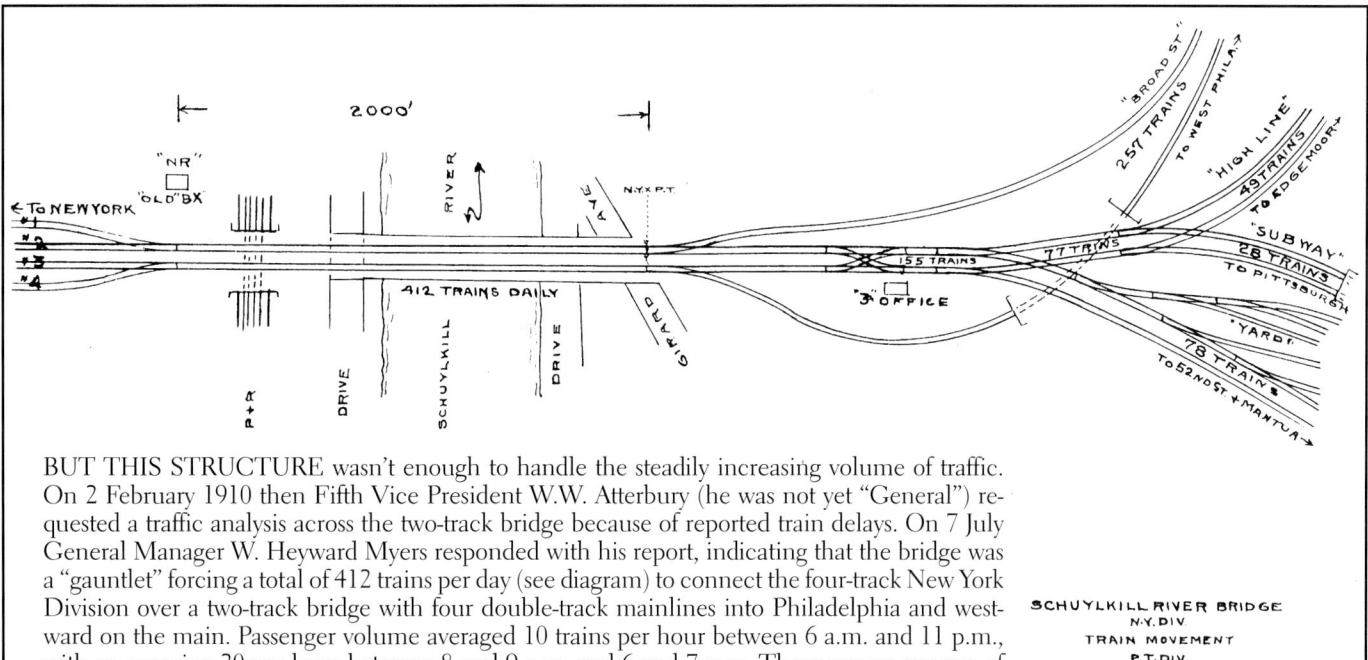

SCHUYLKILL RIVER BRIDGE
N.Y. DIV
TRAIN MOVEMENT
P.T. DIV.

Hagley Museum and Library

BUT THIS STRUCTURE wasn't enough to handle the steadily increasing volume of traffic. On 2 February 1910 then Fifth Vice President W.W. Atterbury (he was not yet "General") requested a traffic analysis across the two-track bridge because of reported train delays. On 7 July General Manager W. Heyward Myers responded with his report, indicating that the bridge was a "gauntlet" forcing a total of 412 trains per day (see diagram) to connect the four-track New York Division over a two-track bridge with four double-track mainlines into Philadelphia and westward on the main. Passenger volume averaged 10 trains per hour between 6 a.m. and 11 p.m., with an amazing 20 per hour between 8 and 9 a.m. and 6 and 7 p.m. There was an average of 54 trains per day (13%) known to be delayed as a result, with at least an additional 7% slowed up approaching the bridge as far back as North Philadelphia on the east and 52nd St. on the west. These delays were estimated to cost over $30,000 per year, and the traffic volume was expected to increase by 10% annually. His recommendation was a statement of the obvious: to build a replacement four-track bridge of stone or concrete, estimated to cost about $600,000. It would soon pay for itself. Note NR (formerly BX) Tower at the east end of the bridge.

Ted Xaras Collection

PRR EMBARKED on a major rebuilding of the Connecting Railway bridge. The new bridge was a massive 11-arch, 5-track structure, extending 1230 ft. from the west side of Girard Avenue to the east side of River Drive near Engleside. W.L. Ziegler, PRR Engineer of Construction, noted the following precautions taken during winter construction: "We used hot water, hot sand and hot stone, kept portable stoves at full blast, and covered the concrete as soon as laid with salt hay and tarpaulins, and kept the stoves under full draught until the concrete had set." Two tracks were opened in 1913, with the remaining three-track portion (occupying the site of the old bridge) completed the following year. This view looking west shows a westbound passenger moving across the bridge during the expansion project ca. 1911. Girard Avenue extends across the river and under the tracks at the left edge of the photo. East River Drive is in the foreground.

THE APPROACH on the west side crossed over Girard Avenue on a bridge constructed in 1911 and shown here in a 1917 photo. It consisted of four steel spans, encased in concrete and totaling 206 ft. An interesting incident relates to work done by PRR in this area in April 1903. It seems that a woman had a candy and cigar stand located on PRR property on the south side of Girard Avenue, just west of the bridge. She was asked to remove the stand several times prior to construction to extend the south abutment. She apparently refused and on 21 April had to be forcibly removed. This prompted a suit against PRR, which she claimed "unlawfully, maliciously and with great force and violence . . . threw said fixtures and property belonging to said defendant into the said street and removed and destroyed plaintiff's building or store property which she had erected thereon . . . ." We have no information on the outcome of the suit, although we can be sure the construction went as planned.

National Archives

Herbert H. Harwood, Jr.

THE COMPLETED BRIDGE over the river is shown here 70 years later as the second section of Amtrak Train No. 913 heads southbound in a June 1984 view. The catenary poles were initially erected when the Chestnut Hill Branch was electrified in 1918.

NORTHERN CONNECTIONS

AFTER CROSSING over the Reading main on the east side, the line passed under 33rd Street, shown here in a ca. 1948 view as a husky Consolidation moves a diner westward.

Harry Albrecht/Ted Xaras Collection

JUST TO THE EAST the line passes under Cecil B. Moore Avenue. Here, in a May 1994 photo looking westward, we see an outbound SEPTA train. This is now SEPTA's R7 line all the way to Trenton. The track at left is the Conrail Engleside connection.

Herbert H. Harwood, Jr.

WE WILL now tour the Chestnut Hill Branch, constructed in 1883-4 as the Philadelphia, Germantown & Chestnut Hill RR to compete with the Reading line (see map) to that growing fashionable suburb. The branch was constructed as a double-track line 6.5 miles long. It was substantially built, costing about $2 million. There are nine curves (maximum 9° at Germantown Junction), 10 northbound grades (maximum 0.3%) and three southbound ones. The terrain is generally hilly, with a steady rise to the north. The soil is mostly clay at the southern end, terminating in the Germantown and Chestnut Hill ridges of mica schist. The lower end is industrialized, but most of the line is suburban, bordering the eastern edge of Philadelphia's Fairmount Park, located in the rugged Wissahickon Creek valley. The branch has heavy suburban commuter traffic, with 32 trains daily (in 1917) to Chestnut Hill, with six to Fort Washington, totaling 230 cars. The freight traffic was largely derived from the Midvale Branch near the southern end, serving several industries including Midvale Steel and later the Budd Company; this averaged 150 cars per day in 1917.

This branch is now SEPTA's Chestnut Hill West (R8) line, to distinguish it from the ex-Reading Chestnut Hill East (R7) route, which roughly parallels the ex-PRR line to the east.

NORTHERN CONNECTIONS

A FOUR-UNIT MU train swings onto the Chestnut Hill Branch in this 1933 photo looking westward from the platforms of the North Philadelphia station. The substation for the branch is on the right, framed under the large signal bridge.

J. Harold Geissel/Ted Xaras Collection

CHESTNUT HILL BRANCH patrons were served by these platforms and shelters at the west end of North Philadelphia station. The main waiting room for the branch has been removed by the time of this undated view. The concrete-encased girder bridges over the Reading tracks are in the foreground; also note the tight (9° curve).

Railroad Museum of Pennsylvania (PHMC)

JUST AFTER LEAVING North Philadelphia the branch crosses over the Reading line to the same destination, shown here looking northward in a 1917 photo. This is a 125-ft. steel truss with massive members built in 1916.

National Archives

Ted Xaras Collection

THE FIRST STOP on the branch is the station at Westmoreland (MP 6.1), shown here not long after it was constructed in 1885. The somber gentlemen in dark coats and hats await the next train. A second story was added in 1890 for agent's quarters.

National Archives

SHORTLY THEREAFTER it crosses over Reading trackage again, this time the line to Port Richmond, that road's massive coal pier. This was a 73-ft. one-half through plate girder structure constructed in 1911 and shown here in a 1917 view.

NORTHERN CONNECTIONS

W.N. Jennings/Ted Xaras Collection

QUEEN LANE (MP 7.5) is the next stop. It was also constructed in 1885 and is shown here in an 1896 photo looking southward. Midvale Yard and the short Midvale Branch, completed in 1893 to the Midvale Steel Works, was just south of this facility. In 1915 the Edward G. Budd Manufacturing Co. located its plant on the line and began shipping steel auto bodies. In the 30s and 40s this plant shipped large numbers of stainless steel rail cars, which made up the consists of many famous name trains. After World War II the plant returned to production of body stampings for cars and trucks. Note the outcroppings of Wissahickon schist encountered on the line.

National Archives

IN 1889-90 several of the stations on the branch had second stories added for agent's quarters, as shown here in a 1917 northward view of Queen Lane. Note that a covered pedestrian footbridge to the southbound side has also been added.

CHELTEN AVENUE station (originally Germantown - MP 8.1) was built in 1886 and looked like this in 1917, showing construction work in progress to eliminate the grade crossing. Most of the stations on the branch were designed by Philadelphia architect W. Bleddyn Powell to fit in with the elegant neighborhoods and make their patrons feel right at home.

National Archives

WHEN THE grade crossing elimination and electrification project was completed in 1918, the station took on quite a different character, as shown in this photo showing the new station platforms at the depressed track level and the old structure still in place on the street level. This view shows the brick freight station and Adams Express office, a frame foreman's tool house and the small yard.

Ted Xaras Collection

TULPEHOCKEN station (MP 8.5), built in 1888, had acquired a Penn Central-style sign when this photo was taken in 1972, but it needed a coat of paint on the wooden portions. The license plate on the Oldsmobile station wagon reads "Rizzo." We wonder if it belonged to the late (some would say infamous) mayor of Philadelphia.

Herbert H. Harwood, Jr.

NORTHERN CONNECTIONS

Joseph Morsello/Ted Xaras Collection

WE DON'T HAVE many shots of steam on the Chestnut Hill Branch, but here is a prize one. It shows the locomotive, identified on the photo as either No. 817 (Class H1, Altoona 1879) or 917 (Class D11-A, Altoona 1884) heading southward past the station at Upsal (MP 9.1) ca. 1900. The second story was added to the structure in 1889.

A COMMUTER scans the headlines of the *New York Times* while waiting for his Philadelphia-bound train at Carpenter (MP 9.7) in November 1974. This structure, built in 1885, is virtually identical to the one at Tulpehocken.

Herbert H. Harwood, Jr.

AN AFTERNOON COMMUTER LOCAL hustles northward in pre-electrification days past an immaculately landscaped Allen Lane station (MP 10.1) ca. 1910. Allen Lane Tower (formerly AQ) was housed within the station, located just south of the junction of the Fort Washington Branch with the Chestnut Hill Branch. Built in 1890, it controlled commuter movements on these lines as well as freight movements in and out of Midvale Yard.

IN 1912 an interesting "flying bridge" was built to allow southbound passengers to safely cross over the tracks. Here we see a Penn Central Silverliner headed north in October 1969 as lack of maintenance allows the vegetation to close in.

Herbert H. Harwood, Jr.

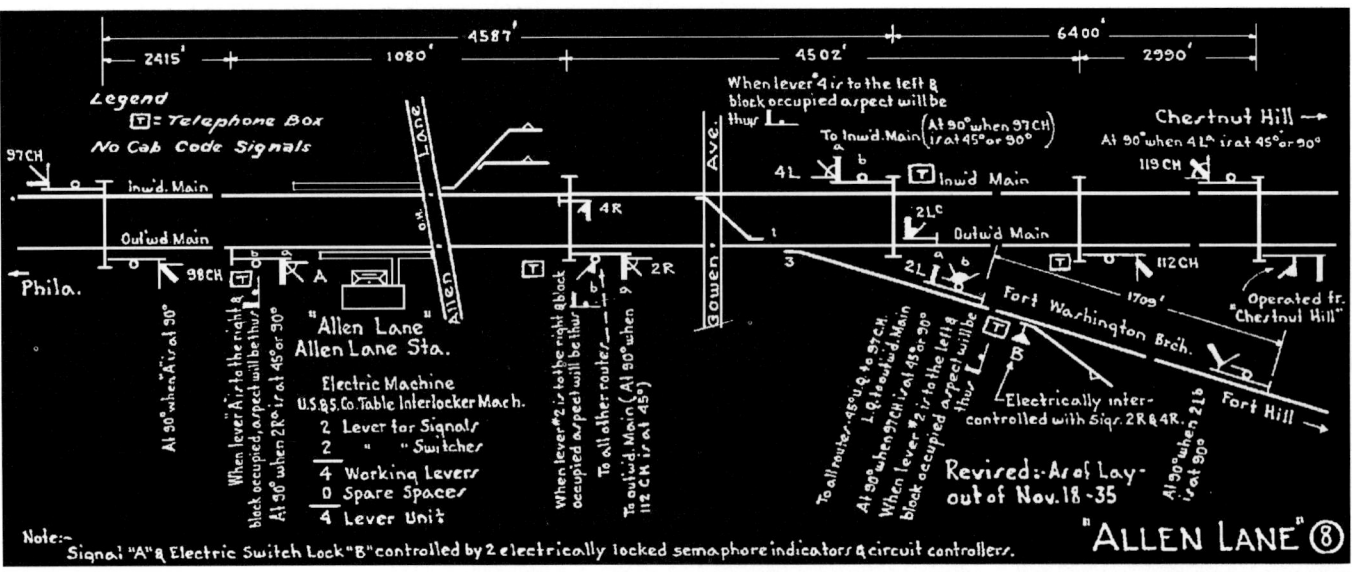

Hagley Museum and Library

THE INTERLOCKING at Allen Lane looked like this in 1935, controlled by an electric machine. The tower operator (who was also the station agent) also controlled power to the Ft. Washington Branch, under instructions from the Power Director located in 30th Street Station.

NORTHERN CONNECTIONS

AT THE JUNCTION — It's exactly 11:41 a.m. on 26 January 1957 and Train No. 821 runs southbound on the Chestnut Hill Branch at the junction with the single-track Fort Washington Branch, just north of Allen Lane station. This intersection was variously known as Fort Washington Branch Junction or Cresheim Junction, and was protected by the interlocking known as CW. Note the open substation (unlike the ones on the Main Line, which were enclosed).

John J. Bowman, Jr./Fred W. Schneider, III Collection

JUST NORTH of the junction the line crosses over Cresheim Creek on a 433-ft., 13-span deck plate girder trestle. The structure was built in 1884 and is shown here with a southbound train in November 1974.

Herbert H. Harwood, Jr.

PERFECT SHOT - After crossing the creek the branch enters St. Martins (originally Wissahickon - MP 10.9). John Bowman has captured a southbound train at the station in a photo combining superb timing, composition and light conditions. The station was constructed in 1887 and is portrayed here on 26 January 1957. VX Tower was originally housed in the station.

John J. Bowman, Jr./Fred W. Schneider, III Collection

COMPLETION of the electrification of the Chestnut Hill Branch was delayed because of World War II and other factors, but was finally finished in early 1918. Here we see the inaugural run approaching the end of the line on 30 March of that year. The gentleman in the doorway of the rear MU is track foreman Anthony A. Lepping, grandfather of the photo contributor, who entered PRR service on 1 December 1903.

Norman J. Lepping Collection

NORTHERN CONNECTIONS

A NORTHBOUND SEPTA train moves past Austin Tower (originally GK) into Chestnut Hill station on 20 August 1998. SEPTA refers to this terminal as Chestnut Hill West, to distinguish it from Chestnut Hill East, which is the former Reading facility.

THE STREET SIDE of the terminal at Chestnut Hill (MP 11.9) is shown here as it looked in February 1917, before the spire and center gable were removed. It was built in 1886. Note the vintage automobiles.

National Archives

END OF THE LINE – A trio of surprisingly clean owl-faced MP54 units sits on the not-so-clean track at Chestnut Hill Station in September of 1960, awaiting its return trip into Philadelphia. A car inspector checks the equipment.

THERE WAS a small yard, a 60-ft. turntable (constructed in 1891, replacing a smaller one built in 1884), a water tank (but no coaling facility) and a freighthouse, all located south of the passenger station. The attractive freighthouse was built in 1885 and is shown here in a 1917 photo.

National Archives

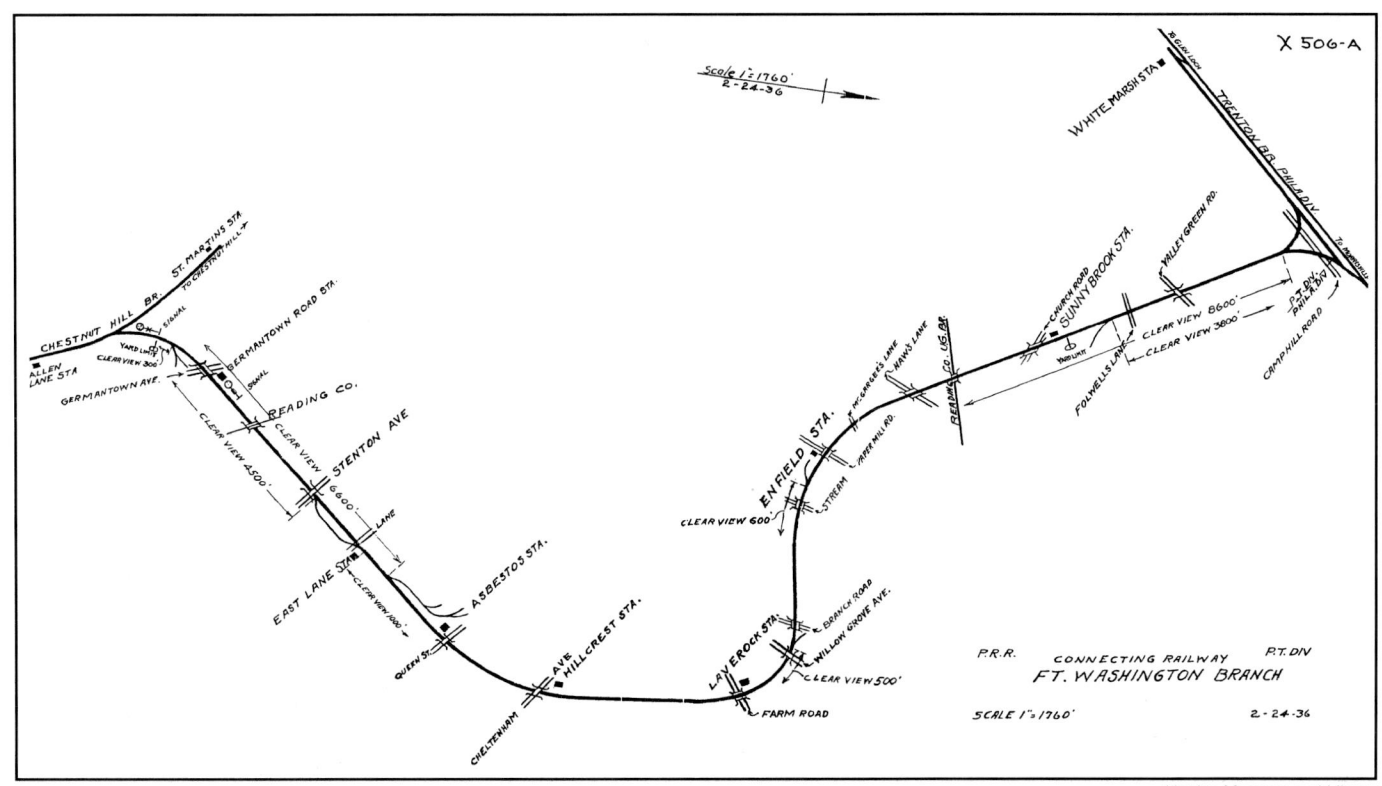

Hagley Museum and Library

THE FT. WASHINGTON BRANCH (sometimes known as the Cresheim Branch) was begun in 1892 and opened on 30 July 1893 as an alternate route to the Trenton Cutoff. It ran from Cresheim Junction, near Allen Lane on the Chestnut Hill Branch, 6.2 miles to Whitemarsh on the Trenton Cutoff (Philadelphia Division), which it joined at a wye. It was crossed by the Reading's Chestnut Hill Branch at its lower end and crossed over the Reading Plymouth Branch near the upper end. Because of the relatively light traffic, passenger facilities on the branch were limited – the only enclosed stations were at Germantown Road on the southern end and at Fort Hill and Whitemarsh on the northern end, where the branch connected with the Trenton Cutoff. The rest were either small shelters or just platforms. The only locomotive service capability was south of Germantown Road, where a storage track and ash pit were located. Electrification of this branch was initiated in January 1924 and MU operation began on 27 February 1924.

NORTHERN CONNECTIONS

AT HILL CREST (MP. 12.5) the single-track line ran through some hilly terrain, shown here in a May 1952 view looking southward. The open shelter is typical of most of the rudimentary stations on the line. The right-of-way was designed for double track, but the traffic level never justified construction of the second track. In the early years six to eight trains daily ran in each direction, including through runs from Broad Streeet to Trenton via the Trenton Cutoff. This was later reduced in frequency and required changing trains at Allen Lane.

Hugh Jenkins/Rob Piligian Collection

PHOTOS of the lightly-traveled Ft. Washington Branch are rare enough, but here's an extra bonus. The location is Whitemarsh, at the western end of the siding where the branch joined the Trenton Cutoff (Philadelphia Division). What we have is a GG1-led, New York City-bound mainline passenger train detouring on the Cutoff – usually considered a freight-only line – on 28 January 1952.

When the line was originally built it connected with the Trenton Cutoff at Ft. Hill to the east, allowing only eastward movement onto the Cutoff toward Trenton. Sometime after the turn of the century a wye was constructed, allowing westward movement as well. This was accomplished by connecting to a passing siding extending 0.7 miles west to Whitemarsh, parallel to the Cutoff. In addition a short run-around track was built at Whitemarsh, allowing steam locomotives to run eastward to Ft. Hill, around the wye and back to Whitemarsh to couple to trains for the return trip to Philadelphia. Both tracks appear in the foreground of this photo.

Hugh Jenkins/Rob Piligian Collection

Hugh Jenkins/Rob Piligian Collection

PASSENGERS and crew gather to have their pictures taken at Whitemarsh (MP. 16.6), the last station on the branch. The occasion was the last morning train on the line, 28 March 1952. Note the superb station sign. In July of that year a large section of the line was taken out of service; three years later only stubs remained at either end. A portion of the upper end of the right-of-way subsequently became part of PA Route 309.

WE NOW RETURN to the mainline at Germantown Junction (later North Philadelphia), the point where the Chestnut Hill Branch diverges from the Connecting Railway. In a late 1880s view we see a southbound train from New York City led by an immaculate D4 Class 4-4-0 pausing at the original station, which was constructed in 1884. A freight depot had been built here as early as 1869.

Ted Xaras Collection

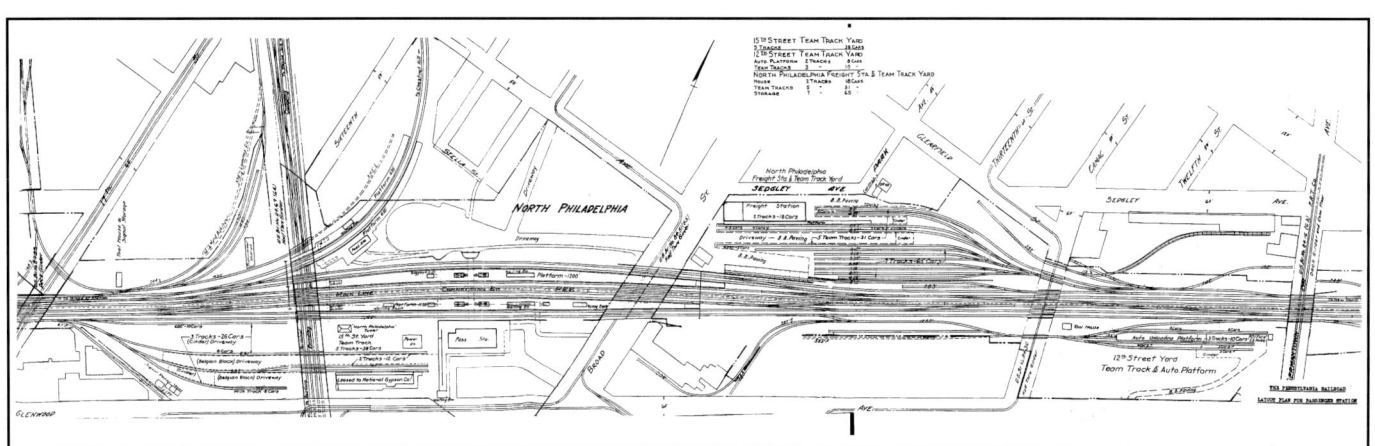
Ted Xaras Collection

THE LAYOUT of the facilities at North Philadelphia shows us both the diversity and complexity of the Division in microcosm. We have mainline passenger action, commuter operations (Chestnut Hill and Trenton), as well as though and local freight movements. North of the main at the far left in this 1935 diagram is the short (1/4-mile) Stifftown Branch, industrial spurs, the Reading main undergrade crossing, and then the Chestnut Hill Branch curving northward through the station platforms. South of the main is the NORTH PHILADELPHIA Tower and the 15th Street Yard and Team Track. The old freight shed is leased to National Gypson Co. East of that area is the main station and waiting room. Moving farther east we find the new North Philadelphia Freight Station and Yard, and still farther east is the 12th Street Yard and Auto Unloading Platform (remember this is 1935, when autos were carried inside boxcars). This entire area has several undergrade highway and rail crossings, typical of the Connecting Railway in general across the City.

NORTHERN CONNECTIONS

William J. Coxey

NORTH PHILADELPHIA (formerly GD) Tower was one of the most demanding towers on the Philadelphia Terminal Division because of the number of conflicting moves. This two-story concrete structure was built in 1913, replacing the old wooden one. A two-man operation, it handled all passenger trains through the station, plus MU's off the Chestnut Hill Branch. It also handled freights that served six yards and adjacent industries between the tower and SHORE. This photo looks eastward as Train 221, led by freshly-painted GG1 No. 4864, moves out from the station platforms under the massive signal bridge in July 1963. This train was one of the heaviest rush hour "Clockers" from New York, with 8-10 coaches, a bar lounge and a couple of parlors. The first car on this run is a business car, probably being deadheaded.

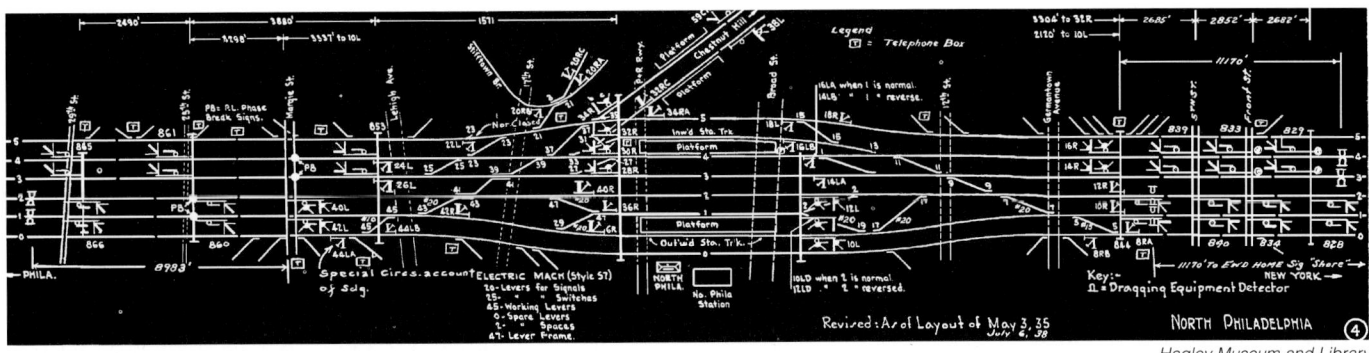

Hagley Museum and Library

THE INTERLOCKING diagram confirms the complexity of the trackage through North Philadelphia, a six-track electrified thoroughfare (Tracks 0-5), with two additional tracks in the platform area. Note the profusion of approach signals in both directions. Upper-quadrant semaphores were installed on the Connecting Railway from the end of the Schuylkill Bridge to Frankford Junction in 1913, and converted to position lights when the line was electrified. The tower housed an electric interlocking machine as of July 1938.

131

NORTH PHILADELPHIA was a growing area when this new passenger station was opened on 16 June 1901. It was the first of two new facilities built just after the turn of the century (West Philadelphia being the other one, in 1903) to better serve passengers on through trains, which were not effectively handled by Broad Street Station. The new station replaced the previous one at Germantown Junction, as the area was previously designated, built in 1884. It measured 50 x 136 ft., with a 49 x 80 ft. waiting room. It was attractively constructed of brick with terra cotta trim, as shown in this postcard view when new.

Hagley Museum and Library

AS PART of the initial program to improve traffic flow, a project to raise the tracks through North Philadelphia was begun in 1912. New elevated platforms were constructed in 1913 when the grade was raised 4 feet. The station itself was enlarged, with platforms and shelters serving both the mainline and the Chestnut Hill Branch. This view looking north shows the results as the project was nearing completion in 1915. Although it wasn't convenient to Center City, North Philadelphia then became the primary facility for through trains from New York City to the west, avoiding the delay associated with the moves in and out of Broad Street Station.

NORTHERN CONNECTIONS

Hagley Museum and Library

THIS AERIAL VIEW shows us the layout of the station area in North Philadelphia looking northeastward on 25 June 1939. At left is the complex of one-half through steel plate girder bridges used to carry the passenger (and abandoned freight) tracks over the Reading main in the cut. The Chestnut Hill line curves northward through the branch platforms. To the right of that is NORTH PHILADELPHIA Tower, the old freight shed, the power house and the main station. Across Broad Street on the north side of the tracks is the new freight station and team tracks. Note the long station platforms to accommodate passengers on the Blue Ribbon Fleet.

L1s NO. 3499 provides us a dramatic look at steam power under the wires as it thunders past the tower at North Philadelphia in a mid-30s view looking east. The track at left serves industrial spurs in the area.

Edward Trebino/West Jersey Chapter, NRHS Collection

133

TRIUMPH III

THE OVERHEAD was installed through North Philadelphia to Trenton in 1930 as part of the Philadelphia Improvements. It was extended to New York City in 1933 and Washington, DC in 1935, allowing through passenger service between these two terminals. Here we see modified P5a No. 4750 pulling a southbound passenger through the station ca. 1937.

Edward Trebino/West Jersey Chapter, NRHS Collection

GG1s OF COURSE were the predominant through power in North Philadelphia once they assumed their sovereign rule at the head of the Blue Ribbon Fleet. Here GG1 4896 accelerates Mail and Express Train No. 17 westbound past the Chestnut Hill Junction in July 1963. This train ran from New York City to Pittsburgh via 30th Street Station daily except Sunday.

William J. Coxey

NORTHERN CONNECTIONS

GG1s also took their turn in freight duty. Here a pair – one grimy, the other clean – lead train MD18 eastward through the junction on a late afternoon in June 1965. The massive signal bridge again provides the frame. MD18 ran daily from Potomac Yard (Washington, DC) to Harsimus Cove Yard (Jersey City).

William J. Coxey

FOURS GALORE – In another late afternoon shot, E-44 No. 4444 leads Train NF4, with a long string of K9 stock cars, eastward through North Philadelphia in July 1963.

William J. Coxey

Train NF4 (NF = no feed) was a Chicago to Jersey City livestock express that ran through Philadelphia on Tuesdays and Thursdays only. The cars were converted from no longer needed X-32 box cars in the PRR shops. Suffice it to say that North Philadelphia was a great trainwatching location!

TRIUMPH III

THE PARADE CONTINUES – A pair of AEM-7's hustle a southbound Amtrak train through North Philadelphia on 26 October 1998. Amtrak uses the station primarily for east-west trains, its traditional role during PRR days. Note the concrete ties on the two Amtrak main tracks; SEPTA uses the outer two.

National Archives

PRR CONSTRUCTED an imposing brick freight station at North Philadelphia, shown here in a 1917 photo. It was built in 1903, replacing the earlier one erected in 1889. It was 51 ft. wide and extended 229 ft., with a two-story office building. Note the World War I-era B&O boxcar on the team tracks alongside.

K2 PACIFIC 3345, one of the predecessors to the K4's, accelerates a passenger train eastward from the North Philadelphia area in this busy photo ca. 1910. Oil headlamps and lower-quadrant signals are still extant at this time.

Railroad Museum of Pennsylvania (PHMC)

NORTHERN CONNECTIONS

WE NOW MOVE to North Penn Junction, named for the Reading line that crossed under the PRR tracks. The passenger station at the junction (MP 6.4) was constructed in 1889 and is shown in a 1917 Valuation photo looking westward.

National Archives

THE FREIGHTHOUSE at North Penn Junction was constructed in 1882 and is depicted here in a 1917 photo. It replaced an earlier one built in 1873.

National Archives

JUST EAST of North Penn Junction are two more PRR branches. Curving to the left in this eastward view ca. 1950 is the Oxford Road Branch (former Philadelphia, Bustleton & Trenton RR) to the northeast and on the right the short Fairhill Branch serving several industries to the south. In the center of the photo are the Fairhill yards and freight station; to the right of that is the Philco plant. The Delaware River is in the haze in the background.

Tom Hollyman Aerial Photos/Penn Central RR Collection/ Pennsylvania State Archives

THIS PHOTO shows two structures, one embracing the other in 1917. The first is a three-span, one-half plate girder bridge over Kensington Avenue, constructed in 1890. The second is the Kensington Viaduct, which carries the Frankford Elevated (traction) line overhead. Note the trolley tracks underneath, along cobblestoned Kensington Avenue. SHORE Tower is just visible at the right edge of the photo, perching on the fill.

National Archives

SHORE (VN) TOWER controlled movements to and from the Delaware River RR & Bridge Co. line that ran east across the Bridge to Atlantic City and Jersey shore points and also south to Camden. It was built in 1894. Here we see a four-unit Metroliner set, its PRR keystone replaced (almost) with the PC logo, moving eastbound under the Kensington Avenue viaduct and past the tower in August 1972.

Herbert H. Harwood, Jr.

NORTHERN CONNECTIONS

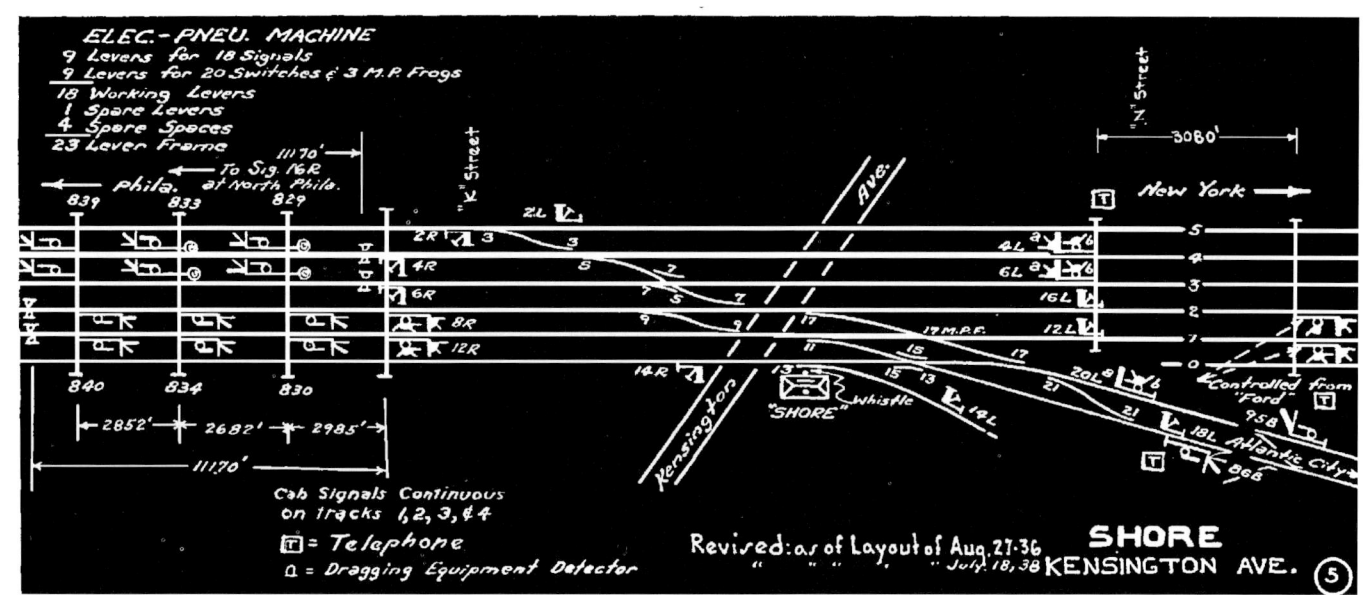

Hagley Museum and Library

AS THE INTERLOCKING diagram attests, the primary function of SHORE was to move inbound trains from the Delair Bridge across the busy main to the southbound tracks, as well as getting freights in and out of the south end of Frankford Junction Yard. It also serviced the riverfront trackage from the north, including transfer freights between Camden Yard and Greenwich Yard in South Philadelphia.

John F. Born

OPERATIONS AT SHORE could be rather busy at times. Here we see a southbound Metroliner, northbound and southbound SEPTA trains, and at right an E44-led Conrail freight from Camden waiting its turn to enter the interlocking, all under the maze of overhead on 17 September 1980.

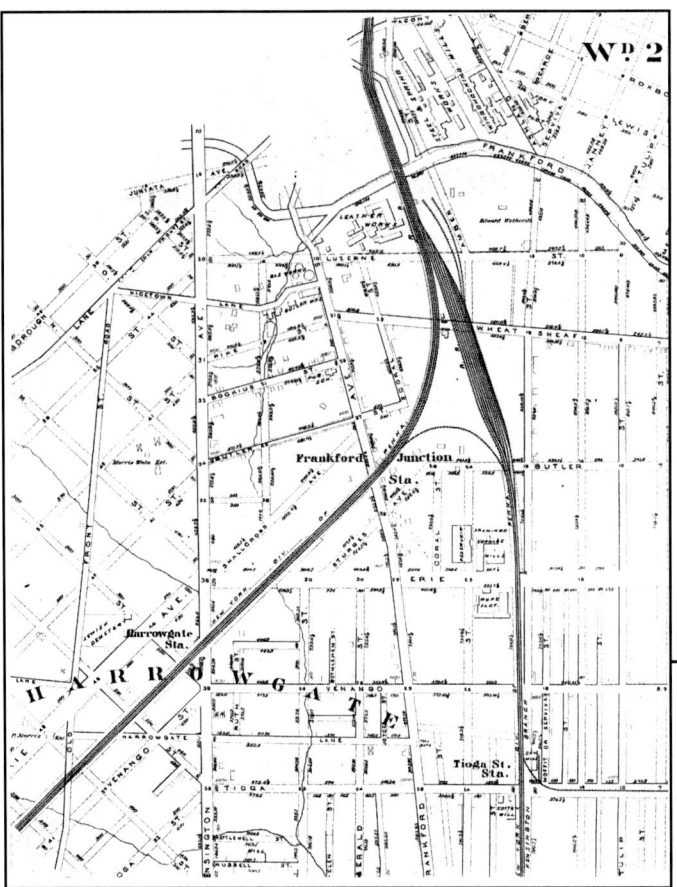

Ted Xaras Collection

FRANKFORD JUNCTION, where the Connecting RR met the Philadelphia & Trenton, is shown here as it appeared in the 1888 Atlas. At this point in time it is little more than a wye and a small freight yard. The station is located at the western end of the wye; the Kensington Branch extends southward. All of this trackage was still part of the New York Division at this time.

BY 1910 the yard trackage has grown in two directions, the Delaware River RR & Bridge Company line extends eastward across the yard and toward the river, and the Kensington & Tacony line has been added to the east, parallel to the river. Interestingly, on 5 April 1902 the Philadelphia City Council approved a little-known PRR proposal for a new junction of the Connecting Railway with the P&T main, eliminating the tight 4° curve. This would have involved a line running due east from the junction with the Oxford Road Branch, entering a very broad curve and joining the P&T farther north at Adams Street. Property acquisition took place, Erie Avenue was realigned to connect with Torresdale Avenue and even some grading took place from G Street to Kensington Avenue (Note "Connecting RW Co." on map). However, the change was never made, remaining one of the mysteries of PRR in Philadelphia. PRR chose to superelevate the curve instead.

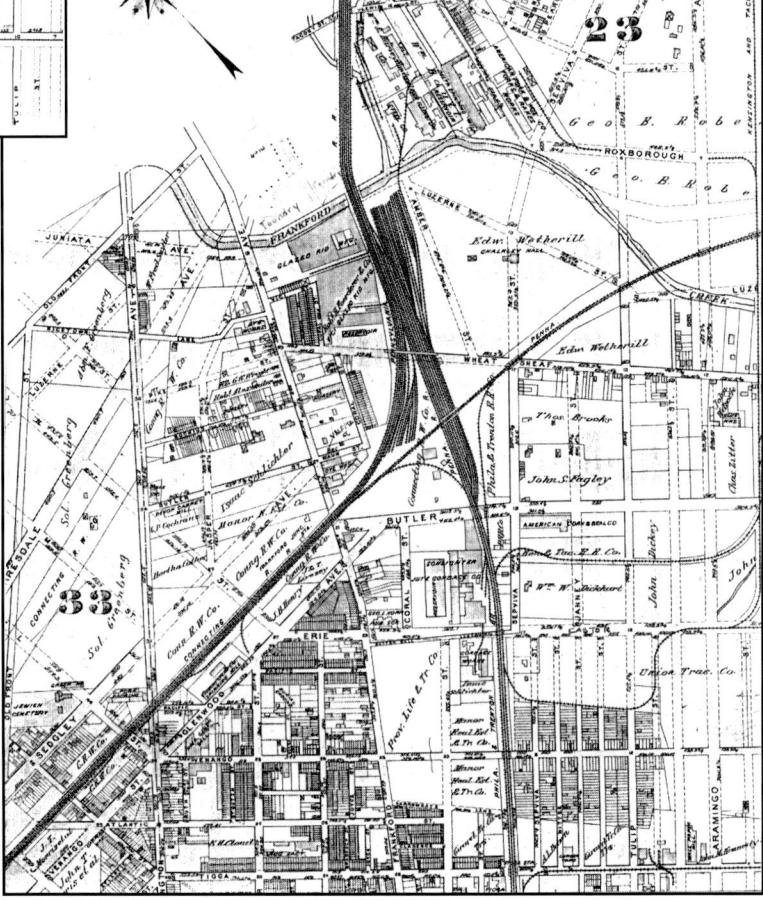

Ted Xaras Collection

NORTHERN CONNECTIONS

FRANKFORD JUNCTION passenger station (MP 8.5) is boarded up but still intact in this October 1968 photo. It was constructed in 1896. This view, taken from the rear of an eastbound Pennsylvania-Reading Seashore Lines train, shows the relationship between the station and the mainline and Shore tracks.

John F. Born

J. R. Quinn/Ted Xaras Collection

AN EASTBOUND passenger train headed for New Jersey thunders past Frankford Junction station in this May 1956 photo. K4s 5497 leads a long string of P70 coaches onto the Delaware River RR line.

141

TRIUMPH III

HERE WE HAVE a remarkable view of Frankford Junction, looking southward ca. 1890. The original passenger station is straight ahead on the curve, and the freight yard at left is already a busy place. Note the triple-masted bracketed signal post and to the right of it a northbound train, presumably off the Kensington Avenue line (original P&T).

E.P. Alexander Archive/Ted Xaras Collection

TAKEN AT ABOUT the same location over 100 years later, although without the benefit of a photographer's car to stand on, we are looking at the northern entrance to Frankford Yard where it joins the main (site of FORD interlocking) on 26 October 1998. The Wheatsheaf Avenue footbridge passes over both.

NORTHERN CONNECTIONS

STANDING on the footbridge looking north we capture a southbound Amtrak train heading into the sweeping curve as it passes Frankford Yard on 26 October 1998. This is a great location to view Corridor trains, SEPTA locals and Conrail action in the yard and on the Delair Bridge line.

SPEAKING OF CONRAIL, we see a switcher working Frankford Yard on 26 October 1998 while another freight moves eastward onto the Delair Bridge approach.

TRIUMPH III

WE'LL TAKE a brief look at the Delaware River Railroad & Bridge Co., a short connecting line (the name was longer than the railroad) that runs from Frankford Junction across the Delaware River to the division post in New Jersey. Opened 19 April 1896 and costing $145 million to build, it served to connect with the original north-south Camden & Amboy line as well as for through trains to Atlantic City and other Shore points. Here we see abbreviated Conrail Train PT85 moving toward Philadelphia to pick up cars with E-44 4404, still in PC paint, and a transfer cabin in October 1976. The mainline curves sharply to the left here and heads northward toward New York City; the grade and curvature were both reduced through this area in 1903.

William J. Coxey

National Archives

THE LINE crosses over the Frankford freight yards and onto the approach to the Delair Bridge. The west approach to the bridge, shown here in a 1917 view, is an imposing 2131-ft, 52-span deck plate girder structure. It was erected in the summer of 1895, in just 7 weeks!

THE BRIDGE ITSELF, shown here in a 1917 photo, consisted of three fixed Pennsylvania truss spans plus a through truss swing drawbridge totaling 1932 feet. The division post with the Atlantic Division was just at the east end of the bridge.

National Archives

NORTHERN CONNECTIONS

THE MASSIVE stone center pivot of the swing bridge is shown here in a 1917 view. These four sections of the main bridge were constructed in 1896.

National Archives

TO INCREASE CLEARANCE for river traffic, PRR constructed a new vertical lift span in 1958 just west of the swing bridge. The 542-ft. span was floated into place in one piece to facilitate installation and minimize delay. It was the longest double-track and heaviest lift bridge in the world. It is shown here in a photo looking eastward across the Delaware on 7 August 1987, with the Tacony-Palmyra highway bridge to the north. Note how the end of the first truss section has been "chopped" to allow installation of the new lift towers.

Thomas Barnett/Ted Xaras Collection

TRIUMPH III

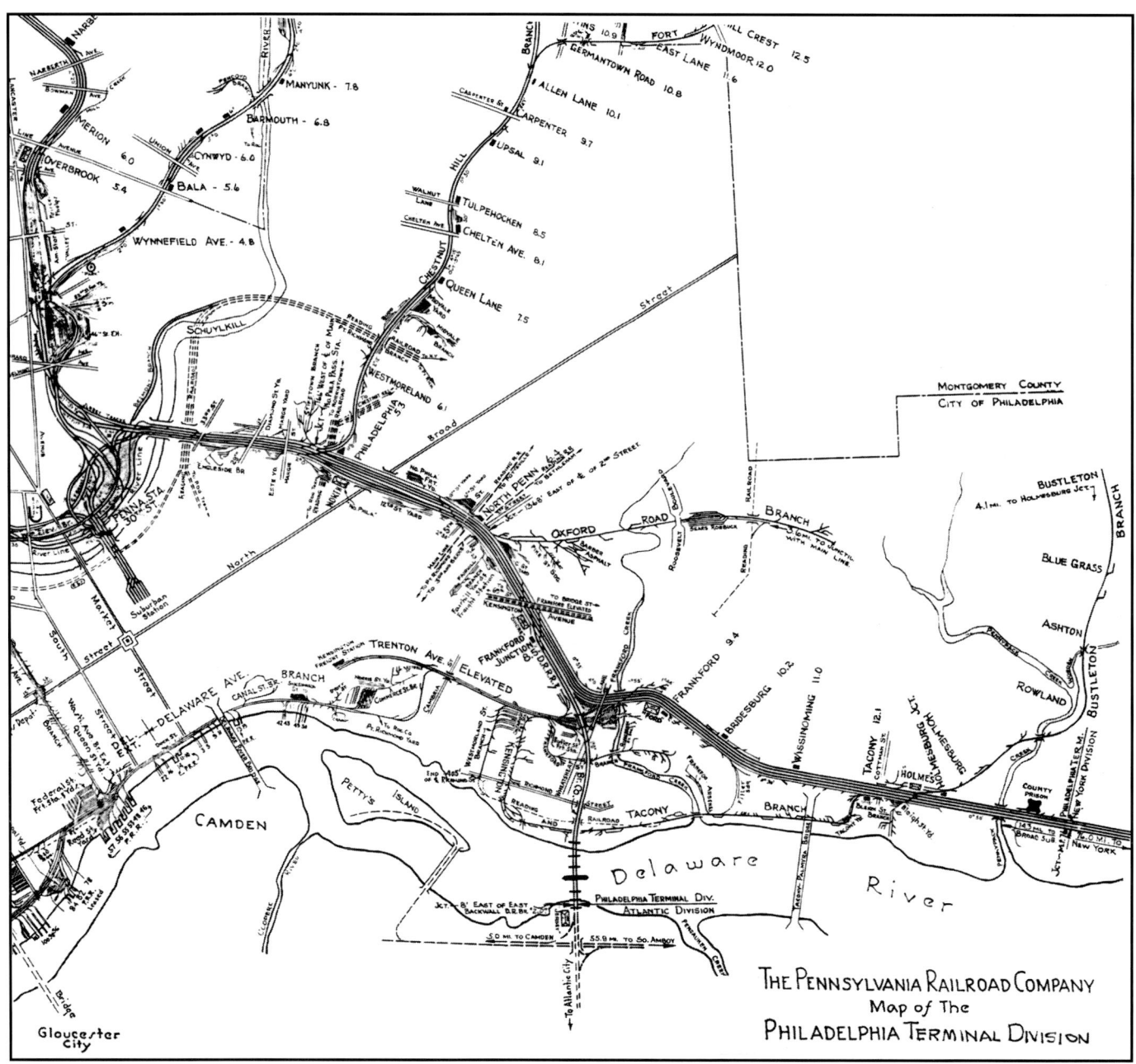

Andrew M. Wilson

THE SECTION of the Philadelphia & Trenton that became part of the Philadelphia Terminal Division is shown in this portion of the divisional map, which shows the entire Connecting Railway. The Tacony Branch (formerly the Kensington & Tacony RR) runs south from Tacony, serving industries along the Delaware River waterfront, and the Bustleton Branch (Bustleton RR) runs northeast from Holmesburg Junction to its namesake city. Note the division points with the New York Division at Liddonfield and the Atlantic Division at Delair. Note also the location of the towers controlling the main tracks – NORTH PHILADELPHIA, SHORE, FORD and HOLMES.

The P&T RR was incorporated 23 February 1832 and was originally constructed in 1834 on the right-of-way of the old stage road from Philadelphia to Morrisville, NJ. It started at Kensington and ran northeasterly, crossing the Delaware Division of the Pennsylvania Canal in the borough of Bristol and continued to the borough of Morrisville. This portion of the line was completed in 1833 and utilized horses until November 1834, when authorization was granted to use locomotives. A second track was laid in the 1860s, and a third and fourth added from Frankford to Holmesburg in 1882-4, and from Holmesburg northward in 1887-9. The P&T became part of the United New Jersey Railroad & Canal Co., which was in turn leased by PRR in 1871 – in a bold strategic move by John Edgar Thomson. It and the Connecting Railway became part of the New York Division, although subsequently the Philadelphia Terminal Division was extended to a point just north of Pennypack Creek in Liddonfield.

The terrain of this line is generally level, and curvature is light north of Frankford. The soil is clay at the southern end and gravel and light sandy loam for the northern reaches.

NORTHERN CONNECTIONS

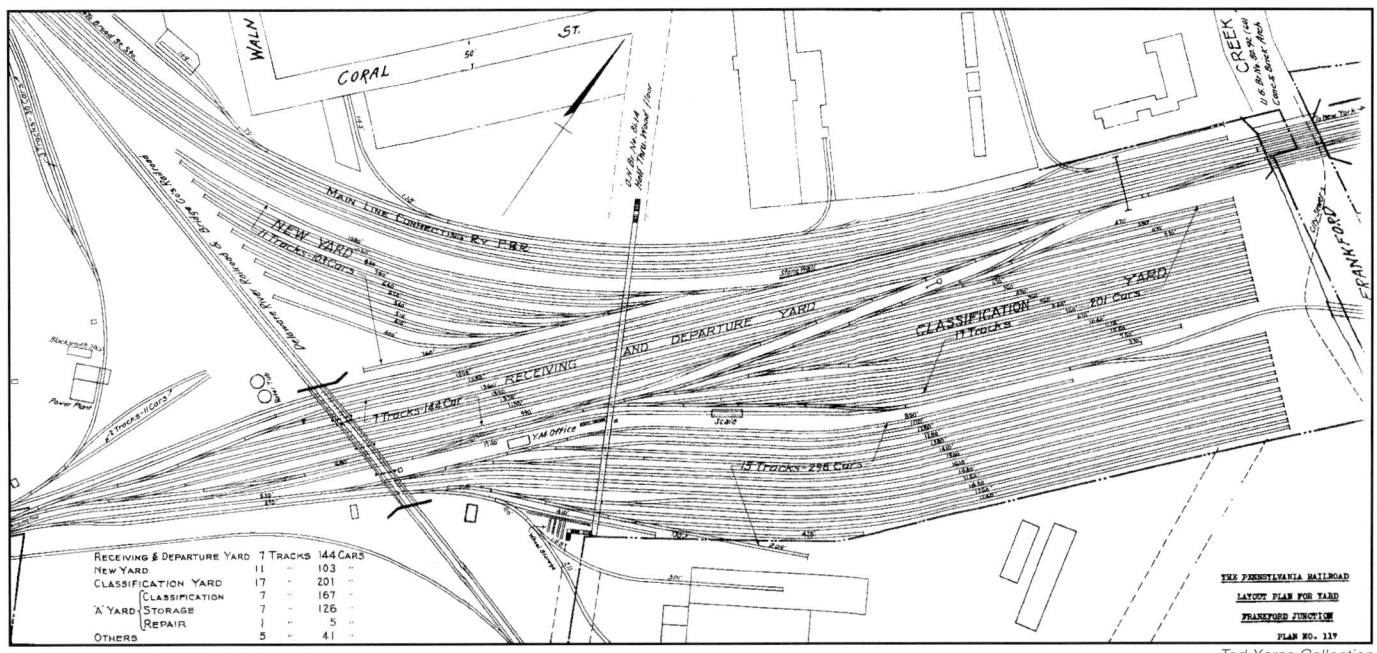

Ted Xaras Collection

NOW WE'LL TAKE a closer look at the facilities in the area from Frankford Junction to Kensington that was originally part of the P&T mainline. The most extensive is the Frankford Junction Yard, which serves as a receiving point for freight originating on the Kensington Branch, on the Connecting Railway and the numerous short industrial lines in the vicinity of Frankford. The yard was originally constructed in 1890 as a freight storage yard and enlarged over the years. In 1900 a new enginehouse and 75-ft. turntable were built, replacing the facilities at Kensington. A new Adams Express building and platform were built in 1912, and the yards were electrified in 1937.

This diagram shows how the yard looked in 1935. The Classification Yard is at right, the Receiving and Departure Yard above and to the left of that, and the "New Yard" along the curve in the main. The Delaware River RR & Bridge Co. crosses at left.

147

Tom Hollyman Aerial Photos/Penn Central RR Collection/Pennsylvania State Archives

HERE'S AN AERIAL VIEW of the Frankford Junction yards ca. 1950. We are looking southeastward: the five-track main sweeps around the curve at right, the classification yard is at left, with the receiving and departure yard between them. At the top of the photo, above the DRRR&BCo. tracks, are the engine terminal and the yard office.

NORTHERN CONNECTIONS

Andrew M. Wilson

IN 1953 PRR constructed a new $2 million freight facility with separate inbound and outbound freight sheds. Known as the Butler Street Freighthouse, it was located at the southern end of the yard. It is shown here as it appeared in May 1998. If you were to pose the question where PRR's freight facilities in Philadelphia were located, the short answer would be, "wherever they needed to be." The longer answer we are attempting to document.

National Archives

THE ONTARIO STREET freighthouse was located in a small yard south of the main yard at Frankford Junction. It was constructed in 1890 and is shown here in a 1917 view. The early motor truck belonged to the Schwarz Wheel Co., Frankford.

THE TRACKS from Frankford Junction to Kensington, known as the Kensington Branch, were elevated starting in 1899, but the complex project was not completed until 1910 (most of the construction work was done between 1907 and 1910). This was a joint endeavor between the railroad and the City of Philadelphia to eliminate grade crossings in this congested area. Operations on the line were maintained during construction, so a temporary track was constructed to one side of Trenton Avenue (at grade), which involved relocation of several Reading sidings in the area.

This 1917 Valuation photo looking southward shows the 5472-ft., 127-span steel viaduct above Trenton Avenue, known as the Trenton Avenue Elevated. It was constructed by American Bridge Co. (Pencoyd) in 1909. The land under the viaduct was sold to the City for $750,000, as the city's contribution to the project.

National Archives

THIS THREE-SPAN, 64-ft. one-half through plate girder bridge constructed over Westmoreland Street in 1908 is typical of the grade crossings on the fill portion of the line.

National Archives

THIS REMARKABLE PHOTO of the grade crossing of the Kensington line along Trenton Avenue with the Reading Port Richmond Branch has been published before, because of the quaint P&R windmill tower, but it is also of interest to students of PRR history. It is one of only a few photos extant taken on this section of the original P&T line during the late 1890s. We are looking northeast – in the distance at left is the connection to the Reading branch that allowed New York trains to pass through Philadelphia before construction of the Connecting Railway (see Chapter 6).

Philadelphia City Hall Archive / Ted Xaras Collection

NORTHERN CONNECTIONS

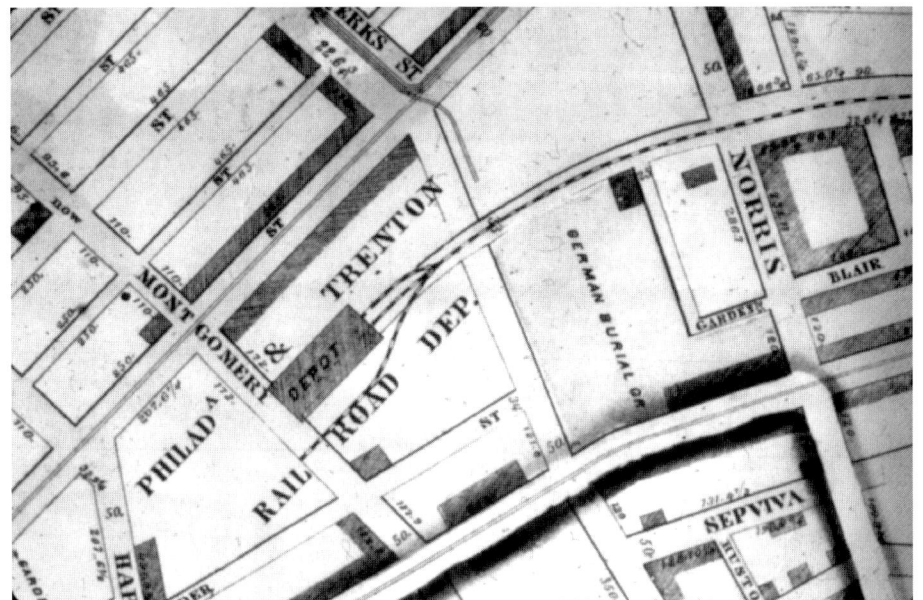

THE LAYOUT of the facilities at Kensington is shown here in a map from Smedley's 1862 Atlas. The P&T originally constructed its depot at Montgomery Avenue, between Front Street and Frankford Avenue, from which service was inaugurated on 1 November 1834. This was supplemented during the 1840s and 1850s by a second depot at 3rd and Willow Streets for horse-drawn equipment. With the opening of the Connecting RR in 1867, however, the route into Philadelphia from the north was drastically altered. Through trains to and from New York City shifted to the "New York Depot" in West Philadelphia. The use of the Kensington station for this service was discontinued in that year; it remained in use for local service.

Ted Xaras Collection

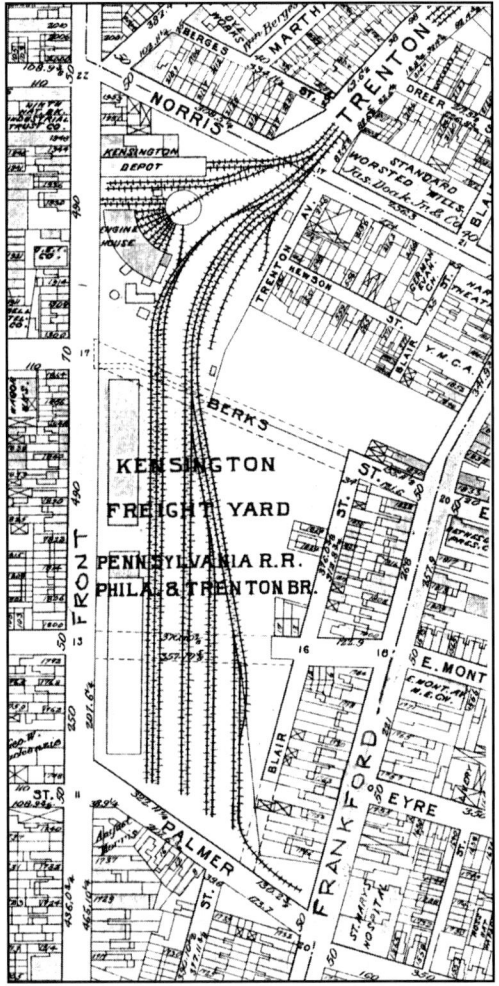

A NEW STATION, separate from the freight facilities, was opened on 1 May 1882. This consisted of a brick waiting room attached to a two-track trainshed, farther north at Front and Norris Streets. The layout is depicted here in a map from the 1910 Atlas.

Ted Xaras Collection

THIS DEPOT is shown here in a rare 1890s photo, looking west through the shed toward the front. The enginehouse is at left. The Kensington Station continued in use – certainly unheralded given its heritage – into the 1920s.

Ted Xaras Collection

ALTHOUGH it doesn't need further identification, a freight shed was constructed in Kensington in 1887 and is shown here in a turn-of-the-century view looking north at the Palmer Street end. Motor trucks would of course later replace Dobbin and the interesting horse-drawn wagons.

Railroad Museum of Pennsylvania (PHMC)

E. S. McKeown

(left) RETURNING to the main, FORD (FJ) Tower was located just north of Frankford Yard, at the junction of the Connecting Railway with the P&T mainline to Trenton. This tower controlled movements in and out of the yard from the north. FORD is shown here in an August 1961 photo. When the tower was closed the board was moved to SHORE.

(below) FORD interlocking was the mirror image of the unit at SHORE, controlling movements across the main in the opposite direction. It was one of three towers on the Philadelphia Terminal Division (the others being NORRIS and BRILL) still housing Armstrong levers. Moving a local freight from one side to the other required considerable work, particularly if a through train appeared in the meantime! Upper quadrant signals were installed from Frankford to Holmesburg Junction in 1914, completing the Connecting Railway/P&T project. Note the lead to the north end of Frankford Junction yard.

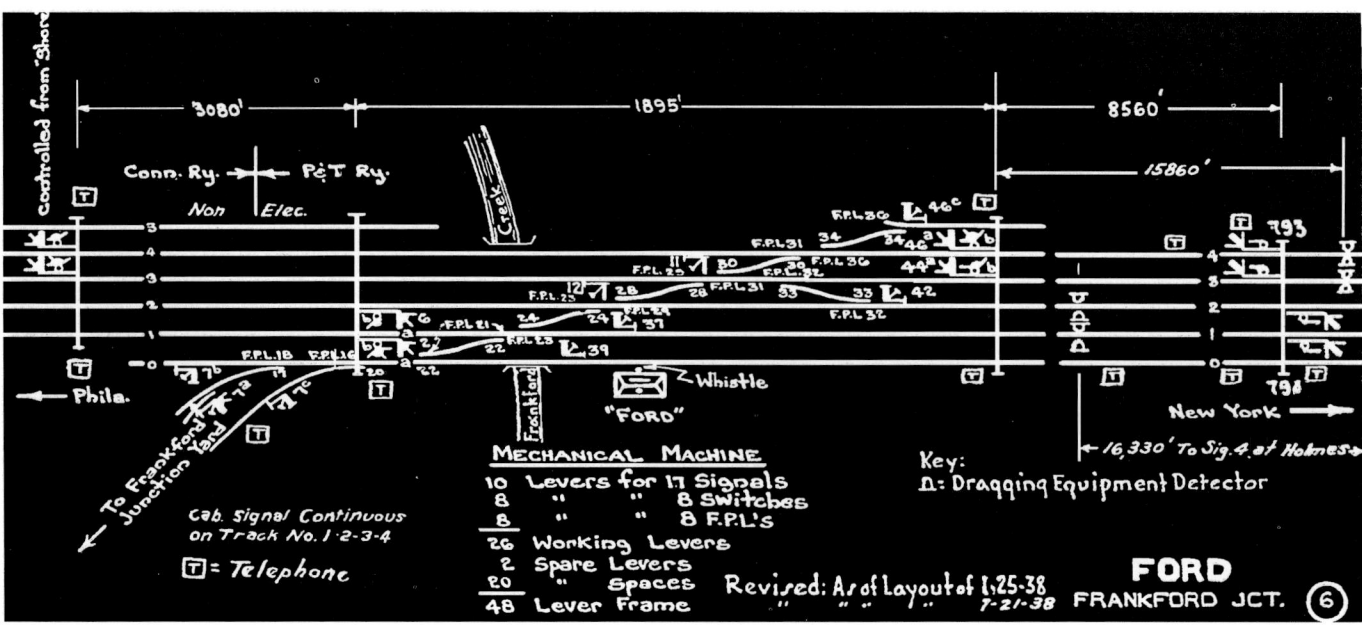
Hagley Museum and Library

NORTHERN CONNECTIONS

THIS VIEW looking northward shows the main Frankford Station (MP 9.4) in 1917. It was constructed in 1883.

National Archives

THE SOUTHBOUND SHELTER was added in 1886. Note the boxcars on a siding behind the station. A freight depot was built by the P&T in 1845.

National Archives

AN ADAMS EXPRESS COMPANY building was added at Frankford in 1914 and is shown here in a 1917 photo.

National Archives

WE CAN'T IDENTIFY the locomotive, but this undated photo is labeled "Fast Express, PRR, Frankford," so let's just enjoy the action as the train heads southward towards Philadelphia.

Railroad Museum of Pennsylvania (PHMC)

BRIDESBURG (MP 10.2) passenger station is shown here in a 1917 photo. It was constructed in 1896, replacing an earlier depot built in 1883. A freight depot was located on the P&T near this location as early as 1845.

National Archives

THE WISSINOMING (MP 11.0) passenger station constructed in 1889 is reminiscent of similar two-story structures on the Chestnut Hill Branch.

National Archives

NORTHERN CONNECTIONS

THIS UNIQUE structure served as the station at Tacony (MP 12.1). It was constructed in 1886 and is shown here as it appeared in 1917. The view looks northward. An early freight depot was built here in 1849.

National Archives

AT THE TIME the P&T was constructed there were numerous grade crossings. Although a few overhead bridges were probably built before that time, a major grade crossing elimination program was initiated in 1891. This effort was largely completed between Frankford and Holmesburg Junction by 1895 and elsewhere on the P&T within the City limits by 1900, except for the Kensington Branch. In some areas the old line was retained for use as yard and connecting trackage, but the main was elevated on structures such as this 80-ft., three-span, one-half through plate girder bridge over Princeton Street in Tacony, typical of several on the line. It is shown here in a 1917 view.

National Archives

TRAIN NO. 29, the westbound *Broadway Limited*, moves south through Tacony in July 1966. Observation Mountain View holds its customary position at the rear of the pride of the PRR. Note the long length of welded rail awaiting installation as part of the upgrading of the Corridor for Metroliner service.

William J. Coxey

155

TRIUMPH III

THE ORIGINAL passenger station at Holmesburg Junction was located on the west side of the main, just north of the interchange with the Bustleton Branch. Virtually identical to the one at Wissinoming, it was constructed in 1886 and is shown here in a 1917 view.

National Archives

FRAMED by the PRR signal bridge, an Amtrak train rockets past the northbound platform at Holmesburg on 26 October 1998. The fence is there for good reason!

NORTHERN CONNECTIONS

HOLMES (HG) Tower was originally located on the east side of the tracks at the junction with the Bustleton Branch. It was the division post tower on the Philadelphia Terminal Division and therefore interacted with both PT and New York Division dispatchers. The current tower, on the west side, is shown here on 26 October 1998; the northern portion serves as the SEPTA ticket office and southbound waiting room on the R7 Trenton line.

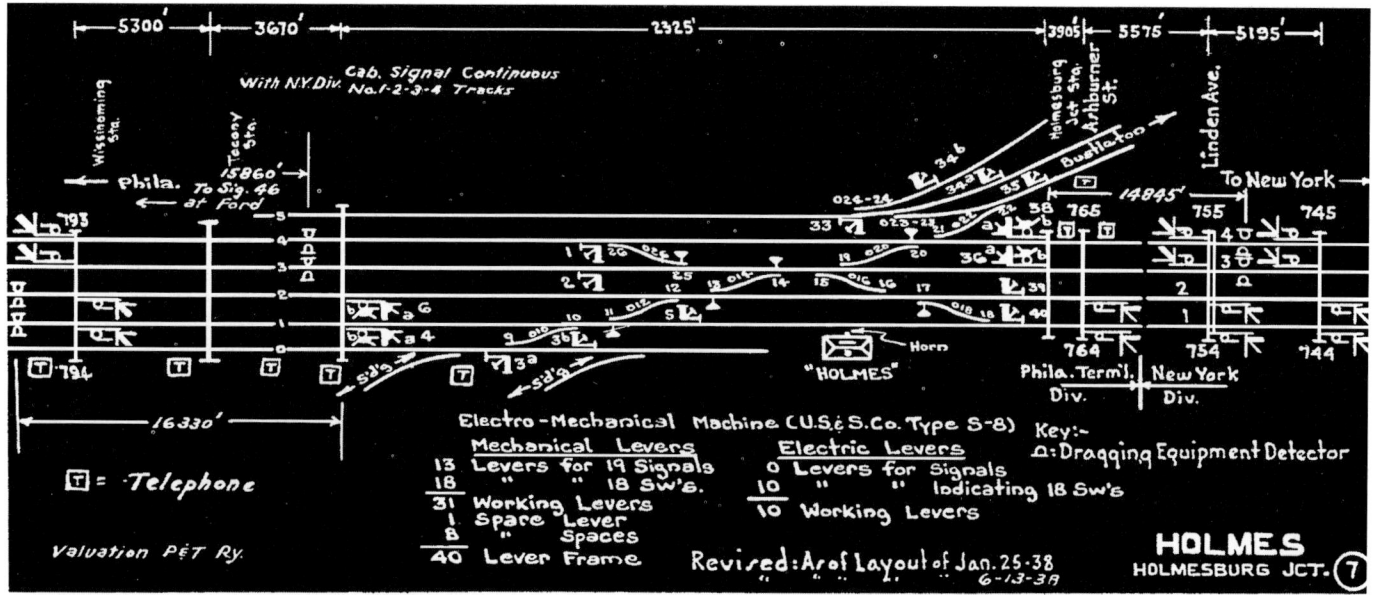

Hagley Museum and Library

HOLMES controlled a full interlocking across the four-track main in both directions as well as serving the Bustleton Branch and Bleigh St. yard. It housed an electro-mechanical machine as of June 1938.

TRIUMPH III

LEAVING NO DOUBT about the identity of the structure, the sign tells the story. The shiny vehicle adds a touch of class to this late 1930s photo.

Edward Trebino Collection / West Jersey Chapter, NRHS

A SHORT Conrail local moves off the Bustleton Branch, past HOLMES Tower on 26 October 1998. The sign on the tower reads, "Warning, Active Tracks."

WE WON'T SPEND much time on the short Bustleton Branch, running from Holmesburg Junction northward to Bustleton, but this interesting structure warrants a look. It served as both passenger station and Adams Express agency in Bustleton, at the end of the branch. It is shown here in a 1910 photo; note the wooden passenger cars.

Ted Xaras Collection

NORTHERN CONNECTIONS

THIS PEACEFUL SCENE shows the masonry bridge over Pennypack Creek, although a large prison complex is just a short distance away. This 183-ft., 4-span structure was constructed in 1887 and extended in 1914.

THE LIDDONFIELD passenger station was constructed in 1891 on the P&T but included in the Philadelphia Terminal Division in 1916 at the junction with the New York Division. It resembles its neighbors to the south.

Chapter 3
The Golden Arm

The Main Line

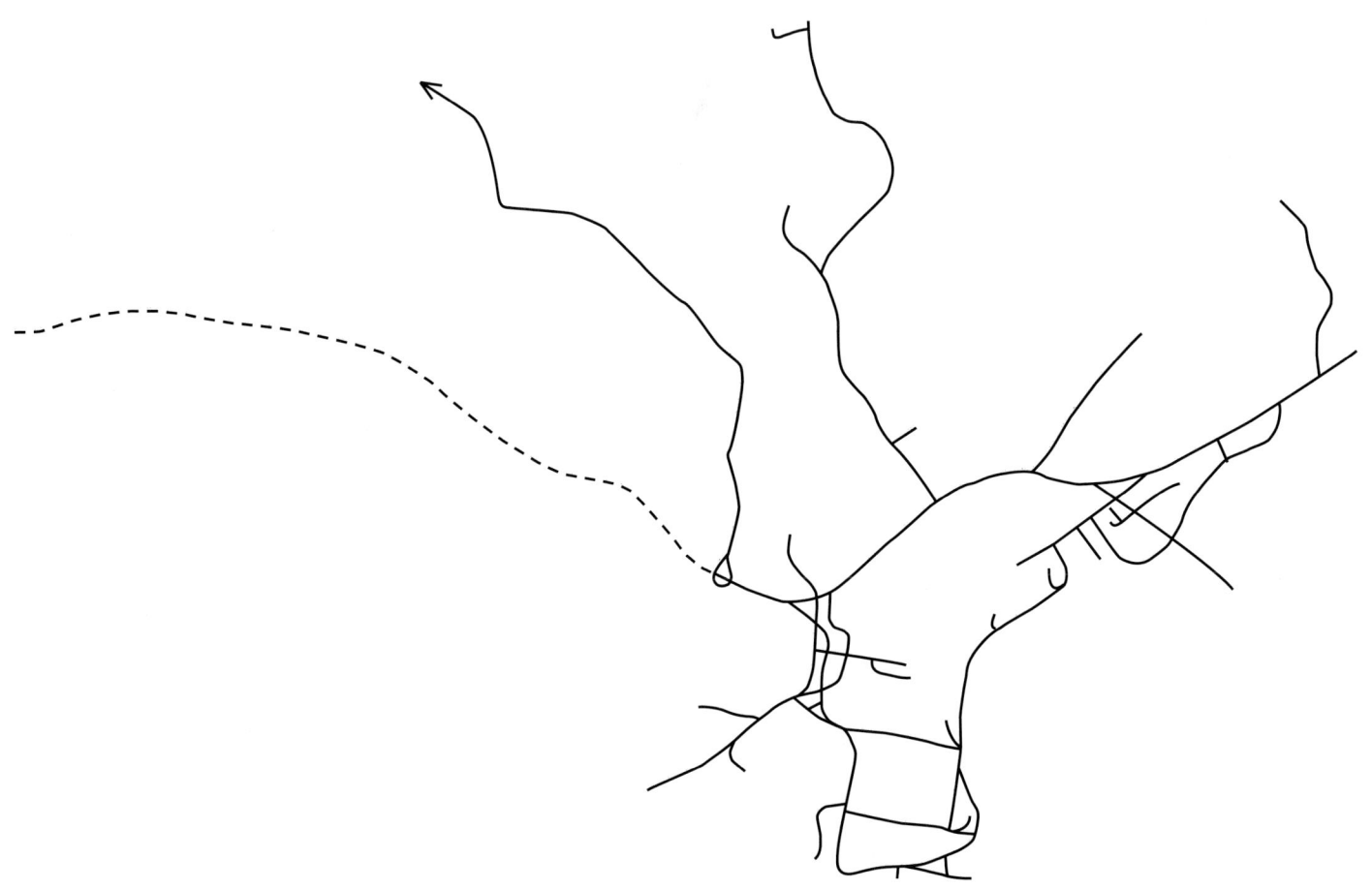

THE GOLDEN ARM

Andrew M. Wilson

THE ARROW POINTS to PRR's Golden Arm, *the* Main Line portion of the mainline from Philadelphia westward. Arguably the most famous section of railroad right-of-way in the United States, the Main Line runs from Overbrook at the Philadelphia city limits 14.4 miles westward to Paoli, destination of untold namesake local commuter trains. Curves on this line are fairly easy, but it was not always so. PRR undertook a realignment of the winding trackage originally laid out by Major Wilson shortly after purchasing it from the P&C in 1857, and then launched upon a major program to four-track the eastern end of the line for the Centennial Exposition. This was subsequently extended as far west as Paoli in 1893. Note the location of the three surviving towers at Overbrook, Bryn Mawr and Paoli.

"American railroads did so much to establish modern American life–our ongoing economy and social structure, even the basic physical underpinnings of city and countryside–that even when we ignore them, a large part of the country's "whereness" will probably be forever in their debt. Long before the interstate highways, railroads opened the frontier and populated the continent. Then they connected 48 states, hundreds of landscapes, and thousands of communities so that we could manage ourselves as a single country.

Railroads greatly accelerated urbanization: They helped giant 20th century cities coalesce, and by encouraging compact suburbs to sprout, they also gave birth to our even more immense new metropolitan regions, which already serve as home base for about 80 percent of Americans."[1]

[1] Tony Hiss, The Ideal City, in Preservation Magazine, January/February 1997. Copyright, the National Trust for Historic Preservation. Used with permission.

Perhaps nowhere else in the United States did a railroad shape a city's surrounding communities than PRR did on The Main Line, that segment of the mainline between Overbrook, just at the Philadelphia City limits, and Paoli, PA. For a distance of 20 miles, PRR influenced the physical layout, politics, architecture, social and cultural patterns, and economic forces affecting these communities. It virtually created them by locating, building and naming the stations and laying out the towns. These were (and still are) distinct from the political entities (townships) of which they are a part, becoming home to generations of PRR executives and ordinary citizens alike.

Sometime in the summer of the long-ago year of 1832, the first (of countless number since) Paoli local trains made its maiden trip from Philadelphia to Green Tree (just west of Paoli) on the not yet completed Philadelphia & Columbia, reportedly stopping along the way to appropriate fence rails to feed the locomotive's hungry firebox. It just made it to its destination before running out of that other essential commodity, water. The crew and hardy passengers formed a bucket brigade to bring water from a local well for the return trip. It took 11 hours to make the 40-mile round trip, which would not be satisfactory to even the most patient of today's commuters.

The P&C was initially viewed as a part of the state Public Works system linking Philadelphia and Pittsburgh and ultimately the Midwest. It was subsequently viewed by PRR as a vital link to the port city in *its* transportation system serving the same purpose. It was only as the City of Philadelphia began to grow and increasing numbers of people began to forsake the City for the lure of the surrounding countryside that The Main Line took on a significance of its own. Utilization of the West Philadelphia RR route, replacing the Belmont Plane in 1850, greatly facilitated train operation in and out of the city, not only for the transport of freight, but also for passengers.

When PRR purchased the Columbia Railroad in 1857, passenger service consisted of three through trains to Pittsburgh, one each to Lancaster and Harrisburg and two to West Chester (via the West Chester RR). Local service was minimal, as very few business people then had residences outside Philadelphia. Land adjacent to the railroad right-of-way was very reasonably priced, generally valued as farmland. Development was slow during the 10 years after PRR assumed ownership, but with the Civil War over and the postwar building boom getting underway the railroad in 1868 began a program of inducement to stimulate "suburban" travel.

As an example of this development PRR purchased several tracts of farmland adjacent to the line in Lower Merion Township, about 9 miles west of Philadelphia. This land had sold for $100 per acre in 1847, which was considered a reasonable price at the time. This same tract was purchased by PRR in 1868 for $730 per acre. A new town was laid out, including gravel streets, shade trees, a large hotel and other improvements. The streets were maintained by PRR until 1886, when most of the lots had been sold. This responsibility was then turned over to the Township, although PRR continued to handle other aspects.

The name Bryn Mawr, the "Great Hills," was chosen by W. Hasell Wilson (son of Major John Wilson, who originally laid out the P&C in 1827), who by then was Chief Engineer of Construction for PRR. It was named after the old Welsh home of Rowland Ellis, a Quaker minister and an early Philadelphia landowner, because of the large number of Welsh settlers in the area. Wayne Estate, one of the earliest and largest planned residential developments, was another well-known Main Line community.

The pattern continued, and PRR subsequently located additional stations at short intervals along the right-of-way and also increased the frequency of local train service, both of which in turn caused a further increase in real estate values. Desirable locations for country homes convenient to the stations increased over a few years from around $700 per acre to more than double that rate.

In 1868 the number of through trains was increased to five, and there were eight locals. By 1895 the daily service on the mainline consisted of nine through trains, two to Harrisburg, one each to Lancaster and Columbia, and 36 locals. The land adjacent to the railroad, which was formerly devoted to farming, was now rapidly becoming settled with attractive homes, including many which belonged to PRR officials. The Panic of 1873 slowed things for a while, but development soon resumed.

PRR established a Department of Real Estate in 1874 under W.H. Wilson to handle the administrative details. Many Class I railroads had real estate departments, but usually for commercial development. PRR's operation handled the preparation of town maps, deeds, leases, rentals and even settlement of tax issues.

Thus the Main Line was born – created and nurtured by PRR.

As we have noted in Chapter 1 the program to implement the four-track system was completed as far west as Merion in time for the Centennial Exposition. This was extended as far west as Villanova in 1882. In conjunction with realignments through Wayne (eliminating a reverse S-curve) and Upton (between Villanova and Radnor) the four tracks were completed to west of Berwyn in 1887. The program was finally completed as far as Paoli by 1893, resulting in a four-track superhighway able to simultaneously handle commuter locals, the through passenger fleet, and local and manifest freights. We should note here that the Trenton Cutoff was completed by this time, allowing through freight traffic to and from New York City to divert to that line at Glen Loch and thus bypass the Main Line corridor. With completion of the new bridge at Coatesville in 1904 the four-track system extended all the way from Philadelphia to Lancaster. This was followed by the construction of the Low-Grade Line, providing parallel freight trackage to Harrisburg and in effect extending the four-track system all the way to that city and beyond (see *Triumph II* for a complete discussion of this important saga).

Although the migration had already begun before that, construction of Broad Street Station in 1881 allowed further expansion of PRR's commuter service to businessmen who had begun to move from the City itself to rapidly growing towns along the Main Line.

PRR constructed a series of ornate stations for its clientele, each one a distinctive example of Victorian architecture, and often becoming attractions in themselves.

Not only did wealthy businessmen find Main Line neighborhoods a proper and desirable environment in which to live; PRR virtually mandated its leaders to locate their estates there. A.J. Cassatt constructed "Cheswold" in Haverford for his family (and horses), General Atterbury established "Boudinot Farms" in Radnor and even Stuart Saunders, PRR's last Chairman, selected a $195,000 (in 1963 dollars) Norman-style mansion in Ardmore.

The PRR elite not only lived and worked together, but they also joined the same exclusive (and white male Protestant) social clubs, golf clubs, cricket clubs, hunt clubs, etc. Most of them even made it into The Philadelphia Club, the City's oldest (founded in 1834) and most prestigious bastion of the upper crust elite – and the Republican Party.

Along with suburban growth came heavy traffic on the railroad as well as the roadways, notably the Lincoln Highway (now Route 30). We have noted above the steps PRR undertook to significantly increase the capacity of its lines. To facilitate movement of the growing number of commuter trains at the end of their run at Paoli, a wye was constructed in 1864 allowing these trains to turn, and a duckunder was added in 1903 (some sources say 1906) to allow them to switch over to the eastbound tracks for the return trip without interference with mainline operations. This essentially completed the trackage changes on the Main Line during the PRR era, but the railroad turned to another solution to further improve operations on the Golden Arm and into Broad Street Station.

PRR had used electrification (via outside third rail Direct Current) as the answer to increasing traffic congestion and tunnel and smoke abatement problems in the New York City area in the early years of the 20th century (to be covered in a subsequent volume in the *Triumph* series). After addressing its largest metropolitan commuter operation, it then turned to Philadelphia, its second largest. As we have noted PRR had vigorously promoted the expansion of communities along the Main Line just before the turn of the century. The resultant growth in such communities as Bryn Mawr and Wayne brought an increased patronage of its suburban commuter trains. The increased traffic into already congested Broad Street Station had to be relieved, and space for enlarging this facility and its approaches was severely limited by the high price of real estate within the growing city.

In addition, the stub-end nature of Broad Street Station required a large number of switching moves for each train in and out of the terminal's throat. Because this was a typical commuter operation with morning and evening rush hours, dozens of steam locomotives were required to meet peak demand, which consumed large amounts of coal and water and produced significant quantities of smoke that hung in the downtown area.

After becoming convinced of the efficiencies of electrification and debating the merits of A.C. vs. D.C., PRR finally selected an 11,000-volt A.C. catenary-type system and awarded the contract to on-line customer Westinghouse, with Gibbs & Hill as consulting engineers. Electrification of the Main Line to Paoli, 19.9 miles, was started in the spring of 1913. The overhead wires were supported on tubular steel catenary poles. Power for the Main Line electrification, and subsequently the Chestnut Hill branch, was initially obtained from the Philadelphia Electric Company's facility located at Christian Street, on the east bank of the Schuylkill River in southwest Philadelphia. Power was routed from the Philadelphia Electric generating station via four submarine cables under the river to a railroad-owned substation at Arsenal Bridge where it was stepped up from 13,200 to 44,000 volts and distributed by means of transmission feeders (located atop the catenary poles) to substations at West Philadelphia, Bryn Mawr and Paoli (and also to Chestnut Hill for that branch), where it was stepped down to 11,000 volts, 25 Hz. for the catenary system.

The initial catenary installation was divided into three sections. The first included Broad Street Station and approach tracks and the mainline north and east of West Philadelphia Station, supplied from the West Philadelphia substation. The second included the main between West Philadelphia and Bryn Mawr, fed from the substations at those two locations. The third, consisting of the main between Bryn Mawr and Paoli, was supplied by the substations at either end. In addition to the main tracks, a portion of the West Philadelphia yards and the entire yards and shop area at Paoli were also electrified.

In addition to the erection of catenary, PRR decided to make other improvements to this line. To improve traffic flow and safety, grade crossings were eliminated and a new automatic signal system was installed. This utilized a newly developed position light signal in place of the semaphores that had been in place for many years. The engineers felt that these would be more visible than the semaphores among the maze of wires. In addition, the semaphores, being mechanical, were subject to continuing maintenance of moving parts, whereas the position lights were all electrical, requiring only an occasional bulb change. We should note that the original design utilized four lights in an offset configuration similar to a semaphore blade, but this was later changed to the centered three-light configuration still in use today. Position light signals would prove so successful that they were installed systemwide and became an enduring symbol of PRR.

While the catenary was being installed, the railroad removed 93 of its steel suburban coaches from service and sent them to Altoona Shops for conversion to electric-powered multiple-unit cars, which became the famous MP54's. These Tuscan Red "owl-faced" units (for their dual round front windows) shouldered the immense burden of suburban service for multitudes of commuters.

The catenary system on the Main Line was completed in the summer of 1915 and thoroughly tested. All of the MP54's were run between Paoli and Broad Street Station before being put into regular service. Then at 5:55 a.m. on 12 September of that year regular service was initiated as a four-car MU set made its way from Paoli to Broad Street Station. The first westbound train left the station at 7:45 a.m. Service was phased in (sorry!) gradually, starting with eight trains (four in each direction).

During the transition period the electric trains were run on steam schedules. This required the MU's to spend considerable time coasting to avoid waiting in stations, thus providing the first indication of the more efficient operation possible with this new mode of motive power. The schedules were subsequently adjusted to reflect this advantage. By October MP54's had replaced steam locomotives on all 78 scheduled Main Line trains, marking the end of an era – and the historic beginning of another.

During the first winter considerable difficulty was encountered because of the formation of ice on pantographs, preventing proper contact with the overhead wire. PRR tried greasing the pantographs without success. Finally it settled on the use of steam directed at the pantographs from the car roofs at terminals (after they had been locked down and grounded!). In addition, extra trains were run during ice storms to keep the wires clear.

Difficulties were also encountered with flashovers occurring at insulators located under highway bridges, coincident with the passing of a steam-powered train (freights and through passenger trains were still hauled by steam during this period). This problem was eliminated by the installation of double insulators of larger diameter. This was a learning experience for PRR, but it learned well, and instituted engineering modifications and extensive safety procedures for all aspects of electric operation and maintenance.

PRR invested $4.5 million in this complex 20-mile project, which, although not the first of its kind, was still a pioneering effort that served as a prototype for electrification of additional lines. It involved installation of a network of 660 miles of wires, 760 poles and 36 signal bridges – all above tracks in almost constant use, amazingly with no interruption of traffic. Construction was carried out utilizing between 800 and 1200 workers. After completing the Main Line, electrification of the Chestnut Hill branch was begun in 1916 and completed in 1918 and subsequently the Fort Washington Branch in 1924, and finally the Norristown line (the lower end of the Schuylkill Branch) in 1930, as part of the Philadelphia Improvements.

The Main Line project was a triumph in and of itself, and a prelude to an even larger one.

Based on the success of its metropolitan commuter electrification projects, PRR then turned to exploring the feasibility of electrification of the mainline from New York to Washington. After a dramatic announcement by General Atterbury, wires were extended southward to West Chester (via Media) and Wilmington, DE in 1928 and northward to Trenton, NJ in 1930. Power was provided by local utility companies from several locations. Transmission voltage was increased from 44,000, used on the Paoli line, to 132,000. In the 1940s this was again increased to 138,000 and the catenary voltage to 12,000, to improve control of reactive power.

The mainline electrification project will be covered in detail in subsequent volumes in this series, but on 28 January 1935, 10 years (and $125 million) after the initial study to extend the electric territory, GG1 locomotive #4800 was given the honor of pulling the first electric-powered mainline passenger train from Washington to New York City, inaugurating service that still runs today along what is now termed the Northeast Corridor. A few weeks later Gen. Atterbury retired, satisfied that PRR was foremost among U.S. railroads in this regard.

An example of the fruits of electrification was the schedule of PRR's premier New York-Chicago train, the *Broadway Limited*. The schedule time was steadily reduced from 20 to 18 hours on 24 April 1932, to 17 hours three years later, and to 16 hours on 15 June 1938, after completion of the electrification to Harrisburg (and introduction of new lightweight equipment).

Before we begin our journey on the Main Line, it might be useful to make use of the following old mnemonics to help us remember the order of stations: For the first group of towns as we head west out of Philadelphia, "Old Maids Never Wed And Have Babies" stands for Overbrook, Merion, Narberth, Wynnewood, Ardmore, Haverford and Bryn Mawr. The second group is covered by "Really Vicious Retrievers Snap Willingly, Snarl Dangerously; Beagles Don't - Period," for Rosemont, Villanova, Radnor, St. Davids, Wayne, Strafford, Devon, Berwyn, Daylesford and Paoli.

Only on *the* Main Line!

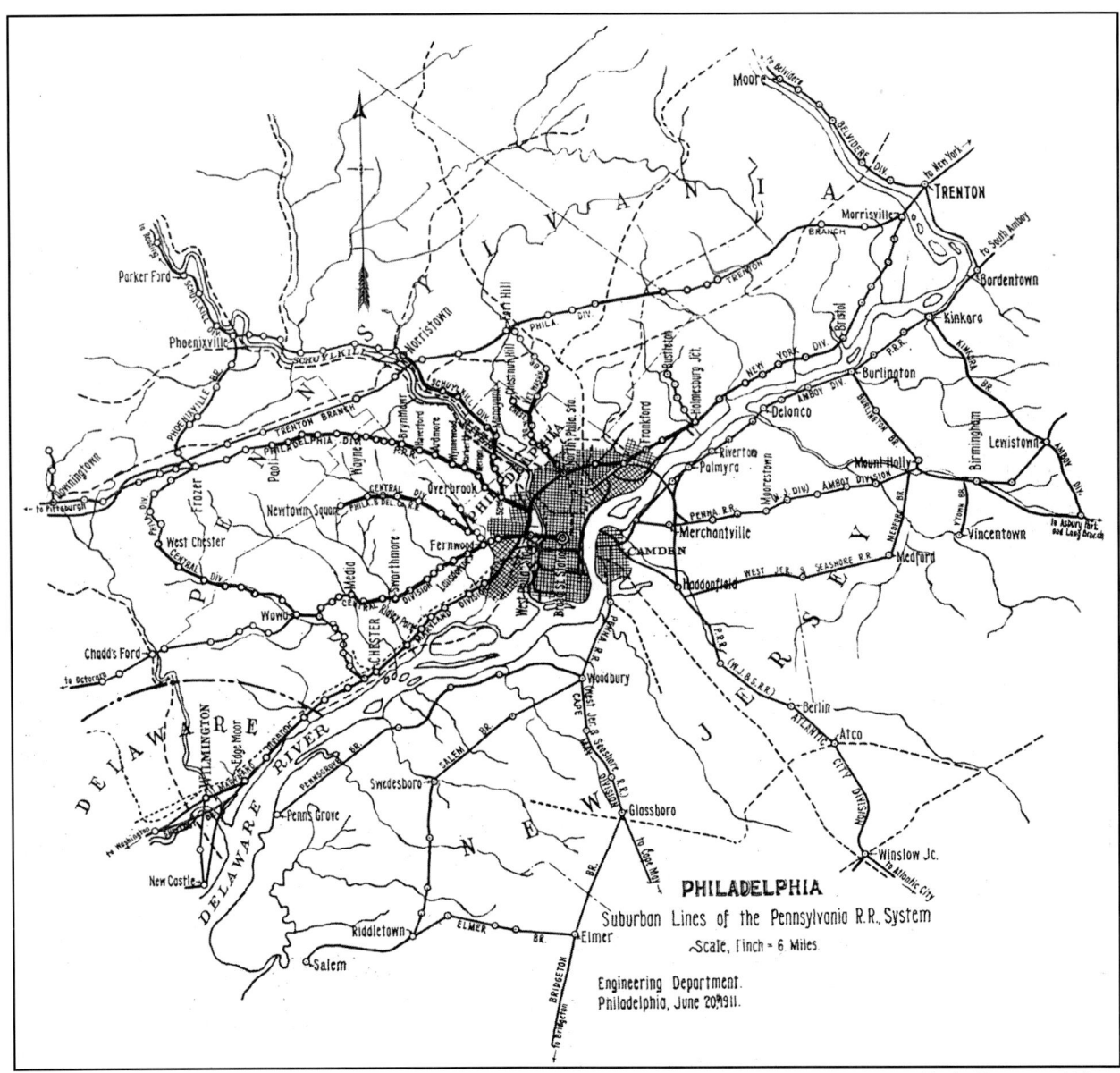

Hagley Museum and Library

AS TRAFFIC in and out of Broad Street Station continued to grow at the turn of the century it became apparent that continued expansion of the station was not feasible. In 1910 a Board of Engineers was appointed with the assignment of evaluating various alternative plans for the improvement of the passenger terminal facilities in the City. As a result of these deliberations a program to improve traffic flow in and around the city was approved by the Board of Directors on 19 December 1911. This program consisted of widening the station approach to Cuthbert St., adding additional tracks on the Connecting Railway including widening the Schuylkill Bridge, improving facilities at North and West Philadelphia and notably, electrification of the suburban commuter lines shown on this map. This latter effort represented a bold step, even though PRR had just completed the monumental tunnel project under the Hudson River and electrification of its trackage into New York City.

The work on the Connecting Railway and the Girard Ave. Bridge was completed, but widening of the Broad Street Station approach was delayed by prolonged negotiations with the City in obtaining the expanded right-of-way. On 5 June 1912 electrification of the suburban lines was supported by the Board of Engineers, the Transportation Committee and Gibbs & Hill (Consulting Engineers) as a solution to this problem. Specific recommendations were made by Gibbs & Hill on 7 August and 31 December of that year, after reviewing other options, that PRR adopt a 11,000-volt, single-phase A.C. system based on estimated lower costs of both installation and operation. These recommendations were approved by the Advisory Committee on Philadelphia Passenger Terminal Improvements, headed by Vice President Samuel Rea. On 12 March 1913 the Board gave final approval for electrification of the 20 miles from Broad Street Station to Paoli, at an estimated cost of $3.5 million. It also reinforced efforts to complete necessary negotiations with the City to allow final plans to expand the approach to Broad Street Station to proceed. Construction of the overhead was initiated shortly thereafter, and after a period of phase-in and testing, service was inaugurated on 12 September 1915. It was the beginning of a Herculean 25-year effort that would change the face of eastern railroading!

THE GOLDEN ARM

WINTER'S TASK – An E3a fights the elements as it moves an ice-encrusted New York Express westbound through the interlocking just east of Overbrook ca. 1910. Montgomery Avenue is at the left.

Railroad Museum of Pennsylvania (PHMC)

OVERBROOK is the first tower on The Main Line – although probably the least known. It is located on the south side of the tracks east of the City limits and the inbound station. It is shown here in excellent shape in August 1972.

Herbert H. Harwood, Jr.

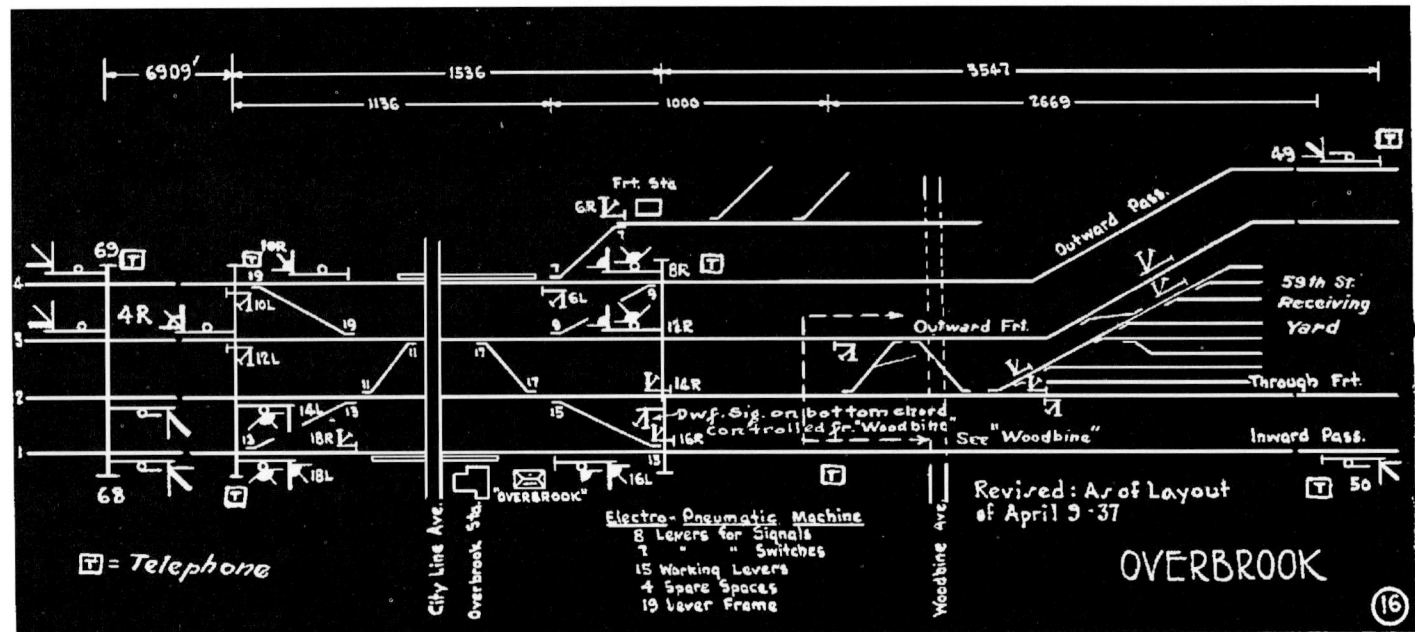

Hagley Museum and Library

ALTHOUGH not one of the better known towers on the Division, OVERBROOK had a tough job. The electro-pneumatic machine controlled a full interlocking in both directions on the main; all freight traffic in and out of the west end of 59th St. Yard; PARK interlocking (two miles northwest on the Schuylkill Branch, not the one at Parkesburg on the Philadelphia Division), which controlled the freight traffic in and out of that trackage; as well as the Maintenance of Way yard just east of the tower.

OVERBROOK (MP 5.4), located just inside the Philadelphia City limits – hence its original name, City Avenue – is the first station stop on the Main Line proper (or should we say the proper Main Line). It is shown here in an 1869 photo as it was constructed initially in 1866 (a small frame station was built here in 1858, but this is the later structure, including agent's quarters). The road crossing beyond the station is City Line Avenue.

Ted Xaras Collection

THE GOLDEN ARM

EVERYTHING is in first-class condition as gleaming engine No. 1000, a D-Class 4-4-0, has the honor of escorting an inspection train on the Main Line. The train is headed eastward as it pauses at Overbrook on a sunny day ca. 1910.

Ted Xaras Collection

THIS IS THE SAME building, with subsequent modifications and extensions to the shelter in 1912, making it the oldest surviving station in the Philadelphia area. A handful of commuters are perusing the *Philadelphia Inquirer* in this August 1972 view. The City Line Avenue overpass is now a concrete structure, replacing the original bridge constructed in 1880.

Herbert H. Harwood, Jr.

THIS TRIM freight house at Overbrook is shown here in a 1917 view. It was constructed in 1882 and located on a siding on the north side of the main tracks, opposite the passenger station.

National Archives

169

THIS PHOTO gives new meaning to the term "high stepping." The date is ca. 1899 and we have the *Pennsylvania Limited*, resplendent in its "Yellow Kid" livery, highballing westward behind D16a No. 296 near Merion. This was mainline railroading on *the* Main Line!

Ted Xaras Collection

THE GENERAL WAYNE INN, built in 1704 and basking in the winter sun in a March 1985 view, was originally used by the P&C as its ticket office serving Merion, although it probably was not the station stop because of the distance from the line. When the P&C was originally built it snaked around the low hills in the area. When PRR took over the line it began straightening out the curves and relocating the track, thus requiring a new station to be built. The inn is named for General Anthony Wayne, who was born in Easttown, south of Paoli, and distinguished himself in several Revolutionary War battles.

Herbert H. Harwood, Jr.

THE GOLDEN ARM

Ted Xaras Collection

THE ORIGINAL wood-frame Merion station was constructed in 1864. It is shown here at the left in this fascinating view, as a westbound train led by a gleaming Class D 4-4-0 pauses in front of MR Tower in the early 1870s. Note the pristine RPO with classic eagle emblem.

E.P. Alexander Archive/Ted Xaras Collection

HERE WE HAVE a morning view of the original Merion station looking westward during the 1890s, with later canopies and eastbound shelter added. Note the beginning of the curve toward Narberth.

BY WORLD WAR I a new brick and stucco station had been constructed on the other side of the tracks at Merion, shown here looking eastward ca. 1917. This would be the last new station on the Main Line until Paoli was rebuilt in 1953. The heavy trunk looks like it would be a load for the vintage auto.

Ted Xaras Collection

SEPTA TRAIN No. 115, a pair of Silverliner IV's obtained from GE in 1974-5, heads past the westbound shelter in Merion on the R5 line to Paoli. The date is July 1989.

Herbert H. Harwood, Jr.

NARBERTH (MP 6.8) was another Welsh name courtesy of President George Roberts, who renamed several Main Line stations with more upscale designations, usually after English estates, commensurate with the image he was creating for the area. The original stone station was built here in 1870 to serve city residents who favored the area, originally known as Libertyville and then Elm, as a close-in summer locale. It is shown here shortly after it was constructed, with wooden platforms at rail height, before the line was four-tracked.

Ted Xaras Collection

THE GOLDEN ARM

Ted Xaras Collection

THIS SCENE might be entitled, "Station and Towers at Narberth." A platform shelter has been added to the original structure, plus a small freight shed to the west. But the most interesting aspect of the photo is the two towers – the original octagonal MQ Tower is being replaced with a new square one ca. 1890. To the west is the beginning of the "Great Fill" toward Wynnewood. Additions were made for a post office in 1904, the shelters were extended in 1906 and a freight station was constructed in 1913.

IN 1969 the old station was replaced with this attractive modern facility, making it the newest one on the Main Line. It is shown here in March 1999 with a Silverliner approaching the eastbound platform.

R.S. Short/Herbert H. Harwood, Jr. Collection

A STRING of classic PRR MP54 commuter cars is headed west into the curve at Narberth in July 1967. PRR initially created 93 of these venerable units to serve the newly electrified territory by converting steel suburban coaches at Altoona Shops. The fleet of MP54's became a workhorse carrying millions of suburban commuters in and out of Broad Street Station starting with electrification of the Main Line in 1915 and later into Suburban Station when it was constructed in 1930. The fleet continued to grow until nearly 450 units were built. These included a variety of combines, full baggage and even baggage-RPO's. By World War II some were upgraded with roller bearing trucks and a few were air conditioned. Most remained the same, however, causing much consternation among commuters after the war when the long distance fleet was being replaced with new equipment. Finally in 1950 PRR initiated a rebuild program at the Wilmington Shop, resulting in 99 units with equalized trucks, stainless steel window frames and modernized interiors. The owl-faced units (derived from their twin round windows on the ends) were gradually retired starting in 1958 when the first of a new generation of Budd-built commuter equipment came on line. The last of the MP54's were taken out of service in 1981.

THE GOLDEN ARM

IN A STIRRING PORTRAYAL of Main Line action, a fast-moving westbound passenger behind D1b No. 98 overtakes a slower freight on the "Great Fill" between Narberth and Wynnewood. They are both passing steel bracket post signal No. 72. Note the sharp ballast line in this superb ca. 1910 photo.

John S. Powell/Ted Xaras Collection

WYNNEWOOD (MP 7.4) is near the end of the big curve in the Main Line. The community – originally known as Libertyville – was named for Thomas Wynne, president of the first colonial assembly of Pennsylvania convened by William Penn on 21 January 1683. This is another original stone station shown here shortly after it was built in 1870.

Ted Xaras Collection

THIS VIEW dated February 1971 shows the station with the shelters added and then extended in 1910. Note that the track grade has been raised and the door moved to the side.

Herbert H. Harwood, Jr.

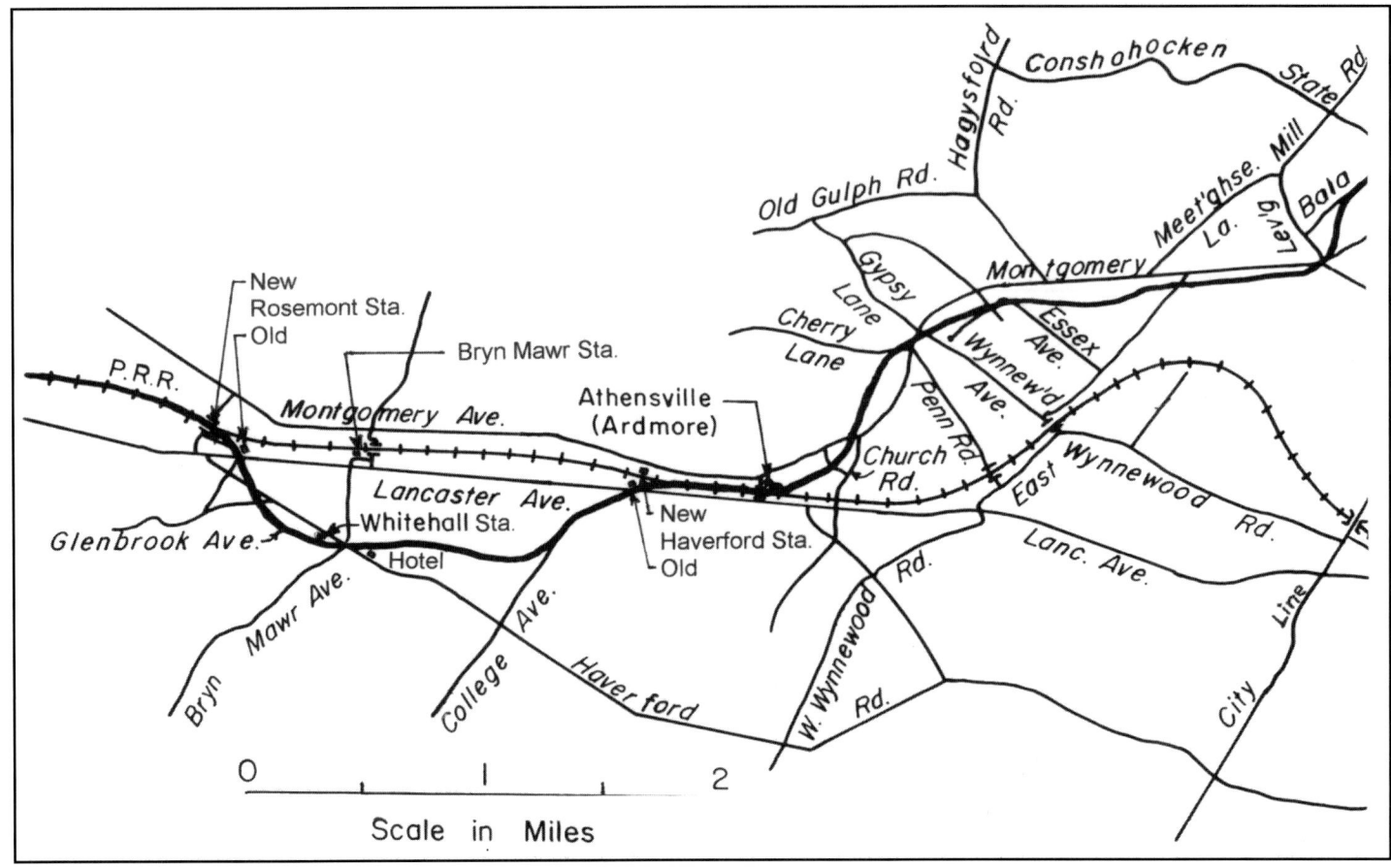

WHEN PRR finally acquired the P&C in 1857 it found itself the owner of a railroad not only badly in need of repair, but also a line with many curves. A track relaying program was undertaken starting in 1856 (actually before the purchase) to resolve the clearance problem, enlarging the track centers from 9'9" to 11'3" or 11'6," closer to PRR's 12'2." The repairs and the track realignments west of Paoli are discussed in *Triumph II*, but PRR embarked on a series of track relocations on the Main Line after the Civil War. Chief Engineer William H. Wilson prepared a plan to straighten out the curves between Athensville (now Ardmore) and West Haverford (Rosemont). The old right-of-way (dark line) and the new alignment (cross-hatched line) are shown here. The plan was approved by the Board on 28 April 1868 and work was initiated in the summer of that year. However, reminiscent of earlier construction local farmers objected to the proposed new line, particularly the deep cut required east of the small community of Humphreysville. PRR, in a strategic move that would have far-reaching effects, bought up several tracts of land in 1868-9, not only for the right-of-way, but also for future residential development. This laid the groundwork (literally) for the transformation of rural Humphreysville into fashionable Bryn Mawr. The project continued during 1869 and the new line was opened on 27 March 1870.

Once the first project was begun, plans were developed for further realignment west of Rosemont, through Villanova and Morgan's Corner (Radnor) to a point west of the present Radnor Station. This included not only reduction in curvature but also involved cuts and fills to reduce grades and grade crossings. The entire double-tracked main was opened on 13 July 1873, eliminating nine curves and bringing the Main Line to its present-day alignment east of Radnor (except for the 2° 58" curve at Radnor, which was straightened by Amtrak when I-476 was constructed through the area in 1989, requiring a new bridge across the highway).

The program to complete the realignment west of Morgan's Corner to Green Tree was approved on 14 June 1876 (during the Centennial Exposition). This involved the elimination of 15 curves and elevation of the line on a fill, particularly from east of Berwyn through Devon to Daylesford, eliminating many grade crossings. This program was completed by the beginning of 1878, and except for some minor relocation between Wayne and Paoli in the 1880s the Main Line assumed its present-day alignment.

ATHENSVILLE is shown in an old photo looking westward ca. 1868. The little frame building on the right has an interesting history, out of proportion to its size. Perhaps representing the closest thing to a P&C "standard" structure, it served as the station stop here until 1873, when it was moved westward to Upton (between Villanova and present-day Radnor) to serve as a trackside flag stop because of the track realignment. It was abruptly removed in 1902 – never to be seen again – reportedly (perhaps apocryphally would be a better word) under direct orders from President Cassatt because of complaints from an irate Main Line resident over PRR service at Upton.

Ted Xaras Collection

Ted Xaras Collection

ARDMORE (MP 8.5), in the author's judgement, was the most architecturally stunning of all the Main Line stations. It was built in 1873 by Wilson Brothers and is depicted here ca. 1880 in all its Victorian splendor. The expanse of the wooden platforms between the tracks has been partially removed to make way for additional tracks. When this station was erected, the original small frame structure was then moved west to Upton. A tower was located in the right-hand turret for a number of years.

TRIUMPH III

Ted Xaras Collection

THE PLATFORMS were extended in 1906 and again in 1909 to accommodate increased patronage to the area, which also a summer haven for city residents. Ardmore was originally known as Athensville when it was a stop on the P&C. It is shown here in a post-electrification view ca. 1917.

IN A TRAGIC LOSS the old station was sold for a shopping center in early 1957. It was replaced by a utilitarian one-story brick structure. The new 13 x 124-ft. eastbound station, which became the main waiting room and ticket office, was opened on 10 October of that year. It is shown here in a 1998 view as an eastbound Silverliner passes.

THE GOLDEN ARM

Herbert H. Harwood, Jr.

HAVERFORD (MP 9.1) has an interesting configuration. This view shows the westbound station, originally built in 1870 and extended in 1906, with a baggage shed added in 1913. The community is the home of early woolen mills and Haverford College, founded by the Society of Friends (Quakers) to promote classical education. This view was taken in February 1971.

National Archives

IN 1916 a two-story brick and concrete station was constructed on the eastbound side, with a post office on the first floor and the waiting room on the track level. Haverford was another Main Line community with summer boarding houses for city residents.

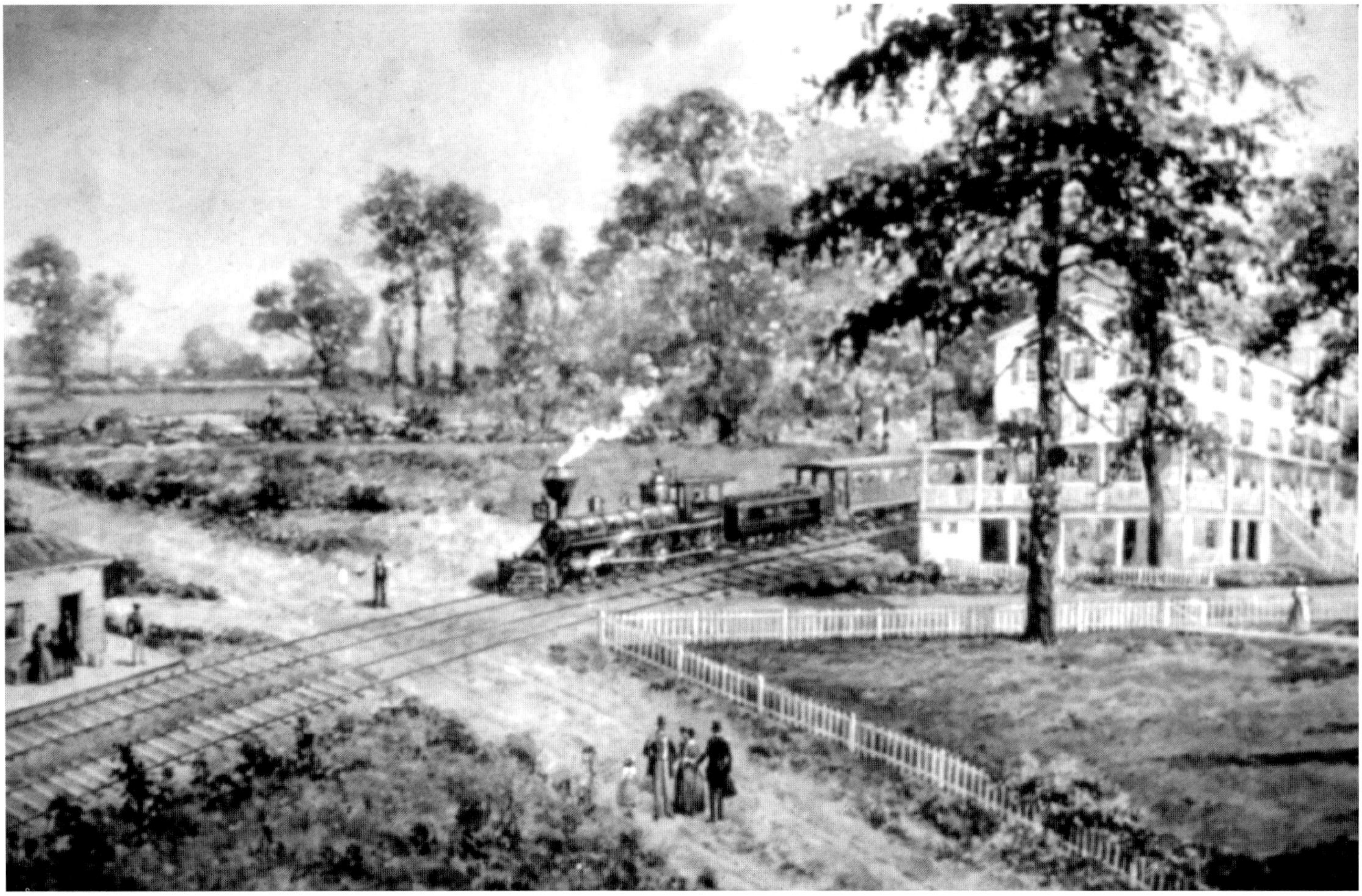

Ted Xaras Collection

THIS MARVELOUS painting shows the White Hall area ca. 1868, looking north. At the right is the White Hall Hotel, the original P&C station from 1830 facing Haverford Road. The replacement 1859 PRR station is just visible at the far left. Bryn Mawr Avenue is in the foreground of the picture, and the old right-of-way is now Glenbrook Avenue.

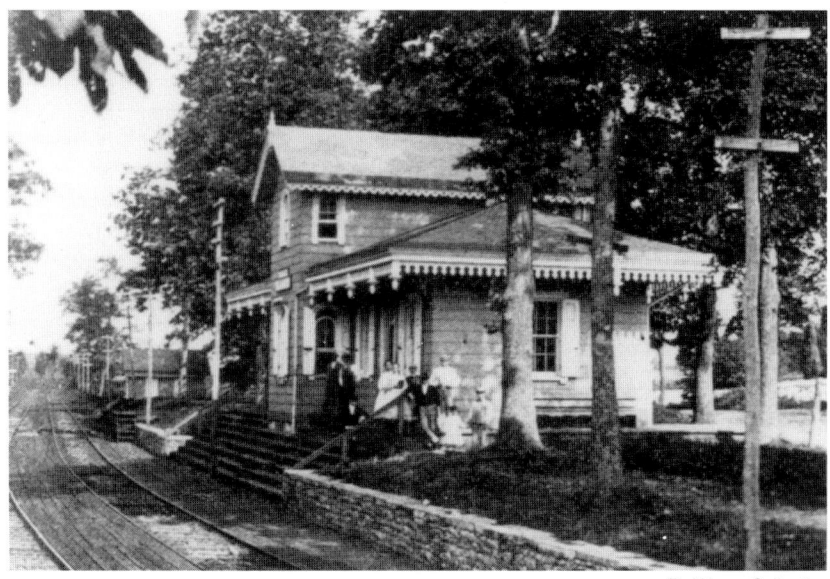

WHITE HALL is another example of a station abandoned when the line was relocated in 1870. The area, now known as South Bryn Mawr, was named after the hotel. The 1859 station is shown here in a ca. 1869 photo looking westward, with its classy Victorian trim.

Ted Xaras Collection

THE GOLDEN ARM

Herbert H. Harwood, Jr.

(below) THE DESTINATION of many of the genteel members of Philadelphia society was the Bryn Mawr Hotel (also known as the Keystone Hotel), an elegant resort designed and constructed by Wilson Brothers in 1873. Both the station and the hotel attracted visitors and residents to the area, causing the community to grow and prosper, which of course was PRR's intent. The hotel was destroyed by fire in 1877 and was then rebuilt by Frank Furness. It finally became the home of the Baldwin School in 1896. The hotel's "courtesy wagon" stands in the driveway in this undated photo, we believe of the rebuilt structure.

(above) WHITE HALL station still exists today, the last surviving structure on this segment of the line. It serves as the Thrift Shop of the Bryn Mawr Hospital, still showing touches of its Victorian origins.

Railroad Museum of Pennsylvania (PHMC)

THE ELEGANCE of the early PRR clientele is depicted at the equally elegant Bryn Mawr (formerly Humphreysville) station as it appeared shortly after it was constructed – also by Wilson Brothers – in 1870. Note the expansive right of way – plenty of room for additional tracks as soon as the traffic warrants. The third track was extended as far as this location in 1873.

HERE ARE TWO more views of the illustrious station and complex at Bryn Mawr, rendered shortly after the 1870 opening and before arrival of the third track in 1873. An ornate gem by any standards.

Eugene DiOrio

BRYN MAWR STATION was remodeled and enlarged in 1900, with the addition of a baggage house and extended platform canopies. A signal bridge (in the background) has replaced the pedestrian walkway and an underground passageway added. Note BRYN MAWR (originally WH) Tower at the right in this photo taken 19 August 1961.

EVEN THE FREIGHT HOUSE, also constructed in 1870, evoked a touch of elegance in resembling the passenger station. It was enlarged in 1916-17 and is shown here reasonably intact over 100 years later in May 1975. It still stands today, converted to a restaurant.

Herbert H. Harwood, Jr.

SADLY the grand old station at Bryn Mawr was replaced in the winter of 1963-4 with a modest but attractive brick building. The new station is shown here adjacent to the old one, shortly before it opened.

Railroad Museum of Pennsylvania (PHMC)

BRYN MAWR (WH) Tower is located at the midpoint of the Main Line, opposite the station. It was built in 1896 and is shown here in an October 1969 view. Note the tubular catenary pole, which was the original design installed on the line to Paoli.

Herbert H. Harwood, Jr.

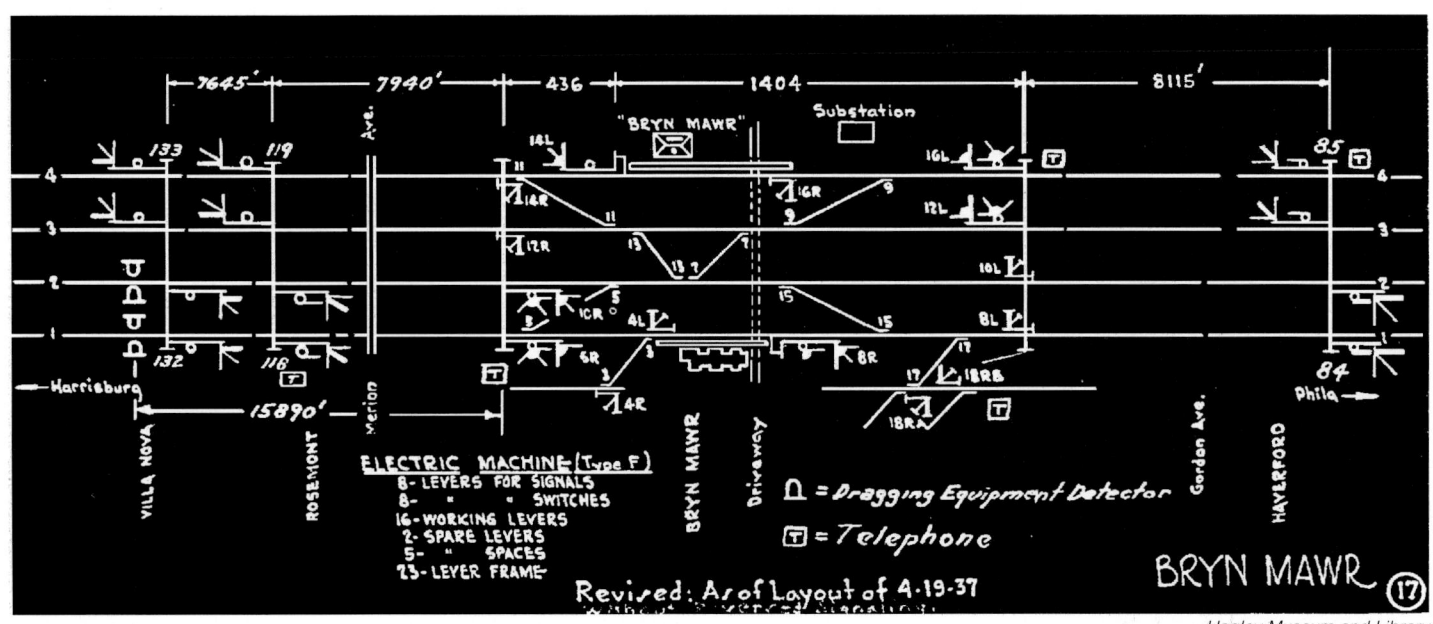

Hagley Museum and Library

BRYN MAWR, an electric machine, controls a complete interlocking for mainline operations, as well as outbound MU trains that terminate there. They then require a switchover from Track 4 to Track 1 for the return trip to Philadelphia. Note the location of the station and the electric substation (built in 1915), as well as the dragging equipment detector.

THE GOLDEN ARM

Pennsylvania State Archives

ON 16 September 1863 Joshua Ashbridge donated a piece of land at the intersection of Railroad and Lancaster Avenues for the construction of a passenger depot at West Haverford. In return for this gift PRR named the station Rosemont, after the Ashbridge estate. The station location was moved a short distance westward in 1871, after the Bryn Mawr cutoff was completed. The original structure then became a private dwelling, shown here in a ca. 1950 photo looking eastward. The road follows the old right-of-way.

THE CURRENT Rosemont station, constructed in 1891-2, extended in 1906 and with a second story added in 1909, is shown here in a 1949 view looking westward. The station still stands today, although somewhat modified in appearance.

Ted Xaras Collection

Fred W. Schneider, III

UGLY DUCKLING – Here we see a modified P5a hauling a mixed freight westbound through Rosemont station on 26 June 1955. Having been eclipsed from their intended role in passenger service, the P5a's – both boxcabs and the GG1-like center cab units – served out their days performing freight duties.

185

TRIUMPH III

THE STONE STATION built at Villanova (MP 12.0) in 1872 and extended in 1906 is shown here in a view looking westbound in February 1971. Originally known as Radnor (when present-day Radnor was called Morgan's Corner), the town is the home of the university of the same name, whose buildings are just visible through the trees at the left of the station. It is the first stop in Delaware County, part of the original area settled by William Penn and established as a separate county in 1789. The third and fourth tracks were completed to Villanova in 1882 and extended as far as Devon in 1886.

Herbert H. Harwood, Jr.

ORIGINALS - Pioneer III Nos. 150 and 151 were new when this photo was taken at Villanova Station in October 1958. These units were originally built as an experiment by Budd to determine if they could serve as a satisfactory replacement for the aging MP54's. The six units (Nos. 150-55) originally had ignitron tubes to convert overhead current to D.C. for the four traction motors, but these were replaced in 1961 by silicon diode rectifiers. They were originally called Pioneer III's but were later designated Silverliner I's when PRR bought 38 more (called Silverliner II's) in 1963. They indeed proved satisfactory and 20 more were purchased in 1968, this time from St. Louis Car Co., designated Silverliner III's. An order of 270 new cars, called Silverliner IV's, were delivered by General Electric to Penn Central in 1974-5, finally signaling the end of the by-then obsolete MP54 units. The original six are identified by their conventional pantographs; all the rest are equipped with Faivelys.

Bruce Bente/Fred W. Schneider, III Collection

It had become increasingly apparent during the 1950s that the "Red Cars" were in dire need of replacement, but neither PRR nor the Reading were in a financial position to purchase a new fleet of equipment for their money-losing commuter operations. In 1960 the City of Philadelphia set up the Passenger Service Improvement Corporation to assist in purchasing new equipment, which would be leased back to the lines (thus the term "PSIC Cars" sometimes applied to the Silverliner II's). Finally in 1968 all Philadelphia area suburban lines were placed under contract with the Southeastern Pennsylvania Transportation Authority (SEPTA).

THE GOLDEN ARM

Herbert H. Harwood, Jr.

SEPTA NO. 9110, an ex-Reading MU unit, heads west through Villanova station toward an original PRR tied arch truss, now being used as a highway bridge for Spring Mill Road (see *Triumph II* for a discussion of these unique early trusses). The photo was taken in November 1988.

William D. Middleton/Fred W. Schneider, III Collection

TRAIN NO. 75, the westbound *Duquesne*, is framed in the signal bridge as it moves east of Radnor in 1964. Note the two New Haven ex-troop sleepers converted for mail use.

THIS STRUCTURE served as the station at Upton (located between Villanova and Radnor). The station was closed in 1900 when the track was relocated to the south, and is serving as a residence in this 1975 view.

Herbert H. Harwood, Jr.

THE ORIGINAL STATION at Morgan's Corner (originally Brookeville, later Radnor, MP 13.0) was built in 1862. It is shown here in a late 1860s view looking westward. Passing the station is engine 217, a unique and elegant combination passenger car and early 4-4-0 locomotive.

Ted Xaras Collection

THE FRAME STATION was replaced in 1871 by the brick structure shown here. It was extended in 1902 and 1906 and is shown as it appeared in February 1971.

Herbert H. Harwood, Jr.

THE GOLDEN ARM

Herbert H. Harwood, Jr.

BLACK PC GG1 No. 4931 leads an eastbound into Radnor station, three years into the merger in February 1971.

Railroad Museum of Pennsylvania (PHMC)

ON THE FLY – K2 No. 3373 takes on water at the track pans in Radnor ca. 1910. The pans were installed on Tracks 2 and 3 in 1903 to replenish water after the climb out of the City. They were supplied by tanks to the west that we will look at shortly.

MU TRAIN No. 341 moves west between Radnor and St. Davids on 10 August 1967. Note that several cars in this train have replacement stainless steel window frames and keystone decals in place of lettering. The second and seventh units in this lashup are trailers.

John J. Bowman, Jr./Fred W. Schneider, III Collection

ST. DAVIDS was previously known as East Wayne, and the original frame station is shown here ca. 1868, after the name was changed (note the apostrophe). The sign indicates 13 miles from Philadelphia and 339 miles to Pittsburgh.

Ted Xaras Collection

THE GOLDEN ARM

Ted Xaras Collection

THE SECOND St. Davids station (MP 13.7) is shown here in an 1890s photo looking eastward. Similar to the one at Rosemont, it was constructed in 1890 and extended in 1913. St. Davids was the site of an early planned community in the late 1880s designed to attract well-to-do Philadelphians to the attributes of healthy country living. The agent awaits the arrival of a westbound train headed by E2a 1047. Note the bank of four tanks in the direction of Radnor. The tanks were built there in 1887 to supply the track pans to the east. They were removed in 1908, with water subsequently purchased from the Springfield Water Co.

R TOWER, a classic early PRR octagonal design originally located in Radnor, stands tall and proud in this 1890s photo. It is equipped with a recently-added signal mast, coal bin and the requisite array of awnings – it also served as a telegraph office. Need we mention the purpose of the little house?

Ted Xaras Collection

TRIUMPH III

HERE WE SEE the later incarnation of R Tower, moved from Radnor to west of St. Davids in 1905 and then rebuilt in 1909, in a 1917 view.

National Archives

Ted Xaras Collection

THE ORIGINAL Wayne station was built in 1873 at an early milk stop (note the milk platform at left) known originally as Cleaver's Landing. After the Civil War a Philadelphia real estate developer by the name of J. Henry Askin had purchased a large tract of land surrounding Cleaver's Landing and built a small community he called Louella. In 1880 Askin sold his holdings and the community was renamed Wayne Estate, which became one of the earliest and largest planned residential developments in the country.

THE GOLDEN ARM

Fred Westing/Ted Xaras Collection

THE SECOND Wayne station (1880-82) is now located at Strafford (which we'll look at shortly). In the 1883 the Childs and Drexel real estate development called for a larger and more imposing structure, resulting in the construction of the third Wayne station in the popular Queen Anne style at MP 14.5. A westbound shelter was built in 1902 and a baggage house added in 1905. The entire complex is shown here in a crisp view looking eastward ca. 1908, with activity in both directions.

National Archives

HERE'S A CLEAR LOOK at the long westbound shelter. It was built in 1902 and extended in 1906, and is shown here in a 1917 photo.

William D. Middleton/Fred W. Schneider, III Collection

WAYNE STATION in recent times as well as the westbound shelter are shown in this 1987 shot as Amtrak Train No. 47, the *Pennsylvanian*, speeds westward.

Fred W. Schneider, III

MANIFEST – E44s 4447 and 4457 haul a long string of totally open autoracks westbound through Wayne Station. The date is 27 March 1970, two years into the PC merger.

Fred W. Schneider, III

LOOKING THE OTHER WAY on the same day, we see GG1 4873 hustling mail through the station. Note that the cars are the ill-fated New York Central Flexi-Van units.

THE GOLDEN ARM

THE EAGLE INN, shown here in a March 1998 view, was another old tavern used by the P&C as a ticket office. It is one of the oldest of several early inns on the Lancaster Turnpike, most of which had large farms associated with them. The area was originally called Eagle, after the inn.

Herbert H. Harwood, Jr.

WE FIND the station at Eagle in the woods ca. 1870, at a grade crossing where Old Lancaster Road (now Conestoga Road) crossed the main, about one-third of a mile west of the present Strafford Station. It was a two-story brick structure, housing the waiting room, express and telegraph offices, and the "Spread Eagle" Post Office. The grade crossing was later turned into an underpass.

Ted Xaras Collection

Fred W. Schneider, III

STRAFFORD STATION (MP 15.4) is one of the most frequently photographed on the Main Line because of its elegant ornate detail. Not only is an architectural gem, it has had a fascinating history. It was constructed originally as a building on the Centennial Exposition grounds, possibly for catalogs (other sources indicate it was the Japanese, later the Illinois Building). After the Exposition closed it was moved to Wayne as a flag stop ca. 1880. Later (ca. 1885) it was again moved to the present site, where it was called Eagle, after the original station, and then in 1887 it became Strafford, after an estate owned by the Wentworth family. This 1967 view looks eastward as nine-car Train No. 350 accelerates past the exquisite jewel of a structure.

Fred W. Schneider, III

WESTBOUND Train No. 331 is nicely framed in the canopy arch at Strafford as it moves toward Paoli on 27 March 1970. MU 751 has been repainted in Penn Central commuter green.

National Archives

SZ TOWER was built east of Devon in 1900 when interlocking was installed. It is pictured here in a 1917 Valuation photo.

Railroad Museum of Pennsylvania (PHMC)

HEAVYWEIGHT ACTION – A P5a moves a long string of heavyweight varnish westbound through Devon in the 1920s. Air conditioned cars bring up the rear.

THE CURRENT Devon station (MP 16.4) was constructed in 1883 and extended in 1906. This 1917 view looks eastward as an MP54 moves toward the city. Several communities joined together in the 1890s to form the Devon Horse Show Association to show off their fine animals. The first show was held in grounds across from the station in July 1896, and the tradition continues today. (*Editor's Note:* We lived in Devon in the mid-1960s while running a newly acquired subsidiary in Willow Grove and we used this station frequently when traveling to Center City. Being Marylanders from the Land of Pleasant Living, we will have to say that we did not find the Main Line a hardship area. Delightful people, schools, scenery, food and neighbors. In a word, civilized.)

National Archives

National Archives

A SHELTER was built on the westbound side in 1902 and a baggage house was added in 1905 for the convenience of Devon residents traveling to the west, both shown here in a 1917 photo looking eastward.

TRIUMPH III

A FREIGHTHOUSE was added to the facilities in Devon in 1887 and is shown here in a 1917 view.

National Archives

HIGH FLYER - Two high-stepping units, led by E2-Class 4-4-0 No. 1979, doublehead a long train westward out of Devon ca. 1910. We are especially fond of this photo, with the twin signal mast outlined against the smoke plume, as well as the angle and overall composition - first class in every way!

Ted Xaras Collection

THE GOLDEN ARM

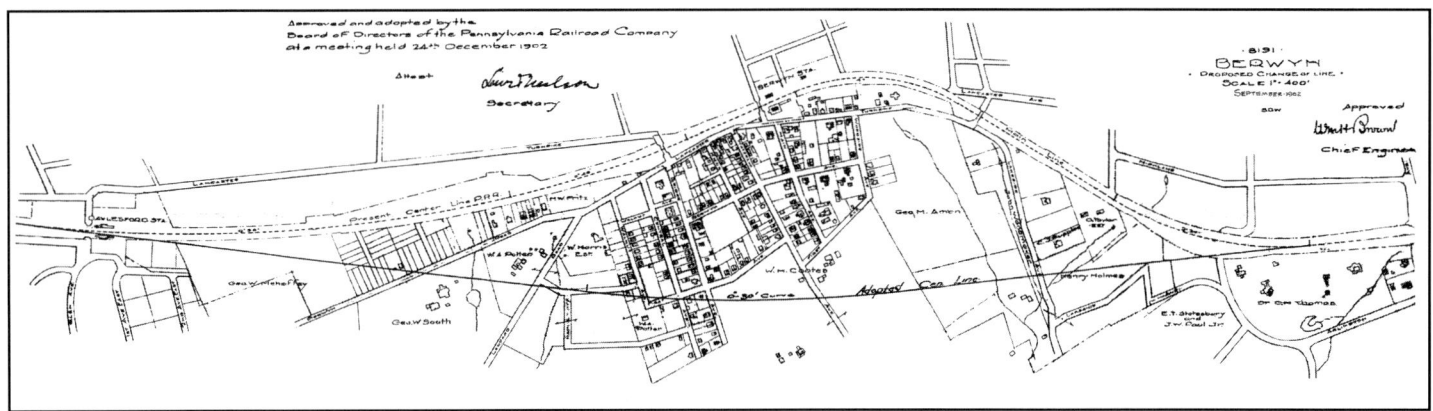

Jim Brazel

THE BERWYN CURVE was on the list of projects for Cassatt's massive 1902 Improvement Program to reduce grades and curvature and eliminate grade crossings on the mainline between Philadelphia and Harrisburg. It was one of the last major curves on the Main Line segment not realigned in the 1876-8 program. The 2° 20' curve east of town and the limiting 4° curve approaching the station would be replaced by a proposed new alignment to the south with a broad 0°30' curvature, necessitating a new station. The project was duly approved by Chief Engineer William H. ("Stone") Brown and by the Board on the day before Christmas 1902, as shown in this map. Most of the property for the new right-of-way was purchased, but with declining economic conditions the railroad had to prioritize its projects, and this one was of lesser importance compared to the critical Penn Station project in New York City, construction of the Low-Grade Line, new stations in North and West Philadelphia and yard extensions in Altoona – even mighty PRR couldn't do everything it wanted! And so the Berwyn curve and the vernerable station remain.

Fred W. Schneider, III

THE ENGINEER is framed in the owl-eyed window as westbound Train No. 333 rounds the curve approaching Berwyn on 27 March 1970. Note the nearly horizontal catenary support wires on the curve.

Herbert H. Harwood, Jr.

THE STATELY station at Berwyn (formerly Reeseville - MP 17.5), one of the few brick depots on the Main Line, was constructed in 1881. The shelters were extended in 1906. This view shows the track side of the main structure in 1975.

Fred W. Schneider, III

THE LATE AFTERNOON SUN highlights Train No. 352, with a quartet of venerable MP54 units, as it pauses at Berwyn on 27 March 1970. This photo looks west at the Cassatt Avenue overpass. A westbound shelter was constructed here in 1912.

Ted Xaras Collection

WE ARE LOOKING eastward at OV Tower, another classic PRR installation near Berwyn. The tower is located at a beginning of a section of four-track line recently installed in this 1890s view. The third track was laid from Berwyn to the end of the division at Green Tree in 1871, and the four-track system completed to that point in 1893.

THE SHELTER that perched on the edge of the fill in Daylesford (MP 18.6) was constructed in 1890 and is shown here in a 1917 photo looking westward. Daylesford was named after the nearby land owned by Richard Graham, who in turn named it after the English estate of Warren Hastings, Governor General of India in the latter half of the 18th Century.

National Archives

AN EASTBOUND Silverliner train pauses at the replacement shelter in May 1998. This enclosure was built about 100 years after the original.

Railroad Museum of Pennsylvania (PHMC)

DOUBLEHEADER - An interesting combo of K2 No. 927 and H-Class No. 442 move an equally interesting consist up the grade toward Paoli in this stirring view ca. 1910. The lower-quadrant signals are entwined with smoke and not a particle of ballast is out of place on the immaculately-groomed roadbed.

E.P. Alexander Archive/Ted Xaras Collection

AND NOW we come to Paoli (MP 19.8), named after a hotel built on the Lancaster Turnpike in the 1770s which in turn honored General Pasquale di Paoli, a Corsican revolutionary hero. The area is noted for the Paoli Massacre, in which 150 Continental soldiers under local native General Anthony Wayne were killed or wounded on the night of 20 September 1777. The main station, shown here in a crisp 1891 view looking eastward, was constructed in 1883. Note the manicured lawn, and that we have three tracks at this point in time.

THE EASTBOUND SHELTER at track level was added in 1898. North Valley Road crosses overhead on a girder bridge in this 1917 view.

THE SHELTER on the north (westbound) side was extended in 1909.

A FREIGHT STATION was constructed in 1888 and shown here in a 1917 photo.

SHORT-LIVED – The P5a's days in passenger service were numbered when this photo was taken in September 1933 of the *Spirit of St. Louis* pausing in Paoli.

W.R. Osborne/Herbert H. Harwood, Jr. Collection

Hagley Museum and Library

A NEW STATION was built in 1953, replacing the old one with a spartan one-story brick building, shown here in a ca. 1955 photo looking west. A GG1 (which replaced the P5a's) leads an eastbound through the facility. The canopy covering the stairway on the westbound side still contains elements of the original construction. Paoli was the original terminus of PRR commuter operations on the Main Line, and for a few years was the changeover point for electric to steam power for through trains prior to the extension of electrification westward to Harrisburg in 1938. Because of exurban growth, current SEPTA service extends farther west to Downingtown, on the former Philadelphia Division (covered in *Triumph II*).

THE GOLDEN ARM

THIS IS Train No. 75, the *Duquesne*, accelerating westbound through the crossovers west of Paoli station in October 1969. It is led by GG1 4935, still in the PRR wide-stripe scheme.

Herbert H. Harwood, Jr.

Bob Lorenz

PAOLI (formerly PA), perhaps the best known tower (and location) on the Main Line, was the division post between the Philadelphia and Philadelphia Terminal Divisions. It was constructed in 1896 and shown here on 11 June 1966, guarding the interlocking and entrance to the MU yards. The tower is located on the north side of the tracks, west of the station. Note the curved bay window (later removed). Beyond is the Paoli substation, one of two, 2-story brick substations feeding power to the overhead on the Main Line (the other one being at Bryn Mawr). They were both built in 1915 when the line was electrified.

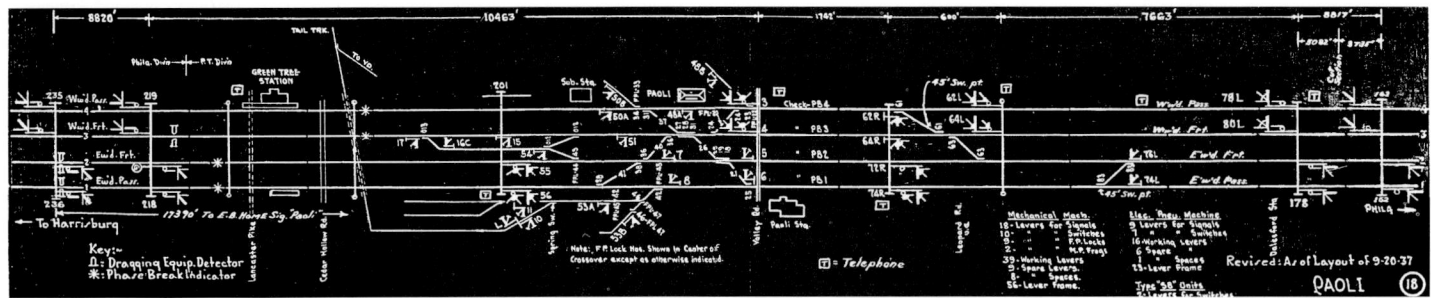

Hagley Museum and Library

PAOLI TOWER, which had both a mechanical and an electro-pneumatic machine, controlled normal diversions on the main, but its major responsibility was movements of MU cars to and from the car shops. The track to the east of the tower extends into the storage yard and the wye; the track west of the tower also runs into the yard. The wye was constructed in 1864. Note the location of the substation, as well as Green Tree Station, the latter illustrated in *Triumph II*.

Elmer Keinard / Glenn Cagle Collection

THE CREW poses in front of their steed as an eastbound passenger train pauses near the rail and tie storage area at Paoli during October 1901. The almost-new locomotive is No. 1968, an uncommon Juniata-built Class E2 4-4-2 with a radial stay boiler giving it a bit of a European look. The boys are decked out in the attire of the day.

PAOLI CAR SHOP, seen here ca. 1917, was constructed in 1915 to service PRR's MP54 MU fleet for its newly-electrified Main Line. (An early brick enginehouse and shops was located here, built in 1865 to replace an even earlier one destroyed by fire the previous year.) Located at the western end of the new car storage yard, the new shop building was 282 ft. long and 110 ft. wide. It had five run-through track bays with full-length pits. An overhead crane was located over two tracks to lift carbodies for major overhauls. It was also equipped with a blacksmith shop, an electric rebuilding shop and a small machine shop.

National Archives

An air brake shop, storage area and general office were added in later years. Electric power for the shop originally came from its own on-site powerhouse, which also supplied "Wrecker's Row," a small group of houses on the property for wreck train employees.

Conrail assumed operation of the Paoli Shops (along with the ex-Reading Wayne Electric Shop in North Philadelphia) when it took over operation of the bankrupt Penn Central on 1 April 1976. On 1 January 1983 SEPTA assumed responsibility for all commuter operations in the Philadelphia area, including shop facilities. The stations on the Main Line are now owned by Amtrak and leased to SEPTA.

THE GOLDEN ARM

Fred W. Schneider, III

AS THE MP54's diminished in the lineup the Silverliners moved in. Here we see representatives of three Silverliner models (I, III and IV) at Paoli Shops in the mid 1970s.

Chester D. Fuhrman

WEST OF THE SHOPS a tail track lets MU trains move out of the yard and then onto a duckunder running under the main, allowing outbound trains turning or returning from the shops or yard to head eastward without crossing the busy thoroughfare. This was built in 1906 to facilitate traffic flow through this busy area. This view looks eastward in April 1968.

Chapter 4
The Big Gamble

The Schuylkill Division

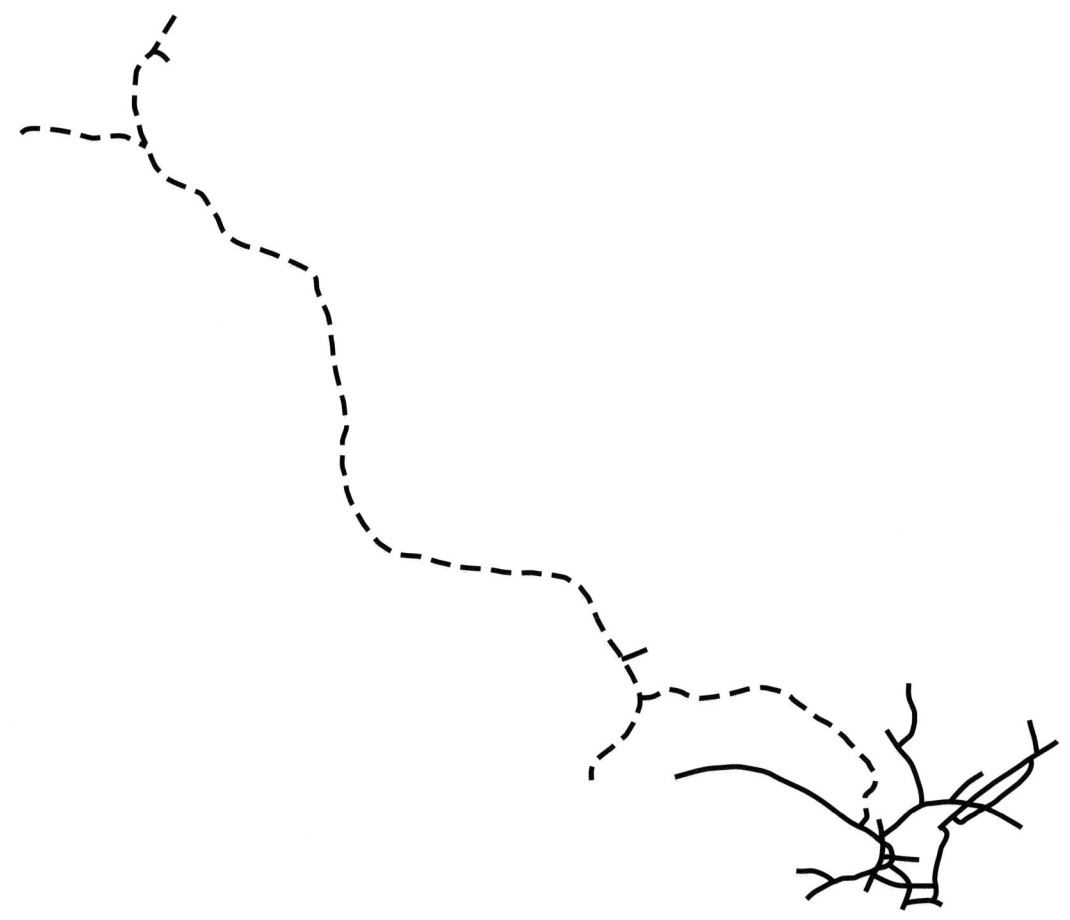

THE BIG GAMBLE

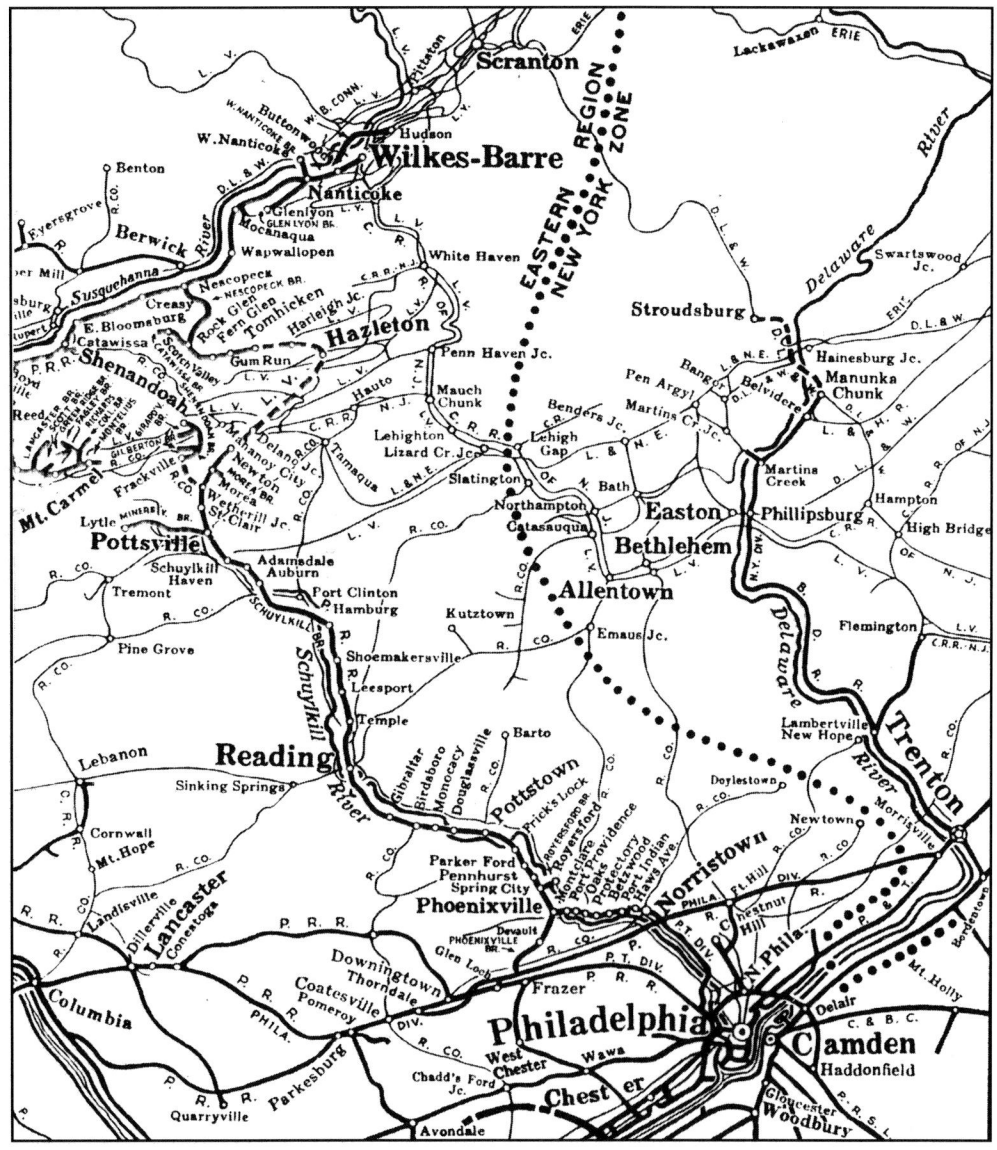

THE SCHUYLKILL BRANCH, at 105-plus miles, was by far the longest component of the Philadelphia Terminal Division. It followed its namesake river valley from just above the outlet to the headwaters, and in so doing traversed heavy industrial districts, lush suburbs, small towns and rural countryside before plunging into the mountainous coal regions of Schuylkill County. It began at Valley Tower, just west of 52nd Street Station on the mainline, crossed over the river (the first of twelve times) and then passed through the industrial towns of Norristown, Phoenixville, Pottstown, Reading and Pottsville to its junction with the Lehigh Valley RR at Newton, (formerly New Boston Junction). In its heyday during the early decades of the 20th Century it saw frequent passenger and freight service, but slowly declined in later years.

The Schuylkill River Valley in eastern Pennsylvania winds northeastward from Philadelphia, where it empties into the Delaware River, nearly 100 miles inland to its headwaters in the mountain ridges rising above Pottsville. It was used by Native American tribes and early European settlers and has been a major transportation corridor for nearly 175 years, and in particular played a key role in the movement of anthracite (hard coal) from the vast deposits surrounding Pottsville to distribution centers in Philadelphia. This was done initially by means of the Schuylkill Canal, completed in 1824 (the year before New York's famed Erie Canal) and later by railroad.

The Schuylkill Valley was also the site of early ironmaking in the U.S., established in the second decade of the 18th Century. This was prompted by the deposits of good quality iron ore and a plentiful supply of hardwood to make charcoal, used in the early smelting process. The industry struggled along with its crude methods until a diminishing supply of accessible wood and cheaper iron made in England by a new process began to foster a technological revolution in the valley and elsewhere. That process was the hot blast method of producing iron, using anthracite – found in the U.S. only in the five contiguous counties in northeast Pennsylvania, with the largest and highest quality deposits in Schuylkill County, at the head of its namesake river.

As the advantages of anthracite became known, not only for ironmaking but also for domestic use, the demand for quantities of the hard material increased dramatically. The first result was the Schuylkill Navigation Company, which was chartered in 1815 and eventually opened 9 years later, thanks to a large infusion of cash from Philadelphia financier Stephen Girard. The canal – and the industries it served – prospered, leading directly to the second result: The Philadelphia & Reading Railroad Company was chartered on 4 April 1833 to challenge the canal by constructing a railroad between those two cities.

After several setbacks, the railroad was completed in 1842 to Mt. Carbon (near Pottsville), at the head of navigation of the canal. It immediately met the competition head-on by hauling anthracite – more tons of it, and faster, than the canal. The Reading would go on to purchase vast areas of anthracite and involve itself heavily in the mining, processing, transport, marketing and even export of its most valuable commodity – black diamonds. In addition to the line down the Schuylkill Valley, the Reading also developed routes to the north and east to ship anthracite from the region, giving it a clear competitive advantage in this trade.

All of this was not lost on arch-rival PRR. Having completed its line to Pittsburgh and then consummated its connection to Philadelphia by acquiring the Philadelphia & Columbia, it turned its sights to new markets after the Civil War. These included the anthracite coalfields and the growing trade in the Schuylkill Valley. Not to be outdone by the P&R, in the early 1870s PRR invested in 28,000 acres of anthracite coalfields of its own. However, these had to be accessed via a time-consuming, circuitous route utilizing a variety of leased lines connecting to the Northern Central RR, and then to the PRR main west of Harrisburg. There was no direct PRR line to Philadelphia.

President George Brooke Roberts (who could be considered an obsessive Reading hater) made the following statement in the PRR Annual Report for 1882 as public justification for a railroad venture into the Schuylkill Valley:

> "This valley produces more local traffic than any other portion of the state, and that in the affiliation between the lines now traversing that district and other trunkline systems [i.e. the P&R and its sometime ally New York Central, which provided a route for shipment of anthracite into central New York state], your Company is gradually being deprived of the advantages of carrying any of this local traffic to more distant points, made it necessary, in the judgement of the Board, to promote the construction of the road."

An unspoken objective, although it certainly became apparent as the line progressed, was to obtain a more direct route into the lucrative anthracite regions of Schuylkill County, which heretofore had been the exclusive domain of the Reading – and perhaps to remind that road that PRR still considered it to be only a second-class operation, even though in 1879 it gained access to New York City by putting together a series of shortlines, plus gaining control of the Central Railroad of New Jersey. At the time the Reading was in one of its periodic financial crises and would accordingly take some time to respond. President Roberts must have swallowed hard, because he was 50 years late and playing catch-up, into territory where the Reading had the best routes and had already established itself with passengers and shippers alike, but the lure was clearly too great to resist.

The Pennsylvania Schuylkill Valley Railroad was formed 1 June 1883 as a consolidation of four lines progressing up the valley: The Philadelphia, Norristown & Phoenixville; the Phoenixville & West Chester Railroad; the Phoenixville, Pottstown & Reading; and the Reading & Pottsville. This company was then leased to PRR.

The first venture in this endeavor to gain a piece of the anthracite traffic was the Phoenixville & West Chester Railroad, which actually began on the mainline in the Chester Valley at Frazer (the junction was depicted in *Triumph II*) and extended northward over the intervening hills into the Schuylkill Valley at Phoenixville, a burgeoning iron (and later steel) center. Construction began in late 1881 and was completed on 1 August 1883. This line later became known as the Frazer Branch (the lower 1-mile segment was designated the Phoenixville Branch, part of the Philadelphia Division).

Construction of a second segment, the Philadelphia, Norristown & Phoenixville, began in the summer of 1882 at 52nd Street Station on the mainline in West Philadelphia, with surveys and grading extending up the valley, along a route envisioned as early as 1830. The line was opened as far as Bala on 1 April 1884. The bridge across the river was completed on 19 April of that year and the line was opened to Manayunk on the north side on 12 May ("Mannaiyunk" was the Indian word for the river; Schuylkill is a Dutch name). Construction proceeded rapidly and the line was opened to Norristown on 23 June, to Pottstown on 22 September and as far as Reading by November. This was clearly a blitzkrieg invasion of P&R territory!

Completion of this portion of the railroad was duly noted in the 1884 Annual Report, which also publicly confirmed the intention to extend the line into the anthracite areas by "looking ultimately to a connection with a branch of the Northern Central Railway at Shamokin, and with the North & West Branch Railway near your Susquehanna Coal Company's properties."

Initially the line was considered part of the Philadelphia Division, but on 15 November 1884 the line was known as the Schuylkill Division, headquartered in Reading. By the end of the following year the line was opened to Hamburg and to Pottsville on 15 November 1886. With completion to Pottsville, the Schuylkill Valley acquired the Pottsville & Mahonoy RR to New Boston Junction (later Newton). This section of the line had a maximum grade of 3.1% and included the 750-ft. St. Clair Tunnel and a 150-ft. high, 530-ft long trestle over Mill Creek Valley. PRR then made an agreement with the Lehigh Valley RR for a connecting track and trackage rights to actually reach the anthracite fields in 1887.

Completion of this line gave PRR access to the manufacturing and agricultural products of Chester, Montgomery and Berks counties as well as the coal region of Schuylkill County. It allowed PRR to avoid the circuitous routing out of the anthracite fields to compete with the Reading in this area and to develop its own extensive coal reserves above Pottsville. It also served the industrial areas of Conshohocken, Norristown, Phoenixville, Pottstown, Reading and Pottsville along the way. To handle the traffic, double track was laid from 52nd Street yards to Phoenixville; short sections were also installed on either side and extending through Pottstown, Reading and Pottsville. Numerous sidings, some holding over 100 cars, were also laid along the line to handle local industries.

Although there were a few inevitable encounters with the Reading during construction and afterwards, at least the PRR line escaped the fears of local residents that the P&R had faced 50 years earlier. At that time (according to an early history of the valley) rumors abounded that, "iron horses would go shrieking through their hitherto peaceful neighborhoods to scare their teams, set fire to their timber, crops and houses, and careen over the county in haphazard fashion to the mortal danger of life and limb."

To control the growing traffic, block signals were installed as far as Phoenixville in 1906 and extended to Mt. Carbon the following year. At peak activity 29 block stations were in operation along the busy line. Upper quadrant signals and mechanical interlocking were installed in 1913, along with 13 interlocking stations. The division operated primarily under train orders except for two short sections of automatic signals from NQ (later NORRIS) Tower to Franklin Avenue (subsequently farther west at Haws Avenue) in Norristown and from the east end of Mount Carbon Yard to Pottsville.

For a while the Schuylkill Valley line prospered, operating at its peak (around World War I) six through passenger trains daily, ten local trains Philadelphia to Norristown, seven Philadelphia to Phoenixville and five Philadelphia to Reading. Two through trains, the *Mountaineer* and the flagship *Anthracite Express*, ran from Philadelphia to Wilkes-Barre, utilizing Lehigh Valley trackage rights north of Pottsville. Both trains offered parlor car service in direct competition with the Reading through the Schuylkill Valley. To serve this traffic there were an unbelievable 52 stations between 52nd Street and Pottsville at this time!

Freight service peaked in 1929, with 14 regular trains daily, plus frequent coal extras. After 1929 the Great Depression took its toll, although World War II traffic provided a brief improvement, but business declined thereafter. The traffic moved predominately eastward, with long coal trains originating at Mt. Carbon Yard and iron and steel products coming out of Reading, Pottstown, Phoenixville and Conshohocken. Most trains terminated at the 52nd Street yards in Philadelphia, although substantial tonnage was dropped off at Norristown yard to be transferred to the Trenton Cutoff freight line for movement either east or west.

Although the Schuylkill Valley line attained divisional status for a while, it always operated – literally and figuratively – in the shadow of the Reading mainline (and Norristown Branch), whose trackage was visible for much of the way. In most areas of its territory the P&R was a poor second to PRR, but in the Schuylkill Valley it largely reigned supreme, having gained the prime water-level route, while PRR had to settle for less desirable locations, often requiring sidehill cuts for its right-of-way. The close proximity of the Reading lines led to many interactions with PRR through the years, not all of them friendly.

Troubles began early. A letter on 13 August 1884, while the line was still under construction, from H. K. Nichols, Chief Roadmaster of the P&R, to J. N. DuBarry, President of the Schuylkill Valley RR, expressed concern over the potential damage to his line (actually the Reading Plymouth Branch) from a proposed track connecting to the Plymouth Rolling Mill Co. siding and the Conshohocken Stone Quarry: "For the protection of the property of this Company, I hereby notify you to refrain from the work contemplated and failing to do so, your Company will be held liable for any injurious consequences and damages which may ensue to the property of this Company by reason of such action."

The matter was referred to PRR Chief Engineer William H. (Stone) Brown – we do not know the response, but construction of the line proceeded nevertheless. This exchange was representative of the Reading's reaction to PRR invading its heretofore sacrosanct territory. It was a harbinger of many such encounters in the years to come.

The Schuylkill Division line follows its namesake river almost from mouth to source, and the general characteristics of the terrain traversed varies from water level to hilly, becoming mountainous on the western end. The line involved digging two tunnels (at Phoenixville and St. Clair, north of Pottsville) and constructing numerous bridges, twelve of which cross the Schuylkill River.

After crossing the river to Manayunk much of the line consists of side hill work, often through rock and numerous quarries (later abandoned); most of these were limestone quarries that operated in the early years of the steel industry in the valley.

Of the 90.7 miles (to Pottsville) 48.7 miles are tangent and 42.0 miles are curved, totaling 52 curves. The average curvature is a bit over 3°, with a maximum of 10°. The maximum grade is at Bala Hill into the Schuylkill Valley, with a 1.8 % grade westbound and 2.1% eastbound. The remainder of the line has a maximum grade of 0.8% in both directions. North of Pottsville the maximum grade is the third steepest on the entire PRR system, a hefty 3.1% above St. Clair.

Traversing the line, it leaves the main at VALLEY interlocking, just west of the 52nd Street jumpover bridge in West Philadelphia, on a broad curve and heads north, passing through the suburban area of Bala-Cynwyd before descending through Barmouth on a curve into the river valley. It immediately crosses the river in a broad sweeping S-curve over a high, 1818-ft. long concrete arch viaduct. In so doing it crosses over the Reading main on the south side and the Norristown Branch (former Philadelphia, Germantown and Norristown) on the north side. Connecting to the Reading main on the south side is the tiny Pencoyd Branch (named after President Roberts' estate in the vicinity), which also served the Pencoyd Iron Co. (later the American Bridge Co.) and a small quarry near West Manayunk.

It then swings through Manayunk, closely paralleling the curves in the river and the P&R Norristown Branch (although initially higher up on the valley shoulder) all the way to Norristown. We should note here in passing that in constructing the Schuylkill Valley line through this section, a considerable amount of waste fill from cuts was dumped into the river, in the process completely tying up traffic on the P&R Norristown line for two days.

Both lines served the heavy Alan Wood steel complex (via the company-owned Upper Merion & Plymouth RR), paper mills and other industries between Conshohocken and Norristown. Before entering the seat of government of Montgomery County the line interchanges with the PRR Trenton Cutoff via a wye and yards at Earnest (depicted in *Triumph II*) before passing under that line, which crosses over the river on a heavy truss bridge. At Norristown the P&R branch cuts across the river and joins the Reading Schuylkill main west of Bridgeport.

From here the PRR line closely follows the river's edge until west of Betzwood, where it passes through Valley Forge National Historic Park (site of the 1950 Boy Scout Jamboree) and as the river bends sharply the line crosses over Perkiomen Creek, just above where the creek empties into the Schuylkill River. The line passes over the P&R Perkiomen Branch and runs through Oaks and Mont Clare, and then crosses over the river again – as well as the Reading main – on another long concrete arch viaduct into Phoenixville. In this area it parallels a section of the abandoned Schuylkill Canal (owned by the Reading in the canal's later years).

In Phoenixville it served the large Phoenix Iron & Steel complex and then connects at a wye with the northern end of the Frazer Branch, as well as the Reading Pickering Valley Branch. This gave PRR two connections into the industrial town of Phoenixville, previously considered sacrosanct Reading territory. The PRR line heads westward (actually north) out of Phoenixville through an 813-ft. tunnel just west of the Reading's longer Black Rock Tunnel and emerges into the Schuylkill Valley again at Cromby, where a small yard is located, serving a Philadelphia Electric Co. power plant.

From a construction standpoint, the short section between the river and the tunnel was one of the most difficult parts of the line because of a large amount of waste material and few places to dump it because of both French Creek and the river twisting through the hilly terrain. The engineers finally resorted to filling in an old quarry pit east of the station, the gully east of the tunnel, between the legs of the wye and even on top of the tunnel.

West of Cromby the terrain opens up into a broad, pastoral valley lying between gently sloping hills. The line then runs through Spring City, where a short branch cuts across the river to Royersford (residence of the author), serving the stove and glass manufacturing industries in that community. It then passes through Parkerford, where another short spur extends across the river to Linfield. It follows the river and finally crosses it again on another concrete viaduct to reach Pottstown, still another industrial community and location of another steel complex and the largest yards on the line. Within the Pottstown area it closely parallels the Reading main again, which at this point is also on the north side of the river. The line was built through this area on slag fill from the Eastern Steel Company.

West of Pottstown the line continues to parallel the river, crossing over it again at Douglassville and then intertwines with another section of the abandoned Schuylkill Canal as its approaches Birdsboro, where another steel mill is located. In Birdsboro it intersects with the Reading Belt Line and the Wilmington & Northern Branch to the south, as well as a yard at the base of a wye.

The line crosses hairpin loops in the Schuylkill River twice and the Reading Belt Line three times as it approaches the city of Reading, and then crosses the river again as it enters the city, the largest on the branch. It then follows the riverbank – and the Reading (which it crosses over and under) – northward to Hamburg, where it again crosses to the west side of the river. At Port Clinton it – along with the Reading – follows the Schuylkill river as it slices through Blue Mountain in a cut reminiscent of the Susquehanna and the east-west mainline (through the same long mountain ridge) west of Harrisburg.

It then follows the twisting river through the valley, crossing the Reading and the river once each south of Auburn and the river twice again north of the town. It then winds through Adamsdale and Schuylkill Haven before cutting through Second Mountain and Sharp Mountain before finally entering Pottsville.

At Pottsville it intersects with the Minersville Branch extending to the west and the Morea Branch to the east (The 7 1/2-mile Minersville Branch was constructed from Pottsville to Primrose in 1892 to access coal deposits). North of the city the line encounters more rugged terrain – it passes through the 750-ft. St. Clair tunnel and then climbs a stiff 3.1% grade. It then traverses Mill Creek Valley on the 150-ft. high, 530-ft. long Darkwater trestle, hitting a 3.0% grade before finally reaching Newton (formerly known as New Boston Junction), where it connects with Lehigh Valley RR for access to the anthracite fields.

In 1888 the trackage north of Pottsville was included in the Sunbury Division, made up of mostly Northern Central RR lines. This configuration lasted until 1927, when the short section was returned to the Schuylkill Division, leaving the PRR-controlled LV linking the two divisions.

For all its effort in building the line, however, PRR's venture in the anthracite business was relatively short-lived. The first blow was the passage by Congress of the 1906 Hepburn Act, regulating the nation's railroads. Among other provisions the Act made it "unlawful for any railroad to transport an article or commodity manufactured or mined or produced by it, or in which it may have an interest, directly or indirectly." In 1909 the Justice Department filed suit against all of the coal-hauling rail lines, except the Reading, which was to receive special attention because of its profound involvement in anthracite production. Finally in 1912 the District Court ordered the Reading-controlled Temple Iron Company to get out of the coal mining business altogether. The glory days of black diamonds were over!

On 26 September 1913 PRR announced its intent to divest its holdings. They were first consolidated into the existing Schuylkill Coal Co. and then sold to Susquehanna Collieries in 1917, thus ending PRR's involvement in the mining and marketing of anthracite.

The Reading and the other anthracite roads continued the legal battle for several more years, but the handwriting was clearly on the wall. The use of anthracite, particularly for home use, had been declining steadily. The decline was temporarily halted by World War I, but resumed thereafter. The long strikes of 1922 and 1925 were the fatal blows to the industry, and many mines closed for good. By the end of World War II most home use of coal had ended, further reducing the demand for anthracite.

On 26 September 1913 PRR announced its intent to divest its holdings. They were first consolidated into the existing Schuylkill Coal Co. and then sold to Susquehanna Collieries in 1917, thus ending PRR's involvement in the mining and marketing of anthracite.

The commuter portion of the Schuylkill Division as far as Norristown was electrified in 1930 as part of the Philadelphia Improvements and the final phase of suburban electrification. It was initially proposed to extend the wires as far as Phoenixville, and this was included in the Board resolution approving overall suburban electrification on 10 December 1924. However, as patronage west of Norristown began to decline it was decided to end suburban service at that point. This reduced the cost from over $3 million to approximately $2 million. A substation and transmission lines between Arsenal Bridge and 52nd Street were installed to power this branch, costing an additional $800,000. This project was finally approved by the Board on 26 June 1929.

On 16 May 1932 the Schuylkill and Sunbury Divisions were consolidated to form the Wilkes-Barre Division, which extended all the way from Philadelphia to Lewistown (via Sunbury). This arrangement lasted until 28 October 1949, when the Schuylkill Branch became a part of the Philadelphia Terminal Division, headquartered in Philadelphia.

Passenger service beyond Reading dropped to minimal levels in the early 30s with the growing popularity of the automobile, although the *Mountaineer* and *Anthracite Express* soldiered on for a while longer. A shaky consolidation of PRR and Reading passenger service was carried out in 1934. On 21 August 1941 all service west of Reading was discontinued. Weekday passenger service from Norristown west to Reading ceased on 5 February 1951; Sunday service remained until the fateful day of 4 October 1953. From this date on all remaining passenger service on the Schuylkill Branch was by MU equipment, terminating at Haws Avenue.

In conclusion we are tempted to ask whether or not PRR's gamble to lay tracks up the Schuylkill Valley was worth it. The answer is – like so many others – yes and no. Yes, the line did "carry the flag" into heretofore sacrosanct Reading territory to tap into the valley's industrial and passenger traffic; yes, it did transport its share of anthracite from the fields to Philadelphia, at least until the double-barreled blasts of government regulation and the decline of domestic anthracite use after World War I. But no, it was not a long-term strategically-viable move, for any of the above traffic. We don't have the numbers, but maintenance costs on the many bridges alone must have been high (although considerably reduced after many of the iron bridges were replaced by concrete), and it was one of the lines hardest hit by the decline of heavy industry and both passenger and freight traffic because of the lure of automobiles and trucks. The close proximity of the better-situated Reading mainline certainly didn't help.

Perhaps the honest answer should be that the Schuylkill Valley line was *not* one of PRR's triumphs.

THE BIG GAMBLE

Fred W. Schneider, III

AS WE BEGIN our journey on the Schuylkill Division, we see the 52nd Street jumpover bridge again as SEPTA/Conrail Train No. 289 heads west towards Manayunk on 23 June 1978. The division begins at VALLEY Tower and diverges from the westbound main at the west end of the bridge. This junction in its early years, before the bridge was built, is shown near the end of Chapter 1 photos.

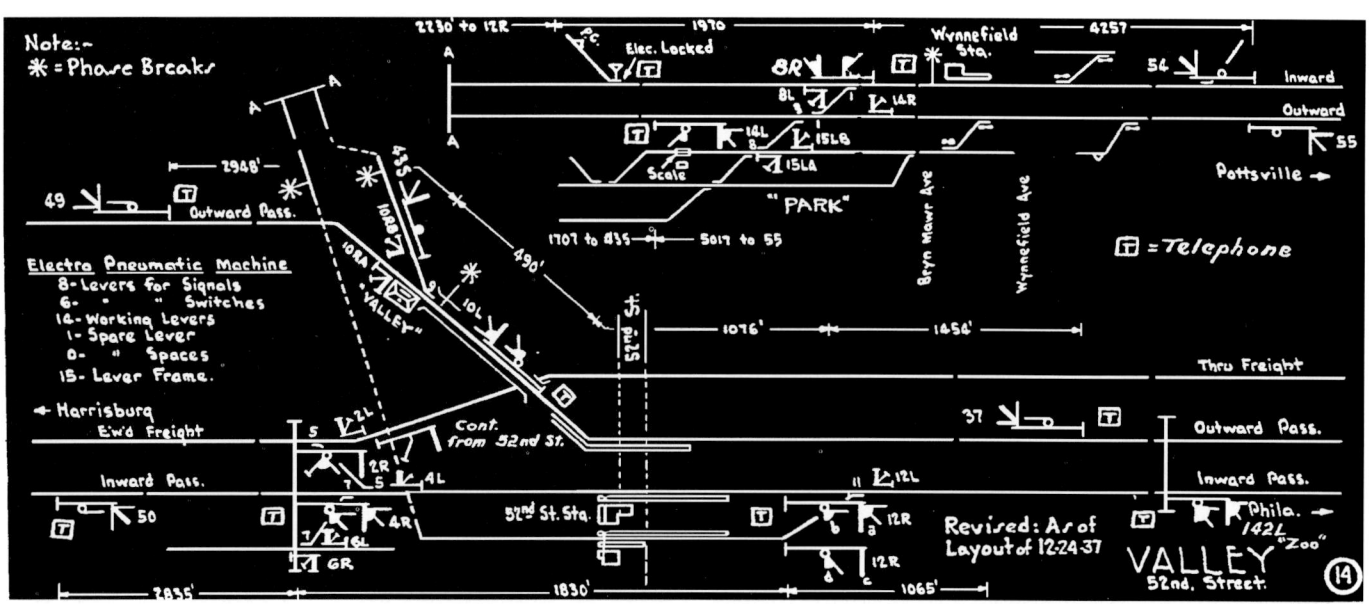

Hagley Museum and Library

VALLEY TOWER controlled passenger movements at the junction of the Schuylkill Division with the east-west mainline at the end of the jumpover bridge. These moves involved a tunnel for the inward (eastbound) passenger tracks under the main and an overhead bridge for the outward (westbound) tracks. Farther out,

PARK (later JEFF) interlocking remotely controlled freight movements in and out of 52nd Street Yards from the Schuylkill Division. This responsibility was subsequently transferred to OVERBROOK. Note the location of Wynnefield Station.

215

BALA Station (MP 5.6) is shown here in a westward view ca. 1890, a few years after it was built. There are a number of large homes visible in a growing suburban area.

Ted Xaras Collection

Andrew M. Wilson

THE EPISCOPALIAN CHURCH OF ST. ASAPH, located on Conshohocken Avenue in the Bala (now Bala Cynwyd) section of Philadelphia, has had a remarkable association with PRR. It was built in 1888, at a time when the area was still rural but beginning to develop as a residential area as a result of the Schuylkill Division running through it (Conshohocken Avenue runs along a portion of the previous right-of-way of the P&C). It was located on land donated by George Brooke Roberts, then President of the railroad. His estate, "Pencoyd," was located a short distance to the east, part of a 150-acre tract originally purchased by John Roberts, one of George's ancestors, who came to the area in 1683 from Bala in Wales. He was a founding member of the Board of Trustees, and the first meeting of the Vestry took place at Pencoyd. The cornerstone was laid on 1 May 1888, and the Conshohocken stone edifice was completed in the fall of 1893. The designer was noted Philadelphia architect Theophilus P. Chandler and the interior of the sanctuary was graced by Tiffany windows and high relief panels flanking the altar, modeled by the Viennese sculptor, Karl Bitter (and donated by George Roberts). Mr. Bitter would later sculpt a number of the relief panels for Broad Street Station, at the behest of – you guessed it – George Roberts. Only one of these, the large allegorical panel, "Progress of Transportation," dated 1895, would survive the demolition and be moved to 30th Street Station. Irony abounds. Mr. Bitter also did some work for the Vanderbilt mega-mansion "Biltmore" in Asheville NC. Prelude to Penn Central?

As the Bala Cynwyd area grew into a genteel suburb, the church would become the place of worship of generations of PRR executives. Photographer Andrew Wilson, who contributed a number of photos and other information for this volume, is not only a member of St. Asaph's, but his great-grandfather was George Pepper Wilson (1866-1935), who began as a telegrapher for PRR and ascended to the level of vice president.

The elder Wilson lived in Ridley Park, another "PRR suburb" (like Chestnut Hill and the Main Line) where railroad executives were encouraged to live in order to build traffic.

THE BIG GAMBLE

CYNWYD (another Welsh name courtesy of George Roberts) was located at MP 6.0, just west of where the tracks of the former P&C line passed through. It was completed in 1884 and enlarged in 1909. This view looks westward ca. 1890, with the main station on the left and the westbound shelter across the tracks.

W.N. Jennings/Ted Xaras Collection

BEFORE DESCENDING through the cut into the Schuylkill Valley, the line passes through West Laurel Hill (Barmouth) at MP 6.8. The attractively-landscaped station is shown here in an early 1890s view looking westward.

E.P. Alexander Archive/Ted Xaras Collection

A VISITOR on this line, GG1 4872 leads a special west of Barmouth on 20 July 1957. This was at least the second trip for this train on the branch on this day to pick up Boy Scouts at the Valley Forge jamboree.

John J. Bowman, Jr./Fred W. Schneider, III Collection

THE PENCOYD BRANCH (named after George Roberts' estate - is there a pattern here?) was completed in 1891. It served a quarry and other industries in West Manayunk, and the Pencoyd Iron Works (later known as the American Bridge Co.), which was responsible for a number of PRR bridges. We should note that this company was originally known as the A&P Roberts Co., for founders Algernon and Percival Roberts, cousins of the PRR president. The branch extended off the Schuylkill Division just before it crossed the river, and curved into West Manayunk. It also had a switchback connector that crossed the Reading main and curved down to the Iron Works and an interchange with the P&R tracks. This 1917 photo looking eastward shows the bridge over the Reading, a 173-ft. steel Pratt truss built in 1891. In the background is the main PRR bridge over the river, which we'll look at next.

National Archives

E.P. Alexander Archive/Ted Xaras Collection

THE BRIDGE TO MANAYUNK, the first of twelve across the Schuylkill River on the branch, was also the largest. It was a 14-span deck truss and girder structure erected by the Phoenix Iron Company in 1883 and totaling 1410 feet in length. This spectacular turn-of-the-century view captures the panorama, including the 6° curves at either end of the bridge, forming a giant "S." The single track on the trestle near the river is the Pencoyd Branch connection to the Reading main. The collection of wooden trestles looks a bit precarious, and in fact some others at the time thought so as well. Fear not, things are about to change. Note the large number of mill buildings in Manayunk, which developed along the Schuylkill Canal.

THE BIG GAMBLE

E.P. Alexander Archive/Ted Xaras Collection

THE NORTHERN END of the bridge in Manayunk, less often seen, is shown in a ca. 1890 photo. The S-shaped structure is supported on 14 piers and rises 80 feet above water level. The Reading Norristown Branch (Philadelphia, Germantown & Northern) is just visible at bottom right.

PRR HAD DETERMINED as early as 1910 that many bridges on the Schuylkill Division were not strong enough (in fact management was concerned that they didn't *look* strong enough) to support heavy steam power, and so a program was initiated to replace all the lighter trusses with concrete arch structures. The line between 52nd Street and Phoenixville was often used as a detour for through passenger trains, and PRR wanted to use heavier freight power as well; therefore this section was given top priority for this undertaking. We will see several replacement bridges completed or under construction as we move up the valley.

National Archives

On this sunny day in June 1917 our Valuation photographer has captured the construction of a massive new bridge across the river into Manayunk, which cost close to $1 million. Note that the alignment of the new bridge is somewhat different than the old one. This was done to reduce curvature and minimize disruption of traffic during construction.

TRIUMPH III

Herbert H. Harwood, Jr.

THE MASSIVE STRUCTURE is shown 76 years later in a June 1993 photo looking toward Manayunk. Overhead poles were erected when the line was electrified, but the 1818-ft. long viaduct is still elegant, although the concrete shows signs of deterioration.

THE BIG GAMBLE

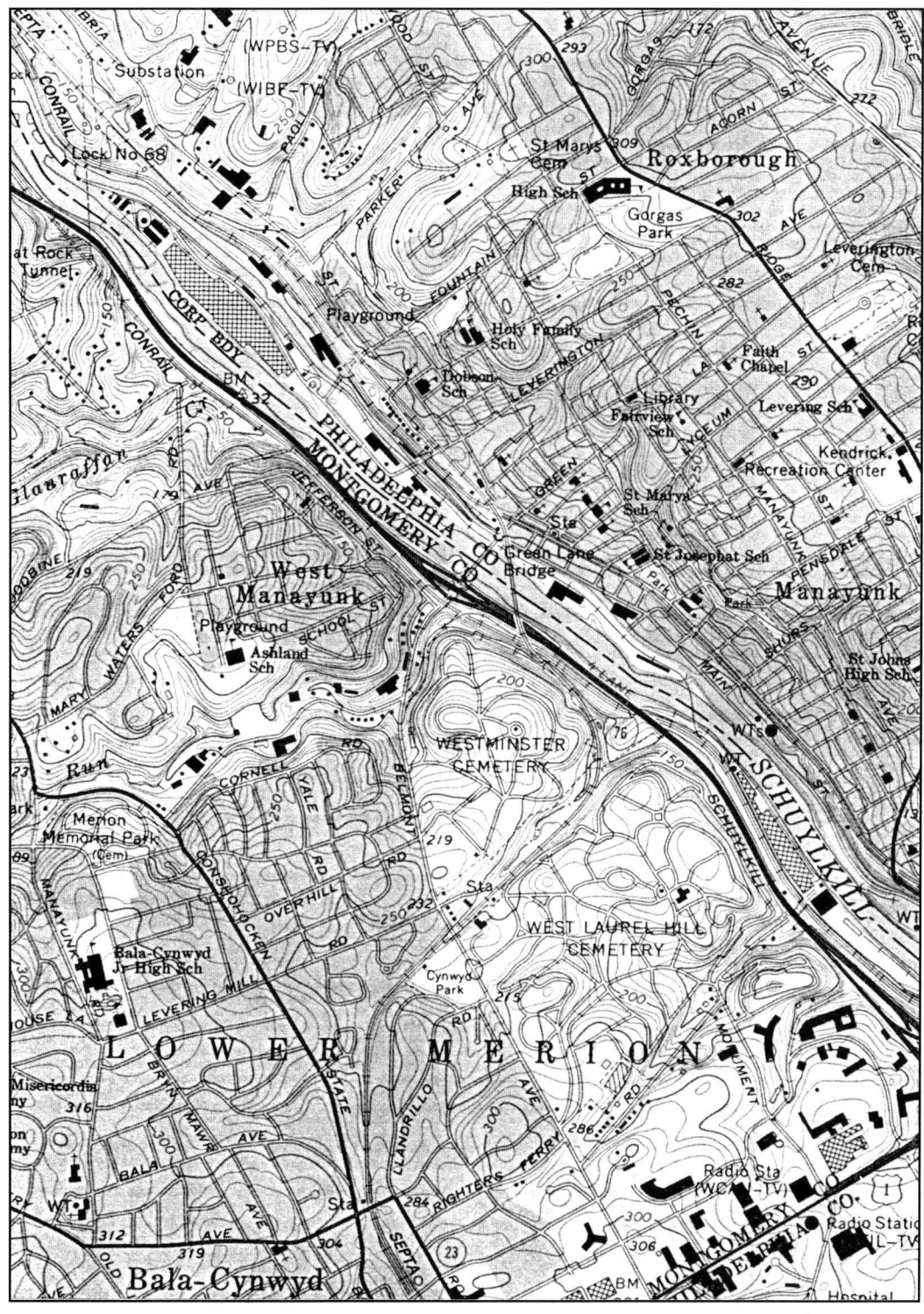

THE AREA around the bridge is shown as it appeared in 1967 (photorevised 1983). The Schuylkill Branch curves and descends into the valley and crosses the bridge as the Pencoyd Branch extends into West Manayunk and down under the bridge to a connection with the Conrail (ex-Reading) main. The bridge curves across the river over the Reading Norristown line. Note Lock No. 68 on a remaining section of the Schuylkill Canal. We will discuss the canal as we move up the valley.

MANAYUNK was settled in 1819 around the Schuylkill Canal, which passed along the north bank of the river at this location. A dam upriver provided waterpower for flour, cotton, woolen and paper mills, as well as the beginnings of the iron industry.

Ted Xaras Collection

A LINEUP of local constabulary keeps a watchful eye on the photographer at Manayunk station (M.P. 7.8). The photo was taken soon after the structure was erected in 1884, when the line was built. Note the curved wooden platforms.

THE BIG GAMBLE

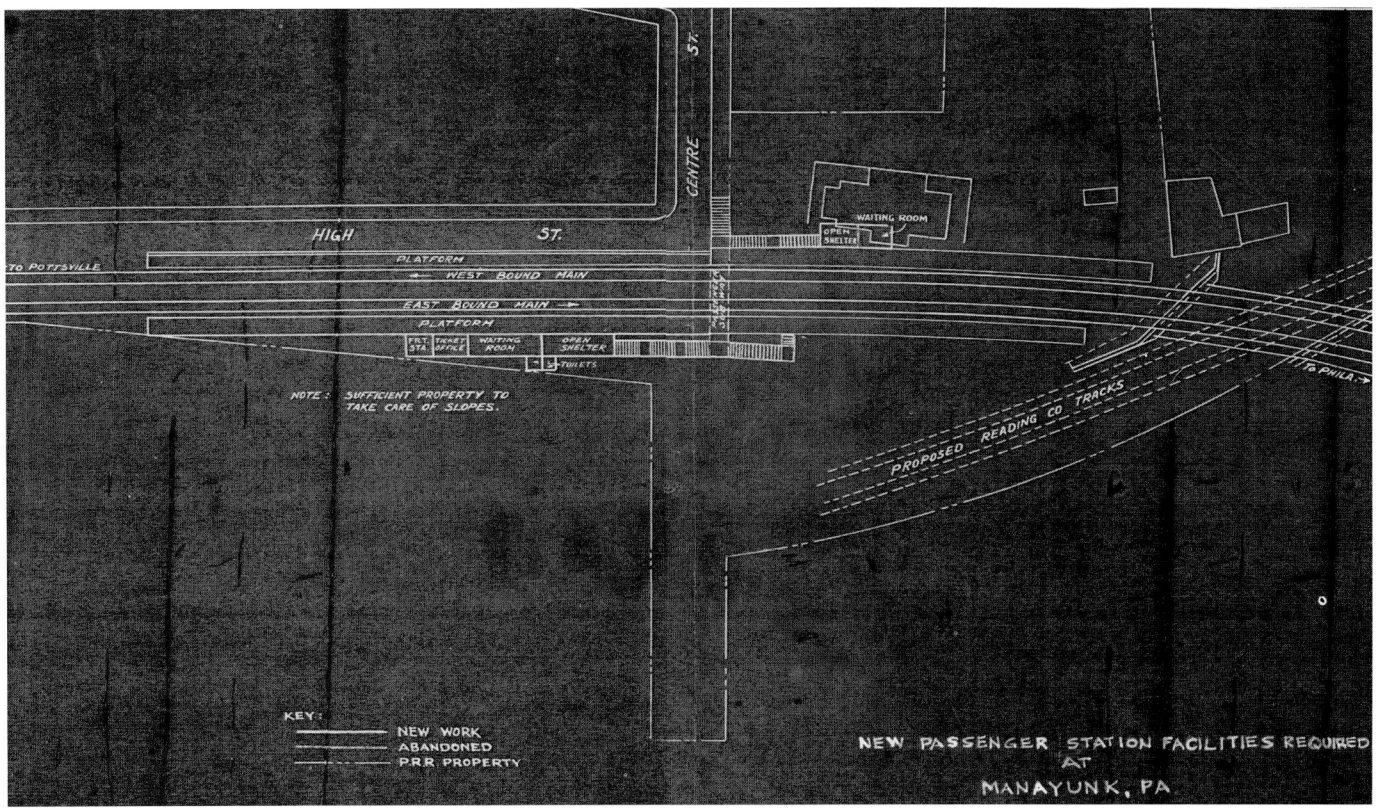

Hagley Museum and Library

R.S. Short/Herbert H. Harwood, Jr. Collection

(above) BECAUSE of the close proximity of the two lines in the Schuylkill Valley, whenever PRR wanted to make changes it had to deal with the Reading. This sometimes involved years of negotiations – often acrimonious – as we shall see shortly. However, the changes at Manayunk in conjunction with the bridge construction were relatively free of these kinds of problems. To reduce costs, a new combination station and shelter was built on the eastbound side, a new waiting room and shelter added on the westbound side, and the 1884 station was abandoned. This involved some realignment of the Reading tracks through the area.

(left) AN EASTBOUND Penn Central (ex-PRR) Silverliner moves past the shelter in October 1969. Note the upper portion of a stone mill building at left.

223

AN EXTENSIVE early anthracite furnace complex was located just west of town, part of the overall iron (and later steel) industry that developed in the Schuylkill Valley. This was because of the ready availability of the raw materials: brown hematite (iron ore), limestone and water power, plus abundant hardwood and later anthracite shipped down the Schuylkill Canal. Both the Reading Norristown Branch (PG&N) and 50 years after that the PRR Schuylkill Valley line were laid through the heart of Manayunk.

National Archives

THIS SMALL STATION and shelter was also built in 1884 at the equally small community of Shawmont (MP 9.5). This view, suffering from "Valuation Focus," looks westward in 1917.

THE BIG GAMBLE

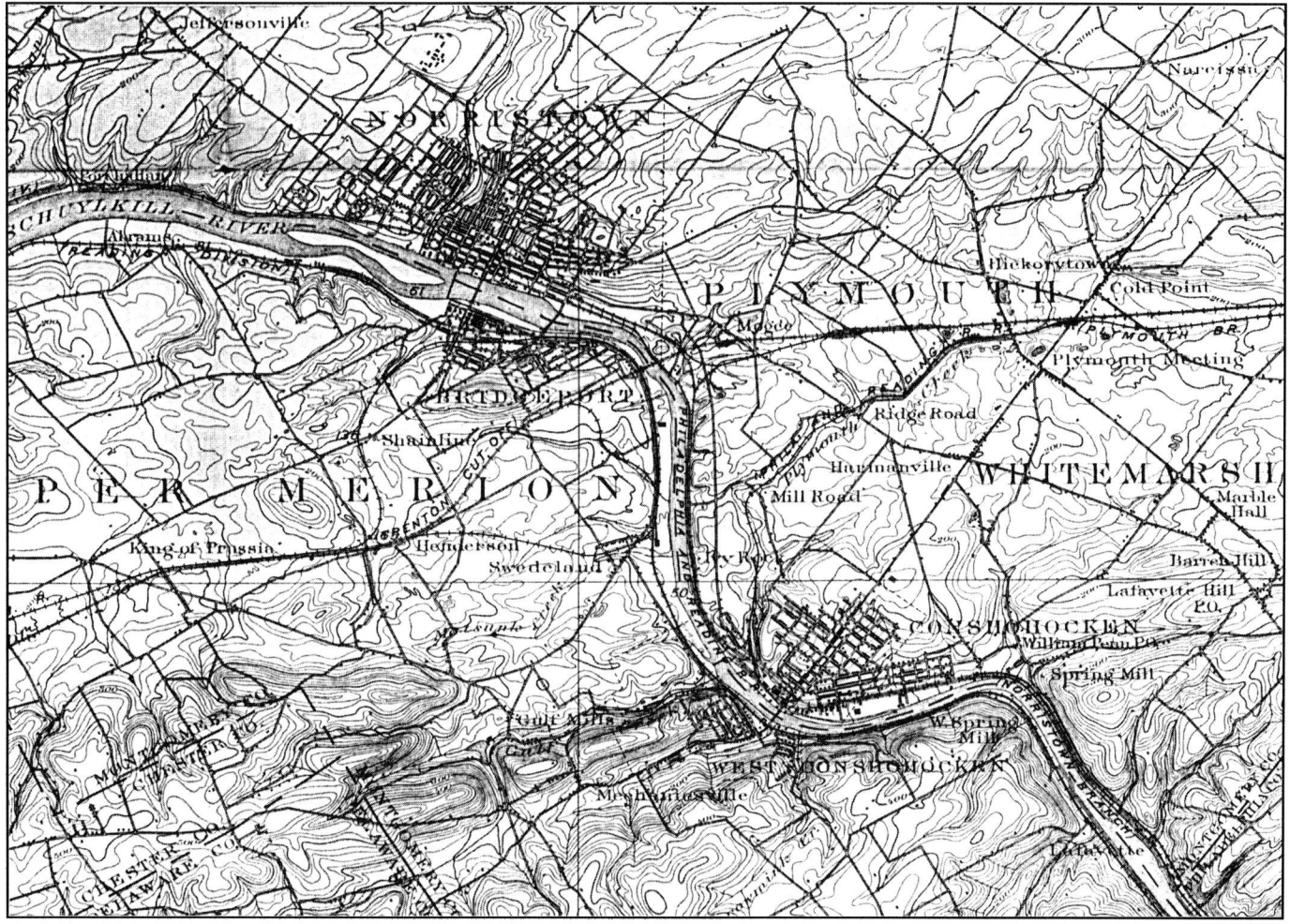

THIS MAP shows the area approaching Norristown up the Schuylkill River Valley. The Reading mainline runs along the south bank of the river, while the Norristown Branch (former PG&N) follows the north bank into its namesake borough. The PRR Schuylkill Division runs alongside the Reading branch, just to the right on this map. The PRR line connects with the recently completed (at the time of the map survey in 1894) Trenton Cutoff (Philadelphia Division) via a wye and small yard at Earnest, just before both lines pass under the PRR freight line, which runs on a high truss bridge across the valley. The lines then continue on into Norristown.

Two branch lines, one from each railroad, serve the industrial complex north of Conshohocken. The Reading Plymouth Branch runs southwestward along Plymouth Creek and then turns southward into Conshohocken. The PRR Swedeland Branch extends eastward from Henderson on the Trenton Cutoff, serving the area on that side of the river. We will examine this fascinating area in more detail as we proceed.

Martin S. Zak/Ted Xaras Collection

WE HAVE another scene at train time, this one at Spring Mill sometime in the 1940s. This station was built - along with many others on the line - in 1884. Spring Mill was the location of a grist mill that dated back to the early 1700s and operated for well over 200 years. In 1839 an iron furnace was constructed adjacent to the grist mill. Limestone was quarried in the area, giving rise to lime kilns which in turn supplied white ash used as a flux in the blast furnaces that were established in the Schuylkill Valley. G5s 5716 represents typical steam passenger power on the line until service was discontinued.

THIS PHOTO illustrates just how close the Reading Norristown Branch and PRR Schuylkill Valley lines were in the valley. The view looks west at Spring Mill in 1895, with a Class H1 (old Class I) No. 740 highballing eastward. When the two lines were electrified the catenary poles were so close that they were joined in some sections.

Ted Xaras Collection

E.P. Alexander Archive/Ted Xaras Collection

STILL ANOTHER scene with passengers waiting for train arrival, this one at Conshohocken (MP 13.5), a few years after the station was constructed in 1884. Conshohocken was the location of several early industries in the valley using water power from the Schuylkill Canal, as well as extensive lime kilns.

National Archives

TROUBLE SPOT – This bridge crossing over Plymouth Creek and the P&R Plymouth Branch was near the site of one of the earliest encounters between PRR and the Reading in the Schuylkill Valley, discussed in the text. The bridge, originally built in 1883 by Cofrode & Saylor (as were many of the bridges between here and the city of Reading) and renewed in 1905, is a 220-ft. long, four-span, one-half through plate girder structure. The Conshohocken Road overpass is visible just behind the PRR bridge in this 1917 view looking northward.

TRIUMPH III

Michael Rabbit Collection

THE EARLIEST BEGINNING of the Alan Wood Steel Co. was a water power mill built in 1832 in Conshohocken by James Wood and his son Alan for rolling iron plates from bar iron. In 1857 Alan Wood formed a partnership, known as Alan Wood & Co., establishing the Schuylkill Iron Works. In 1901 a new company known as the Alan Wood Iron & Steel Co. was formed, this one owned by Howard and Richard Wood, Alan's son and grandson, respectively. Open hearth furnaces and a blooming mill were constructed upriver from Conshohocken at Ivy Rock to produce the blooms to be rolled into sheets at the Schuylkill Iron Works.

In 1911 the company bought out Richard Heckscher & Sons Co., which had built a blast furnace on the west (Swedeland) side of the river. A second furnace was built in 1912 and a third in 1920; the original mill was abandoned in 1925. An 84" plate mill was constructed at Ivy Rock in 1914, and two batteries of coke ovens were built on the Swedeland side in 1918, with a third battery added in 1929. In 1929 operations on both sides of the river were consolidated as the Alan Wood Steel Co. In 1950 a 30" continuous hot strip mill was put into commercial operation, and an additional open hearth furnace was added that same year. The plate mill was modernized in 1954, allowing introduction of a new line of cold rolled products.

This aerial photo taken in the early 1960s shows the complex on the west side of the river looking southeastward. We can identify the following in this picture: The Reading main runs from the left edge of the photo to the upper right and the interchange yard extends behind the stacks; the coke ovens are below the twin stacks and the quencher is beyond the ovens, emitting the cloud of steam; the car dumper is to the right of that with a string of cars extending from it; the crusher and conveyer system is below that; the blast furnaces are in the upper right, with multiple stacks; below that is the PRR Swedeland Branch (curving into the plant from the Trenton Cutoff – Philadelphia Division) and providing carloads of coal and ore; the domestic coke bins are below the tracks; finally at center right is a remnant of a second connection to the Trenton Cutoff (curved track with cars stored on it), which ran up through some early quarries and lime kilns. The Upper Merion & Plymouth RR bridge extends across the river to the Ivy Rock facility on the east side.

THE BIG GAMBLE

Michael Rabbit Collection

DURING THE EARLY 1960s the rolling mill complex on the Ivy Rock site was expanded and the old mills removed. In the mid-60s a basic oxygen furnace was constructed, which began operation in 1968; shortly afterward the open hearth furnaces were removed. Despite these efforts at installing new technology, Alan Wood Steel Co. filed for bankruptcy in June 1977 and discontinued operations. Several years passed, and the plant was eventually sold to Lukens Steel Co. of Coatesville, PA (see *Triumph II*) in 1990, and operations at the plate mill were started up again. Lukens was in turn taken over by Bethlehem Steel in 1998, and the plate mill continues to operate under the Bethlehem Lukens name.

This early 1960s photo shows the Ivy Rock complex on the east side, looking south down the river valley as it curves to the east around Conshohocken. From right to left: The Reading Norristown Branch runs along the river, and the PRR Schuylkill Valley line runs closer to the plant, with a lead extending upgrade to the plant, primarily for shipping finished product; the rolling mills run parallel to the river, with the blooming mill and slab-plate mill at right angles; the offices are at lower left, with the open hearth furnaces above; to the right of the open hearths is the machine shop; the Reading Plymouth Branch enters from the north and curves around the open hearth furnaces, primarily providing scrap metal and limestone. The site of the future BOF plant is out of the picture at the left edge.

Hagley Museum and Library

PLANT SWITCHING OPERATIONS are carried out by the Upper Merion & Plymouth RR, a subsidiary of Alan Wood Steel Co. established in 1907. It serves the plants on both sides of the river by means of a bridge built in 1910. Portions of the plant were also served by narrow gauge trackage, but this was all removed when the open hearth furnaces were dismantled. A new standard gauge yard was constructed east of the basic oxygen furnace in the mid-60s. The railroad remained in operation during the bankruptcy, serving other plants in the area. Today it is owned by Bethlehem Lukens, operating at a reduced scale from the 70s. Most incoming loads originate at the Coatesville plant and arrive via the Conrail (ex-Reading) interchange at Swedeland, using the bridge to access the plant. This photo shows 0-4-0T switcher No. 34 and hot metal transfer cars ca. 1925, dwarfed by the blast furnace and looming stacks and towers.

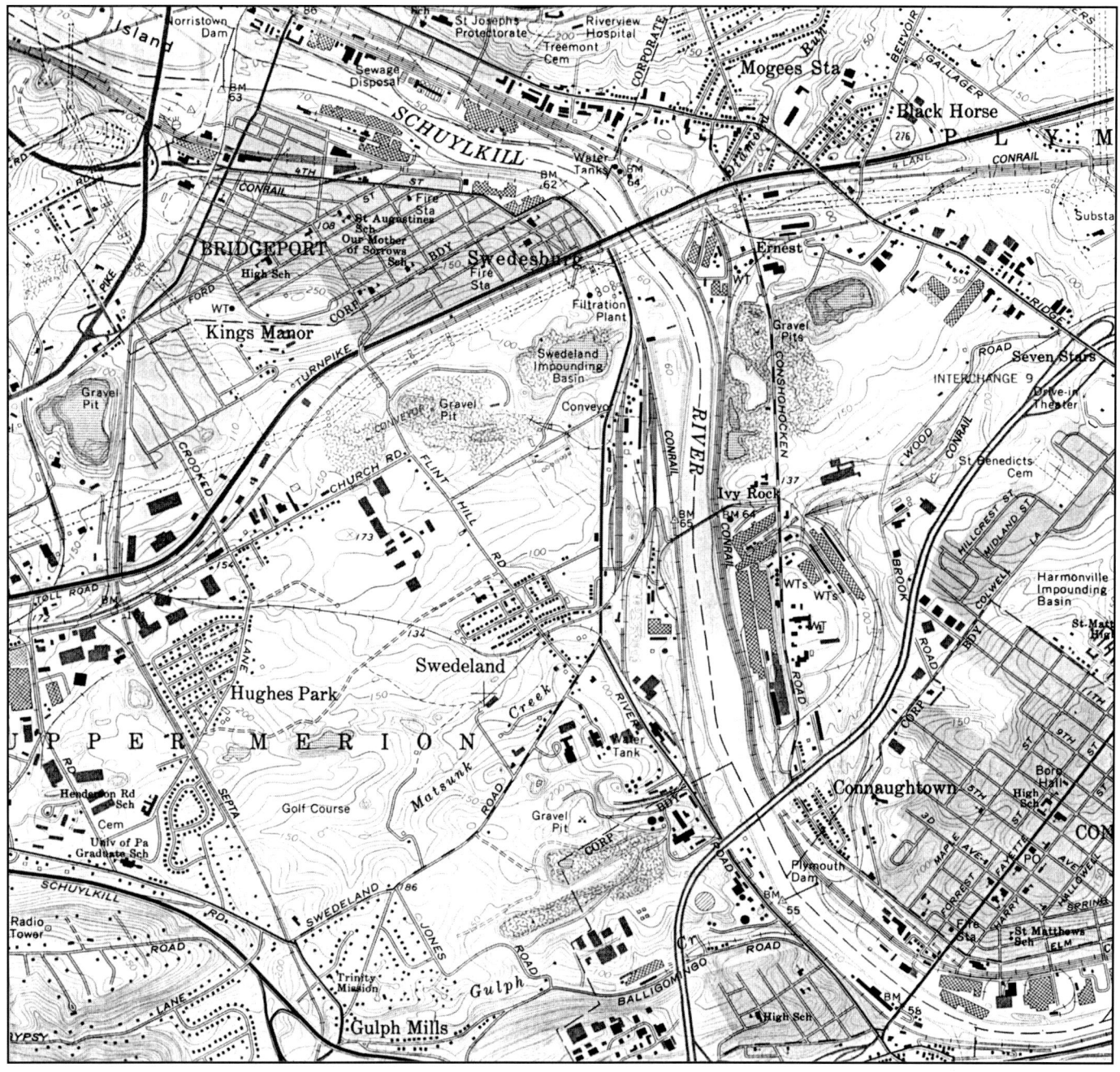

A CLOSER LOOK at the trackage in the area of the steel complex is shown here in a 1966 survey map (photorevised in 1983). The Ivy Rock complex is clearly shown on the right (east) side of the river, accessed by four Conrail lines, two on either side of the valley. The ex-Reading Plymouth Branch extends down from the right, and the ex-PRR Schuylkill Branch serves the plate mill from along the river. On the left (west) side the ex-Reading Schuylkill main runs alongside the plant, while the ex-PRR Swedeland Branch extends east from the Conrail Morrisville line (ex-PRR Trenton Cutoff). The gravel pit and impounding basin are remnants of early limestone quarries; there is also a vestige of a spur that at one time provided a second connection to the Trenton Cutoff. Note the UM&P bridge connecting the two sites. The PRR Schuylkill Branch continues through Norristown and along the river bank westward, while the Reading line cuts across the river and joins the main west of Bridgeport. The trackage entering Norristown from the south is the SEPTA Norristown High Speed Line (former Philadelphia & Western traction line).

NORRISTOWN was named after Isaac Norris, who purchased the land from William Penn, Jr., and was laid out by William Smith in 1784. It was the site of the beginnings of the Schuylkill & Delaware Canal ca. 1792, the first public canal in the U.S. It was intended to connect the two rivers, but was abandoned after about 15 miles and heavy expenditure. The enterprise was later incorporated into the Schuylkill Navigation Co. Norristown eventually became the seat of government of Montgomery County. This view looks across the river, with a westbound Philadelphia & Reading train in the foreground.

Ted Xaras Collection

THE FIRST Norristown Station (MP 17.5) that PRR built is shown here soon after it opened on 23 June 1884. It was located on the corner of DeKalb and Lafayette Streets, where freight transfer platforms had been located for many years. The tracks ran in the pavement of Lafayette Street, in the foreground. The freight station is to the left.

After the station had been in place for 20 years it was relocated farther west to the middle of the block between DeKalb and Swede Streets, to alleviate blocking of the critical grade crossing at DeKalb Street, about which we will hear more shortly. This second facility was opened on 21 February 1904.

THE BIG GAMBLE

Hagley Museum and Library

ELIMINATION of grade crossings in Norristown was an issue that arose as early as 1915 and simmered for nearly 15 years. Both PRR and the Reading put forth many tentative plans, but agreement among the borough, Montgomery County and the two railroads could not be reached. Finally, after fatal accidents occurred at the DeKalb Street crossings near the two stations and pressure from the Norristown Chamber of Commerce, several conferences were held resulting in a plan dated 9 November 1928. This plan was finally approved by the Borough, County and the Public Service Commission early in 1929, and by the PRR Board on 22 May of that year. However, with declining passenger revenues the railroads delayed implementation of the project, considering the elimination of one or the other's trackage from Manayunk westward to Norristown, and/or the use of a joint station in Norristown. The two railroads could not agree on either consolidation option, so the crossing elimination project finally got underway. This photo shows the PRR tracks in Lafayette Street looking east from the DeKalb Street crossing ca. 1925.

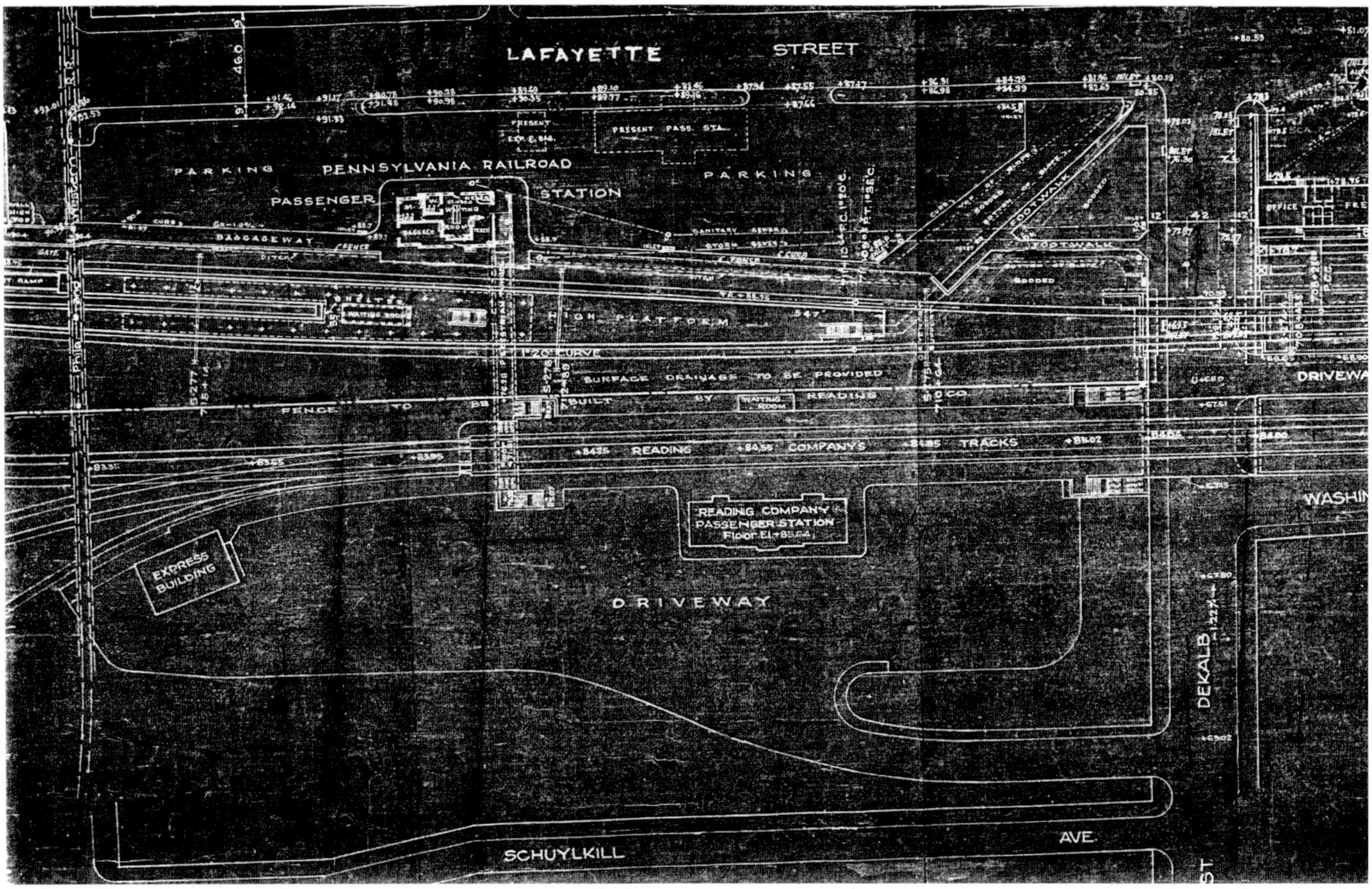

Hagley Museum and Library

THE NORRISTOWN IMPROVEMENTS, as they came to be called, consisted of elimination of seven grade crossings in the downtown area. In the station area it involved relocation of PRR trackage along Lafayette Street about 150 ft. southward to lie adjacent to the Reading tracks, elevation of both right-of-way plus depression of DeKalb Street to allow an undergrade crossing. New passenger and freight stations for both railroads were also required. The diagram shows the location of both new passenger stations, plus the site of the previous (1904) PRR facility. The new freight house shown on the diagram at upper right was opened on 1 December 1934, the last part of the Improvement program. Note the Philadelphia & Western RR, an interurban line now utilized as SEPTA's high-speed line from the south.

THE NEW STATION opened 30 July 1934, just 50 years after the first PRR station in Norristown. It was a one-story building measuring 32 by 69 ft., facing Lafayette Street halfway between DeKalb and Swede Streets. A 550-ft. long high-level concrete platform was constructed between the relocated eastbound and westbound tracks, with a 12 by 40 ft. shelter in the center. Pedestrian subways connected to the main waiting room and the intersection of DeKalb and Lafayette Streets. This photo shows the station as it appeared in the early 1950s.

PRR Publicity File/Penn Central RR Collection/Pennsylvania State Archives

THE BIG GAMBLE

THE LAST TRAIN to Reading (down to Sunday only) is shown here at the high level platform in Norristown on 4 October 1953. The station itself is just visible to the left of Atlantic No. 1600 and three P70 coaches. Lafayette Street is at the left.

Ted Xaras Collection

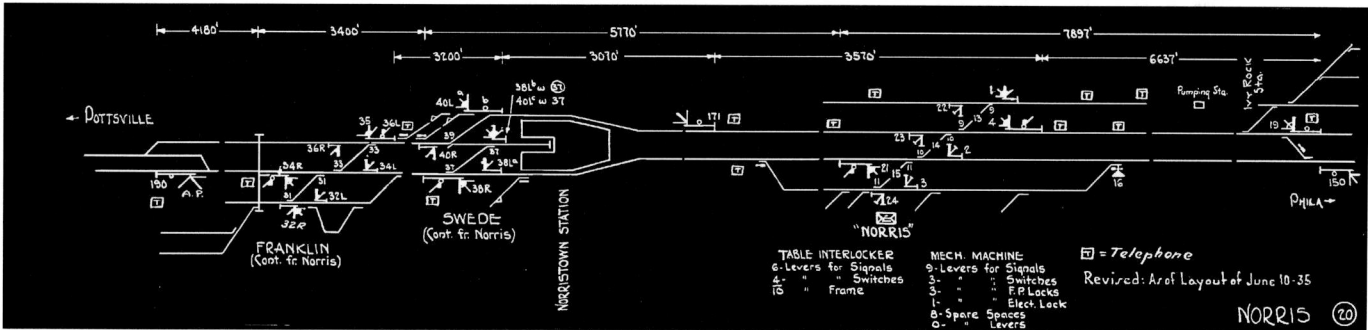

Hagley Museum and Library

NORRIS TOWER controlled movements through Norristown Station (by means of SWEDE and FRANKLIN interlocking), a small freight yard and the wye interchange between the Schuylkill Division and Earnest Yard on the Trenton Cutoff. This freight-only line crossed over the river, the PRR Schuylkill Division and the Reading Norristown Branch on the north bank and the Reading main on the south side (see *Triumph II* for a discussion of the Trenton Cutoff and Earnest Yard). Eastbound traffic from the west destined for the Schuylkill Division would be brought into Earnest Yard and then moved either towards Norristown or to the Conshohocken industrial complex.

HERE'S A LOOK at NORRIS Tower as it appeared in July 1957. The view looks eastward.

Winfield Gross Collection

235

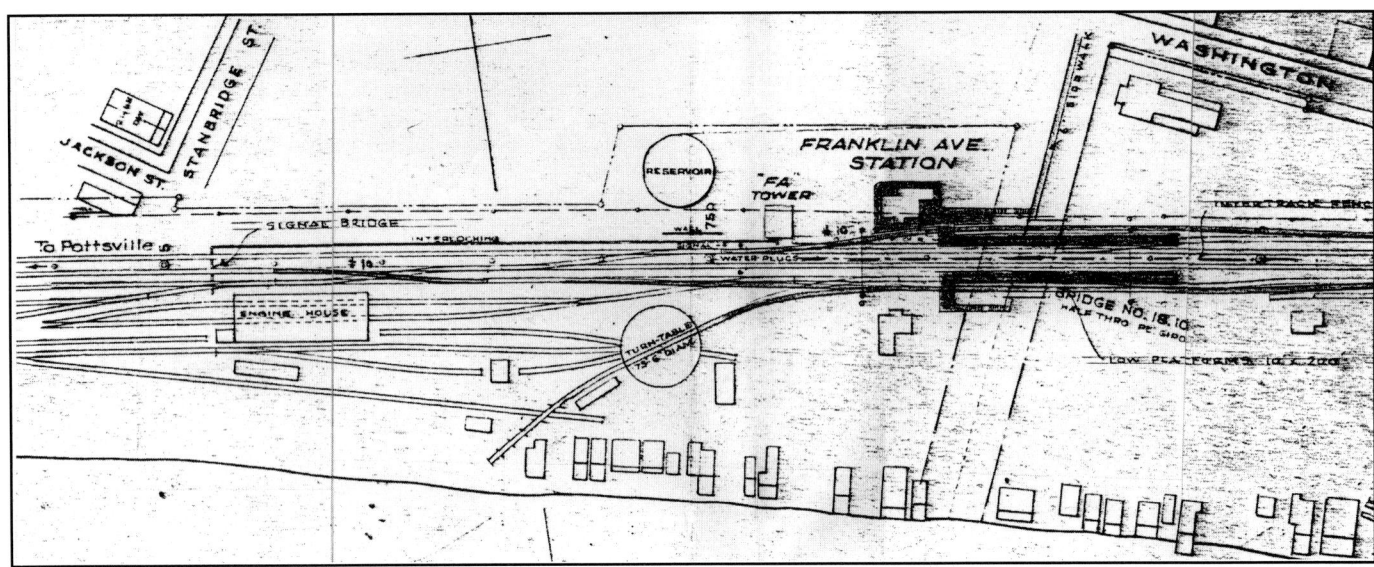

Hagley Museum and Library

IN 1903, as part of an earlier program to improve facilities in Norristown, an additional passenger station was built about a mile to the west at MP 18.3. This was originally known as the Franklin Avenue Station, later known as Haws Avenue, which subsequently became the terminus of electric service on the branch. A 75-ft. turntable was constructed in the engine terminal at the same time. FA Tower was built in 1907, and the station and coaling facility were enlarged in 1910. This diagram shows the layout of facilities in the area as of 5 February 1932.

MU TRAIN No. 660 heads east toward Philadelphia after pausing at the Haws Avenue Station on 20 July 1957. Note the 660 hp. Baldwin switcher, Class BS6 (S6), which along with the 1,000 hp. S10's were typically assigned to the yards at Norristown, Phoenixville, Pottstown and Reading during this period. Through freights during the early diesel era were usually headed by massive 2,400 hp. Baldwin Class BS24 (RT624) center-cab road switchers. In later years 1,750 hp. EMD Class EFS17m (GP9) road switchers appeared in freight service on the branch.

John J. Bowman, Jr./Fred W. Schneider, III Collection

BETZWOOD (MP 21.8) was a tiny community just east of Valley Forge. The picturesque station, also built in 1884 and shown in a 1917 view, was the destination of thousands of Boy Scouts attending a jamboree in the National Park in the summer of 1950.

National Archives

THE BIG GAMBLE

WITH CLEAN STACK, E6s No. 1611 hustles a westbound two-car local through Betzwood in February 1951. This area is now the beginning of a popular bike and jogging trail eastward out of Valley Forge Park.

E.P. Street/Herbert H. Harwood, Jr. Collection

WEST OF BETZWOOD the line crosses the lower end of the Perkiomen Creek, just above its outlet into the Schuylkill River. Shown here in a peaceful view ca. 1890 looking west toward Oaks is the 387-ft., three-span Warren Truss and plate girder bridge constructed when the line was built in 1883.

E.P. Alexander Archive/Ted Xaras Collection

IN 1910 the truss was replaced with the concrete arch structure shown here in a 1917 photo. A traction line was constructed under the west end. The Schuylkill Division right-of-way has been obliterated by a four-lane expressway through this section, but this bridge survives today, albeit looking rather forlorn.

National Archives

Railroad Museum of Pennsylvania (PHMC)

ALTHOUGH Oaks (formerly Perkiomen - MP 24.8) was another small community in the valley, it was just across the river from Perkiomen Junction, the interchange between the Reading Perkiomen Branch and its Schuylkill main. This ca. 1910 view looks eastward when the station was still known by its earlier name.

MONT CLARE (MP 27.4), another small Schuylkill Valley hamlet formerly known as Quincyville, is the site of this picturesque station. It was built in 1884 and shown in a 1917 view, which suffers from severe "Valuation Focus." The name of the community was changed to Mont Clare - after the estate on the hillside - when the Schuylkill Valley tracks were laid through town.

The Schuylkill Canal ran parallel to the line at this point, just south of the station. The section in this area, completed in 1821, was known as the Oakes Reach, after Thomas Oakes, the Schuylkill Navigation Co.'s principal engineer. The entire canal was finally completed in 1825 (the same year as the Erie Canal) and prospered for some 45 years moving anthracite, lumber and manufactured goods to Philadelphia. Canal usage gradually declined with the coming of the railroads, and in 1869 a coal miners' strike, summer drought and fall floods were a near-fatal blow. In 1870 the P&R bought the system and began to abandon it. The last known boat passed through this area in 1918, and the canal was taken over by the Commonwealth of PA in 1931; large sections of the canal were then filled in or drained. Most of the Oakes Reach was spared this fate, although the lower end was filled in as a silt basin for a river dredging project. The section through Mont Clare is still extant in 1999, and the locks are being restored as an historic attraction.

National Archives

THE BIG GAMBLE

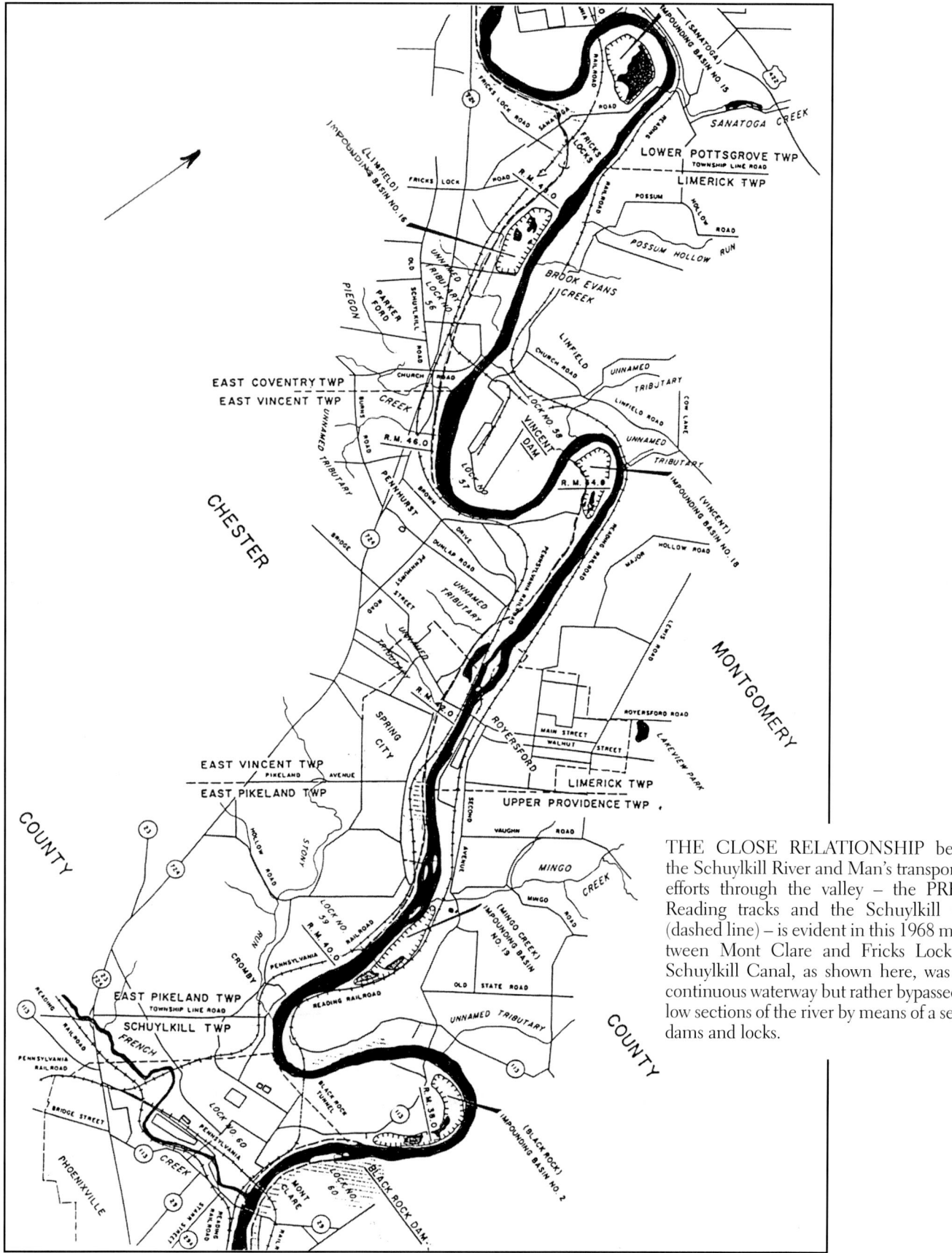

THE CLOSE RELATIONSHIP between the Schuylkill River and Man's transportation efforts through the valley – the PRR and Reading tracks and the Schuylkill Canal (dashed line) – is evident in this 1968 map between Mont Clare and Fricks Lock. The Schuylkill Canal, as shown here, was not a continuous waterway but rather bypassed shallow sections of the river by means of a series of dams and locks.

Spring-Ford Area Historical Society

TRIUMPH III

Elmer Keinard/Glenn Cagle Collection

A WESTBOUND passenger train heads across the truss bridge from Mont Clare toward Phoenixville in the fall of 1894. This 1330-ft. iron truss and girder bridge was constructed by the Phoenix Iron Company in 1884; portions of the bridge were replaced with steel girders in 1897. The Schuylkill River has the look of glass on this early fall day. The P&R Schuylkill main, with passing passenger train, is at the bottom of the picture.

THE BIG GAMBLE

Historical Society of the Phoenixville Area

THIS VIEW of the same bridge into Phoenixville taken in 1906 shows the south bank of the Schuylkill River and the Reading line passing underneath. Note that there are two trains visible on the Reading tracks. The one facing eastbound looks like a switching move with a brakeman sitting atop the boxcar. The other is headed westbound, under the PRR through truss.

A NEW BRIDGE was built in 1915, replacing the trusses. This was a graceful 15-span concrete structure 1230 ft. long. Note the PRR keystone at the south end. The Reading main is in the foreground and the Oakes Reach section of the Schuylkill Canal passes under the northern end.

National Archives

AT THE PHOENIXVILLE END is an 83-ft. steel one-half through plate girder span over the Reading main. The track to the left curves into the Phoenix Iron Works, which we will examine shortly. We trust the Reading patrons (and crews) got a good look at the PRR keystone.

National Archives

TRIUMPH III

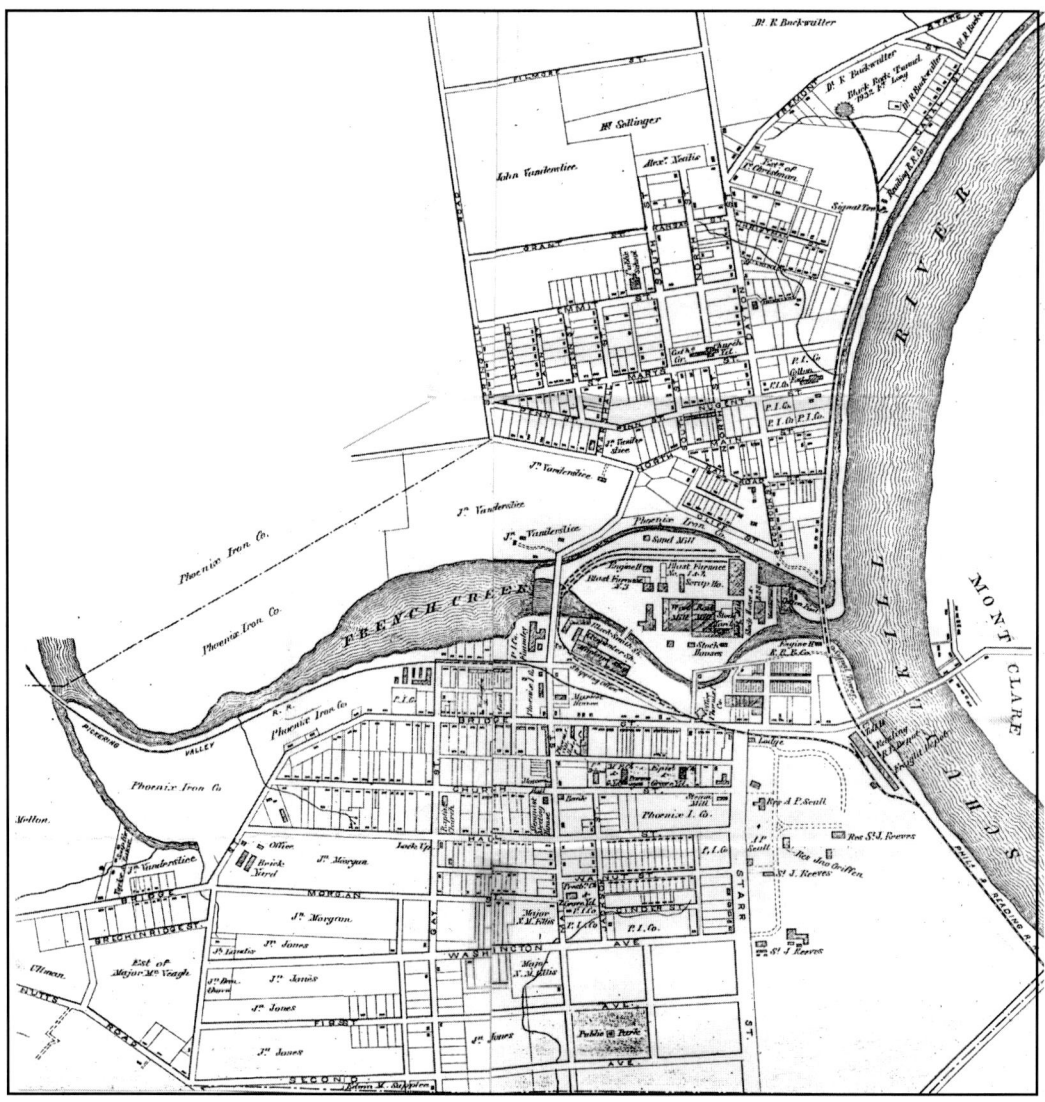

Historical Society of The Phoenixville Area

PHOENIXVILLE is shown in the Witmer's 1873 Atlas with the P&R main extending along the river and the Pickering Valley Railroad (later the Reading Pickering Valley Branch) connecting behind the passenger and freight depot. PRR has not yet arrived on the scene. Note the Phoenix Iron Works, which is beginning to fill up the space between the main settled area and the North Side, and that French Creek is dammed up to occupy considerable space in the valley. Note also the canal extending into the works.

The Phoenix Iron Works traces its origins back to 1783, when an old grist mill on French Creek was acquired by Benjamin Longstreth, a Quaker, for the purposes of establishing an iron rolling and slitting mill. In 1790 he also built the first nail factory in the U.S. on this site, and installed machinery which, by the turn of the century had almost completely supplanted hand-wrought nails. At this time the mill consisted of only one furnace, one pair of rollers and one pair of slitters. The entire output – about three tons per day – was carried the 300 ft. to the nail factory on the back of one stalwart donkey. In 1809 a larger nail factory was constructed and the facility named the French Creek Works.

The works was sold in 1813 to a group of Philadelphia investors including Lewis Wernwag. Wernwag, one of the first professional bridge builders, had gained fame as the builder of the Upper Ferry Bridge over the Schuylkill River in Philadelphia, known as the "Colossus," the largest wooden bridge in the U.S. at the time. Wernwag expanded the works and built a school and housing for the workers. He also experimented with anthracite as fuel at the plant.

The story has it that Wernwag, looking down upon the works one evening from his mansion on the bluff, saw the fire of the furnace light up the sky and was reminded of the mythological Phoenix, the bird that arose from its own ashes. He was so moved that the next day he renamed the plant The Phoenix Works. Fifteen years later the town became Phoenixville; it was incorporated as a borough in 1849.

Despite Wernwag's efforts, financial difficulties arose and the works were sold in 1821 to Jonah and George Thomson of Philadelphia, two of Wernwag's partners. Wernwag himself returned to the design and construction of bridges. The Thomson's again expanded the works, increasing output to 40 tons per week. By 1825 the nail factory was the largest in the U.S. In 1826 the Thomson's installed the first steam power plant in the region and the first anywhere designed to use anthracite.

THE BIG GAMBLE

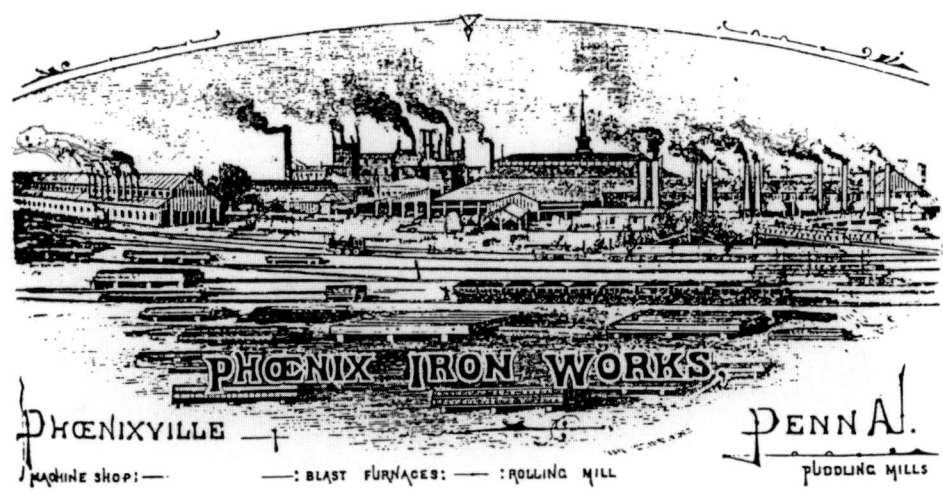

Historical Society of the Phoenixville Area

A NEW ERA BEGAN in 1827 when the works were sold again to Benjamin and David Reeves. The Reeves family was to guide the Phoenix Works through 118 years of growth and change, prosperity and recession. The brothers built a new rolling mill and puddling furnaces, and in 1837 constructed the first anthracite blast furnace built for the purpose. It produced 1,500 tons per year starting in 1840. Rolling mill production grew to 3,000 tons per year and nail production to 32,000 kegs annually.

The arrival of the P&R in 1839 spurred (sorry) interest in production of iron rails; the works began operation of its rail mill in 1846. David Reeves and his chief engineer developed the gag press, which became universally used for straightening rails as well as structural shapes for the next 60 years.

In June 1848 the entire nail factory was destroyed by fire. It was the end of the nail business at the site, but like its namesake, the Phoenix Iron Works arose again and by 1851 construction of the first structural shape mill in the U.S. was started, along with new rolling mills. The first structural beams in the U.S., the largest of which was 9" across, were rolled at the Phoenix Iron Works in 1855.

In 1861 the works started production of 15-inch wrought iron beams, the largest in the U.S., and a large I-beam measuring 9 x 5-3/8 inches, known as the Great Beam. Both of these products were used extensively during the Civil War in cannon and mortar emplacements. Phoenix Works also produced large quantities of the Griffen Gun for Union forces. It was a rifled field cannon with a 3" bore invented by John Griffen, superintendent of the works.

This view of the Phoenix Iron Works from an early company letterhead – when belching smokestacks equated to prosperity – shows the Machine Shop on the left, the blast furnace at center left and other mills on the right. P&R tracks serving the mill are in front.

Historical Society of the Phoenixville Area

THE GRIFFEN GUN is shown in this photo of the weapon on the lawn in front of the Phoenix Iron Works. It was a cannon with a 3" rifled bore, invented by John Griffen, General Superintendent of the company from 1854 until his death 30 years later. The barrel was made of laminations of wrought iron, formed hot between rolls around a mandrel and then machined. This resulted in a weapon of accuracy and great strength against bursting. The barrels weighed approximately 800 lbs. each and cost $350. Between 1861 and 1865 some 1,400 of these field pieces were manufactured at the works and sold to the Union Army for use during the Civil War. The first Union shot in the decisive Battle of Gettysburg was made by a Griffen Gun on 1 July 1863, part of a group of 75 with Battery A, 2nd U.S. Field Artillery. The use of these guns to defend against invasion of Pennsylvania was fitting because reportedly one of General Lee's objectives was to destroy their site of manufacture.

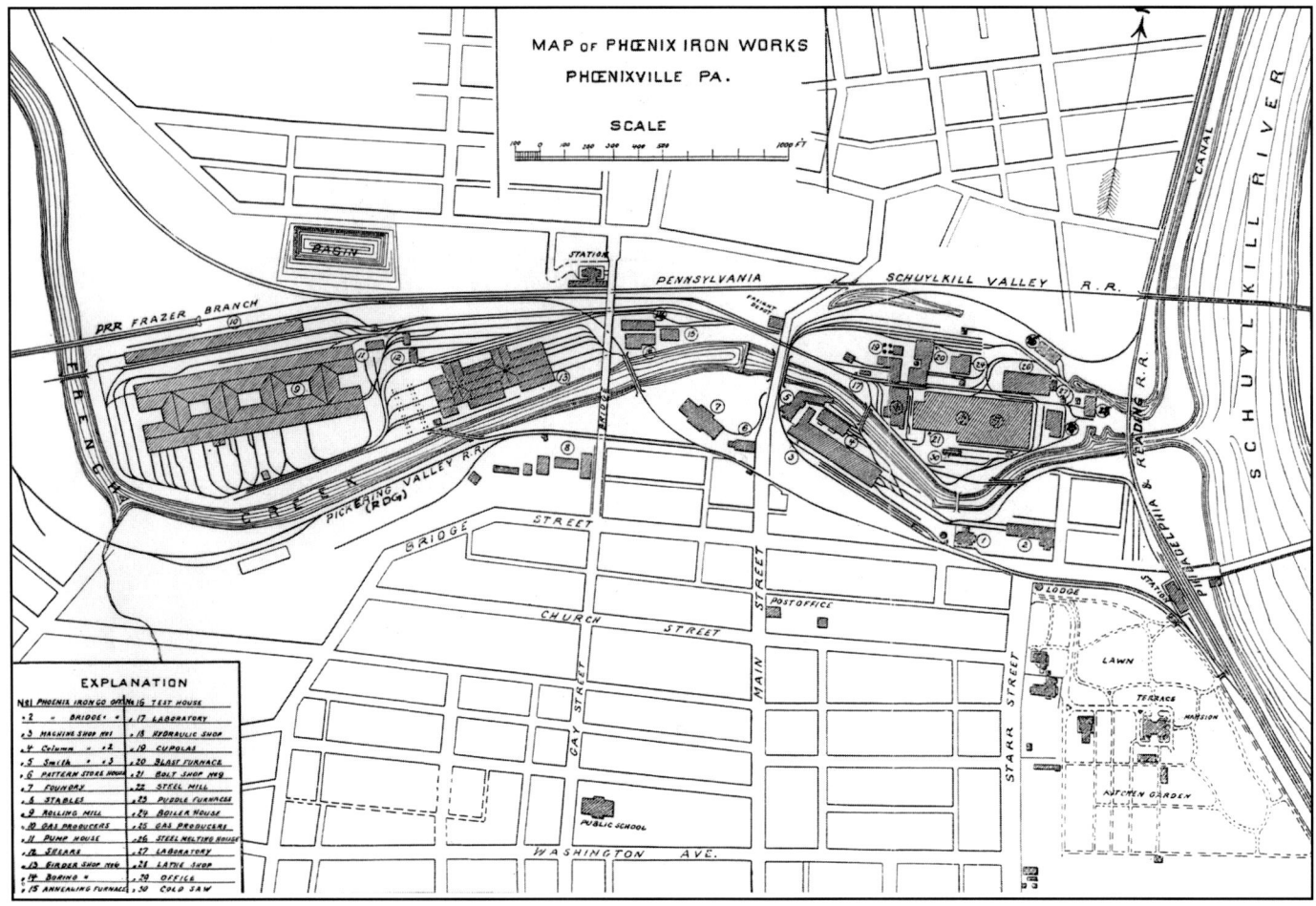

Historical Society of the Phoenixville Area

IN 1871 Phoenix began construction of the largest rolling mill structure in the world, covering 6 1/4 acres under a single roof. Built of iron, glass and slate, it was to serve as a model for the Centennial Exhibition buildings erected in Philadelphia. Its huge capacity allowed Phoenix to become the largest producer of iron shapes in the U.S., typified by the contract for the New York City Elevated in 1879. During the 1880s the mill produced large quantities of wrought iron for shipbuilding, which led in 1884 to the rolling of steel shapes for the U.S. Navy. In 1886 Phoenix began construction of a new steel plant, and in 1889 two 10-ton open-hearth furnaces began production. By the following year the works had four furnaces of 15-20 ton capacity and 18 new puddle furnaces. By 1890 the Phoenix Works was one of the few fully integrated plants in the U.S., serving as a model of international renown.

At the turn of the century Phoenix Iron Co. was faced with increased competition because of the formation of the large steel corporations. David and William Reeves, grandsons of the original president, began a plant modernization program in an attempt to remain competitive. They installed the first fully electrically operated rolling mill in 1901, a new 150-ton furnace in 1911 – the largest open hearth facility in the world – and by 1926 under the leadership of Samuel Reeves (the fourth generation of his family) the works became fully electrified.

This map of the Phoenix Iron Works shows how the facility has expanded into the area along French Creek, which has been filled in with slag from the furnaces. Note the large Girder Shop (No. 13) and the immense Rolling Mill (No. 9), constructed in 1871.

Note also that the PRR Schuylkill Valley line has arrived and laid trackage to serve virtually the entire works. The passenger depot (top center) is located at the intersection of Gay and Vanderslice Streets.

Historical Society of the Phoenixville Area

THE GIRARD AVENUE BRIDGE in Philadelphia was one of the earliest – and most beautiful – bridges built by Clarke, Reeves & Co. (predecessor of the Phoenix Bridge Co.) in 1874. Here it crosses – most elegantly – over the Schuylkill River in the City's famed Fairmount Park, allowing Philadelphia residents to access the Centennial Exposition in 1876. The three middle spans are 197 ft. long and the two end ones are 137 ft. It is 100 ft. wide, with seven wrought iron trusses forming each span.

The Phoenix Bridge Co. was the oldest and one of the best-known firms of its type in the U.S. From its beginnings it had a close affiliation with the Phoenix Iron Co., which had successfully entered the field of bridge construction with the initiation of structural shape rolling in 1855. Samuel J. Reeves, vice president of Phoenix Iron Co, reinforced this affiliation in 1862 with the invention of the Phoenix Column. This consisted of a hollow wrought iron column made up of segmental channels riveted together at their flanges. It was the first wrought iron column to be patented and provided a strong, lightweight and economical design.

The first official bridge company was formed in 1868 as Kellogg. Clarke & Co. A reorganization took place in 1871, and the name was changed to Clark, Reeves & Co., reflecting the partnership of David Reeves II, also president of the Iron Works. In 1873 the firm signed a contract with Phoenix Iron Works to carry out all that firm's bridgebuilding. In 1884 the firm became known as the Phoenix Bridge Co., with David Reeves as president and William H. Reeves (general superintendent of Phoenix Iron) as general superintendent.

Among the notable bridges designed and constructed by the firm are two large bridges for the Connecticut AirLine Railway (later part of the New Haven) at Lyman Viaduct (1112 ft.) and Rapallo Viaduct (1378 ft.). Other major spans are the New York Central bridge across the Hudson River at Albany, NY (1873); elevated railway structures in New York City (1879) and Brooklyn (1890); Ohio River bridges at Cincinnati (1887) and Louisville (1889); the Manhattan Bridge, New York (1909); and the PRR Schuylkill River Bridge on the Trenton Cutoff (1914).

Later structures include the Reading Co. viaduct in Manayunk, PA; the PRR vertical lift bridge over the Hackensack River in Jersey City; the Arlington Memorial Bridge in Washington, DC (1931); portions of the Pulaski Skyway near Newark; the Troy-Menands Bridge, Troy, NY; the Boston & Maine draw spans over the Charles River, Boston; and notably the Buzzards Bay Bridge (1936) over the Cape Cod Canal, the largest vertical lift span ever constructed.

Phoenix Bridge Co. was noted not only for the quality but also the beauty of their structures. However, the company's fortunes declined after World War II and it was sold to the Barium Steel Co. in 1949 along with the Iron Works itself. No longer able to remain competitive in changing world markets, it finally closed

TRIUMPH III

DURING BOTH WORLD WARS the works operated at top capacity and turned out large quantities of materials for the war effort. However in 1944 Samuel Reeves died suddenly, culminating 118 years of leadership by the Reeves family. The plant changed ownership several times over the next 5 years and on 3 June 1949 it shut down. However, on 19 August of that year both Phoenix Iron Co. and Phoenix Bridge Co. were purchased by Barium Steel Corp. The company became Phoenix Iron & Steel Co. and began production of steel pipe, which was very profitable for a number of years. In 1959 the plant was sold again and renamed Phoenix Steel Co. It struggled valiantly against both foreign and domestic competition. In 1982 the open hearth furnace was shut down, and Phoenix Steel closed in 1985, leaving only the tube-rolling mill still in operation. Finally, on 28 March 1987 the remaining works were shut down for the last time. This ended nearly 200 years of iron and steelmaking in a town where generations had grown accustomed to the throb of furnaces and mills in the French Creek valley

Historical Society of the Phoenixville Area

– and depended on it for their livelihood. At Phoenix, "The people made the difference." In this aerial photo of Phoenix Iron Works looking east ca. 1949 the PRR Schuylkill Valley line is clearly visible on the left, with the passenger station and trackage into the plant. The Reading mainline can be seen along the river, with the depot in the upper right. The large rolling mill is at the lower right, and the girder shop is in the center of the photo.

Elmer Keinard/Glenn Cagel Collection

AN IMMACULATE PRR 4-4-0 No. 210 poses for its portrait near the Phoenix Iron Co. on 30 September 1894, 10 years after the line was opened. The identity of the locomotive behind No. 210 can't be determined, but it looks like a tank engine, possibly a plant switcher.

PHOENIX IRON CO. No. 12, an 0-4-0T locomotive used for moving cars within the plant, rumbles across Main Street near the scrap yard. This ca. 1949 view looks northward toward the PRR overpass bridge. This was a 96-ft. one-half through plate girder span originally built in 1884 and rebuilt in 1914.

Historical Society of the Phoenixville Area

Ted Xaras Collection

WHEN PRR BUILT the Schuylkill Valley line through Phoenixville a number of already historic landmarks were sacrificed to make room for the second railroad. The right-of-way and the bridge across the river detracted from the previously unimpaired view of the valley from "Mont Clare," the Whitaker family mansion across from the borough. Cutting the right of way through North Phoenixville resulted in the destruction of the mansion built by the ironmaker and bridge engineer, Lewis Wernwag, and subsequently occupied by successor George Thomson and then by Dr. Isaac Pennypacker. One of Dr. Pennypacker's sons, Samuel W., became governor of Pennsylvania in 1903.

Perhaps in atonement for this deed, PRR built this attractive depot (MP 28.1) on the side of Black Rock Hill in 1883 and landscaped the grounds with flowerbeds. This early 1900s view looks north (eastward on the line), with the station and lower level platforms on the left. The interior contained a central ticket office flanked by separate men's and women's waiting rooms. During its heyday the depot served as the gateway for visitors and patients from all over the U.S. to the nearby Valley Forge General (Army) Hospital. When passenger service on the Schuylkill Valley was discontinued in the early 50s the station interior was remodeled for freight use. It was razed in 1986.

On the right is PN (later PHOENIX) Tower, which controlled the junction with the Frazer Branch west of the station as well as movements in and out of the Iron Works. Note the water columns on both sides of the tracks.

Historical Society of the Phoenixville Area

THE FREIGHT STATION is located on Bridge Street, west of the Iron Works. Once the decision was made in 1885 to extend the line to the coal fields, PRR constructed a spur into Phoenixville's coal yards (previously supplied only by the Reading) and located a freight station there, just west of its competitor's facility. This photo shows the structure still standing 100 years later, being used as a home and garden shop.

(next page)

WE'LL BRIEFLY EXAMINE here the short Frazer Branch (originally the Phoenixville & West Chester RR), which ran south from Phoenixville to connect with the mainline at Frazer. The lower end of the line (about 1 mile) was known as the Phoenixville Branch and was part of the Philadelphia Division (The intersection of this branch with the main is depicted in *Triumph II*). Although serving a sparsely populated area of Chester County, this line had a colorful history. When it was originally opened in 1883, there were no stations, although platforms were built at Nutt Road, Harveyville, Pickering, Devault Beaver's and Swedesford Road. A year later sheds were constructed at Pickering and Beaver's, "for the accommodation of passengers," according to the West Chester *Daily Local News*, which characterized them as neither "very extensive nor very inviting."

Meanwhile, the citizens of Charlestown, the largest community on the line, protested that no station was planned for their village. They threatened to continue to use the Reading line (Pickering Valley RR) if PRR ignored the town. And so, in 1884 a siding was installed at Rees' Paper Mill and a platform and flag stop established. A station was finally erected in 1886, named Aldham to avoid confusion between Rees' mill and Reeseville (the original name of Berwyn, on the Main Line). In 1887 the station at Beaver's was renamed Devault to avoid confusion with other locations named Beaver. Subsequently two additional stations, Sidley and Bacton, were added. Sidley was added in 1888, named after the nearby Sidley Silica Sand Co. This name was chosen rather than Cornog, who was once owner of the land, because of his opposition to building the line.

The name Bacton was reportedly selected after a stockholder complained that this road only served back towns.

Operations on this backwoods line were not known for their speed. The folklore that trains would wait for a hen to lay an egg so a local farmer could have an even dozen to ship is most likely just that. However, it is known that one Frank Norris raced a northbound train from Frazer to Phoenixville in his horse-drawn wagon and won!

The branch had its share of wrecks, including one at the new iron trestle over Buckwalter Road. The new structure, replacing a wooden one, was still under construction when at noon on 16 December 1896 a northbound freight derailed and rolled down the embankment. Several cars were left hanging from the trestle. Four individuals were hurt, although the crew survived by jumping from the locomotive before it rolled over. Service was restored in 2 days.

The line slowly declined after World War I with the advent of cars and trucks. Passenger service was discontinued in 1928, replaced by buses that ran until the Depression. The last station was closed in 1964, although surprisingly Conrail (now NS) still operates a daily freight on the line, which currently ends just south of Devault, no longer connected with the Harrisburg main.

THE BIG GAMBLE

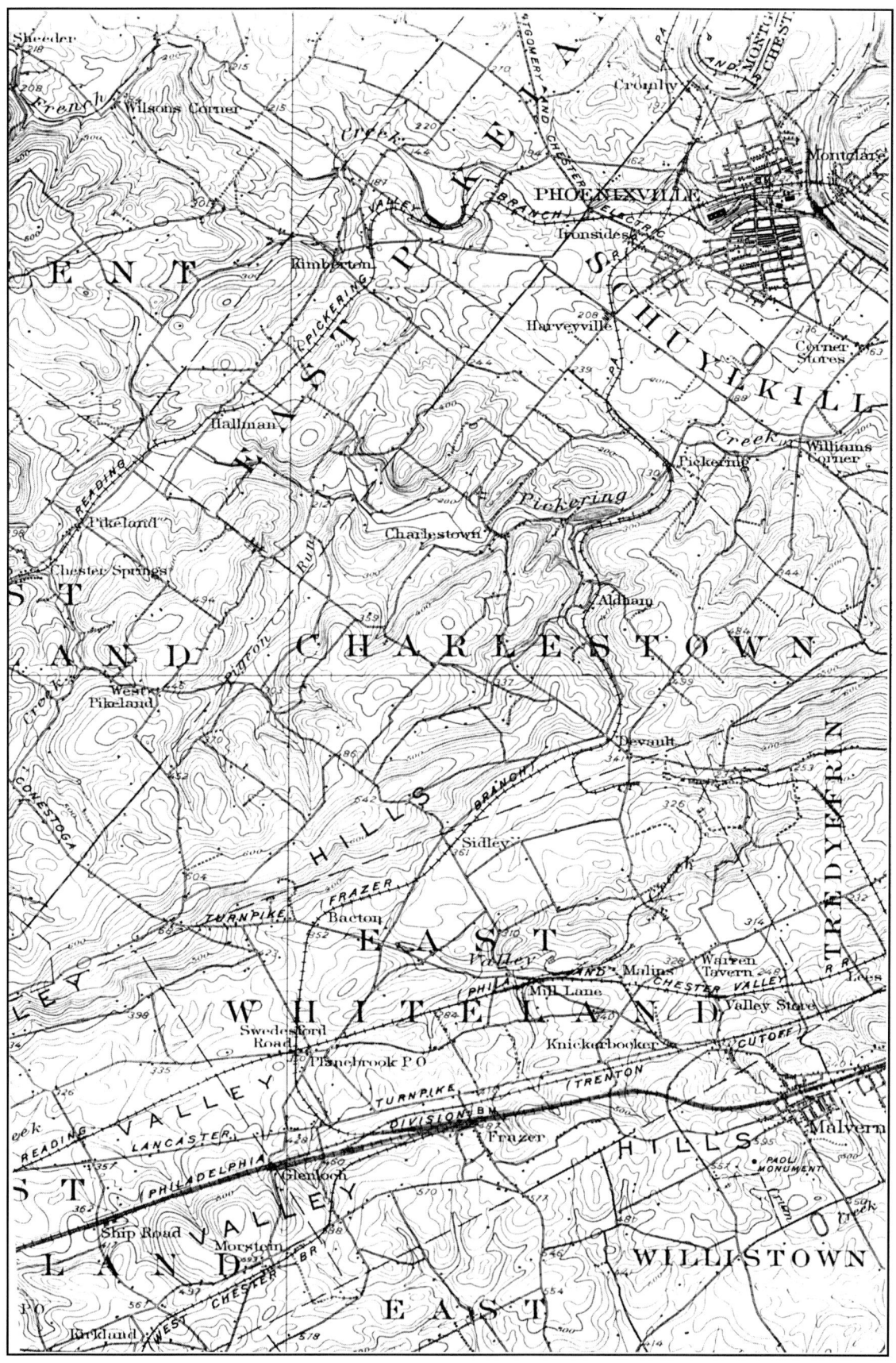

THE FRAZER BRANCH begins at Phoenixville on this long steel trestle, as shown in a 1917 view looking eastward toward the mill buildings. Built with iron girders in 1891, it was renewed in 1898 and in 1913 with steel. Overall it was made up of 32 deck spans totaling 1027 ft., consisting of 15 spans on the east approach, 1 span over French Creek, 1 one-half through span over the Reading Pickering Valley Branch and 15 spans on the west approach.

National Archives

TWO MILES to the south the line crosses over Pickering Creek and Route 29 on this 15-span deck plate girder trestle, known as the Buckwalter Road bridge. This was originally built in 1883 of iron and renewed in 1896 and in 1913 with steel. This 1917 view looks eastward. At one time a spur was located south of the bridge, serving an ice plant. The dam associated with the plant was washed out in the flood of 1902. This area is heavily wooded today and when driving on Route 29 the trestle suddenly looms out of the woods like a black monster.

National Archives

DEVAULT (originally Beaver's) station seems to be getting some repairs in this 1917 photo. It was originally constructed in 1897 to serve the small community.

National Archives

THE BIG GAMBLE

IN ORDER to continue out of Phoenixville westward up the Schuylkill Valley PRR had to tunnel through Black Rock Hill, under Fillmore Street. This view, dated 16 September 1894, looks westward through the tunnel, which at 813 ft. was less than half the length of the Reading's 1932-ft. bore to the north. Although PRR engineers had difficulty finding places to dump the waste material from both the cut and tunnel, the actual tunnel work was considerably less difficult that the Reading's arduous task 50 years earlier, which had required more than one contractor to finish.

Elmer Keinard/Glenn Cagle Collection

Historical Society of the Phoenixville Area

ONCE THROUGH the tunnel the line had easy going through the gently rolling terrain of the Schuylkill Valley. This bucolic early 20th Century view shows an eastbound Reading freight (with a predominance of anthracite hoppers) winding its way across a loop in the river, before it plunges into its own Black Rock tunnel into Phoenixville. In the background a line of cars on the PRR line sits on a siding above the hamlet of Cromby.

251

TRIUMPH III

Elmer Keinard/Glenn Cagle Collection

A CLOSER LOOK at Cromby in September 1925 shows the Philadelphia Electric Co. power plant constructed just west of Phoenixville. A curved yard is located to the left, serving the coal-fired facility. West of this area a short S-shaped track crosses the river to connect with the Reading main. Just west of that are the remains of a segment of the Schuylkill Canal, running west through Spring City to a point above the Vincent Dam.

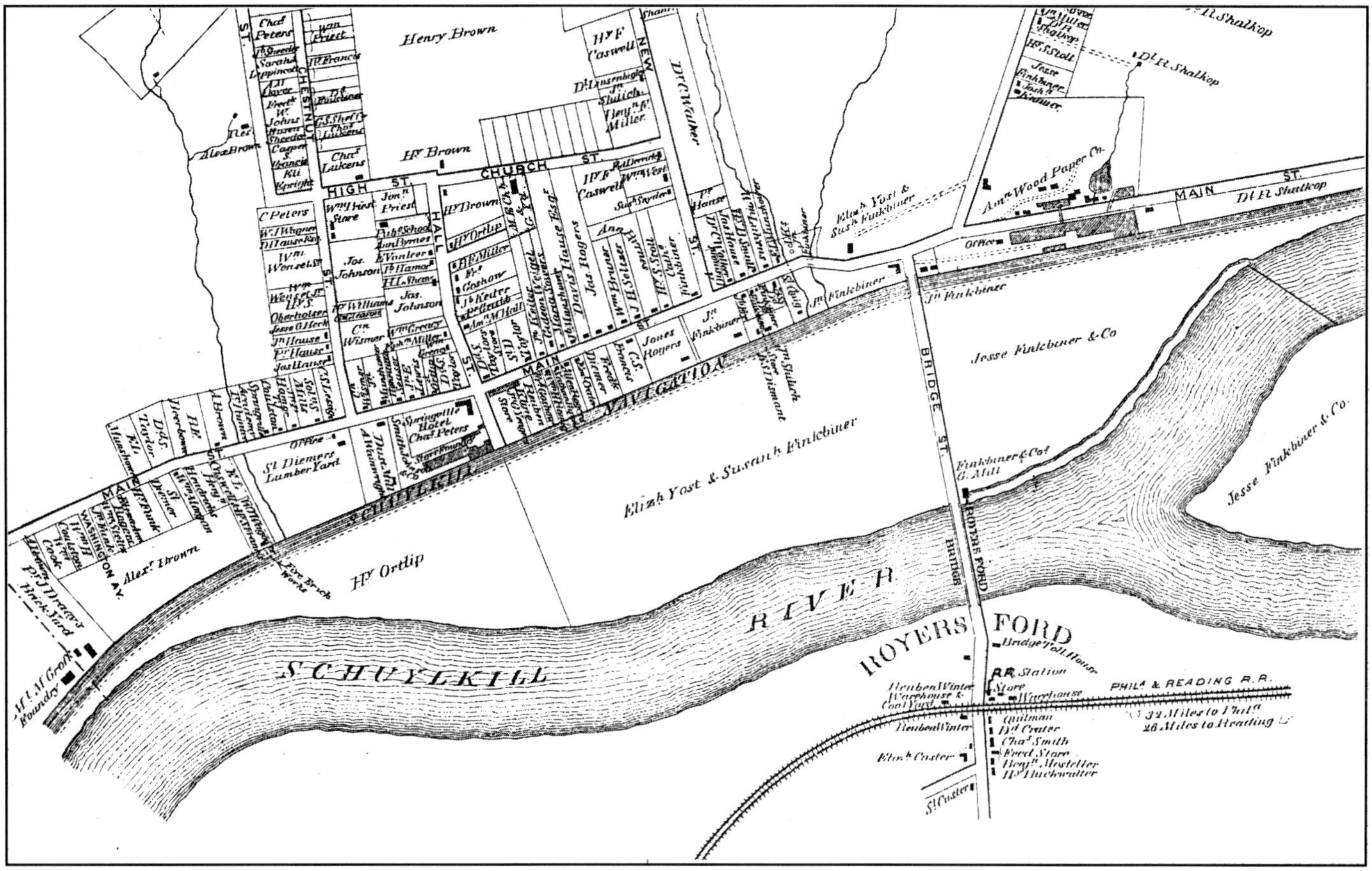

THE BIG GAMBLE

Historical Society of the Phoenixville Area

SPRINGVILLE and Royersford (the latter the residence of the author) on the Schuylkill River are shown on this map from Witmer's 1873 Atlas. Springville was first settled in 1837 on lands along the Schuylkill Canal, originally part of the old William Penn Grant. It was granted a charter 12 August 1867, and the name was changed to Spring City in March 1873. Note the clear orientation of the village area to the canal. The Reading line is already in place on the north side; the PRR right-of-way would later cross over the canal twice to enter the borough and then pass between the canal and the river on the south side, with a branch extending across the river to Royersford (earlier known as Royer's Ford).

THE SPRING CITY (MP 32.3) passenger depot and a small freight station (on the right) are shown in this early 1900s postcard view looking westward on the line. The passenger station was constructed in 1884 and a ladies' waiting room added in 1894; it was again enlarged in 1906. Note the detailing in the iron fence along the platform.

253

TRIUMPH III

THE SCHUYLKILL RIVER is normally placid, but was brought to record high flood levels in May of 1936. The flooding caused considerable damage in the Schuylkill Valley, but it doesn't seem to deter the boys from doing a little wading. One of them even has his Brownie camera to record the scene for posterity. Behind them is the freight station, with a single-sheathed boxcar on the track in front and the work cars beyond. The smaller section at the eastern end, built in 1907, is the same building shown in the early 1900s photo of the passenger depot; the addition and transfer platform were constructed in 1912.

Everett Rarich Collection

Spring-Ford Area Historical Society

IN 1891 the G.S. Bennet Co. built a factory on the hill above Spring City to manufacture window glass. PRR ran a siding from the freight station across Main Street and up along a small stream known as Goose Run to serve the factory. This photo of a high-stacked 0-4-0 is believed to be part of a work train near the factory during construction of the siding.

WEST OF SPRING CITY the short Royersford Branch cuts diagonally across the river to its namesake borough. This branch was built in 1892 in an effort to get a piece of the action where the Reading dominated in serving the local stove foundries and other industries. The half-through girder bridge shown here was constructed in 1902, replacing the original wooden Howe truss sections that were swept away in a flood.

National Archives

THE BIG GAMBLE

Spring-Ford Area Historical Society

THE STATION at Parker Ford (MP 35.1), named after an early river crossing, is a twin of the one at Mont Clare, although built several years later in 1897. It is shown here in a ca. 1910 view as passengers walk out to meet the westbound train.

Dave Cope / Ted Xaras Collection

WEST OF PARKER FORD the line crosses another section of the Schuylkill Canal at Fricks Lock (on a 126-ft through truss). The station (MP 36.8) is shown here in a 1940s view as G5 No. 5716 pauses to pick up two eastbound passengers. These stalwart units had the primary responsibility for passenger trains on the division and continued in service west of electrified territory until discontinuation of service in 1953.

AN L1 MIKADO, typical of heavy freight power used on the line after the bridges were reinforced, heads west through the station area on the same day. Class H9 and H10 Consolidations handled the way freights and beefy I1 Decapods drew helper assignments on the St. Clair grade north of Pottsville, but the Schuylkill Division was best known for the L1's on heavy freights during the steam years.

Dave Cope/Ted Xaras Collection

PRIDE OF THE VALLEY – The flagship *Anthracite Express*, led by E6s No. 1073, heads eastbound through a Christmas Card scene just east of Fricks Lock on 15 January 1939. At its peak this train provided parlor car service between Philadelphia and Wilkes-Barre.

Railroad Museum of Pennsylvania (PHMC)

THE BIG GAMBLE

THE LINE then curves northwest across the river over a four-span, 644-ft. wrought iron deck Pratt Truss built in 1884. This was known as Brooks Crossing (later Campbell's) shown in a ca. 1900 postcard view as a passenger train heads westward toward Pottstown. When the bridge was first constructed, the lowlands on the Chester County side were crossed on a 200-ft. trestle; this was later filled in and the stone abutment shown here was erected.

National Archives

HERE we see the recently completed replacement bridge in a 1917 view of another graceful concrete arch structure, reflected in the placid waters of the Schuylkill. This one was virtually identical to the one at Phoenixville.

Hagley Museum and Library

POTTSTOWN, formerly known as Pottsgrove, was named after John Potts, an early iron maker and prominent citizen who laid out the town in 1752 and then founded an iron works in 1791 on Manatawny Creek, at the western edge. It was also the site of early flour mills on the creek. The town subsequently became the location of several heavy industries, especially early foundries and rolling mills including the Potts Brothers Iron Works, Ellis & Lessig Iron Works, Pottstown Iron Company, Sotter Brothers, Inc. and the Warwick Iron Company.

This marvelous aerial drawing by noted 19th Century urban artist T. M. Fowler looks at Pottstown from the southeast in 1893. In the foreground the landscape is dominated by the large Pottstown Iron Company works. The PRR tracks run close to the river and the Reading line behind the mill; both served the large complex by providing raw materials and a means of shipping finished components. The PRR depot is located at the northern end of the Hanover Street truss bridge crossing the river. West of town the line crosses Manatawny Creek, originally on a seven-span, 207-ft. deck plate girder bridge.

AN EASTBOUND passenger train, with classy engine No. 402, pauses at Pottstown station (MP 40.3) to pick up patrons in an early 1900s postcard view, postmarked 1909.

THE BIG GAMBLE

POTTSTOWN was a commercial center requiring a fair-sized freight house as well, built in 1884. It is shown here in a 1917 view.

BLOCK SIGNALS on the Schuylkill Division were extended from Phoenixville to Mt. Carbon in 1907, and mechanical interlocking plus upper quadrant semaphores were installed starting in 1913. Interlocking machines were installed at several locations, including Pottstown. Here we see WO Tower in that borough, as it appeared in 1917.

WE'LL TAKE a closer look at a few of the companies that were part of the heritage of the iron and steel industry in Pottstown. The Pottsgrove Iron Works was one of the earliest rolling mills in the area. It was started in 1846 by Henry and David Potts, Jr., descendents of early ironmaker John Potts. It later became the Potts Brothers Iron Works and produced iron plates for Civil War ironclad ships. It continued under ownership of the Potts family until 1916, when it was sold and eventually closed. This ca. 1915 view looks north across the placid river at the mill, with WO Tower in the center alongside the PRR right-of-way.

259

THE WARWICK IRON CO. furnace was located west of the Manatawny Creek. It was founded by Jacob and Isaac Fegley, who developed a successful process for producing iron of a high degree of purity. It was leased to the Eastern Steel Company of Pottsville in 1912 and during World War I worked to full capacity, at one time blasting for 750 days straight! After the war it fell on hard times and was abandoned by the mid-20s. This ca. 1900 view of the Warwick Iron & Steel Company shows two blast furnaces, with a variety of railroad equipment in the foreground.

Historical Society of Pottstown

Hagley Museum and Library

In 1863 two pioneers in the iron industry, William Mintzer and John E. Wooten, built a rolling mill that subsequently became the Pottstown Iron Company. Mintzer was a Pottstown banker and Wooten was a shop foreman for the Reading RR. (Wooten later became head of the Reading Shops and developed the successful anthracite-burning locomotive firebox that bore his name.) In 1864 the firm was taken over by Edward Bailey and Joseph Potts, Jr., who obtained financing from Philadelphia capitalists to enlarge the mill. An anvil furnace was constructed, along with a nail plate mill and a nail factory that together employed as many as 1200 workers. In the 1890s the anvil furnace was dismantled and the plate mill converted into a puddling mill. In 1898 the Glasgow Iron Company leased the plant, operating it until 1928, when it was purchased by the McClintic-Marshall Company of Pittsburgh.

The first iron bridges manufactured in Pottstown were fabricated around 1872 in the old Reading Railroad shops. The business was operated by J. Dutton Steele & Son until 1877, when it was taken over by Cofrode & Saylor of Philadelphia. This firm prospered for a time, fabricating several of the bridges used by PRR in building its Schuylkill Division line. Shortly thereafter, however, it went into receivership, was operated briefly by Baird & Company as the Philadelphia Bridge Works, and then in January 1900 was also taken over by McClintic-Marshall (with financial backing from the Mellon family), which began to substantially enlarge the plant.

THE BIG GAMBLE

Hagley Museum and Library

IN 1915 McClintic-Marshall purchased additional property in the east end of Pottstown for the erection of Shop No. 2, which began on 22 November of that year. Fabrication of structural members was initiated a year later. Expansion continued with the erection of Shop No. 3, located east of Shop No. 1; this facility began operation on 14 January 1919. On 1 October 1928 ground was broken east of Shop No. 2 for construction of a 120 x 600-ft. assembly shop building for large bridge sections. The George Washington Bridge, New York, was the first major structure fabricated in this huge shop. In 1929 the old Pottstown Iron Company mill was reworked for the fabrication of welded joists and related components.

On 10 February 1931 McClintic-Marshall Company was acquired by the Bethlehem Steel Company, which operated it as a subsidiary until 1 February 1936, when the Pottstown plant became the Fabricated Steel Construction Division of the parent company. In addition to the George Washington Bridge, this facility, served by both PRR and the Reading for raw materials and shipment of large fabricated sections, constructed many major bridges, including the Bear Mountain Bridge, New York; the Golden Gate and San Francisco-Oakland Bay bridges in California; the Tacoma Narrows Bridge, Washington State; the Chesapeake Bay Bridge, Maryland, as well as several bridges on the Pulaski Skyway, New Jersey and the Pennsylvania and New Jersey Turnpikes. Steelwork for many large buildings was also fabricated by this plant, including the Metropolitan Insurance Company, Lincoln Building and City Bank-Farmers Trust, all in New York City; and the John Hancock Building, Boston.

This superb aerial photo shows the plant looking westward on 2 November 1931, with the large assembly shop in the foreground. By this time only a few of the early Pottstown Iron Co. mill buildings remain at the west end of the complex. The PRR tracks are on the left, the Reading on the right, both with small yards serving the plant.

National Archives

MOVING WEST of Pottstown, we encounter a small shelter of interesting design that served the hamlet of Stowe. It was built in 1887 and is shown here complete with stop sign in this 1917 view.

TRIUMPH III

THE STATION at Douglassville (MP 44.5), shown in an 1890s photo, was similar to the one at Manayunk. It was constructed when the line was built in 1884. Note the large post lamps and the freight platform.

Ted Xaras Collection

JUST WEST of Douglassville the line crossed the river again on another concrete arch bridge, this time of a somewhat different design. It was 627 ft. long, built in 1912, replacing a four-span, 656-ft. Pratt through truss constructed in 1884. It is shown here in a 1917 Valuation photo.

National Archives

AFTER CROSSING the river the line spanned another section of the Schuylkill Canal east of Monacy. This was an 89-ft. steel one-half through plate girder bridge built in 1911 and shown here in a 1917 view. This replaced a 100-ft. through truss constructed in 1884 when the line was built.

National Archives

262

THE BIG GAMBLE

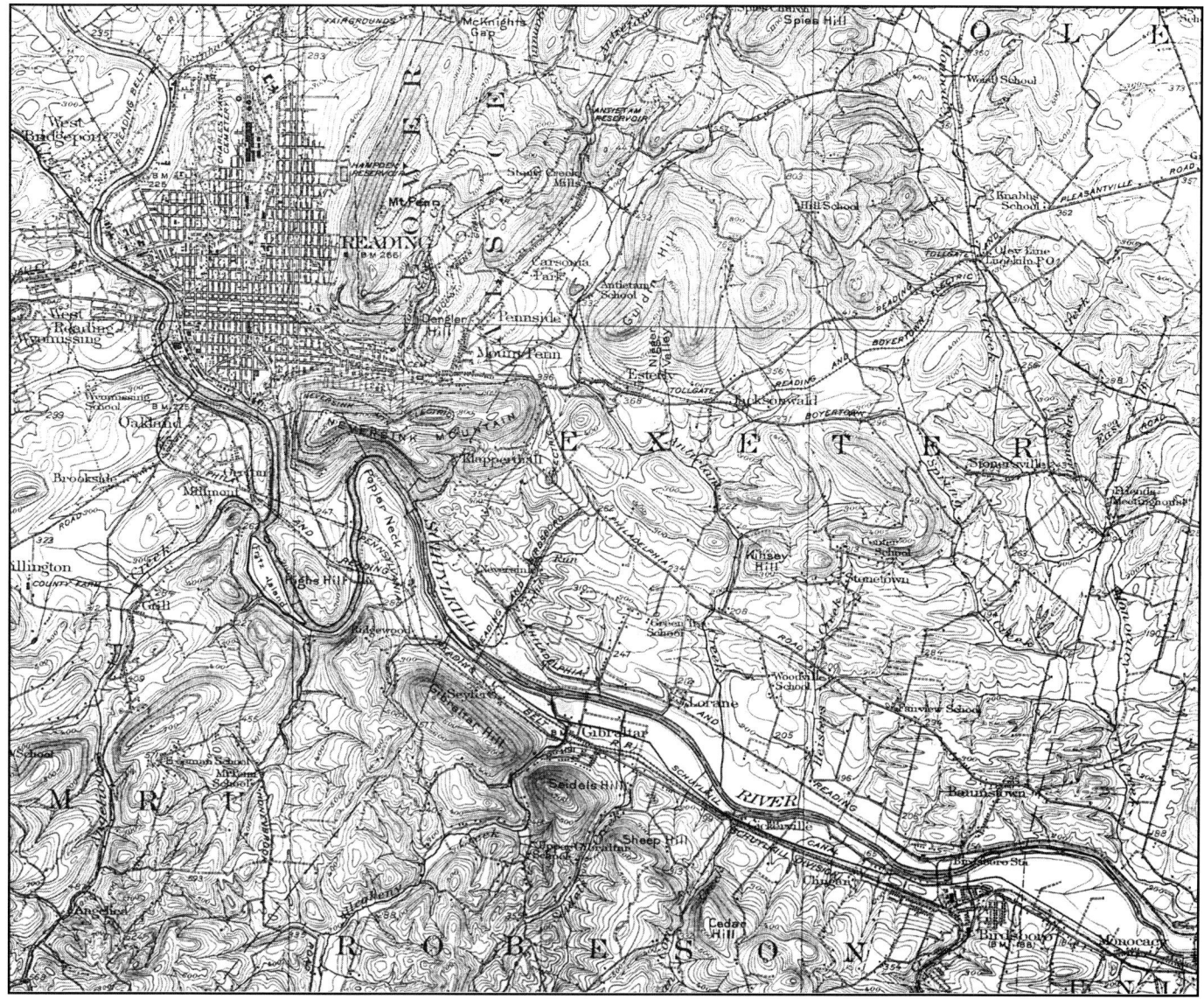

THE APPROACH to the borough of Reading up the Schuylkill Valley is shown here in a 1913 map. Starting at lower right, the Reading main runs along the north side of the river. On the south side a track extends across the river, connecting to the Wilmington & Northern Branch which runs southward through Coatesville. The Reading Belt line then runs along the south (west) bank around the borough. The PRR Schuylkill Division runs from Monacy through Birdsboro parallel to the Belt Line and then intertwining with it, crossing the river twice as it loops upon itself and then crossing the river a third time before entering Reading from the southwest. Note how Mount Penn and Neversink Mountain dominate the borough.

TRIUMPH III

Railroad Museum of Pennsylvania (PHMC)

BROOKE Interlocking in Birdsboro was a Reading tower that controlled the junction of the PRR Schuylkill Division with the former's Wilmington & Northern Branch that extended down through Coatesville. Here we see an eastbound PRR train making the turn and cutting across W&N trackage to head down the Schuylkill Valley ca. 1910. The yards and the wye connection leading across the river to the Reading main are in the background at right.

BIRDSBORO (MP 49.1) was named after Mark Bird, who began what became a flourishing iron business here. It was an important junction point and site of a small interchange yard with both the connector to the Reading mainline and the Wilmington & Northern Branch, which ran southward to Coatesville. The passenger station is shown here in a superb view shortly after it was built in 1887.

Ted Xaras Collection

THE BIG GAMBLE

National Archives

THE FREIGHT HOUSE in Birdsboro was also built in 1887, and extended in 1913. The town was the location of Eastern Steel Company, another Schuylkill Valley steel operation. This 1917 photo shows the other rail facilities that were constructed in the area. These were primarily Wilmington & Northern, as the main Reading station was across the river.

BEFORE REACHING the borough of Reading the line had to cross the river three times and the Schuylkill Canal again before finally reaching the station. At the time these Valuation photos were taken in 1917 PRR was in the process of replacing the first two bridges with concrete arches. This first bridge, at Popular Neck, shown here behind the concrete replacement, was an 852-ft., seven-span deck truss and girder structure built in 1884.

National Archives

Ted Xaras Collection

THE SECOND BRIDGE, also built in 1884, is shown in an 1880s photo looking westward. This one was slightly shorter, with six deck trusses plus a through plate girder span totaling 806 ft. This structure was known as the "Angelica" bridge because of its location near the outlet of Angelica Creek in an area then known as Orrton, south of Reading. The abutment for the parallel Reading Belt Line bridge is just visible at the extreme left; the P&R tracks extend from the Belt Line under the PRR girder span and across the river into an industrial area in the south end of the borough.

265

THE REPLACEMENT BRIDGE gives us a lesson in concrete arch construction. Not unlike masonry bridges, one needs to erect falsework and then build forms to support the poured concrete until it cures sufficiently to support its own weight. Note the temporary wooden pile trestle and trackage for the crane.

National Archives

THE THIRD CROSSING of the river (and also the beginning of the Union Canal to Middletown) finally puts PRR into the namesake borough of its archrival. This was a five-span, 728-ft. through truss and deck plate girder structure erected in 1884, and shown here in a 1917 view.

National Archives

ONCE ACROSS the river the line immediately spanned the Schuylkill Canal along the east bank. This was an 80-ft. through plate girder bridge built in 1884 and rebuilt as a steel structure in 1916, just the year before this picture was taken.

National Archives

THE BIG GAMBLE

THE BOROUGH of Reading, the county seat of Berks County, is located in a wide basin on the east bank of the Schuylkill River. Directly east of the borough is Mount Penn, named after the founder of the Commonwealth. It was laid out in 1748 by the Proprietary, although the settlers were largely German. It sits at the junction of the Schuylkill and the Union Canal to Middletown, the latter the first canal route surveyed in the U.S. Reading was the site of extensive hat manufacturing in early years, but later iron rolling, nail making, and iron and brass casting industries were established, along with the manufacture of farm implements. The borough also became the location of the legendary Reading Shops, where the large fleet of P&R steam locomotives was designed, erected and maintained.

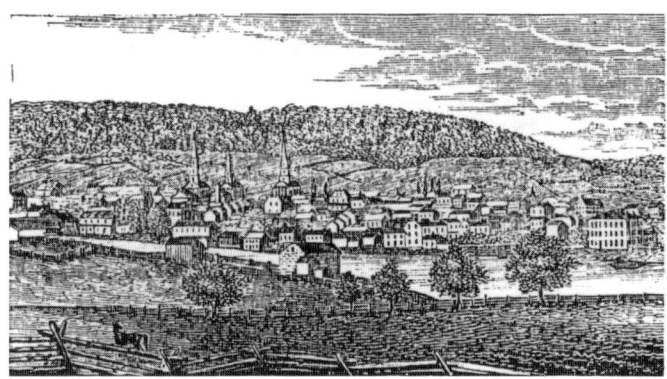

Hagley Museum and Library

READING also had several iron and steel plants. In 1836 Keim, Whitaker & Company built a rolling mill and nail factory along the river. On 12 August 1889 the Reading Iron Company was organized, taking over the plant and expanding it to eventually become the country's largest manufacturer of wrought iron pipe. The company operated two blast furnaces in Reading, along with over 300 puddle furnaces and 36 skelp mills. In 1919 it acquired the puddle mill, plate mill and nail factory of the George B. Lessig Company in Pottstown. Another early works in Reading was J. H. Steinbergh & Sons, which became the American Iron & Steel Manufacturing Company in 1899 and was taken over by Bethlehem Steel in 1917.

This view shows the Reading Iron Company plant on 30 September 1927, looking eastward across the river. It is served by both the Reading Lebanon Valley Branch cutting across the photo and the PRR Schuylkill Branch along the east side of the river at this point. The tracks on the west side, at the bottom of the photo, are the Reading Belt Line. The PRR depot is located at top center of the photo, above the east end of the arched Penn Street Bridge.

267

THE FIRST ENGINE into Reading on the Schuylkill Division was high-stacked No. 390, a Class D3 (old Class C) locomotive shown here with its proud crew and getting its valve gear lubricated in 1885. Perhaps the crew later was lubricated as well.

THE READING DEPOT, or should we say the PRR depot in Reading, was constructed in 1884-5. The 54 x 146-ft. brick structure is shown here in a view looking southward ca. 1890. The five-story building at the Penn Street end was the initial location of the Schuylkill Division Superintendent and general offices. It was certainly not as elaborate as the P&R facilities, but at least it showed the keystone flag in the heart of Reading territory.

THE BIG GAMBLE

Ted Xaras Collection

A LATER PHOTO, ca. 1910, shows an iron Whipple truss bridge has been constructed to carry Penn Street across the canal and Schuylkill River. This fascinating view looking northeast shows a later 4-4-0 moving passenger cars in the station area, as well as a trolley to West Reading passing overhead (several trolley runs terminated at the station). Note the weeds invading the canal bed.

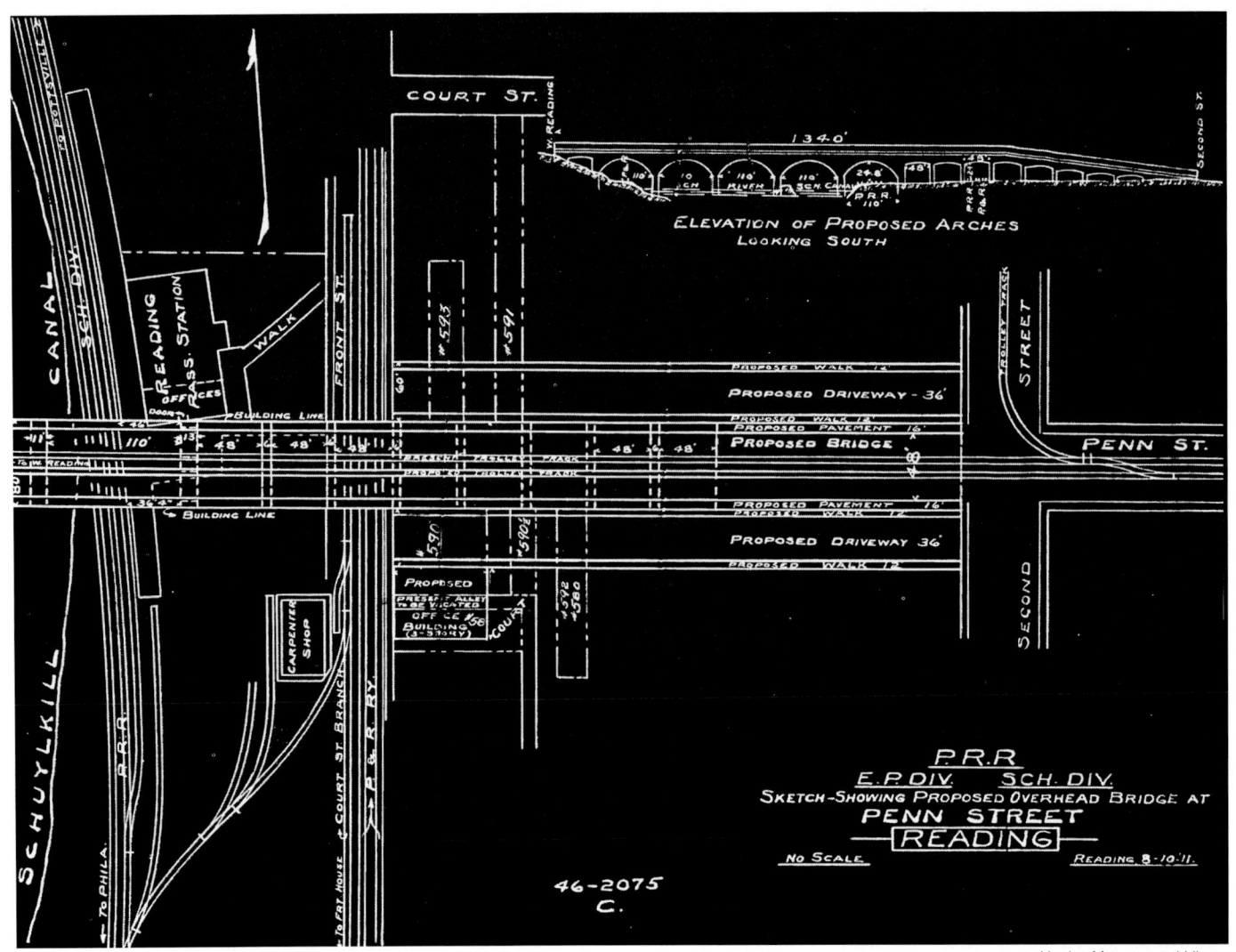

Hagley Museum and Library

IN 1911 Berks County proposed building a new concrete arch bridge on Penn Street from Second Street west over the P&R and PRR tracks, the canal and the river to West Reading. This necessitated modifications to the office end of the PRR passenger station, which interfered with construction of the bridge. The bridge was completed in 1912, and the Division offices were moved to a new site south of the bridge (shown on the diagram). Note the Court Street Branch extending southward to the freight house.

THE BIG GAMBLE

HERE WE MEET Atlantic No. 1600 again, this time at its destination in Reading and turned for its final southbound run to Philadelphia on 4 October 1953. The faithful are perhaps asking for a look in the cab. The locomotive is framed by the concrete arches of the Penn Street bridge.

Ted Xaras Collection

PRR SHOWED its presence in the namesake city of its rival with this nearly-new brick office building for division personnel, built in 1913 and shown here in 1917. Just so everyone got the message, a large keystone is emblazoned over the entrance.

National Archives

G5 NO. 1813 is being turned on the table, constructed in 1907, as the conductor and crew look on near the water tank in East Reading Yard ca. 1950.

Dave Cope/Ted Xaras Collection

271

National Archives

A SECOND combination station was located at Exeter Street, serving the north end of the borough. It was built in 1891 and is shown here in a 1917 view.

NORTH OF Belt Line Junction, where the Reading Belt Line rejoined the main, the PRR line crossed over the Reading tracks to Pottsville. This 1917 photo looks northward as a line of hoppers moves south underneath. This bridge was an 89-ft., one-half through plate girder originally built in 1885 and rebuilt in steel in 1913.

National Archives

National Archives

AS WE MOVE north of Reading the line runs along the east bank of the river through several small towns before curving to the northwest and crossing the river two more times before reaching Pottsville. The first town is Temple (MP 64.2), where the station was built in 1892. Note the window detailing shown in this 1917 photo.

THE BIG GAMBLE

NORTHWEST of Temple the Schuylkill Division crossed the outlet of Maiden Creek on a two-span, 132-ft. stone arch bridge, unusual for this line. It was built in 1891, replacing a Warren Truss constructed in 1885 and shown here in a 1917 view.

National Archives

HERE'S THE small station serving the village of Leesport (MP 67.7). This one, constructed in 1892 and shown here in a ca. 1910 photo, was an atypical design for the division with it's pagoda-like roof.

Ted Xaras Collection

THE PASSENGER STATION in the village of Shoemakersville (MP 71.7) is shown in a 1917 photo looking southward, with the freight station beyond. This structure, built in 1892, shares a similar design with several others in this section - the waiting room, rest rooms and ticket offices on the first floor and agent's living quarters on the large-dormered second floor. The community was named after the Shoemaker family, of whom Colonel George was an early miner and promoter of anthracite to a skeptical public, who considered it too hard to burn. They were both right.

National Archives

Ted Xaras Collection

HAMBURG (MP 76.8) is a town on the east bank of the Schuylkill River just below Blue Mountain, the first of the Appalachian ridges. The valley area is fertile and well cultivated. North of the town the Schuylkill Division tracks cross over the river and then both the railroad and the river slice through the mountain. This ca. 1908 postcard view of the 1892 station looks southward.

National Archives

HERE WE HAVE another bridge under construction, a 563-ft., seven-span deck plate girder and through plate girder structure being rebuilt during June 1917. This one crosses the river just north of the village of Hamburg.

THE BIG GAMBLE

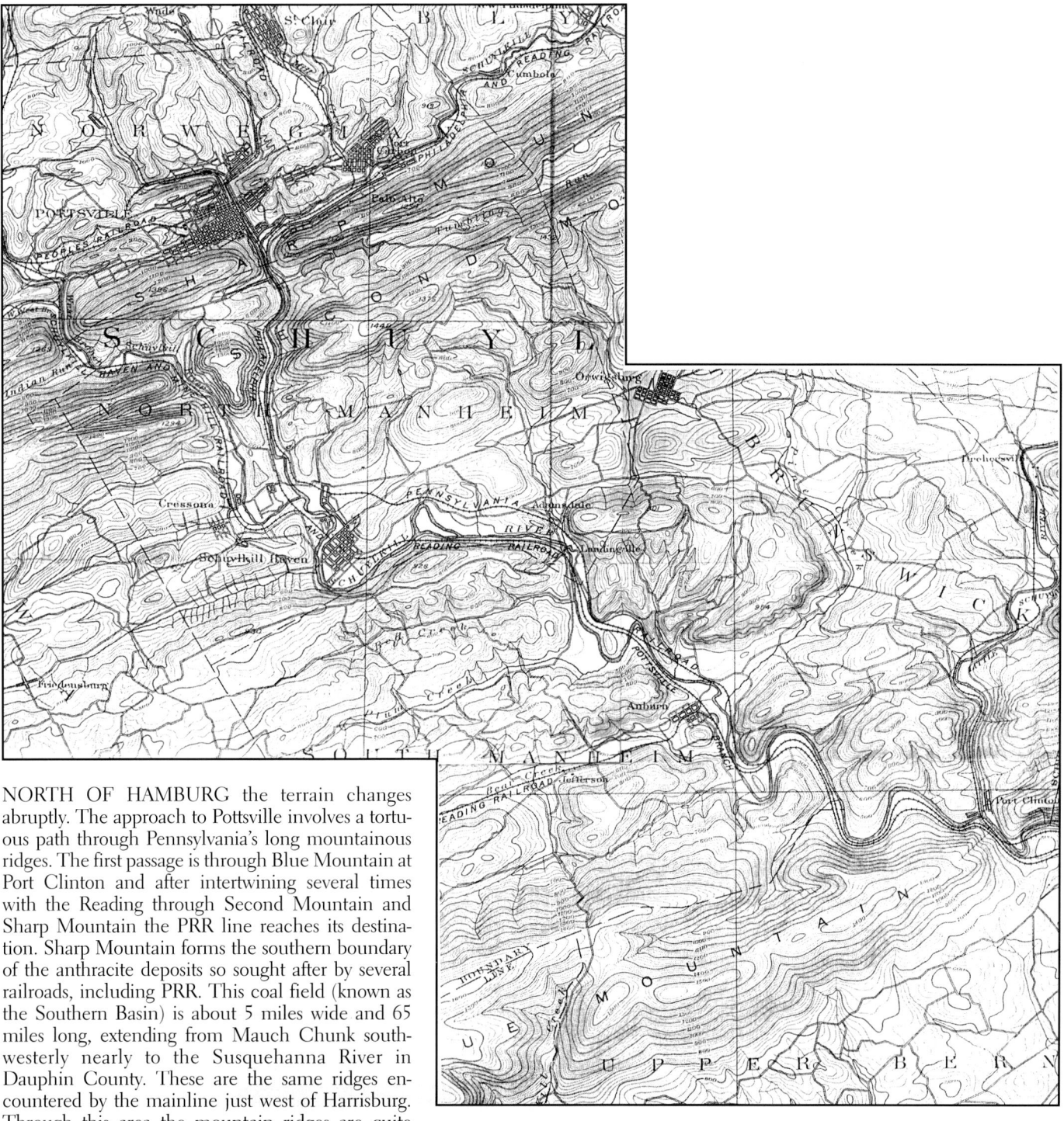

NORTH OF HAMBURG the terrain changes abruptly. The approach to Pottsville involves a tortuous path through Pennsylvania's long mountainous ridges. The first passage is through Blue Mountain at Port Clinton and after intertwining several times with the Reading through Second Mountain and Sharp Mountain the PRR line reaches its destination. Sharp Mountain forms the southern boundary of the anthracite deposits so sought after by several railroads, including PRR. This coal field (known as the Southern Basin) is about 5 miles wide and 65 miles long, extending from Mauch Chunk southwesterly nearly to the Susquehanna River in Dauphin County. These are the same ridges encountered by the mainline just west of Harrisburg. Through this area the mountain ridges are quite steep, rising from 800-1200 feet almost vertically, with the Schuylkill River or its tributaries at the bottom. Layers of hard conglomerate rock alternate with soft red shale, which decomposes and falls into the river (and onto the railroads) below. The Reading line to Tamaqua branches to the right at Port Clinton and follows the Little Schuylkill northeastward. Both lines then wind their way through the valley, crossing the river and each other several times on the way toward Pottsville. North of Pottsville the line bends several times and passes through the 750-ft. St. Clair Tunnel.

TRIUMPH III

A FAN TRIP led by a trio of E7's winds its way up the Schuylkill Valley in June 1955. We believe this is Port Clinton, where the Reading line to Tamaqua splits off to follow the Little Schuylkill, just before both main tracks slice through the gap in Blue Mountain, seen in the background.

I. Cusick/Herbert H. Harwood, Jr. Collection

SOUTHEAST of Auburn the PRR line crosses over the river and the Reading once more. This bridge was a 473-ft. structure, consisting of five deck plate girder spans and a through Pratt Truss built in 1910. This view looks west along the Reading tracks.

National Archives

AUBURN (MP 84.8) is the next stop on the Schuylkill Division, showing a station of slightly different design, built in 1887. A freight house was constructed in Auburn in 1910 and a 35,000-gal. water tank added the following year. This 1917 view looks northward.

National Archives

THE BIG GAMBLE

HALF WAY between Auburn and Adamsdale the line crosses the river again, this time on a 255-ft. concrete bridge built in 1913 and shown here in 1917. This bridge is similar to the one west of Douglassville. Note the stone abutment from an earlier bridge.

National Archives

JUST BELOW Adamsdale (MP 88.0) the Reading follows the river in a large S-turn, while the PRR line takes an easier alignment (but with steeper gradients). Here we see the passenger station, also built in 1887, with the freight house in the background. This 1917 view looks southward. Note the interesting order board.

National Archives

AT THE WESTERN END of the S-curve is aptly named Schuylkill Haven (MP 90.6), a principal site for shipping coal, both by canal and later railroad. It is located in a narrow valley providing the only area of tillable land in mountainous Schuylkill County. This station, constructed in 1887, is shown in a 1917 view looking southward, with the village located to the east. It is almost identical to the one at Hamburg except that it is built on the side of the hill where PRR was forced to build its right-of-way.

National Archives

277

Ted Xaras Collection

PRR MAINTAINED a shop facility for the division at Mt. Carbon, a small town south of Pottsville nestled between Second and Sharp Mountains. The complex was originally built along the river in the late 1880s and expanded with a sand house and 75-ft. turntable in 1907 and rebuilt water tank in 1913. This marvelous 1890s photo shows a collection of early freight cars, bobber cabooses (cabin cars?) and the original 60-ft. turntable. Note the double-track covered bridge connecting the PRR and the Reading tracks on the west bank of the river.

THE BIG GAMBLE

Ted Xaras Collection

BLACK DIAMONDS – A string of early hoppers loaded with anthracite is lined up in the yards at Mt. Carbon, awaiting shipment southward. Many more empties await to be sent to the mines for loading in this 1890s view looking northward.

JUST SOUTH of Pottsville the PRR line crosses over the Reading Schuylkill Valley line, which turns sharply northeastward. The first bridge is a lacy through Pratt Truss built in 1886. This 1917 view looks southward above a line of hoppers on the Reading tracks.

National Archives

JUST TO THE NORTH of the Pratt Truss is a more mundane 61-ft. deck plate girder bridge, also over the Reading tracks. This one was constructed in 1886 and rebuilt in 1916, a year before the photo was taken.

National Archives

Ted Xaras Collection

JUST BEFORE ENTERING the center of Pottsville the line crosses over the Schuylkill River one last time, as it turns northeastward away from the borough. This 1890s view shows the early deck truss over the river to the Orchard section of town.

THE BIG GAMBLE

THE TRUSS was later replaced with a 68-ft. concrete arch span, shown here in a 1917 Valuation photo.

National Archives

POTTSVILLE, located on the lower slope of Sharp Mountain, is the major center of the anthracite coal trade for the area. Schuylkill County, at the peak of anthracite production, contained an extensive network of canals and later railroads to ship out the black diamonds. There were hundreds of miles of trackage, both above and below ground level. As part of its role serving the mining industry, Pottsville was also the center of manufacture of stationary steam engines and other heavy machinery, including some used in the iron works in Phoenixville.

Pottsville was named for the German John Pott, no relation to John Potts of Pottstown, although both were early ironmakers. The settlement grew rapidly after the discovery of anthracite in 1825, resulting in a rapid influx of speculators and entrepreneurs. This early rendering shows Sharp Mountain rising above the town, with a portion of Second Mountain behind it on the left, and the gap between through which the Schuylkill River (and the railroads) pass.

PRR BUILT a substantial, and modestly ornate, stone and brick passenger station in Pottsville (MP 94.7), evidently wanting to impress the industrious local citizenry. One suspects that the real reason was to compete with the Reading's equally ambitious – and similarly underutilized – depot designed by Frank Furness. This structure, most likely by W. Bleddyn Powell, was constructed in 1886 and is shown here as it appeared when new.

Ted Xaras Collection

CONSOLIDATION No. 1151 backs a local up the Minersville Branch during the 1940s. The 7-mile branch serving three coal mines was completed on 1 August 1892. Note the string of hoppers behind the X29 boxcar.

H.P. Albrecht/Ted Xaras Collection

AFTER PASSING THROUGH the St. Clair tunnel, the line climbed a stiff 3.1 percent grade (the steepest on the branch, requiring helpers) cut into the hillside above Mill Creek. At Darkwater it crossed the valley on a 530-ft. long trestle constructed in 1886-7, shown here in an early 1950s view, with a fantrip utilizing Reading equipment rolling across.

Lewis L. Hoy/Herbert H. Harwood, Jr. Collection

THE BIG GAMBLE

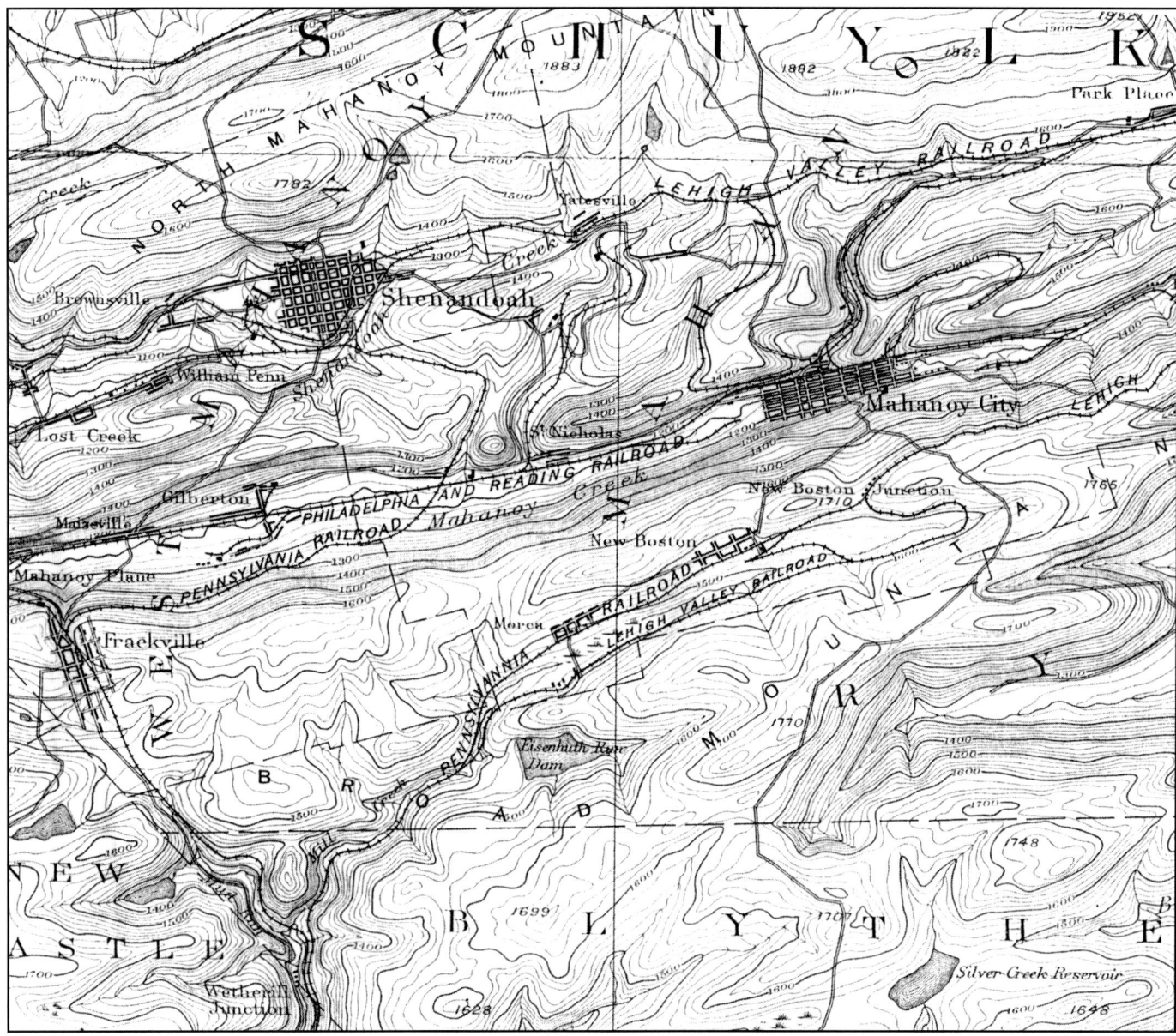

THE FINAL DESTINATION for the Schuylkill Division was finally achieved at New Boston Junction (later called Newton) at MP 105.5, where it connected with the Lehigh Valley Railroad. This connection was made by the acquisition of the Pottsville & Mahonoy RR, which had a maximum grade of 3.1% and a 530-ft. trestle bridging Mill Creek. In addition a line to the Susquehanna fields was opened up in 1887 by obtaining trackage rights over the Lehigh Valley to Tomhickon, where it connected with the North and West Branch RR. This area was rife with rail lines to the mines and collieries, tapping the rich anthracite deposits. Note the Minersville Branch extending to the northwest. Also note the Mahonoy Plane, controlled by the Reading, which hauled coal cars up the steep valley slope.

Chapter 5
Tidewater Saga

The High Line, Delaware Extension and Port Facilities

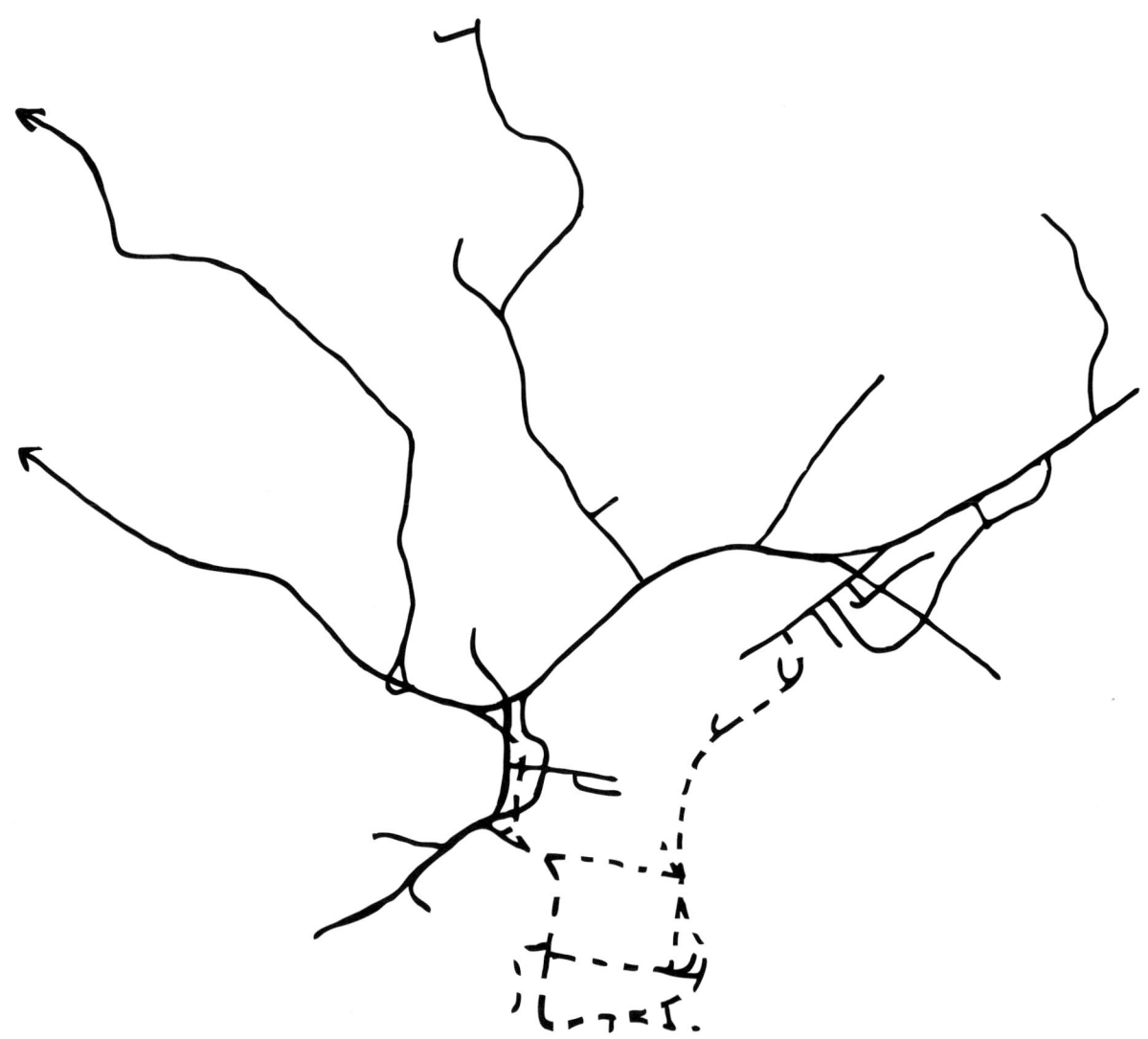

THE LAYOUT OF rail lines serving the South Philadelphia port facilities as of 1898 is shown in this USGS map. The Philadelphia, Wilmington & Baltimore line extends along Washington Avenue. Farther south is the B&O Delaware Branch and below that the PRR Greenwich Branch. The Girard Point Branch runs to that location, and the Schuylkill River Branch Extension continues from there to the Navy Yard on League Island. This map predates the construction of the West Philadelphia Elevated Line, requiring use of the Junction RR (or the Schuylkill River Branch, constructed in 1880) and the Grays Ferry Bridge for access to the terminal facilities.

Even before it had acquired the State Works, PRR had applied to the Pennsylvania Legislature for the right to build a line to the Delaware River (on the east side of the City) from some point on the Columbia Railroad, and this was approved 18 April 1856. After delays caused by both the Panic of 1857 and the prolonged and arduous negotiations to take over the State Works, PRR was "authorized to select the most eligible location on the Delaware River for a terminal depot, to be reached by *locomotive steam power* [italics added], and to cause the extension of the road to the said river to be completed at the earliest practical period." Following considerable internal debate over the location, PRR in 1859 agreed upon a site at the foot of Washington Avenue, just north of the old Navy Yard. This was at the strong urging of John Edgar Thomson, who saw the extension as a way to get around the delays and cost of hauling freight by horse through crowded city streets

To improve freight traffic flow through West Philadelphia, the Schuylkill River Branch to Arsenal was constructed in 1880, bypassing the Junction RR. A new bridge across the Schuylkill River was constructed to this Schuylkill Arsenal and the Delaware Extension (as it came to be known) put into operation on 27 January 1862. According to the 1861 Annual Report, "Its construction was not undertaken a day too soon," because of the delays in passage over the city tracks via horsepower. The following year a grain elevator "for the staple of the West" was constructed at the foot of Washington Avenue, and the Point Breeze Branch to the City Gas Works (for delivery of coal) and other terminal facilities were completed, for an expenditure of a half-million dollars.

The line across to Greenwich on the Delaware River was constructed during the period 1863-66. In 1871 at PRR's request the City widened Delaware Avenue along the riverfront, allowing a double-track line to be built to serve the piers on one side and warehouses on the other. In 1873-4 the line along the river was extended northward to McKean and Dock Streets. Additions to other port facilities were made in 1872-3, including expanded coal docks at Greenwich, provision for the growing petroleum trade and a "commodious" new freight house on Delaware Avenue at Dock Street. The latter was opened on 10 August 1874 for through freight, replacing the facility at 13th and Market (local freight was now handled at a depot at 15th and Market). The Dock Street terminal was expanded in 1881.

In 1875 PRR acquired the old Navy Yard along the Delaware River south of Washington Avenue, at Southwark, which added about 28 acres of land (including 5 acres under water for deepwater wharves). Connecting tracks from this site to the Delaware Extension were laid, and in 1879 a freight shed and three new piers were added.

On 5 May 1876 the Legislature authorized the River Front RR to connect the Delaware Extension at Dock Street with the Kensington Avenue terminus of the P&T RR., provided approval was granted by the City; this was obtained on 31 May 1877. This line was planned to run up Columbia Avenue, but local residents – not to be outdone by their rural counterparts on the mainline – strenuously objected, leading to riots, many injuries and even the deaths of three policemen! PRR wisely chose another route, connecting with the P&T at Lehigh Avenue. The line was constructed jointly with the Reading ... however, when it was finally completed in 1882 it was leased to PRR on 1 May of that year. It was formally merged into PRR on 1 April 1903, forming the Delaware Avenue Branch and completing the loop of freight trackage around the City.

Construction of the Girard Point Branch took place in 1874. As part of an 1873 agreement with the newly-formed International Navigation Company, a new terminal was constructed at Girard Point with warehouses and grain elevators capable of handling a large tonnage of grain. On 1 April 1881 PRR formed the Girard Point Storage Company to take over the river terminal facilities of the International Navigation Company in Philadelphia and to improve the property by construction of an additional elevator. On 28 April 1881 the elevator burned and had to be completely rebuilt ... this was completed by July of the following year. PRR subsequently took over this company and its facilities in 1917.

The Schuylkill River Branch Extension was built in 1900, actually an extension of the Girard Point Branch whose primary purpose was to serve the League Island Navy Yard located at the southern tip of the City. A second track was added in 1917.

In 1904 an innovative connection was completed between the main freight yards in West Philadelphia and the Delaware Extension, eliminating the need to use the passenger main and the Junction Railroad for that purpose. The West Philadelphia Elevated Branch or "The High Line," as it quickly came to be known, was a double-track viaduct arching over the yards on the west side of the Schuylkill River and connecting with both the east-west and north-south mainlines on the north (at Mantua Junction) with the PB&W main southward and the Delaware Extension via Arsenal Bridge. This impressive structure facilitated the movement of eastbound freights, especially coal trains from Enola Yard, directly onto the Delaware Extension to reach the port facilities without interfering with other traffic. The area in West Philadelphia would continue to experience many changes, as we have seen, but through them all, heavy freights – and priority Army-Navy game passenger extras – would move unimpeded to their destination over this line. It was a masterpiece of railroad engineering.

For some years PRR had embarked on a program of grade crossing elimination all along the line and including within the Philadelphia city limits, both from a safety standpoint and to facilitate traffic flow. In 1913 the City decided that the remaining grade crossings on the Delaware Extension and the east-west PB&W and B&O trackage would need to be eliminated. Under an agreement signed on 23 March 1914 (between the City and PRR, PB&W and B&O) the PB&W line along Washington Avenue was to be elevated and the Delaware Extension and the B&O trackage abandoned in favor of a new jointly-operated line running south along the Schuylkill River and then east from the Navy Yard to the Delaware riverfront. New yards were to be constructed for both companies under a jointly-financed plan. The joint line was constructed – and then the City's dollars dried up. PB&W remained at grade, and the Delaware Extension across town continued, used jointly by PRR and B&O. After World War I, work on this project was finally resumed.

During the prewar period, additional improvements were made. A new pier and grain elevator were constructed at Girard Point. In 1917-18, PRR built two branch lines to serve the intense wartime activity occurring at the shipyards on Hog Island and other points on the Schuylkill and Delaware riverfronts. These came to be known as the 60th Street and Philadelphia & Chester branches. In 1928 a new 2,000,000 cu. ft. cold-storage warehouse was built at Oregon and Delaware Avenues. This, along with an adjacent produce terminal opened in 1925, gave PRR significantly-improved facilities for handling fresh food into the city.

The $3 million projected expansion of the South Philadelphia freight terminal was finally completed in 1942, in time to handle World War II tonnage. Work on this project had started more than a decade earlier during the Improvements, but was suspended in 1931. A new Greenwich receiving and classification yard was built, southeast of what was then called Municipal Stadium (later John F. Kennedy Stadium).

In a startling new venture, the first shipload of iron ore from Peru arrived at PRR's newly opened ore pier at Greenwich Point in South Philadelphia on 19 March 1954. Requiring $10 million and two years to complete, the facility gave PRR one of the largest tidewater ore unloading operations in the country. When built initially it had capacity to unload two ships simultaneously at the rate of 3600 tons per hour, with provision for expansion to handle four ships at 10,800 tons per hour. Hopper cars were loaded with ore from the ships via a conveyer and then moved to Greenwich Yard for makeup into trains for westbound movement to the steel centers, replacing iron ore from the depleted Misabi ranges.

In 1957, as part of PRR's efforts in trailer-on-flatcar technology, a TrucTrain terminal was constructed in the port yard area and expanded in 1962. This facility was the beginning of intermodal capability in Philadelphia, which expanded considerably under Conrail and is due for further growth.

It had taken over a century, but Thomson's vision of Philadelphia as a major eastern port city had finally been accomplished.

TRIUMPH III

Railroad Museum of Pennsylvania (PHMC)

THE WEST PHILADELPHIA Elevated Line or "High Line," was part of A.J. Cassatt's strategic plan outlined in the 1902 Improvements program. The overall objective of this massive endeavor was to facilitate the handling of through freight traffic between Pittsburgh and New York City, as well as into the yards in South Philadelphia. The High Line, although much less extensive than the other components, thus ranked up there with the Low-Grade Line and the Trenton Cutoff (described in *Triumph II*) that were both designed to not only handle more tonnage but to handle it more expeditiously and thus *more economically*. The 2.3-mile, double-tracked line extends from ZOO Junction, with connections to the classification yards and New York freight tracks, and runs south to Arsenal Bridge, affording freight trains from the north and west direct access to the Delaware Extension and Greenwich Yard, thus removing this traffic from the heavily congested West Philadelphia yards. There is also a connection to the southbound main. This superb aerial photo looking southward ca. 1953 shows the line threading its way above the coach yards, past 30th Street Station (with its recently expanded lower-level trackage) and the Post Office and then curving onto Arsenal Bridge in the distance. Construction of 30th Street Station resulted in elimination of Schuylkill River Branch trackage.

National Archives

THE ELEVATED PORTION is 7,000 ft. long and reaches a maximum height of 42 ft. The upper end of the line was constructed on a heavy masonry viaduct - brick arches on stone piers. This 1917 photo looking southward captures a late 19th century coach on a siding alongside the massive structure, near Spring Garden Street.

National Archives

THE BRIDGE over Chestnut Street, typical of several structures over city streets extending to West Philadelphia, is depicted here in a 1917 photo with an eastbound trolley headed toward the downtown area. Note the keystone on the bridge, strategically located so street traffic would be reminded of PRR's presence.

THE REMAINDER of the High Line consists of a steel viaduct – deck plate girder spans (and a few truss sections) on steel piers. This 1917 view looks northward.

A FREIGHT led by GG1 4837 rumbles southward atop the High Line on 17 May 1959. The West Philadelphia steam heating plant was constructed in 1929 to provide steam not only to 30th Street Station but also across the river to Suburban Station. It dominates the skyline on the left, while members of the Tuscan Red fleet stand ready in the coach yard below.

TIDEWATER SAGA

WE NOW MOVE south of the Market Street area. This map from the 1888 City Atlas shows us both the lesser-known PW&B trackage in West Philadelphia (note the old West Chester & Philadelphia depot and shops – see Chapter 6) as well as the Schuylkill River branch (labeled the Southern Extension) curving across the river to the Delaware Extension. This line was constructed in 1880 from Haverford Avenue to Arsenal to provide a freight bypass of the Junction RR. The United States Arsenal on the east bank gives the bridge and tower their name. Woodland Cemetery (left) is the burial site of many 19th Century Captains of Industry, including PRR President John Edgar Thomson (see *Triumph II*).

Ted Xaras Collection

TRIUMPH III

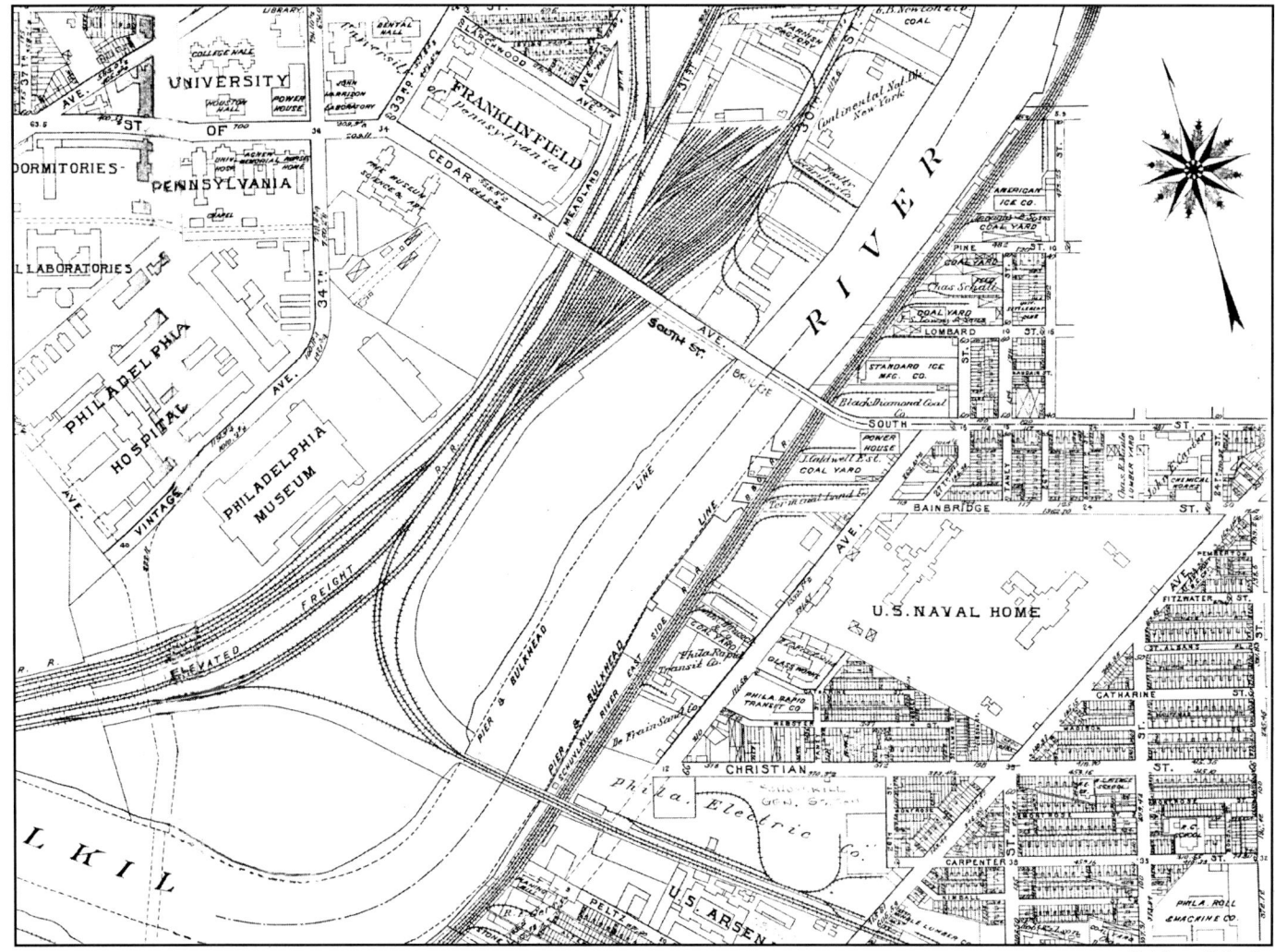

Ted Xaras Collection

THE 1910 ATLAS shows us not only extensive yard trackage development in the South Street (Cedar Avenue) area, but also the addition of the West Philadelphia Elevated Freight Line (which came to be known as the High Line). This critical trackage connected both to the Delaware Extension and the mainline south, enabling freights to move from the east-west or north-south mainline onto either of these lines without passing through the congested West Philadelphia Yards. The Almshouse has become the Philadelphia Hospital.

TIDEWATER SAGA

A WESTBOUND Conrail freight moves across Arsenal Bridge and onto the north leg of the wye on 2 November 1998. The north leg joins the main at CP FIELD (named after the nearby University of Pennsylvania athletic field), while the south leg junction retains the PRR name CP ARSENAL.

(below) ARSENAL BRIDGE provided a critical link between the north-south main via the Schuylkill River Branch (and later the West Philadelphia Elevated line) onto the Delaware Extension. The first permanent bridge at this location, known as the Newkirk Viaduct (see page 333) was constructed in 1837-8 by the PW&B, allowing horse-drawn railcars to move across to city trackage at Broad and Washington Streets. This was replaced by the structure shown here, constructed in 1861 as a three-span iron bridge on stone piers, with a center pivoting draw span. This 1860s photo, looking eastward toward South Philadelphia, captures the lacy elegance of cast-iron bridge construction. Buildings of the U.S. Arsenal are on the right. Note the early ball signal.

E.P. Alexander Archive/Ted Xaras Collection

THE BRIDGE was rebuilt as shown here in 1885-6, most likely in wrought iron. It consisted of nine deck truss spans overall: three on the west approach extending 320 ft., a 192-ft. draw span and five spans totaling 320 ft. on the east approach. This view looks eastward across the placid Schuylkill River in 1917. Looming in the background we see the stacks of the Philadelphia Electric Schuylkill Generating Station which provided power for the initial electrification of Broad Street Station, West Philadelphia and the Main Line.

National Archives

Ted Xaras Collection

WE ARE STANDING along the Delaware Extension looking south at the crossing of the PW&B, which extends east along Washington Avenue to the left and westward across Arsenal Bridge to the right. This rare 1880s photo shows the classy tower guarding the grade crossing. The sign behind the tower advertises Reilly Siding & Storage, with "The Best Facilities."

TIDEWATER SAGA

Ted Xaras Collection

A FEW BLOCKS south we see Class B6sa 0-6-0 No. 544 working the Delaware Extension near Reed Street ca. 1950. These locomotives were ideal for heavy switching duties in the port area during the steam era.

THE NEXT TWO photos give us a glimpse of the then "far south side" of Philadelphia as it was ca. 1890. This first view looks southwestward at the grade crossing and junction of the Point Breeze Branch, which extended from the Delaware Extension, and the B&O Schuylkill East Side Railroad freight branch. The B&O tower seems a bit mundane compared to the elegant Victorian PRR structures. In the background of this photo is the Point Breeze Gas Works, later the United Gas Improvement Company. Tank farms of the Atlantic Refining Company would later populate the area beyond the tower and along the Schuylkill River.

Ted Xaras Collection

MOVING FARTHER SOUTH on the Delaware Extension, we come to the B&O freight branch again at today's 25th and Wolf Streets. This ca. 1890 photo looks north, with a lamp black factory on the left and another plain B&O tower on the right. At this time the square street grid pattern was just being laid out, although most of the property boundaries bore more relation to the geography rather than the grid.

MOVING STILL FARTHER south to Girard Point, near the confluence of the Schuylkill and Delaware Rivers, we are looking at the early Elevator A (left) and B (right) of the Girard Point Storage Company. This company was formed by PRR in 1881 to take over operations of the International Navigation Company. This ca. 1900 view looks southwestward between the piers and the Back Channel, which ran between the mainland and League Island.

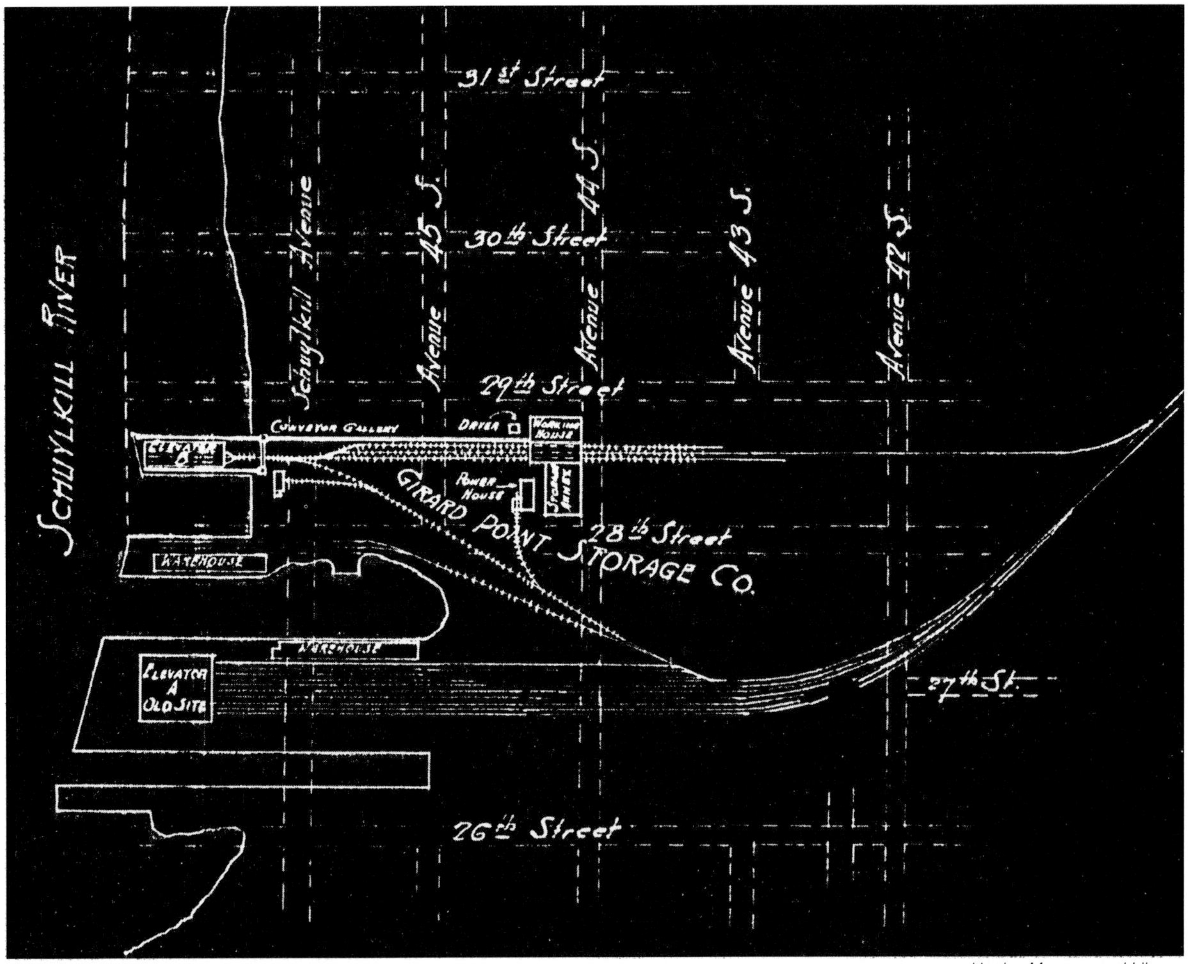

Hagley Museum and Library

IN NOVEMBER 1911 PRR proposed the construction of a new 1 million bushel grain elevator at Girard Point. The cost estimate was $760,000 for the concrete structure (in the center of the diagram). This was the plan preferred over repair of the old elevators or construction of the new elevator farther east at Greenwich Point because of the high cost of river dredging and building new yards at that location. Note that North is to the right on this diagram.

Hagley Museum and Library

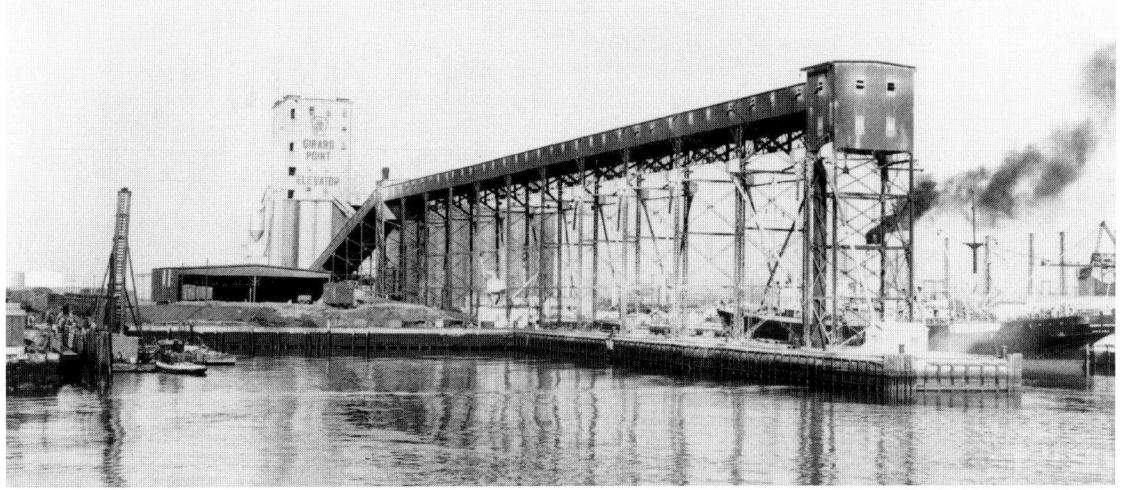

THE NEW ELEVATOR, shown here looking north ca. 1950, is located 200 ft. inland from the dock. Grain is delivered to the ships for export via the conveyor gallery containing four belts, each with a capacity of 15,000 bushels per hour. Ships can be loaded on both sides of the dock. The total complex includes 177 reinforced circular tanks and 143 interstice tanks with a combined capacity of 2,225,000 bushels.

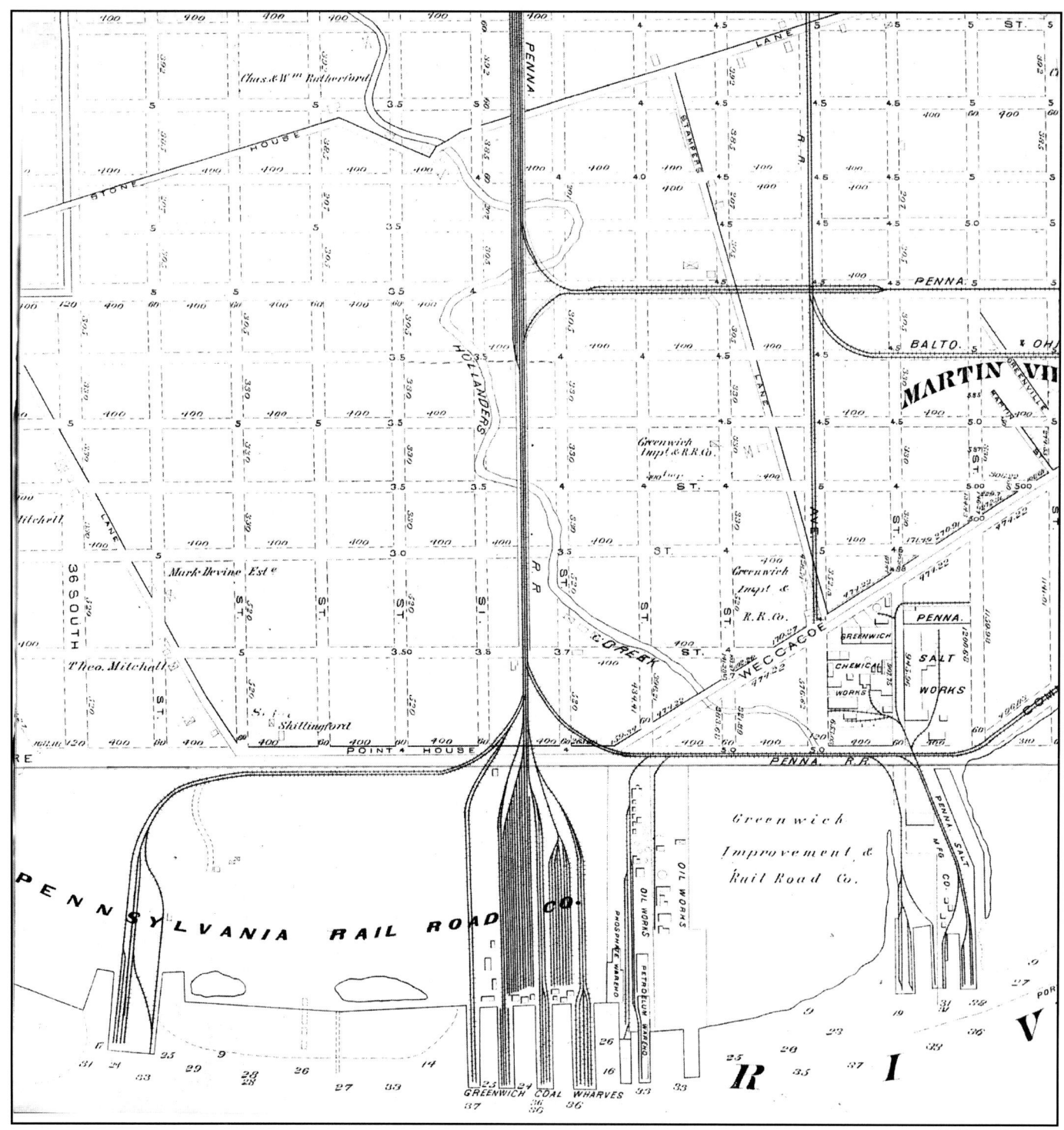

Ted Xaras Collection

WE NOW MOVE eastward across South Philadelphia to the yards and piers at Greenwich, on the Delaware River. This map, taken from the 1888 City Atlas, shows the early configuration of Greenwich Yard and coal wharves. The Delaware Extension runs eastward (top down) to the dock area and then swings northward, becoming the Delaware Avenue Branch. The beginnings of a classification yard extend along the east-west right-of-way. Running northward in the center is the Swanson Street Branch. The B&O Schuylkill River East Side RR extends parallel to and north of the Delaware Extension, and a branch swings northward one block east of Swanson Street. Initially, these lines ran at grade level in the streets. Note that the city street grid is still under development at this time.

TIDEWATER SAGA

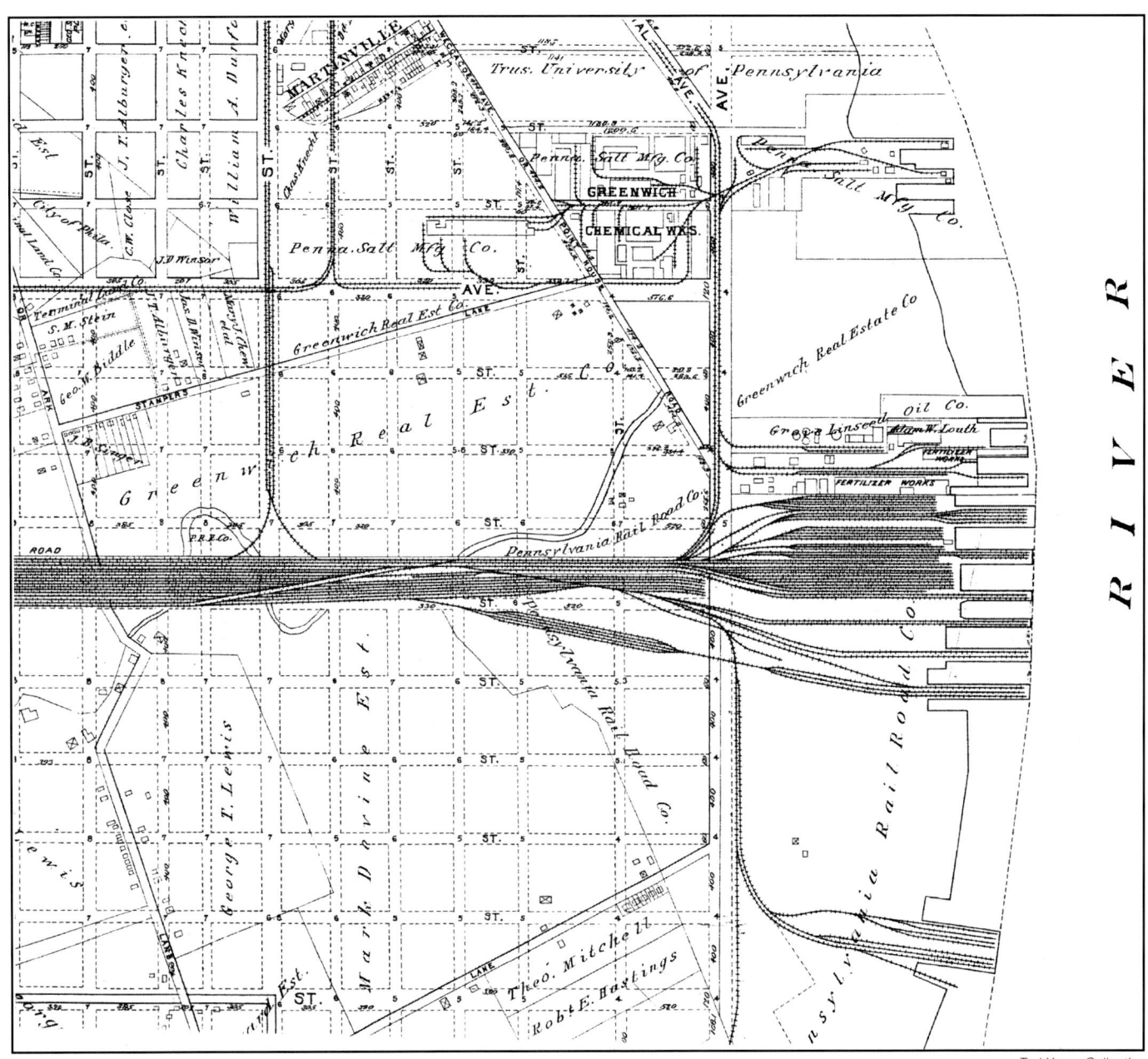

Ted Xaras Collection

BY 1910 the Greenwich Yard trackage has multiplied, as have the pier storage tracks. Note the ladder tracks allowing classification of inbound and outbound cars. B&O trackage has expanded somewhat, although PRR got there first, precluding extensive growth.

THIS REMARKABLE VIEW of "Soft Coal Hollow" in the early 1890s shows the long lines of loaded wooden hoppers in the pier storage yard, awaiting transfer to the coal piers for ship loading. Two cars are sitting on the approach trestle. We would have to classify most of this as mine run coal.

THE EARLIEST freight facilities at Greenwich Point were constructed in 1867. Old Pier No. 4, completed in 1873, is shown here in a 1917 view. The wooden trestle extended for 500 feet. The photo shows the chutes for loading coal into barges or smaller ships in the river.

TIDEWATER SAGA

A BIT farther south we see the approach to Pier No. 6. The tracks diverge into the storage yards for strings of hoppers. Incoming cars roll down a 1% grade toward the pier and are then hauled by a cable attached to a stationary steam engine up the 17.5% incline to a point 75 ft. above water level for unloading.

BEHEMOTH – The immensity of Pier No. 6 is evident in this view showing the 730-ft. structure as it appeared in 1917. This height of this facility allowed the loading of larger oceangoing ships for the export trade.

Ted Xaras Collection

ONE DOES NOT normally think of grain elevators as being architecturally stylish, but this facility at Delaware and Washington Avenues (north of Greenwich Point) has a certain functional elegance about it. The 1870s photo shows several PRR boxcars in the yard, lettered "Grain" and "Merchandise."

Ted Xaras Collection

A LATER VIEW of this facility ca. 1900 shows the conveyor extending to the ship loading wharves on the river. This is Pier No. 48. The fireproof brick elevator (left background) has a capacity of 450,000 bushels.

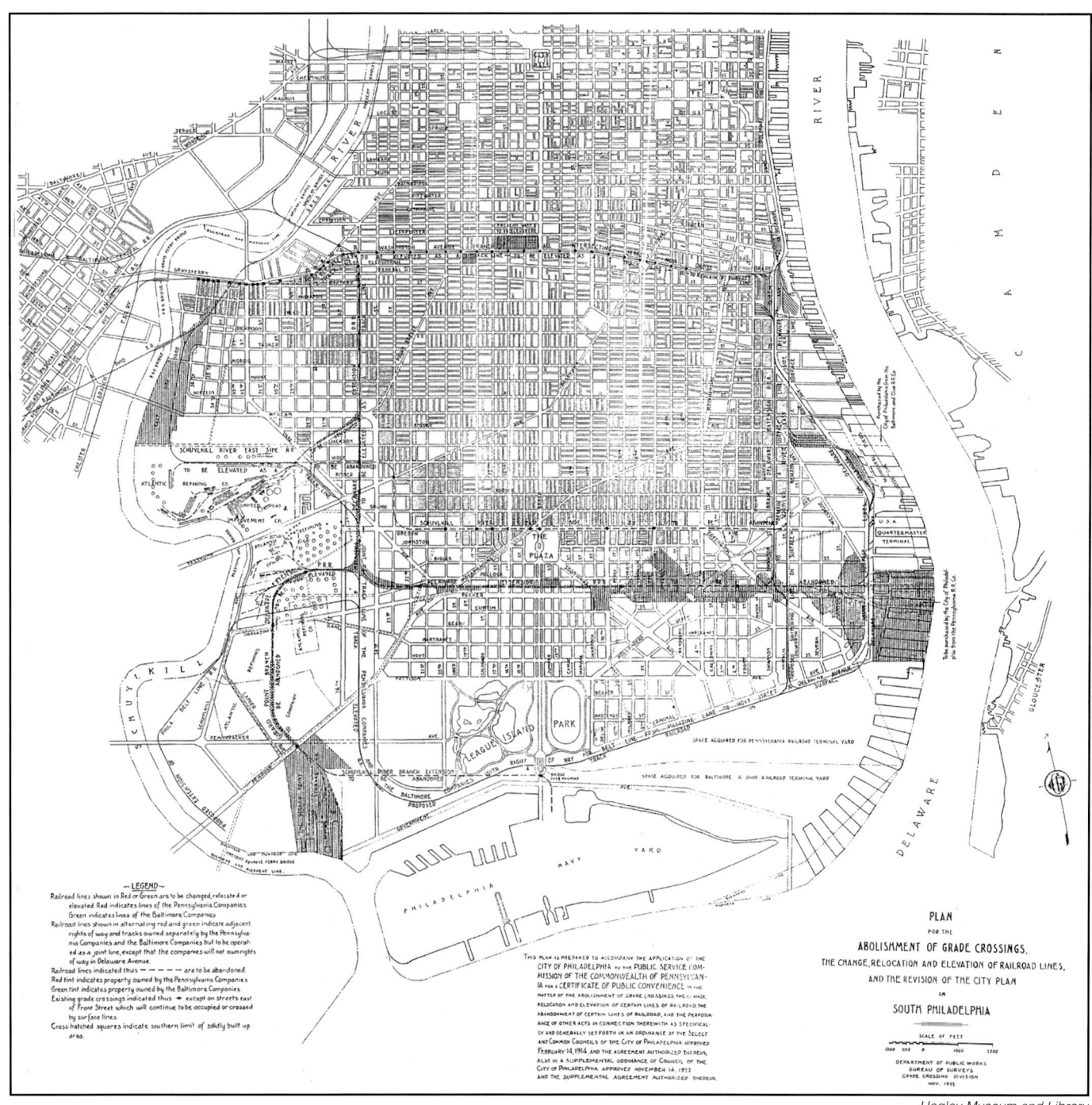

Hagley Museum and Library

THIS PLAN, dated November 1922, details the comprehensive proposal for the abolishment of grade crossings as well as the relocation and/or elevation of several rail lines in South Philadelphia. Work based on an earlier agreement among PRR, B&O, PB&W and the City dated 23 March 1914 had been initiated but suspended before the outbreak of World War I because of exhaustion of City funding. The new plan approved 14 November 1922 encompassed the following elements (top to bottom, left to right on the diagram): 1) Elevate the PB&W Washington Avenue Branch (including the yard at Broad Street); 2) Abandon the Schuylkill River East Side RR (B&O) along Oregon Avenue; 3) Elevate the Delaware Extension along 25th Street to the point where it turns and extends to the Delaware River; 4) Abandon the east-west portion of the Delaware Extension in favor of a new joint PRR-B&O line to extend to the new Navy Yard and then turn east to the Delaware River at Greenwich Point, where new terminal yards for both railroads would be built. The Girard Point Branch and Schuylkill River Branch Extension would then be abandoned.

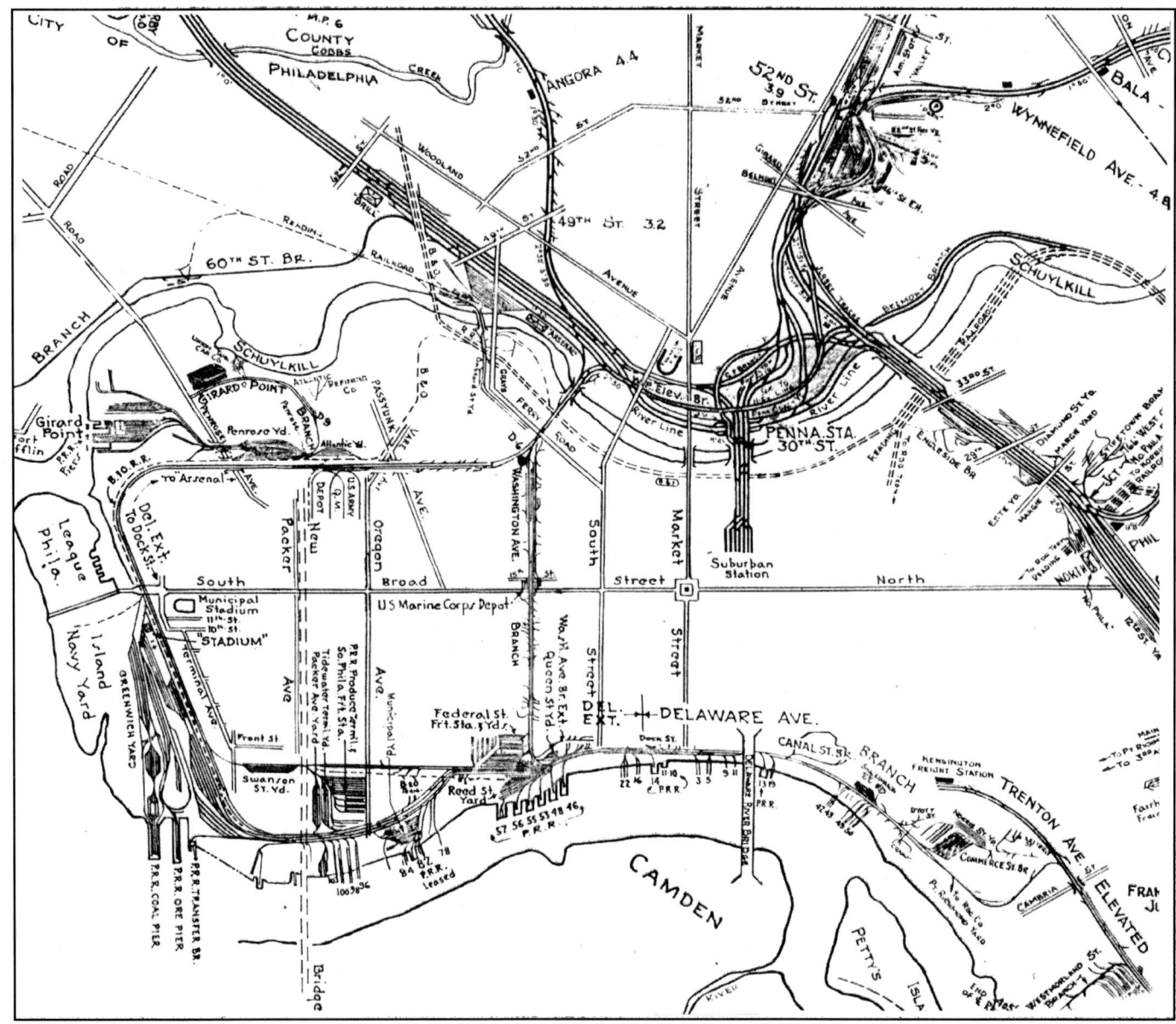

Andrew M. Wilson

IT TOOK A WHILE, but this ca. 1955 diagram shows the eventual outcome of the "South Philadelphia Improvements." Work was not resumed on this ambitious project until the mid-1920s. The north-south portion of the Delaware Extension was elevated to the turn (25th Street Viaduct) and the Oregon Avenue tracks removed, but the Washington Avenue line remained in the street. The new line across to the Delaware River was constructed, and a plan for the new South Philadelphia Terminal Yard at Greenwich Point was developed in 1928. This included a new coal pier, an ore handling facility, two receiving yards, a classification and departure yard and engine terminal. This complex as proposed had an 8500-car capacity and covered 295 acres. In addition to the above, a new produce terminal and South Philadelphia freight station complex at Oregon and Delaware Avenue was completed in 1928. This diagram also shows the Swanson Street Branch, which ran from the Greenwich Point yards northward to Norris Street, providing an alternate route through the riverfront area. It was constructed in 1884 and double-tracked in 1889. Note the extensive series of yards and piers served by the Delaware Extension and Delaware Avenue Branch.

TIDEWATER SAGA

FORMER PB&W trackage along Washington Avenue survives to this day, as evidenced by this June 1998 photo looking west from Broad Street. Philadelphians are used to trackage in the streets, both trolley and freight, but we doubt if very many who drive over these rails are aware of their history.

Andrew M. Wilson

Conrail Public Affairs/Penn Central Railroad Collection/Pennsylvania State Archives

IN 1926 PRR constructed an extensive South Philadelphia freight terminal and produce yard on Oregon Avenue, west of Delaware Avenue. The facility was expanded in 1928 with the completion of a large brick cold storage warehouse that provided 2 million cu. ft. of cold storage space. The entire complex is shown here in a ca. 1950 aerial shot looking to the northwest over South Philadelphia.

TRIUMPH III

Hagley Museum and Library

THE NEW COAL PIER and yard area is shown in this view looking west at the Delaware Riverfront on 8 August 1929. Completed in that year, the facility was equipped with two dumpers having a capacity for handling 96,000 tons daily. Strings of cars are moved on the two outer tracks to the dumpers. After unloading, individual cars roll down the inclines to the ramps at the end of the pier and then return via the two center tracks. They are then returned to the storage yard on tracks around (or through) the center shop structure.

Railroad Museum of Pennsylvania (PHMC)

A LOOK AT Delaware River pier facilities and yards from the air is provided by this photo ca. 1950. We are looking southward along Delaware Avenue, with Pier 43 at the bottom. Entering from the right is the Washington Avenue Branch to the Federal Street freight station and yards. The Reed Street Yard extends southeastward to the American Sugar Refining Co. (with the tall stack), with B&O tracks south of that. The Queen Street Yard branches northward in the foreground.

Chuck Leopold Collection

SADA SAN TURNBULL was one of several hundred women workers hired on by PRR during World War II to maintain operations while their male counterparts were in the armed services. She served from 1943 to 1946 as a freight brakeman, based out of the busy Reed Street Yard. She is shown here performing her unsung role sometime during that period. She was also issued a full uniform for passenger duty. She received her termination notice when the servicemen (with higher seniority) returned to their positions.

In the early 70s she hired on as a passenger trainman on Reading commuter trains in and out of Philadelphia. When Conrail took over she was transferred to freight service and took medical retirement in 1977.

FARTHER NORTH along Delaware Avenue, PRR constructed this imposing six-story freight warehouse in 1883 at the Shackamaxon Street Yard. The building is shown here as it appeared in 1985.

Andrew M. Wilson

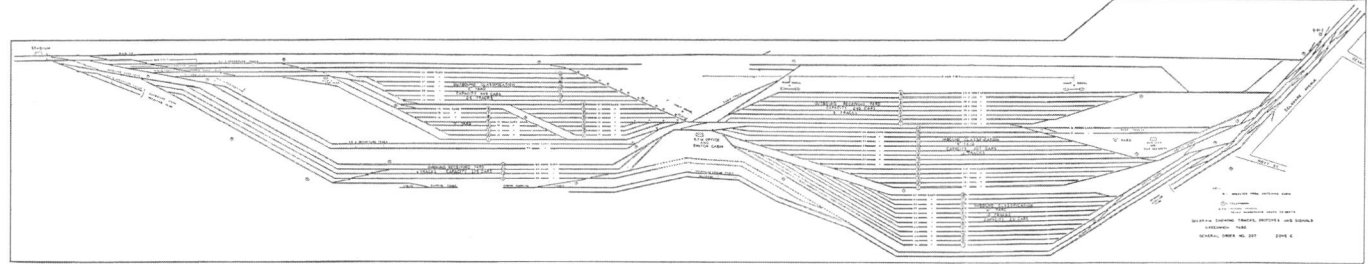

Hagley Museum and Library

MOVING SOUTH again, here's a look at the layout of the Greenwich Yards. The yards were rearranged and expanded in 1942 and again in 1944, as shown here, to accommodate increased wartime export volume as well as to and from the military installations in the Philadelphia area. Traffic over the piers increased from prewar levels of about 250,000 tons to almost 620,000 tons in 1942 and nearly 1.5 million tons in 1943. To handle the staggering load the yard capacity was increased from 2000 to 4500 cars in 1942 and nearly 5000 cars in 1944.

Hagley Museum and Library

IN 1952 PRR began construction of a new ore loading facility at Greenwich Point, just north of the Coal Pier. Constructed on rubble fill from the demolished Broad Street Station (at least it was put to good use) the complex was a bold move by PRR management to capture imported iron ore business from South American mines (to replace depleted domestic sources). The $10 million facility was opened on 19 March 1954 and handled over 1 million tons the first year. A third machine was added in 1955 and a fourth in 1956, increasing capacity to over 10.5 million tons per year. This 1959 photo shows the entire complex with two ships alongside and the Coal Pier at left. Note the expanse of Greenwich Yards beyond.

TRIUMPH III

A PAIR of Conrail EMD units switches Greenwich Yard alongside I-95 on 2 November 1998. To the right a string of intermodal cars awaits departure. PRR first established a TrucTrain terminal in South Philadelphia in 1957. The freight yards in South Philadelphia were electrified in 1937 – here the former catenary supports now hold light fixtures.

Tom Hollyman Aerials/Penn Central RR Collection/Pennsylvania State Archives

ARMY-NAVY GAME trains were inaugurated by PRR in 1936 to accommodate the crowds of fans attending the annual football clash between the two service academies. Philadelphia was chosen as the site because of its location and the availability of rail service close to Municipal Stadium. The operation was a highly organized one, carried out with planning and execution reminiscent of a military campaign (not inappropriate for the clientele). Army-Navy trains were popular from their inception, and they quickly grew to become the most intense mainline passenger operation in the U.S. Weeks of advance preparation each year turned Greenwich Yard, normally a receiving facility for coal and ore, into a temporary passenger terminal. The yard was scrupulously cleaned and roadways and walkways resurfaced. Additional signals were installed, along with activation of STADIUM Tower, to handle the concentrated train movements under a special General Order. This view looking eastward ca. 1950 shows Municipal Stadium, with the Greenwich yards beyond.

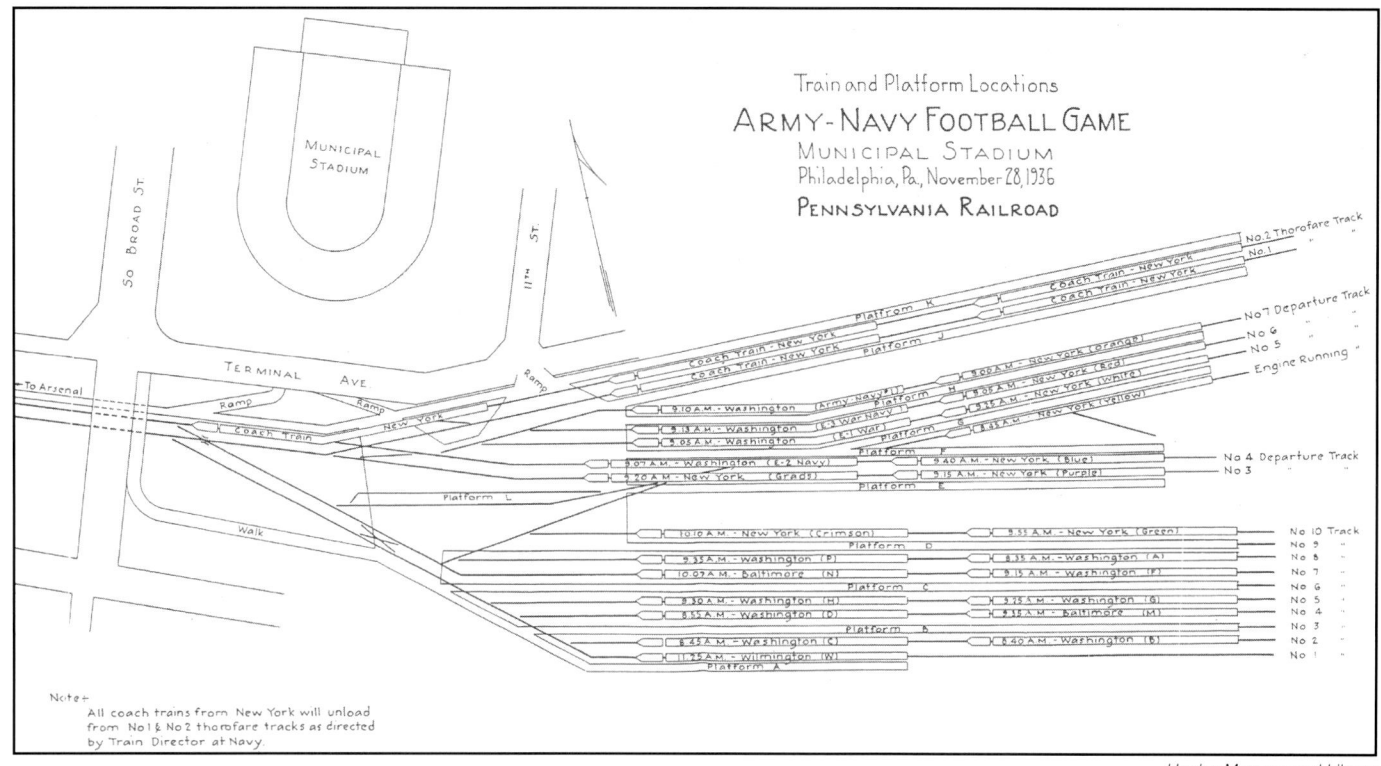

Hagley Museum and Library

A DETAILED TRACK DIAGRAM was prepared, showing the location of each special train entering the yards (the diagram shown here was drawn up for the inaugural operation on 28 November 1936). Platforms were clearly marked for each train. Coach trains were identified by the letters N, W, NK, BA and AC for New York, Washington, Newark, Baltimore and Atlantic City, respectively. Parlor trains were identified by colors. Special trains for dignitaries were scheduled, and the POTUS train carried the President of the United States, who changed his allegiance (and even his seat) at halftime. In 1962 John F. Kennedy had the dubious distinction of being the last president to arrive by rail. In 1963 Municipal Stadium was renamed in his memory.

The primary route for trains from the west and north was via the High Line to ARSENAL Tower and then onto the Delaware Extension to the Stadium yard. Trains from the south swung directly onto the Delaware Extension at ARSENAL Tower. Both the High Line and the Delaware Extension were one-way during the inbound and outbound movements. It should be noted that the B&O also participated in this operation, albeit on a smaller scale, unloading its passengers at a temporary location west of Broad Street Station, and later assigned tracks in the PRR yard. The Army cadets traveled on a New York Central train; the midshipmen used the B&O initially, and after that road's passenger service to Philadelphia ended, PRR in later years.

The operation required a huge collection of equipment, including both PRR and non-PRR cars. Motive power was predominantly GG-1's, but steam engines (mostly K-4's) were also used - all cleaned up for the occasion. In the peak postwar year of 1947, 56 locomotives, 324 coaches, 154 Pullmans and 37 bar and dining cars were used to carry a total of 27,844 fans directly to Municipal Stadium. Assembling this much equipment without compromising regular train service required extensive planning. Some regular trains terminated at the site; other cars were obtained by shortening regular consists and drawing from reserve pools, as well as leasing equipment from other railroads, adding to the color of the day. Extra locomotives were placed on "protect" status at strategic locations in case of breakdowns, and wreck (and even wire) trains were on standby. Pilot engineers were assigned to assist road engineers not familiar with the location. It was a prestige assignment, to say the least. Steam power lasted until 1954. MU equipment was first used in 1975 and Amfleet cars behind F40 diesels took over until declining ridership forced cancellation of special service in 1988, ending a colorful 50-year tradition in Philadelphia.

TRIUMPH III

SOME OF THE CROWDS attending the Army-Navy Game are shown here, moving from their trains toward Municipal Stadium. Both GG1's and one K4 are visible in this 1940s photo. It's hard to believe today that men went to football games in suits and ties and women in stockings and heels – and virtually everyone has a hat!

Railroad Museum of Pennsylvania (PHMC)

William J. Coxey

THEY CAME from near and far to the big game. Here a doubleheaded pair of Penn Central GG1's, Nos. 4923 and 4938 (the latter still with a PRR wide stripe) roll a game special on the High Line in November 1971. The train is running left-handed inbound (on No. 2 Track) between Chestnut and Walnut Streets. Initially, under a General Order switches were spiked so that both tracks were one-way inbound before the game and outbound afterwards, but in 1962 two-way signaling (Rule 261) was installed to facilitate moving coal and ore traffic in and out of Greenwich Yard. Either way, an impressive operation!

William J. Coxey

A 12-CAR MU special brings in the local fans in November 1971. This train, led by Silverliner No. 219 still in PRR lettering, is running right-handed inbound (on No. 1 Track), shown here crossing over Market Street.

Chapter 6

Southern Conflict and Connections

The Junction RR and the PW&B

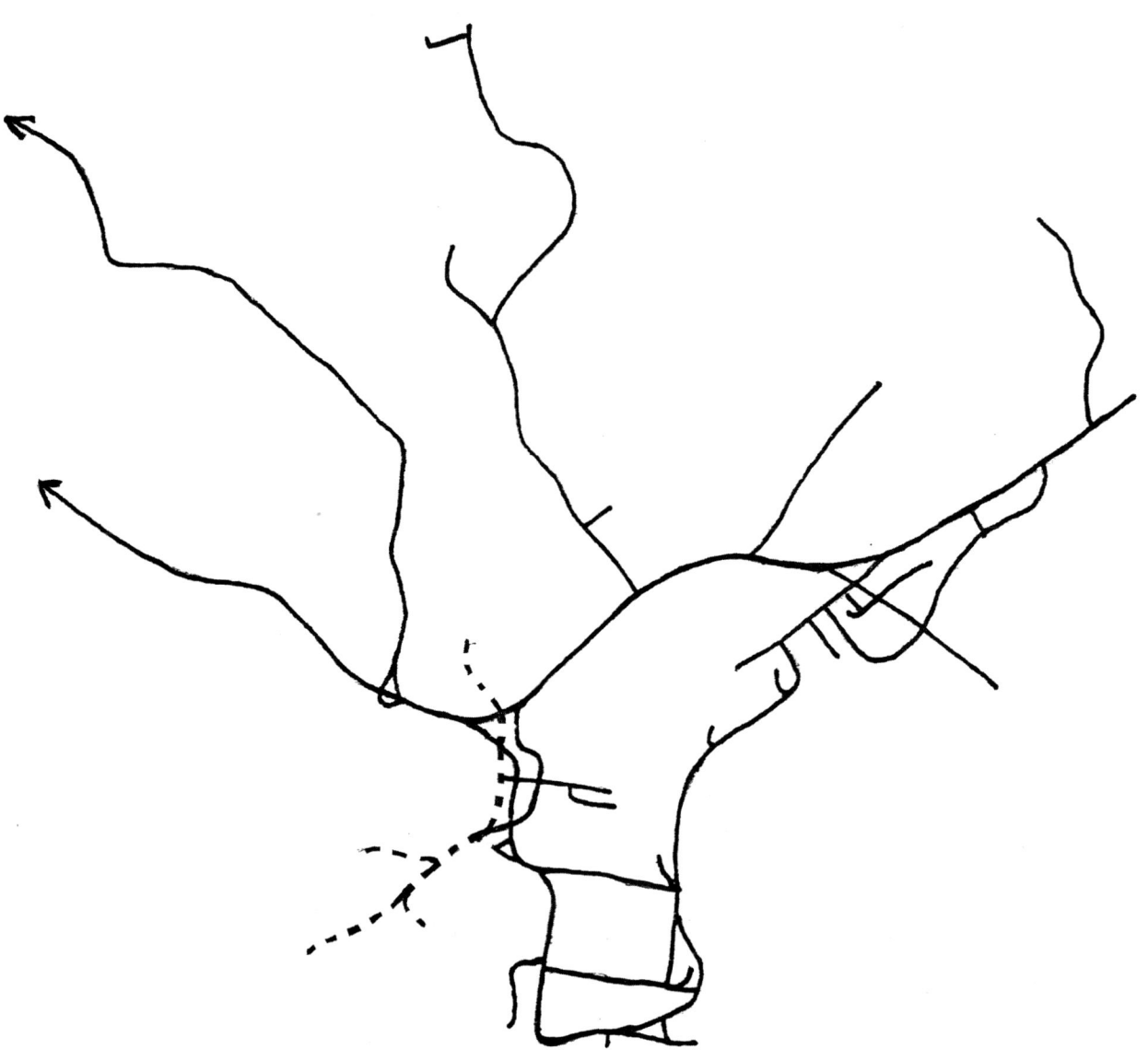

SOUTHERN CONFLICT AND CONNECTIONS

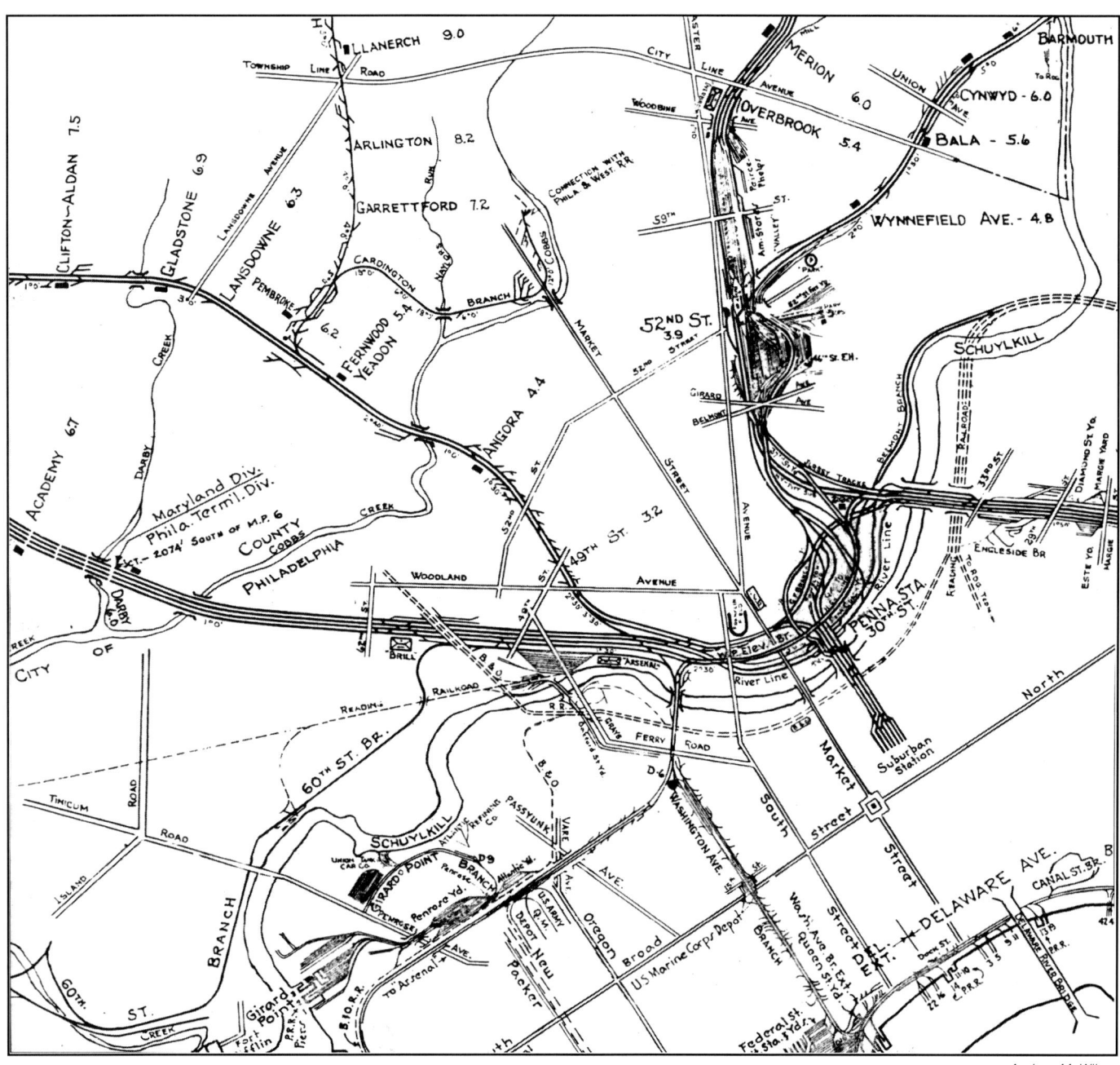

Andrew M. Wilson

THE FIRST IMAGE of PRR approaching Philadelphia that comes to mind is from the west on the Main Line, and then perhaps from New York City on a "Clocker" to Broad Street Station. But there is another approach to Philadelphia, and that is from the south. In this chapter we will attempt to tease out the lines making up the southern approach and explore the complex interactions among PRR, the Junction RR, the Philadelphia, Wilmington & Baltimore and B&O. The PW&B, its successor the Philadelphia, Baltimore & Washington and the subsequent PRR Maryland Division will be covered in considerable detail in another volume in the Triumph series, but Philadelphia played a key role in the north-south traffic on these lines, shown here extending from what is labeled the Belmont Branch north of ZOO Interlocking (right) to the division point with the Maryland Division (left). Note the location of B&O tracks, which cross the PRR (PB&W) main north of BRILL, extend across the Schuylkill River and follow the east bank through the City up to the junction with the Reading. It is another complex but fascinating story.

The short but turbulent saga of a through north-south rail line from New York City to Washington DC through Philadelphia all began innocently enough. In the years before the Civil War the biggest obstacle to such a route was the lack of connections among the four railroads entering Philadelphia – PRR from the west, P&R from the northwest, P&T from the north and PW&B from the south. PRR had connections with the PW&B and the Reading, but these were via tracks of the City-owned railroad in the increasingly congested streets of Philadelphia. Accordingly, after acquiring the P&C and upgrading the east-west main, President Thomson obtained approval from the PRR Board to survey a route on the west bank of the Schuylkill River to make connections with these roads and obtain State authorization for such a line.

A charter was granted by the Pennsylvania Legislature on 3 May 1860 authorizing the formation of the "Junction Railroad Company," organized jointly by PRR, the Reading and the PW&B. The purpose of this line was to connect these three railroads in West Philadelphia and afford interchange capabilities without passing through the congested portions of the City. However, the three roads had difficulty agreeing on a route – strange considering the limited options available, but a fitting prelude to the events that were about to unfold.

The first of these was the Civil War. In January 1862, a few months after the conflict erupted, Congress granted President Lincoln authority to take over the railroads whenever required by events. This was shortly followed by proposals, including a bill from the slick and corrupt Pennsylvania politician and financier – and PRR ally – Simon Cameron, for the Federal government to construct a double-track "Air Line" between New York and Washington. Moving troops from New York to the battle areas, or even to defend the vulnerable U.S. capital, involved circuitous and time-consuming moves, including marching them through Philadelphia's crowded city streets, 3.5 miles from the P&T depot in Kensington to the PW&B station at Broad and Washington.

The Baltimore & Ohio RR, which already had a line between Baltimore and Washington, lobbied against the Air Line proposal but urged its northern colleagues to establish useful connections in the Philadelphia area. All of these pressures finally resulted in the three Junction RR partners agreeing on a route. The line connected with the Reading near Belmont (not far from the original P&C bridge across the river), intersected the PRR near the Market Street bridge and continued southward to a connection with the PW&B at Grays Ferry.

The northern portion, from 35th Street to Belmont, was completed and put in operation on 23 November 1863. This allowed use of a still tortuous north-south route from the P&T through Philadelphia, starting with the Reading's Port Richmond Branch at Kensington, running across the City to West Falls, southward to Belmont, continuing on the Junction RR and then turning eastward across the river again via the Delaware Extension to the PW&B terminal at Broad and Washington. By December 1864 a second portion of the Junction RR was opened, eliminating the eastward trek over the Delaware Extension. By 1865 four through passenger trains each way traversed this path daily, the fastest taking about 10 hours to make the run from New York to Washington, incredible speed for the times. Completing the southern portion to Grays Ferry was delayed during the turbulent Civil War period, but it was finally completed and opened to traffic on 1 July 1866, with all three railroads operating trains over the route.

The final link through Philadelphia was the construction of the aptly-named Connecting RR, between PRR and the P&T, opened in mid-1867 (discussed in Chapter 2). This direct route eliminated the circuitous path over the Reading. Unlike the Junction RR, it was a solely PRR-financed project, leased to the P&T. Completion of this route led to a renewal of the Air Line proposal, which B&O again successfully lobbied against.

The line extending from the end of the Junction RR southward over the PW&B is another, but closely interrelated, story. The short version is that the PRR Board, at its Annual Meeting on 8 March 1881, authorized the purchase of a majority of shares of the PW&B to prevent it from passing "into the hands of parties whose interests were antagonistic" to those of PRR. Those parties were headed by the B&O, which desperately wanted to extend its own line to Philadelphia and continue on to gain direct access to New York City rather than be dependent on a variety of roundabout routes on other lines.

Acquisition of the PW&B was another strategic

move, this time by President George Roberts, that not only gave PRR a line from Philadelphia to Washington (utilizing the previously acquired Baltimore & Potomac RR Co. into the nation's capital) but also provided several added branches and invaluable additional terminal facilities in Philadelphia and Baltimore. With no significant operations along the critical New York-Washington route after the Civil War, PRR began its quest in 1867 and less than 15 years later not only controlled the entire line but had the best route. The story of how this all came about is fascinating and illuminating, not only regarding the railroads involved, but also the individuals who commanded them.

We should pause here and reflect on these giants, who waged the titanic struggle for supremacy in the overall competition for New York-Chicago traffic after the Civil War. The New York Central System, which was being put together by Cornelius "Commodore" Vanderbilt and his son William H., was a competitor of both PRR and B&O in the overall New York-Chicago market, but was never a real factor south of New York City. PRR was driven by the vision and commitment of that giant of the industry, John Edgar Thomson (see *Triumph I* and *Triumph II*) and his aggressive, if less visionary, successors Tom Scott and George Roberts. The third contender was the B&O, led by portly, contentious and slow-witted John W. Garrett. B&O was in reality the weakest member of the three, because of less desirable routes and fewer financial resources at its disposal.

The New York-Washington route became the focus of epic PRR-B&O struggles after the Civil War and involved at least two other major rail systems for this route. We need to examine the situation as it existed at the time and then study the momentous – and often bizarre – events that unfolded on this tumultuous field of battle.

The place to begin is with the PW&B, whose mainline occupied a strategic position in this routing. Between Philadelphia and New York lay the United New Jersey Railroad and Canal Co.'s lines, leased by Thomson in 1871 in a strategic move to obtain control of the line into that vital metropolis. South of Baltimore were two competing lines, the PRR-controlled Baltimore & Potomac, which Thomson had quietly acquired in 1867, and the B&O's Washington Branch, which prior to Thomson's move had what it thought was a state-protected monopoly on traffic to the national capital. Thus the PW&B became the key link for both PRR and B&O between Baltimore and Philadelphia, and ultimately New York City.

There was, however, another even shorter link – the 3-mile Junction RR in West Philadelphia – that had to be reckoned with. All trains between New York and the South had to utilize at least a portion of this line in order to move to the PW&B. Although PRR was only one of the three partners in the Junction RR, the middle portion of the line in fact used trackage owned outright by PRR, through the West Philadelphia yards. The other two parties went to court starting in 1868 over the rights to this key 1-mile section, but PRR prevailed in a decision finally handed down in 1876.

Even after PRR's lease of the United New Jersey "Joint Companies" it maintained the previous traffic agreements with B&O over the line. The PB&W as well remained at least outwardly neutral, accepting traffic from both PRR and B&O. This peaceful situation was about to change, unleashing a cascade of events that would forever change the face of railroading along the New York-Washington corridor.

John Garrett, hungry for an advantage in the struggle, ignored the joint agreements repeatedly negotiated among the major eastern roads and frequently resorted to rate cutting, which aroused the anger of his PRR counterpart and invited retaliation. In a hotly-contested rate war that erupted in late 1874, B&O accused PRR of refusing to sell New York-Washington tickets utilizing the B&O's Washington Branch and worse, not accepting B&O freight traffic to industries located in the Philadelphia area. The general rate settlement of 1875 resolved the issues for a time, but the underlying corporate antagonism persisted.

There was another individual on this battlefield, the highly-ambitious president of the Reading, Franklin Gowen. In response to PRR's success in obtaining a route to New York as well as increasing the chances of corporate (and personal) survival, Gowen in 1879 assembled a patchwork of short lines allowing the Reading to gain its own access for its critical anthracite business. These lines (the North Penn RR and the Delaware & Bound Brook RR), along with trackage rights on the Central Railroad of New

Jersey, allowed him to outflank PRR in its drive for the lucrative New York City market. As soon as traffic over the PW&B began using this route, openly Reading-hostile PRR President George Roberts began making life difficult for the other users of the Junction RR. In April 1879 a lawsuit against PRR from the CNJ and the Delaware & Bound Brook RR resulted, with B&O's public support and the Reading's behind the scenes backing. The case took over a year to settle, but on 28 October 1880 the court directed PRR to cooperate with the other railroads in handling all traffic. However, it did allow PRR a loophole – the use of its own motive power in moving this traffic over the critical mile.

B&O wasted little time in responding. Out of the blue it announced that as of 1 December of that year it would withdraw its passenger traffic from PRR's New Jersey trackage (ignoring the 90-day notice provision) and would do likewise with its freight traffic on the first of the new year. It would henceforth utilize the Reading-controlled trackage (using the Newtown & New York Connecting RR and the Philadelphia & New York Short Line for access) and the allied CNJ to its terminus at Jersey City, across from New York.

This new route still required B&O trains to traverse the Junction RR, including the crucial PRR portion. In retaliation PRR imposed an extra fee and the requirement of utilizing its own motive power for this stretch, along with other delays because of slow (or worse, nonexistent) freights, stalled locomotives, failed switches and other mysterious happenings. What should have been only a few minutes' passage often ended up taking several hours. This, not surprisingly, produced the immediate charge that PRR was delaying B&O trains, which they clearly were. PRR's response indicated that, "the rights of a Baltimore & Ohio train in the Pennsylvania's West Philadelphia yards was quite the same as would be the rights of a Pennsylvania train in the Central Pacific's yards at San Francisco." PRR's lofty position notwithstanding, B&O prevailed, obtaining a Federal court order against delaying any of its trains on this line.

From this point on, the financial machinations began to take on a perverse complexity commensurate with the enormous value of the PW&B to the two rail giants. Enter a Colonel Henry S. McComb, an enterprising Wilmington capitalist who had obtained control of the tiny Delaware Western RR, a "company with a charter but no railroad," to build his own line from Baltimore to Philadelphia. McComb even obtained the backing of William H. Vanderbilt in this venture. Armed with this support, McComb then went to Garrett and his colleagues at the CNJ and secured their commitment as well.

Not surprisingly, PW&B management took a dim view of these threatening developments. What was surprising, however, was their offer to sell an interest in their line to the backers of the Delaware Western scheme. The PW&B then approached one Nathaniel Thayer of Boston, the company's largest stockholder, with their own plan. Thayer, one of five Boston-area directors of the line, duly agreed to deliver a majority of the PW&B stock at a price of $70 a share.

PW&B management (stay with us now) then went to Garrett, who suddenly abandoned the Delaware Western group and joined another investor syndicate made up of a stellar cast of characters including John Jacob Astor, August Belmont, Russell Sage and headed by the slippery but brilliant Jay Gould, who had recently bought his way onto the CNJ Board. On 17 February 1881 this august group agreed to purchase 120,000 shares from Mr. Thayer at the agreed upon price and to do so within a month. Interestingly, PRR Vice President Cassatt was offered a one-third interest in the venture at a meeting on the 19th, but he refused to settle for a minority share. On 22 February it was announced publicly that the deal was closed. McComb, Vanderbilt and the other backers of the Delaware Western plan were incensed at Garrett's pullout (which earned the B&O president Vanderbilt's intense dislike), but they could do nothing. Garrett, meanwhile, was blissfully satisfied and, some say, bragged that the critical PW&B line was his, still another sad example that his tongue and brain were uncoordinated.

Thayer, however, was having difficulty getting stockholders to agree to sell at $72 per share, much less $70. A stockholders' committee was formed with Henry P. Kidder (of Kidder, Peabody & Co.) as chairman, and bids were requested. Suddenly events began to rapidly unfold. On 3 March PRR management deposited "a large amount" of stock with Kidder. On Monday, 7 March the PW&B committee traveled from Boston to New York City for discussion with Roberts and Cassatt, the latter now pushing vigorously for a controlling interest in the crucial line for PRR. Before midnight that fateful night Cassatt had prevailed – PRR agreed to purchase 92,000 shares of PW&B stock at a premium $78 per share, and sweetened the offer by agreeing to buy any additional shares at the same price by 1 April.

On the following day Roberts and Cassatt hurried back to Philadelphia and obtained Board approval of the purchase, and PRR subsequently became the triumphant owner of over 92 per cent of PW&B stock for something over $17 million. Along with it came the second third of ownership in the Junction RR.

A chastened John Garrett returned to Baltimore, once again outmaneuvered by PRR. In a final act of defiance he immediately set about plans for building his own line to Philadelphia, regardless of the cost. On 23 March 1881 he announced that B&O had obtained control of the Delaware Western from Colonel McComb and that construction of the new line would begin as soon as possible. The rate wars returned, however, making financing difficult, and the line was not begun until the spring of 1883.

Its most zealous promoter would not live to see it completed – John W. Garrett died on 26 September 1884, and his vacuous son, Robert, took over the reins of B&O. He had in fact run the railroad during most of his ailing father's last year. B&O had failed once again in the grand scheme of things.

In the meantime, PRR opened its palace in Philadelphia on 5 December 1881, and PW&B trains were routed into Broad Street Station early in 1882, immediately taxing its planned capacity.

PRR did little to ease the efforts of either the older or younger Garrett. After a 3-year grace period, George Roberts' gentlemanly accommodation came to an end, and in 1884 PRR announced it would end the PW&B's contract for B&O traffic on 14 June. The contract was extended to 12 October, but B&O went to court to block the action entirely. In early November – shortly after the elder Garrett's death – it lost its case and gave up. B&O was out of the passenger business north of Baltimore until its own line, appropriately named the Baltimore & Philadelphia RR, could be completed.

B&O fought an endless and tangled series of political, legal and financial battles – including more mysterious PRR obstructions – to complete its line through a decidedly inhospitable Philadelphia. At this point in time one more player added himself to the already star-studded lineup in this drama – New York banker and financier extraordinaire J. Pierpont Morgan. In 1886 Morgan used his considerable financial strength and formidable persona to forge a $15 million deal to lift the Reading out of receivership. Not only did PRR join with rivals B&O and New York Central to provide financial assistance in this endeavor, it also entered into a "binding permanent contract" with the Reading to regulate (read "fix") anthracite prices and avoid tariff wars. Morgan also got George Roberts to withdraw his roadblocks and allow B&O to proceed with its line through Philadelphia.

It finally did so in late 1886, running its new trackage west of and parallel to the PW&B most of the way to Philadelphia, crossing that road and the Schuylkill River south of Grays Ferry and thus avoiding the Junction RR completely. It then ran on the east bank of the river through the City, passing through a tunnel and connecting with the Reading main at Park Junction, south of Girard Avenue. B&O constructed a handsome Victorian station at 24th and Chestnut Streets, designed by noted Philadelphia architect Frank Furness (who subsequently crafted the much larger expanded Broad Street Station). It also extended freight trackage into the South Philadelphia port area, but had difficulty finding piers and industries not already served by PRR or the Reading.

PRR finally obtained complete control of the Junction RR when the Reading gave up its share in 1889. On 1 April 1908 the Junction RR was absorbed into the Philadelphia Terminal Division. The northern portion, from 35th Street to Belmont Junction, then became known as the Belmont Branch and the southern portion, from Market and 32nd Streets to Grays Ferry, as the Grays Ferry Branch. These lines continued on in near obscurity, becoming almost literally buried under the succession of Philadelphia Improvements.

PRR's north-south line was consummated on 1 November 1902 when the PW&B and the B&P were merged and consolidated into a line known as the Philadelphia, Baltimore & Washington RR Co., thus creating a single ownership of the line between Philadelphia and the nation's capital. Earlier that year PRR had further recognized the importance of the

PW&B line by rebuilding several of its major bridges in Philadelphia. The line became an integral part of PRR's north-south mainline and functions today as part of Amtrak's high-speed Northeast Corridor.

B&O finally had its line into Philadelphia, and its traffic agreements on Reading and CNJ tracks, but its problems with PRR through Philadelphia and on into New York City were not over. PRR would deliver a major blow to B&O passenger service to New York with the opening of its magnificent Penn Station in Manhattan on 27 November 1910, eliminating train changes and a time-consuming ferry trip across the Hudson River. However, this competitive advantage was temporarily lost when the United States Railroad Administration moved B&O trains into Penn Station on 28 December 1917, requiring B&O to use the traditional Reading route north of Philadelphia. B&O negotiated a 5-year agreement after the end of Federal control, and extensions lasting until 1 September 1926. After that it had to fend for itself with bus service into Manhattan. PRR's next move was the electrification of its mainline through Philadelphia as far south as Wilmington in 1929-30s, later extended all the way to Washington.

In 1943 PRR considered accommodating B&O passenger trains into either Broad Street Station or 30th Street Station in Philadelphia. Northbound trains would reach those stations via a Reading freight branch that connected with the B&O main at Eastwick, near Grays Ferry Yard. Southbound trains would utilize the PRR Belmont Branch off the Reading main. Both operations would have required backward movements across PRR main trackage at ARSENAL or ZOO and use of the High Line, adding about 1 hour to B&O's already longer schedule between Washington and New York. Fourteen of the sixteen trains would pass through Philadelphia between 9 a.m. and 9 p.m., the period of heaviest train activity. For all these reasons the accommodation was not reached.

B&O passenger service through Philadelphia soldiered on until increasing costs and declining patronage forced the inevitable. The last train left Washington for New York on 26 April 1958. The Philadelphia station remained until it burned in 1963, ending a turbulent 100-year saga.

SOUTHERN CONFLICT AND CONNECTIONS

Ted Xaras Collection

LET US GO BACK – to 1853, when PRR was just beginning to establish itself in Philadelphia, and as yet had no trackage of its own into the City. This map is billed (with a flourish) as the West Chester & Philadelphia Railroad, but it is much more. It shows us of course the Reading (on the old P&C route into the City) and the relocated Columbia RR into West Philadelphia. But our focus here is on routes from the south. We have the pioneering WC&P, and farther south, the original alignment of the Philadelphia, Wilmington & Baltimore through Chester and into South Philadelphia – and even the Southwark RR, which was constructed to the Delaware riverfront as early as October 1834 - but no sign of any B&O presence. There is no north-south route by which through trains could traverse the City, at least not without lengthy and complex maneuvers; the Junction RR is 10 years into the future, and the Connecting Railway 4 years after that. We will now look at the Junction RR and some of the features along the later PW&B route.

Railroad Museum of Pennsylvania (PHMC)

MYSTERY PHOTO – Here we have a fascinating image that warrants close examination and analysis of the location. It is labeled "PRR, Philadelphia 1880s," which helps a little, but certainly doesn't tell us the whole story. If we first establish that the arch truss in the left background is the Connecting Railway bridge as originally constructed (1867) across the Schuylkill River we move a bit closer. Then if we decide from the direction of the sun that we are south of the bridge we are at a dead end because there are no PRR tracks on the east side of the river at that location. If, however, we conclude that the low angle of the sun allows us to be north of the bridge in late afternoon, then we are getting closer to a solution. The right-of-way in the background can then be identified as that portion of the Connecting Railway extending from the bridge westward toward Mantua Junction. Given this location we can then place the train on the Junction RR. So what is a PRR passenger train doing on this part of the Junction RR, heading toward Reading trackage? Our best guess, judging by the vintage of the locomotive and cars, is that this may have been a movement associated with the Centennial Exposition. Any other theories?

(right) THE PHOTOGRAPHER is standing in the rock-walled cut of the Junction RR ca. 1870, looking at the Market Street overpass. These tracks allowed a connection for PRR between the Reading at the northern end and the PW&B at the southern end. Drainage seems to be a bit of a problem here.

Ted Xaras Collection

SOUTHERN CONFLICT AND CONNECTIONS

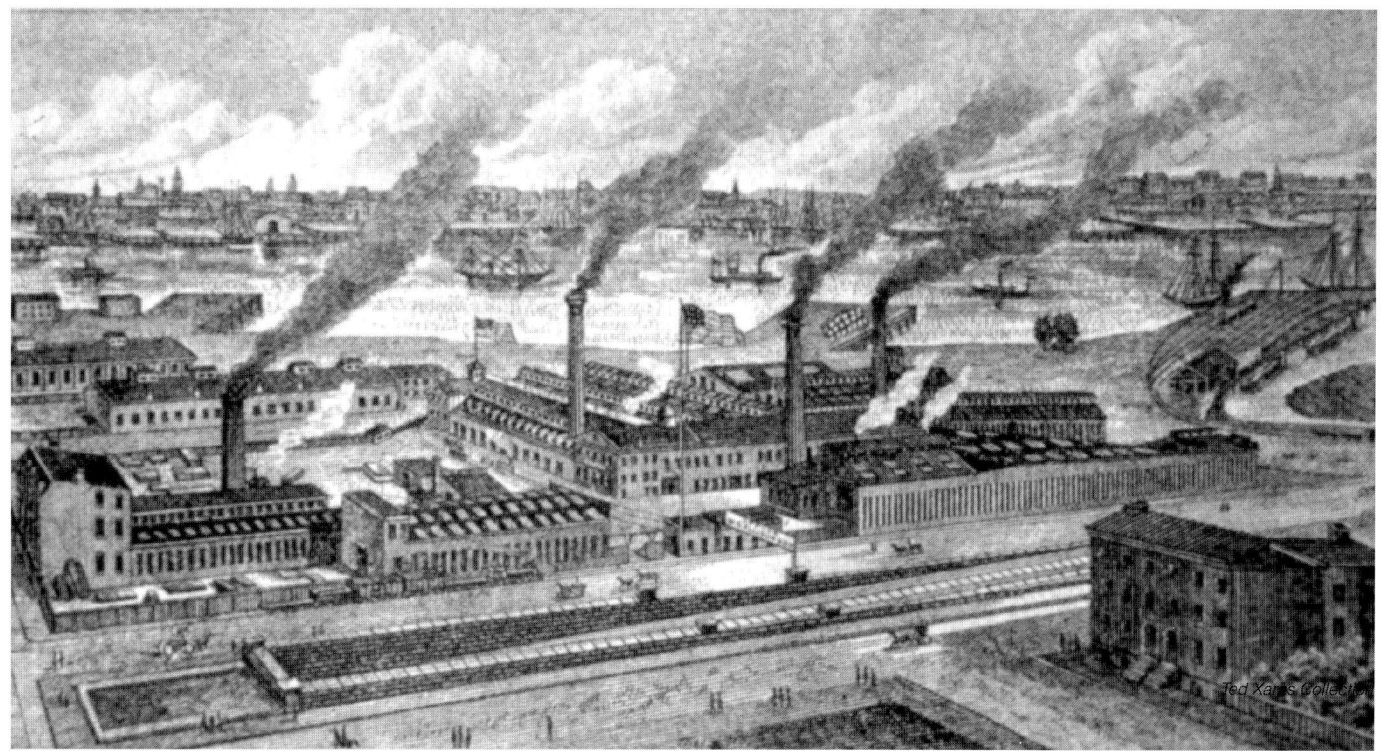

Ted Xaras Collection

THIS DRAWING gives us a superb look at the area in the vicinity of 32nd and Walnut Streets in the 1860s. We are looking east toward the Schuylkill River, with Center City Philadelphia in the background. This is ostensibly a view of the W. C. Allison & Company office and works, but it also shows us some rail facilities. The building at the center left edge of the drawing is the old West Chester & Philadelphia depot, and in the foreground is the southern end of the Junction RR, in the cut.

Philadelphia City Hall Archive/Ted Xaras Collection

HERE'S A CLOSER LOOK – the only one we have – at the WC&P depot, in a rare photo looking north on 29 December 1888. Built in 1866 and extended in 1874, it was closed as a passenger facility in January 1882 when PW&B and WC&P trains shifted over to the newly-opened Broad Street Station. It was reopened briefly during the expansion of Broad Street in 1893-4. This area would later become the location of PRR's West Philadelphia Freight Terminal when the Market Street facility was displaced by the Improvements in the late 1920s.

TRIUMPH III

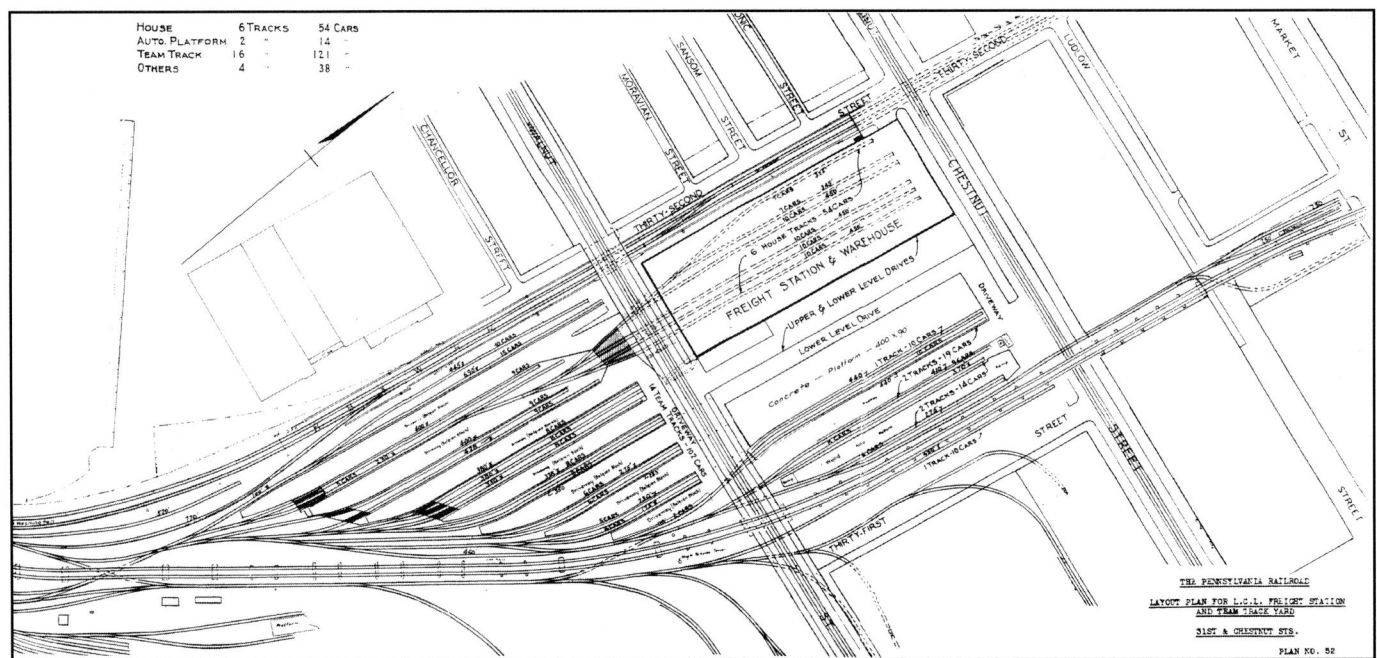

Ted Xaras Collection

HERE'S A LOOK at the layout of the LCL Freight Station and Team Track Yard at 31st and Chestnut Streets in 1935. We are in the same area as the two previous images, showing the Grays Ferry Branch emerging from the tunnel south of Chestnut. The High Line extends across the diagram above 31st Street. The then-new freight facilities are in between these two lines.

Garth Wise Collection

Here's a close-up of the new Freight Station at 32nd and Chestnut Streets. It was opened in 1929, replacing the facility at 30th and Market – where a freight station had stood for so many years – which was displaced by construction of the new passenger complex. The High Line runs alongside at the right.

SOUTHERN CONFLICT AND CONNECTIONS

Tom Hollyman Aerials/ Penn Central RR Collection/Pennsylvania State Archives

THIS AERIAL PHOTO shows us the trackage south of 30th Street Station ca. 1950. The River Line swings into the station, under the Post Office in the center. The freight station and yard are west of that, the white building just above the University of Pennsylvania stadium. And between them is the Grays Ferry Branch (ex-Junction RR).

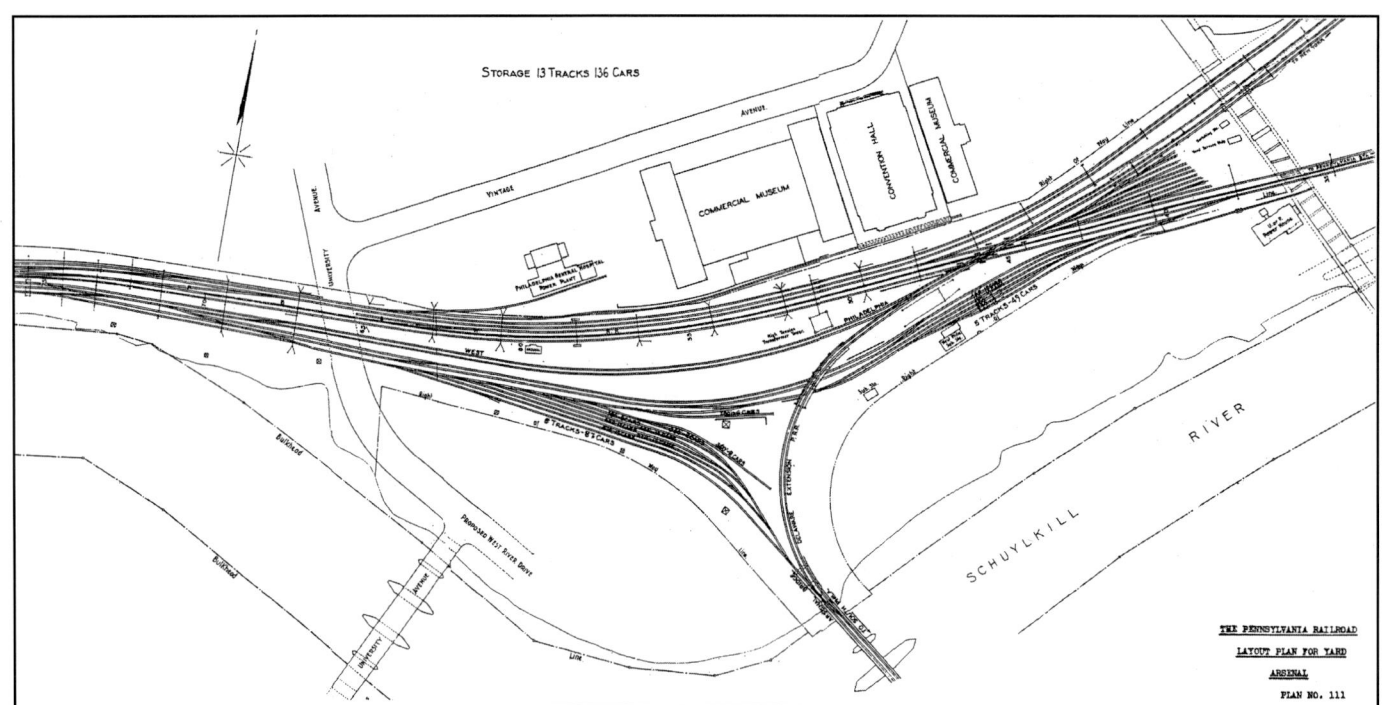

Ted Xaras Collection

MOVING FARTHER SOUTH, we come to the area near ARSENAL Tower (the tower itself is located below the hospital power plant). This was a critical junction - perhaps second in importance only to ZOO - where the Delaware Extension joined the north-south main and the High Line. In this 1935 diagram the High Line, which sweeps down from the upper right, crosses over the main and descends to grade south of the tower. At the wye the Delaware Extension joins the connection to the main and curves across Arsenal Bridge on its way to the yards and port facilities in South Philadelphia.

A SOUTHBOUND passenger train from 30th Street Station approaches ARSENAL Tower on 9 August 1963. We can identify the tracks, left to right, as follows: Outward, Inward (West Chester Branch); Shifting Track leading to South Street Yard area; Southward No. 4 and Northward No. 1 (Main). To the right on the fill are the tracks to the High Line and across Arsenal Bridge to South Philadelphia. The photo was taken looking northward from the tower as the train passes the Philadelphia Civic Center.

John F. Born

SOUTHERN CONFLICT AND CONNECTIONS

ARSENAL Tower took its name from the U.S. government Arsenal formerly located on the east side of the river. It originally protected the crossing (at grade) of the Delaware Extension and the PW&B. Later it fulfilled a role almost as important as ZOO, handling north-south traffic on the main, traffic to and from the West Chester Branch, trains on and off the High Line, movements across Arsenal Bridge to the Delaware Extension, along with freight activity in and out of Grays Ferry Yard (see end papers for the ARSENAL Interlocking Diagram). In this photo also taken 9 August 1963 we see a string of MP54's off the West Chester Branch headed inbound toward 30th Street Station. In the distance is an outbound MU train plus an inbound local freight.

John F. Born

THE SOUTHBOUND *Senator*, led by shiny GG1 4908, passes ARSENAL Tower and heads into 60 mph iron in March of 1952. The train is on southward Track No. 4; immediately behind it is northward Track No. 1, and to the left are the Inward and Outward Tracks. Farther back are the West Philadelphia Elevated (High Line) tracks, which cross over the north-south tracks beyond the tower. The Philadelphia Electric Schuylkill Generating Station is in the background, across the river.

John Pickett/Fred W. Schneider, III Collection

John F. Born

NICELY FRAMED by the signal bridge and under a maze of overhead, a single Silverliner IV - still wearing a PC logo along with its SEPTA markings on 10 November 1978 - heads northward towards ARSENAL. Although traveling northward it is on the southbound passenger main, headed for the line to the suburban (upper) level of 30th Street Station. This excellent photo shows us the High Line connection at left and the West Chester Branch tracks climbing the bank in the background.

SOUTHERN CONFLICT AND CONNECTIONS

LOOKING SOUTH from about the same location, a northbound Amtrak rolls toward Philadelphia. It is 20 years later and the Northeast Corridor has been rebuilt with welded rail and concrete ties on the through tracks. Historic Woodland Cemetery, where several PRR leaders including noted President John Edgar Thomson are laid to rest, is behind the trees at right.

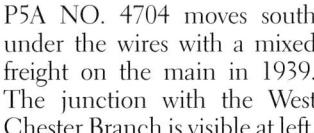

P5A NO. 4704 moves south under the wires with a mixed freight on the main in 1939. The junction with the West Chester Branch is visible at left.

Donald Somerville/Ted Xaras Collection

TRIUMPH III

Ted Xaras Collection

THE DIVERSE ARRAY of lines approaching Philadelphia from the south is shown here in the 1888 Atlas. At top left is the PRR Central Division (originally the West Chester & Philadelphia). Moving left to right we have the PRR Baltimore Division (the former PW&B line) which also extends across to south Philadelphia (note the small engine terminal); the Reading Chester Branch; and the then-new (1886) B&O line into Philadelphia (note the Reading connections).

SOUTHERN CONFLICT AND CONNECTIONS

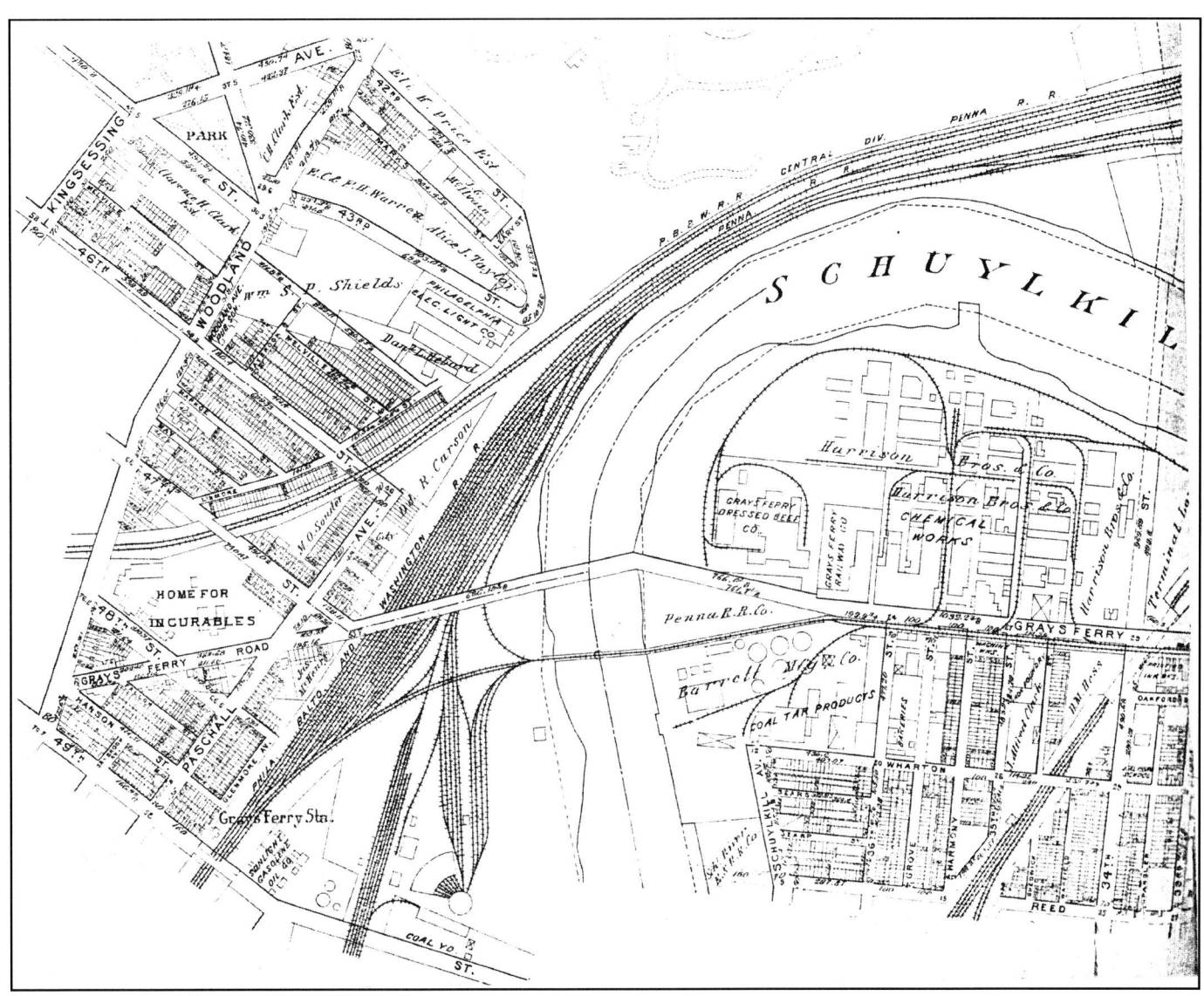

Ted Xaras Collection

BY 1910 the Grays Ferry yard trackage had grown on the west side of the river, and the industrial tracks on the east side had expanded as well.

TRIUMPH III

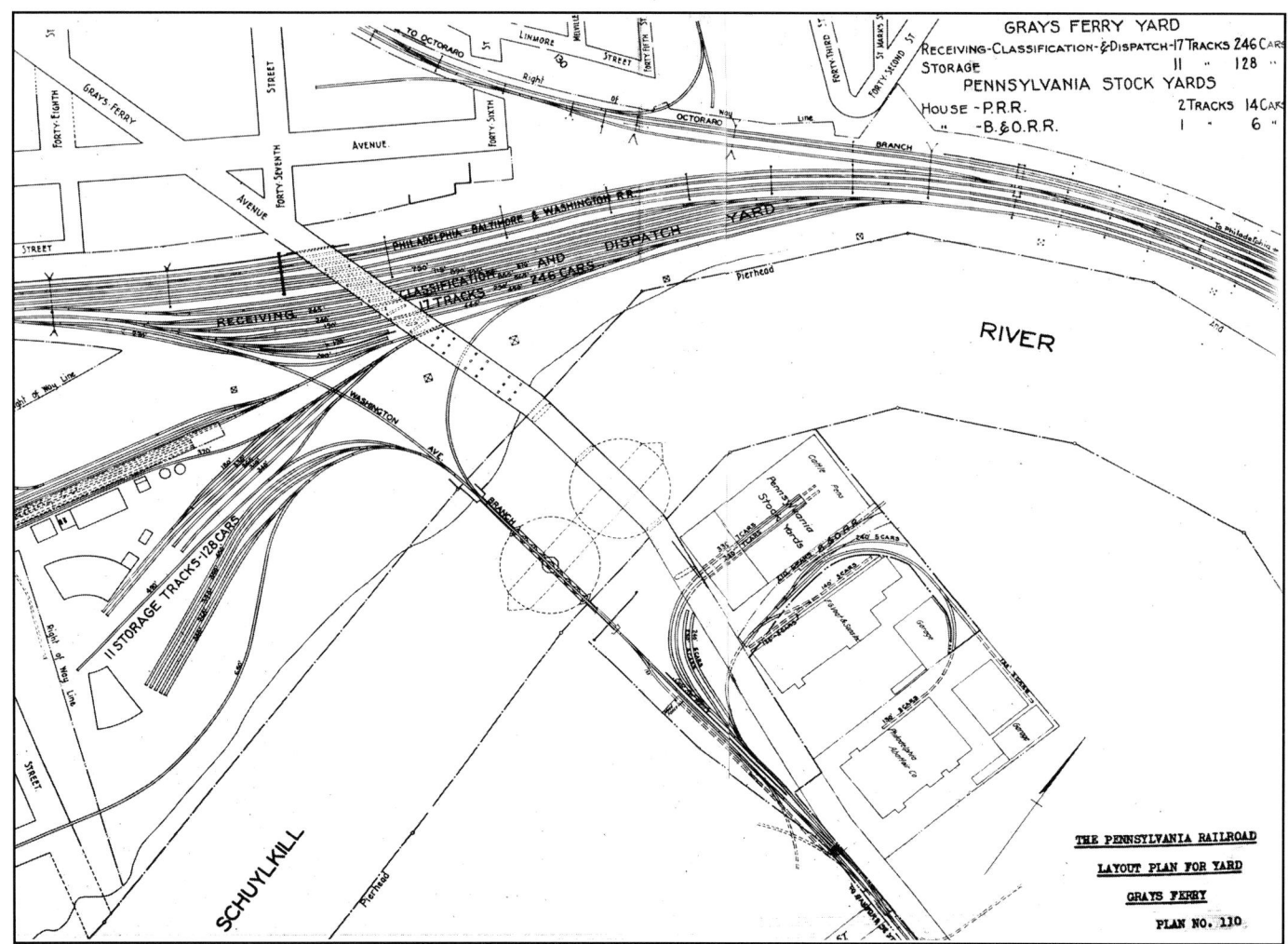

Ted Xaras Collection

THE LAYOUT at Grays Ferry in 1935 is shown here. The yard trackage has only been changed slightly, but we now see the large stockyard complex across the river, along Grays Ferry Avenue. This replaced the old facilities north of Market Street displaced by 30th Street Station trackage during the Improvements. Note the north-south main is still referred to as the PB&W.

SOUTHERN CONFLICT AND CONNECTIONS

Philadelphia City Hall Archive/Ted Xaras Collection

IN 1837-8 the PW&B erected this 800-ft., five-span covered drawbridge over the Schuylkill River at a cost of $200,000. Known as the Newkirk Viaduct, it was a single-track Town truss with one lane for roadway traffic plus the tracks. A stone monument to this line and its builder was later erected just north of the 49th Street overpass along the main. This remarkable photo was taken looking northeastward. Note the telescoping drawspans.

THIS BRIDGE was replaced in 1861 by the iron truss shown on page 293 which was in turn replaced by the wrought iron structure shown on page 294. In 1902 PRR constructed a steel deck truss at this location, shown at the right of this photo. To the left of the bridge is the large new stockyard facility built in 1931 at 36th Street and Grays Ferry Avenue, replacing the ancient complex in West Philadelphia displaced by the approaches to 30th Street Station. This 1939 view looks east across the yards and the Schuylkill River at that impressive structure. The catenary for the newly-completed north-south electrification extends overhead. And oh, yes, that's a Class A5s 0-4-0 in the yards on the west side of the river, one of many of those small workhorses that worked the intricate industrial sidings in the Philadelphia area during the steam years.

Donald Somerville/Ted Xaras Collection

TRIUMPH III

AN ONRUSHING southbound Amtrak is about to duck into the shadow of the 49th Street overpass as it picks up speed south of the City on a sunny day in November 1998. It carries an interesting collection of equipment behind a pair of P-42's running elephant-style, unusual on this electrified thoroughfare. The site of the old Grays Ferry station is at the left, as is the Newkirk Viaduct monument, hidden in the brush.

MOMENTS LATER a northbound R2 SEPTA train from Wilmington heads past the same location.

SOUTHERN CONFLICT AND CONNECTIONS

Herbert H. Harwood, Jr.

THE SOUTHERNMOST tower on the Philadelphia Terminal Division, BRILL (formerly FY) is shown here as it appeared on a sunny day in March 1984. Because of its location it interacted with both Maryland and Philadelphia Terminal dispatchers. Note the complex catenary wire over the equally complex trackwork in this northward view towards the 54th Street overpass.

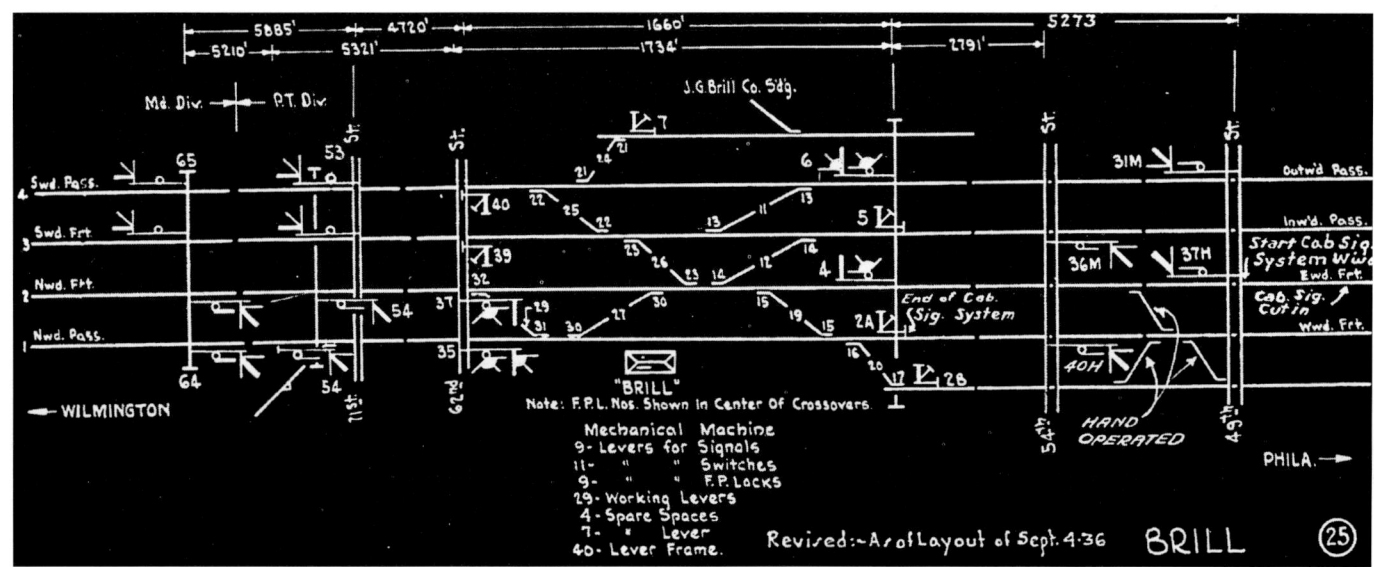

Hagley Museum and Library

BRILL controlled a complete interlocking across the four-track main, as shown here in a 1936 diagram. It also separated traffic off the High Line from the passenger tracks, as well as the interchange with the Hog Island Branch.

TRIUMPH III

Free Library of Philadelphia/Ted Xaras Collection

TO CONCLUDE this chapter, we'll present a few station photos relative to the PW&B and the B&O in Philadelphia. The PW&B vacated its station at 11th and Market Streets and relocated to this impressive Italianate structure at Broad and Prime Streets (Washington Avenue) on 17 May 1852. Known initially as the "Southern and Western Railroad Station," it was over twice the size of the former facility - the train shed covered three platforms and seven tracks and handled both passenger and freight traffic. The PW&B proclaimed that the head house contained "every convenience known or believed to be essential to a station of such prominence." These included a dining room (a first for Philadelphia) as well as the usual waiting room, baggage facilities and ticket office. Most of the Union troops heading south from New York City to meet Confederate forces passed through this depot. Local citizens fed and entertained many thousands of soldiers in a huge canteen located across from the station. This superb view looks northeast on a quiet day ca. 1863, showing horse-drawn streetcars in front of the depot.

SOUTHERN CONFLICT AND CONNECTIONS

Ted Xaras Collection

IN 1876 PW&B rebuilt and enlarged this facility for Centennial Exposition traffic. A separate freight depot was constructed alongside the passenger station and the head house was expanded. When PRR opened Broad Street Station, PW&B trains were shifted over to the new terminal and this facility was no longer used for passengers – it was then remodeled and converted to a freight depot. The front of the remodeled building is shown here in a photo taken on 5 October 1914.

Ted Xaras Collection

THIS VIEW shows the back of the PB&W freight depot ca. 1914, looking east. Note the horse-drawn wagon at the loading door.

TRIUMPH III

Ted Xaras Collection

AFTER B&O finally gained access to Philadelphia, it commissioned noted architect Frank Furness to design this fanciful Victorian edifice at Chestnut and 24th Streets. It was opened in 1887, celebrating B&O's long struggle to reach the city. Its entrance was on Chestnut Street, with tracks below the street level along the east bank of the Schuylkill River. The street level waiting room featured a massive fireplace and a restaurant with an elegant stained glass entrance. On the lower level was a rather plain waiting room, along with ticket office and baggage facilities. A 100 X 300 ft. trainshed spanning four stub-end tracks extended south of the station. This photo looks westward along Chestnut Street in the 1930s, after a light snow had dusted the pavement. (*Editor's Note:* The late Julian W. Barnard made a breathtaking HO model of this station, with lighted interior detail down to an HO railroad display! We had the rare privilege of seeing it at his home in Ohio. Sadly, it did not survive his terminal illness.

SOUTHERN CONFLICT AND CONNECTIONS

Railroad Museum of Pennsylvania (PHMC)

STUNNING – We have many photos of trains in Broad Street Station, but this is one of the best. It shows a gleaming, high-stacked PW&B 4-4-0 No. 98, resplendent with gold striping in front of the original trainshed in the early 1880s, while a PRR colleague waits at left. Note the wooden combine and cast iron detailing on the shed arch. We can't think of a better way to conclude the chapter on the PW&B than to show this photo, which symbolizes its incorporation into the PRR fold.

Chapter 7

Decline and Fall and Reincarnation

PRR in the Postwar Years – and Beyond

Fred W. Schneider, III

DECLINE AND FALL AND REINCARNATION

(Caption for artwork on previous page)

IN THE late 1960s PRR and the federal government embarked on a joint project to improve passenger operations on the New York-Washington corridor, initially for Metroliner service and later in what became known as the Northeast Corridor Project. Most of the cost went to upgrade the roadbed and track – new welded rail and precast, reinforced concrete ties, with heavy rail anchors replacing spikes. Here a southbound train led by AEM-7 945 dashes through the station area at Holmesburg in 1987, typifying Amtrak Northeast Corridor service. Note the concrete ties on the high-speed center tracks, used by Amtrak; the outer ones are used by SEPTA commuter trains and Conrail freights.

In 1945, as World War II moved toward a conclusion, a war-weary PRR reported revenues for 1944 of more than $1 billion but profits were less than 1943 because of government-imposed wage increases combined with restrictions on freight rates and excess-profits taxes. PRR emerged from World War II in better shape than after federal government control during the Great War – however the staggering wartime traffic had taken its toll. Like its competitors it struggled against a variety of post-war monsters. Business boomed, but 1946 saw high expenditures coupled with inflation and rate restrictions that brought PRR's first operating deficit in its 100 years of operation. Although the railroad produced slim profits over the next several years, 1946 was an omen of the future that profoundly shook PRR's ultra conservative management in its centennial year.

After trying a number of experimental steam locomotives without success, PRR belatedly sought the efficiencies of dieselization, but it wasn't enough. Despite the heroic accomplishments of President James M. Symes, including dieselization, opening of a new import ore pier in South Philadelphia, inauguration of TrucTrain trailer-on-flat car service and reconstruction of a state-of-the-art Conway Yard west of Pittsburgh, the handwriting was on the wall for the glory days of the past. Airlines, trucklines and pipelines – and even PRR's old nemesis, canals (waterways as they were now politely called) – all heavily government subsidized, were making strong inroads into the railroad's business.

In addition to the above-mentioned capital expenditures in the 1950s, Symes introduced improved rates and services and better public and employee relations, but none of them were able to stem the loss of traffic, both freight and passenger. Even reorganization from three to nine regions did not bring about the desired economies.

The year 1957 brought a severe economic downturn which struck the Pennsylvania Railroad with severe and unexpected force, leading to the dramatic announcement on 1 November of that fateful year that PRR and its similarly devastated rival New York Central would begin study of a possible consolidation. The recession continued into 1958, resulting in the layoff of thousands of employees and termination of all capital projects. In a shocking development for a road known for its Blue Ribbon Fleet, all long-distance passenger trains were discontinued except the showcase *Broadway*. In an ultimately doomed effort to conserve cash, PRR increasingly deferred maintenance, initiating a vicious cycle that undermined its long-term ability to function as an efficient and competitive transportation system.

Symes characterized 1958 as "one of the most difficult in the history of the company - even more difficult than the depression years of the 1930s."

In 1958 there was no vision other than a singular determination to merge with arch-rival New York Central, which was in a similar financial predicament. The initial contacts between Symes and his NYC counterpart Robert Young were cordial, although neither truly wanted merger of their once-proud railroads to occur. However, an initial study showed that annual savings of $100 million could be achieved by such a combination. Weary from endless proxy battles and legal suits (unrelated to the merger), Young suddenly committed suicide, and his protege Alfred Perlman took over the Central's reins.

Symes turned over the presidency to Allen J. Greenough in 1959, assuming the new position of chairman. He set out to improve service and profits, reorganized the regional structure again, and was rewarded with some modest improvement in operating efficiencies. After a brief increase in profits in Greenough's first year, during which PRR placed its largest rolling stock order for 23,500 freight cars (worth $215 million) the downturn resumed in 1960. PRR posted a loss in that year and again in 1962. In a portent of things to come, income came increasingly from non-railroad sources.

In 1958, with a temporary improvement in the Central's earnings, Alfred Perlman had called off the merger talks. He had other ideas, like modernizing and rebuilding his railroad, although he did talk merger with old PRR rivals B&O and C&O as a "counterweight" to PRR's interests in the N&W. C&O and B&O suddenly announced that they were joining forces, and the N&W moved toward acquisition of the Nickel Plate and the Wabash, *without* the New York Central. Perlman finally agreed to resume the disbanded talks with PRR on 25 October 1961. Agreement came quickly – on 12 January 1962 the boards of both roads approved a merger plan, with PRR holding the controlling interest. The stockholders obediently followed suit.

The ICC began hearings on the merger that were to drag on until 1 October 1963, but it took two and a half years to render a decision, and nearly two years after that for all the court litigation to be resolved.

But the leading characters – and the chemistry – changed again: Symes retired and Stuart Saunders from the N&W, then a PRR-controlled road, assumed the chairmanship on 1 October 1963, the day of the ICC decision. In addition to an intense personal dislike for each other, Saunders and Perlman disagreed on strategy, operations and even the organizational structure of the combined company. Perlman wanted the company to concentrate on railroad operations, abandoning unprofitable branches and utilizing a lean management team to achieve maximum operating efficiency. Saunders on the other hand was interested in the company becoming a conglomerate along the lines of then-successful ITT, Litton Industries and Gulf & Western.

Symes had started with the old Broad Street Station and approach properties in Philadelphia, building the huge Penn Center complex of office towers and shops, to which PRR moved their corporate headquarters in 1957. In New York City the unthinkable became reality when an alliance was formed with the Madison Square Garden Corporation, tragically resulting in Cassatt's landmark Penn Station being demolished to make way for an office tower and a new Madison Square Garden. Symes continued with the development of other PRR land holdings in Chicago and along the Ohio River. Saunders extended the initiative even further by acquiring the Buckeye Pipeline Company, Macco Realty and the Strick Holding Company, as well as a major interest in the Great Southwest Corporation, a builder of amusement parks.

Saunders was turning PRR into a leading land developer – having spent upwards of $200 million on highly speculative investments at a time when large cash reserves would be needed for the merger of the two railroads both badly in need of rebuilding.

And speaking of merger, the ICC had yet to approve it, based partly on objections from several weak New England lines, notably the New Haven RR. The New Haven petitioned the ICC to be included in the merger and finally Saunders, over Perlman's strong objections, was forced to agree. The New Haven, which lost $22 million during 1968, subsequently joined the merged company on 1 January 1969, and Penn Central had to expend a like amount to repair the New Haven's debilitated equipment.

Saunders also agreed to a complex (and grossly expensive) Merger Protective Agreement granting labor huge benefits in return for a meager 5% per year workforce reduction and – paramount to Saunders – the unions dropping their opposition to the merger.

Saunders worked tirelessly in behalf of the merger, overcoming a variety of objections from several quarters, many of them led by Pennsylvania Democratic gubernatorial candidate Milton Shapp. On 17 April 1966 the ICC reached unanimous approval, although the Justice Department held out until November 1967. Finally, on 1 February 1968, 122 years after it had begun, PRR ceased to exist and the Pennsylvania New York Transportation Company came into being. This awkward name was shortened to Penn Central on 8 May 1968 and changed again on 1 October 1969 to Penn Central Transportation Company, which in turn became a subsidiary of the Penn Central Company, which was the holding company, consistent with Saunders' concept of the organization.

Name changes notwithstanding it was soon headed for disaster. Despite propaganda to the contrary, Penn Central was unable to turn things around.

DECLINE AND FALL AND REINCARNATION

Incompatible operating systems and philosophies resulted in huge delays and lost shipments. Commuter operations went from bad to worse, with delays becoming the norm. The road lost $5.2 million from rail operations in 1968, $56 million in 1969 and finally a staggering $431 million in 1970, although the railroad losses were hidden in complex consolidated statements that reflected income from other sources and kept the public, the financial community and the stockholders from discovering the harsh reality. The amusement parks and many of the land holdings were sold to cover operating losses, but it wasn't enough. On 21 June 1970 Penn Central Transportation Company, the largest corporate merger in U.S. history at its inception, declared bankruptcy ... the largest in history to that date, another rueful record for PRR which always did things in a big way.

What had gone wrong?

Just about everything.

Volumes have been written on the subject of the Penn Central bankruptcy, but all agree that it was a combination of internal and external factors, including diverse corporate cultures, poor internal communication at all levels, incompatible computer systems, enormous debt structure, a declining industrial base, intense competition from other transportation modes and costly passenger operations, both commuter and long-haul.

PRR, which behaved through most of its years as a "very proper [Republican] Philadelphia business enterprise," had always prided itself on being able to grow, but there came a time when it could no longer do so. It had always returned a dividend, but its rigid, promote-from-within management culture became insular and stagnant, bent on following traditional policies and procedures long after their validity had disappeared. New talent went elsewhere. Profits from Symes' and Saunders' vaunted real estate investments proved illusory and diluted attention, to say nothing of draining off cash, from the urgently needed rebuilding of the railroad infrastructure.

The New York Central, even in the 1950s, had still exhibited the individual risk-taking fervor from the days of the remarkable Commodore Cornelius Vanderbilt and his son, William H. Its dynamic new leader Alfred Perlman represented a new breed of market-oriented railroad men, willing to innovate and embrace new technologies, and who hired young managers to carry out his ideas.

There were social differences between them as well. We have already characterized the Main Line social order occupied by PRR executives. As authors Joseph Daughen and Peter Binzen describe it, Perlman and other Central executives "lived in posh Westchester County [north of New York City] but they didn't 'occupy it' as their PRR counterparts did on the Main Line." There were age and attitude differences as well, leading to an atmosphere of mutual distrust and even outright disrespect.

Perlman, to his credit, wanted to upgrade the combined railroads' physical plant and modernize systems and equipment, but was frustrated in doing so by David C. Bevan, who as chairman of the finance committee, controlled the priorities of the increasingly lean financial resources, seemingly with Saunders' blessing. While painting a generally rosy financial picture to the stockholders and the financial community, Saunders and Bevan began a program of trying to borrow wherever they could. The reason was that the road was losing a staggering *half a million dollars a day.* A variety of options was explored: The Long Island RR was sold to the State of New York for $65 million, ICC authorization was obtained to sell commercial paper, a $59 million loan from Swiss banks was established, a $300 million revolving credit loan was negotiated with a group of New York and Chicago banks.

After months of political infighting and intrigue, Perlman was given the meaningless position of Vice-Chairman because of his continuing insistence on funds to rebuild the railroad. Paul A. Gorman, the hard-nosed former president of Western Electric, who had earned a reputation as a cost-cutter, was named President to try and turn things around. It was much too little and much too late as the most severe winter in decades engulfed the eastern U.S. and dealt a fatal blow to the already staggering railroad. Saunders, Gorman and what was left of the management team were wallowing in red ink.

If it was possible, the new year brought even worse results. Penn Central lost $102 million in the first quarter of 1970. A $100 million bond issue was offered and then withdrawn because disastrous financial results could no longer be hidden. The road then went to the federal government for emergency assistance. But there was a price to pay to win the reluctant Nixon administration's approval for a bailout – the "old" management team had to go. On 8 June the board elected Gorman chairman, president and chief executive officer; Saunders, Perlman and Bevan were out. But a Byzantine array of politics intervened – the promised government loan guarantees were not to be forthcoming.

Just so you can get a feel for the grim situation that faced Gorman and the board, on 21 June 1970 Penn Central Transportation Co. had current liabilities of some $749 million; current assets amounted to $462 million, with only $7.3 million in cash reserves on hand. There was only one alternative left. The Board passed the following motion:

> "RESOLVED that the board authorizes the Chairman of the Board to sign and cause to be filed a petition in the form presented at this meeting for voluntary reorganization of the company under Section 77 of the Bankruptcy Act."

After 124 years the lumbering giant of eastern railroading had fallen.

Along with most of the railroads in the Northeast, Penn Central was crushed by factors largely outside of its control: a business recession, a general decline in industry critical to the railroad's profits, dramatic increases in subsidized competitive modes of transportation and punishing rate divisions vis-a-vis southern and western railroads. It labored with a decayed physical plant, high labor and terminal costs, particularly the enormous burden of commuter service, and government policies – developed in an era when the railroads were a transportation monopoly – that subsidized their competitors and prevented the kinds of changes needed to run a railroad in the 20th century.

In retrospect, as bad as Penn Central's fall was, it at least served notice to the public and government officials alike that something needed to be done to rescue the Northeastern railroads – Penn Central was the largest, but not the only line in trouble – faced with these onerous burdens.

The remarkably cogent Penn Central trustees' report of 10 February 1971 outlined the following drastic steps that needed to be taken:

1) Reduce route miles by 40%
2) Restructure freight rates
3) Implement labor adjustments
4) Establish a quasi-public agency to take over long-haul passenger service

It echoed the strikingly similar conclusions reached by former Senator George Smathers for the Association of American Railroads issued, not completely coincidentally, nine days after Penn Central had filed for bankruptcy protection.

For money-losing passenger service it was only with successive government intervention, in the formation of the National Rail Passenger Corporation (known initially as Railpax and later as Amtrak) on 1 May 1971 to take over long-distance operations, that the onerous burden began to be lifted. Amtrak received $40 million in government grants, $100 million in federal loan guarantees and some $200 million in cash, loans or equipment from the operating railroads (who were reimbursed for their costs of operation). Several regional authorities (MTA in New York, CTA in Connecticut, NJ Transit in New Jersey, and SEPTA and Patco in Philadelphia) were formed to assume responsibility for local commuter operations.

But it still wasn't enough.

The next step was the Regional Rail Reorganization Act, which was passed by Congress and reluctantly signed by an embattled President Nixon on 2 January 1974. This bill created the United States Railway Association, financed by a $1.5 billion government bond issue. USRA was granted authority to slash unprofitable lines – almost half of the total mileage. We should note that if this had been allowed to be done on the individual railroads 20 years before it *might* have prevented the ensuing debacle.

On 9 November 1975 the Consolidated Rail Corporation was formed to take over Penn Central and six other Northeast railroads, including ownership of trackage used by Amtrak and many of the commuter lines. After its funding was finally guaranteed by the Railroad Revitalization and Regulatory Reform Act of 1976 signed by President Ford (also reluctantly) on 5 February, Conrail began operations on 1 April, supported by $2.1 billion from USRA. It continued to cut unprofitable lines, but still lost $246 million in its first 9 months of operations. From the beginning, it embarked on an aggressive capital improvement effort designed to upgrade its long-neglected trackage, rolling stock and computer systems. It also put in place strong control systems to monitor oper-

DECLINE AND FALL AND REINCARNATION

ational performance. Perhaps the greatest legacy of the early Conrail years - and its first CEO, Edward Jordan - was the landmark Staggers Act, resulting in deregulation of railroad rates, traffic routing and line abandonment And in 1981 L. Stanley Crane, a giant in the mold of Thomson, took command.

It took a while for the payback - deficits increased to $430 million in 1977 and then slowly began to decline until Conrail finally posted a modest profit of $39 million in 1981. In that year the Northeast Rail Service Act (NERSA) was passed, allowing Conrail to completely turn over passenger operations – and the right-of-way – to Amtrak and various regional commuter authorities in 1983. In that decisive year Conrail met two NERSA profitability standards.

Finally on 21 October 1986, after rejecting several outrageous buyout bids, Congress passed the Conrail Preservation Act directing that the federal government's 85% common stock interest be sold to the private sector. In what was then the largest initial stock offering to date, Conrail was sold for $1.6 billion in March 1987. One hundred forty-one years after PRR was chartered its reincarnated successor had a charter of its own. Conrail went on to challenge its critics and become the premier rail system in the northeast and upper midwest, accomplishing what it set out to do – and ultimately doing it very well. Until, of course, it was savaged by CSX and NS.

In Philadelphia, as elsewhere on the line, many shorter branches and yard facilities were abandoned. The 46th Street enginehouse had gradually deteriorated and was abandoned in the late 1960s and demolished in the mid-70s. The yard trackage east of 52nd Street was finally torn up in the 80s.

With declining passenger service (except for the commuter operation at the eastern end) and heavy industry in the valley nearly moribund, the Schuylkill Branch was gradually abandoned and much of the right-of-way from Norristown west to Valley Forge Park subsequently converted to a popular bike and jogging trail. In the mid-80s the Manayunk Bridge was taken out of service because of deterioration of the masonry, and commuter service was cut back to Bala Cynwyd as a result. Remarkably the Frazer Branch, although shortened, was still operated by Conrail, accessed by cutting over the river from the ex-Reading main.

SEPTA, with government financing, finally constructed the long-delayed Center City Tunnel in 1978-84 to connect the former PRR commuter lines serving the western and southwestern suburbs with the former rival Reading lines serving the northern and northwestern areas of the City. This transformed Suburban Station from a terminal to a largely through operation and bypassed the abandoned Reading Terminal (a latter-day triumph in disguise?). Four tracks and platforms of Suburban Station were rebuilt to access the tunnel line, which continued westward through Center City, stopping at Market East station and then surfacing at Green Street to join with the old Reading line at Brown Street. Four stub tracks still remain in Suburban Station, where trains for the evening rush hours are "turned." A fifth track is located in Market East for Media trains.

Interestingly the remaining locals serving former PRR commuter stations originate from Reading territory, e.g. at the end of the line or the former Reading Roberts Yard near the Roosevelt Expressway, while locals serving the former Reading lines to the north and northwest originate in Paoli or the PRR Powelton Avenue Yard near 30th Street Station. Operationally it makes sense but historically it carries a heavy dose of irony.

At this writing SEPTA achieves reasonable success in maintaining on-time service. It has carried out several major upgrade programs – new equipment for the Norristown High-Speed line and new maintenance facilities for the rush-hour push-pull equipment at Frazer and for the Silverliners at Overbrook, replacing the venerable Paoli Shops. However, other projects need attention to reverse a steadily deteriorating physical plant. Heavy netting under several masonry bridges (to prevent falling debris from injuring people or damaging property) is forlorn testimony to their former glory, although some government-subsidized reconstruction work is underway. The mile-long stretch between 30th Street and Suburban stations, at 500 trains a week the most heavily-traveled trackage in the City, is to be rebuilt using new federal and state funding.

Amtrak operates its State-subsidized Keystone Service over the Philadelphia-Harrisburg main, along with the two through trains to Chicago, the *Three Rivers* and the recently-extended *Pennsylvanian*. Hourly Metroliners and a host of through trains ply the high-speed Northeast Corridor through Philadelphia, and new and faster equipment is forthcoming for this service, rendering the upgraded line competitive to air transport between Boston and Washington.

In addition it also appears that SEPTA will need a continuing infusion of cash to arrest the deterioration of its physical plant and even to expand its operations to meet changing suburban and exurban commuter travel patterns. In fact, a Major Investment Study is underway at this writing to explore restoration of rail commuter service in the Schuylkill Valley as far as Reading – to be known as the Schuylkill Valley Metro. It will most likely make use of the ex-Reading right-of-way (now Norfolk Southern) in some manner, but may also utilize short segments of the ex-PRR route.

In addition to Amtrak's superb restoration of 30th Street Station, government and/or private funds are or will be used to restore or rehabilitate several others to their former glory: Overbrook, Merion, Ardmore, Radnor, Wayne, Strafford and Devon on the Main Line and Allen Lane on the former PRR Chestnut Hill Branch. A new North Philadelphia Station waiting room and ticket office have replaced the derelict old building, which is to be rehabilitated for other purposes. A badly-needed new $20 million Transportation Center will be built in Paoli, west of the existing station, which will be closed.

Even yeoman ZOO interlocking has received attention. New Central Instrument Houses with old and familiar names, Girard and Mantua (at the west and east end of the Schuylkill River bridge, respectively), now tie about half of ZOO's previous functions into Amtrak's computerized CETC (Centralized Electrification and Traffic Control) system located in 30th Street Station. Amtrak signal engineers working on the project used old cable ducts to route new ones and paid tribute to PRR engineering in the process. Even with this $6.5 million change the Philadelphia area remains a "tower oasis in a land of railroad computer-control." In addition to ZOO, towers remain active at NORTH PHILADELPHIA, OVERBROOK and PAOLI.

And the saga continues, as we continue to find reasons for optimism – and perhaps even resurgent triumph – in the future of railroading in Philadelphia, PRR's home city.

DECLINE AND FALL AND REINCARNATION

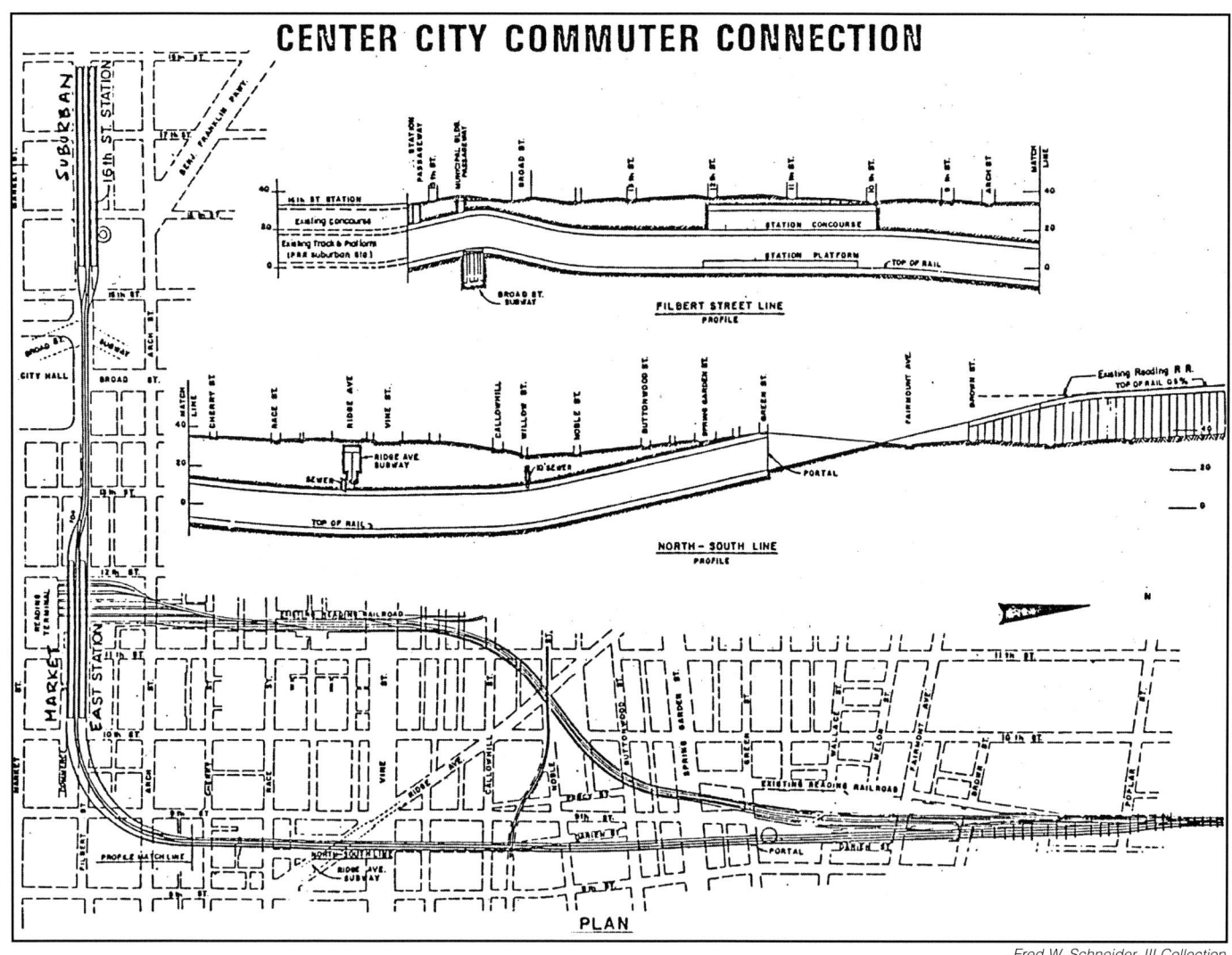

Fred W. Schneider, III Collection

AS FAR BACK as 1888, Samuel Rea (then Assistant to the Second Vice President) proposed a rapid transit connection between the PRR and Reading terminals in Philadelphia. Although the distance between Broad Street Station and Reading Terminal was less than 1/2 mile, the tracks were separated by a vertical distance of 63 feet and aligned at right angles to each other! Although the idea was resurrected several times, it took 90 years, the demise of both railroads, the creation of Amtrak, Conrail and SEPTA, and overcoming local neighborhood opposition before construction finally began on what came to be known as the Center City Commuter Rail Connection in 1978. By that point in time, SEPTA ridership was at 115,000 trips per day and increasing, and the two stub-end terminals were operationally inefficient, with inadequate track capacity to handle rush-hour volume (shades of Broad Street Station!). The four-track line was planned to extend from the previous stub end of Penn Center (Suburban) Station, through a new Market East Station under the former Reading Terminal trainshed, curve northward east of 9th Street, emerge through a portal at Green Street and then onto an embankment and a new concrete viaduct to join the ex-Reading mainline at Popular Street. In the process it eases over the top of the Broad Street subway and then under the Ridge Avenue line.

TRIUMPH III

Fred W. Schneider, III

ALTHOUGH most of the line was constructed using cut and cover techniques, building a four-track line under existing structures in the heart of the City presented many engineering challenges. This photo taken 13 August 1980 shows the concrete beam and grid system supported by concrete caissons used to carry the load of the Reading Terminal train shed. The previously buried caissons then became supporting columns for the new Market East Station.

DECLINE AND FALL AND REINCARNATION

MARKET EAST Station is shown here on 30 May 1988, not long after its opening. The station consists of two platforms, each 35 ft. wide and 850 ft. long, serving the four tracks. Stairs, escalators and elevators lead from the platforms to a concourse level which connects with the Market Street subway and 10th, 11th and 12th Streets. It is a bright, airy facility that contains a variety of restaurants and shops.

The overall Rail Connection project cost over $315 million and took over 6 years to complete. It allowed SEPTA trains to run through from Paoli (ex-PRR) to Doylestown or Lansdale (ex-Reading). What diehard PRR (or for that matter, Reading) fan would have thought it would come to this?

Fred W. Schneider, III

John J. Bowman, Jr./Fred W. Schneider, III Collection

CONNECTING the two lines allowed Reading equipment to run on PRR rails. Here we see a SEPTA fantrip using former Reading "Blue Cars" headed west on ex-PRR trackage at Overbrook on a sunny early June day in 1988.

SEPTA opened a new Overbrook Maintenance Facility in space formerly occupied by yard trackage west of 52nd Street. This state-of-the-art complex, shown here looking westward in October 1998, replaced the venerable Paoli Car Shops.

AMTRAK has constructed a sleek new waiting room and ticket office at North Philadelphia, replacing the venerable structure used for some 90 years. It retains the former north entrance to the passenger tunnel. The high-level platforms have been rebuilt and the canopies refurbished. This October 1998 view looks east (northward) at the new facility.

DECLINE AND FALL AND REINCARNATION

FARTHER EAST, an NJ Transit train from Atlantic City approaches SHORE interlocking on 26 October 1998. NJ Transit runs these push-pull trains seven days a week to and from the Jersey shore.

BOTH CSX and Norfolk Southern plan upgrades of Philadelphia-area facilities to increase intermodal traffic –and improve schedules – on their New York-Chicago routes. Accomplishing this involves expanding terminals at both Morrisville, New Jersey (NS) at the end of the former PRR Trenton Cutoff and at Greenwich Yard in South Philadelphia (CSX). Already completed is a re-grading of the south leg of the wye at ARSENAL. This photo, taken 10 September 1998, shows Conrail crews working to reactivate the connection to the second track on the High Line. With connections at both northern and southern ends, we will have a latter-day reincarnation of the Junction RR, perhaps even replacing the CSX (former B&O) line on the east side of the river. How's that for irony!

TRIUMPH III

AND IN Greenwich Yard, a pair of Conrail GE units move a long string of ballast hoppers in position on 2 November 1998. This is part of CSX's program to upgrade its intermodal capability in South Philadelphia.

AS WE TAKE a final look at Center City Philadelphia, a short two-car SEPTA train moves eastward across the river toward the bridges over the B&O (now CSX) tracks and on into Suburban Station. The towering buildings of Liberty Place, which dramatically changed Philadelphia's skyline in a spectacular latter-day fulfillment of the Philadelphia Improvements, are being completed in this November 1989 photo. They are situated in the area just south of the former Broad Street Station approach tracks.

Herbert H. Harwood, Jr.

Chapter 8
Triumph in Color

WE BEGIN our color journey of the PT Division in the bowels of Penn Center (Suburban) Station on 4 April 1980. Overhead clearances here are very tight!

Fred W. Schneider, III

AN MU TRAIN with red PRR keystone emerges from the subway to Suburban Station and heads westward up the grade toward the upper level of 30th Street Station on 7 August 1967.

Fred W. Schneider, III

TRAIN NO. 23 with a string of MP54s heads out of the upper level of 30th Street on its way to Paoli in September 1958.

William J. Coxey

THIRTY YEARS LATER a Silverliner is framed by the canopies as it heads into the upper level platform area.

Thomas Fuchs

353

TRIUMPH III

William J. Coxey

THE WEST FAÇADE of 30th Street Station gleams in the afternoon sun in September 1958, showing the elegance of the Corinthian columns.

Tom Kane

CLEANED AND RESTORED to original beauty, 30th Street glows like a jewel in this dramatic night shot looking west across the Schuylkill River. PRR's triumphant edifice underwent a $75 million rehabilitation program from 1988 to 1991; this photo was taken shortly after that effort was completed.

TRIUMPH IN COLOR

THE INTERIOR of 30th Street likewise received a complete restoration. This stunning shot looks west over the War Memorial, showing the majestic gold-leaved Corinthian columns towering over the Main Concourse.

Tom Kane

GG1 NO. 4916 shows off its single-stripe scheme in July 1965 against a background of assorted other tuscan red equipment in Penn Coach Yard behind the station.

IT'S NOW 1998 and the color scheme has changed, as a variety of Amtrak equipment has taken up residence.

355

A LONG STRING of Silverliners heads west past the substation at ZOO Tower on 8 December 1963.

SHINY Amtrak P42 No. 102 turns on the wye at ZOO on a frigid 2 January 1999.

Andrew M. Wilson

TRIUMPH IN COLOR

William J. Coxey

TIRED Baldwin Centipede No. 5813 awaits the next helper assignment at the 46th Street Enginehouse in March 1959.

Chester D. Fuhrman

MERGER – Renumbered S1 No. 9443 and freshly-painted cabin car 4720 exemplify the merger as they sit in the 52nd Street Yard in April 1968

TRIUMPH III

MOVING to the Chestnut Hill Branch, we see an inbound Silverliner at Tulpehocken Station on 20 August 1998.

MOVING NORTH on the SEPTA R8 line we come to Allen Lane as an inbound Silverliner picks up passengers on the same day.

TRIUMPH IN COLOR

AN OUTBOUND Silverliner pauses at St. Martins on that pleasant August day in 1998. This station has been lovingly maintained, with attractive flower planters all around.

HERE WE SEE a pair of Silverliners at Chestnut Hill West (in SEPTA terminology), at the terminus of the ex-PRR branch.

William J. Coxey

THE *Broadway Limited* outraces the camera shutter through North Philadelphia in April 1959, blurring the GG1's number. North Philadelphia was the stop for PRR's best east-west trains during this era.

A NORTHBOUND Metroliner, led by AEM-7 No. 942, races past SHORE Tower on 20 September 1998, as a SEPTA commuter train moves on the Frankford Elevated line overhead.

LOOKING the other way we catch an inbound NJ Transit train off the Delair line making its way through SHORE interlocking on the same day.

TRIUMPH IN COLOR

RED-NOSED Amtrak GG1 No. 927 leads a short train southbound through Frankford Junction Station on 15 May 1975.

Dave Hyer

GRIMY S4 No. 8894 moves a local freight around the big curve at Frankford Junction on 8 October 1966.

A TRIO of EMD six-axle units powers a freight eastward toward the Delair Bridge in June 1998.

Andrew M. Wilson

AN ASSORTMENT of Conrail power awaits assignment in Frankford Yard on 13 February 1999. The Delair line is in the background.

Andrew M. Wilson

PENN CENTRAL assigned a freshly-painted GG1 to a long Army-Navy Game special, shown here as it glides southward through Tacony in November 1969.

William J. Coxey

ANOTHER black GG1 leads train No. 172, The *Senator*, northbound approaching Holmesburg Junction in November 1969.

William J. Coxey

TRIUMPH IN COLOR

FRAMED – A pair of Silverliners heads north through Holmesburg Junction on 10 September 1995. Note the derailed Sperry Railcar in the background, on the lead to the Bustleton Branch.

ANOTHER Army-Navy Game special, this time a 12-car string of Silverliners southbound from Trenton, moves past HOLMES Tower in November 1969.

William J. Coxey

BIG P70 No. 600 hustles a mixed Amtrak consist northward through Holmesburg Junction in November 1969.

Andrew M. Wilson

363

TRIUMPH III

MOVING to the Main Line, we see an inbound Silverliner at the immaculate Merion station on 30 May 1998.

SILVERLINER No. 404 pauses at the westbound shelter at Wynnewood on the same date. The restored eastbound structure is now occupied by a small bakery.

BRYN MAWR from the air shows the old freight station at lower left, and proceeding westward the passenger station, and then the tower. This October 1997 view also shows the complete set of crossovers at the midpoint on the Main Line.

Michael Smith/Aerial Views

TRIUMPH IN COLOR

AN OUTBOUND DUO passes the Bryn Mawr substation on 30 May 1998 as it approaches the station platforms.

AS IT PAUSES at the westbound shelter we get a look at BRYN MAWR Tower still standing in 1998.

AN INBOUND PAIR stops at the attractive Bryn Mawr station on 30 May 1998.

TRIUMPH III

A TRIO of Geeps led by No. 7206 works hard as it approaches Villanova at the head of a westbound ore train a few months into the merger in April 1968. *Chester D. Fuhrman*

AS THE TRAIN roars through the station we see the Haupt Truss being used as a highway overpass still in place over the tracks. *Chester D. Fuhrman*

THE WESTBOUND *St. Louisian* approaches Radnor with a full head-end complement on 12 April 1964. Watch out for eastbounds, Fred!

Fred W. Schneider, III

A STRING of eight MP54s moves west of Radnor in September 1967.

Fred W. Schneider, III

AN EASTBOUND pair of Silverliners pauses at St. Davids on 30 May 1998.

TRIUMPH III

Michael Smith/Aerial Views

AN AERIAL SHOT captures a trio of Silverliners at the red-roofed westbound shelter in Wayne during September 1997.

Fred W. Schneider, III

THIRTY YEARS EARLIER a quartet of westbound MP54s stops at the same location.

TRIUMPH IN COLOR

SHINING JEWEL – Touches of fall color set off Strafford Station in this October 1997 aerial shot.

Michael Smith/Aerial Views

AN OCTET of classic MP54s heads eastward toward Philadelphia after stopping at the equally classic Strafford Station on 10 August 1967.

Fred W. Schneider, III

TRIUMPH III

Fred W. Schneider, III

THE EXQUISITE DETAIL of the Strafford Station is worth another look on the same sunny day in 1967.

AMTRAK Keystone Service Train No. 648 roars eastbound through the Devon Station on 30 May 1998.

TRIUMPH IN COLOR

CLASSIC – An inbound MU train is dramatically framed by the platform canopy at historic Berwyn Station on 7 August 1967.

Fred W. Schneider, III

THIRTY-ONE YEARS later a pair of Silverliners stops at the same location. The station has been restored and houses an art gallery.

TRIUMPH III

THIS AERIAL VIEW looking westward at Berwyn clearly shows the relationship between the Main Line and Lancaster Turnpike (Route 30). The Cassatt Avenue overpass is being rebuilt in this October 1997 photo.

Michael Smith/Aerial Views

THE LAYOUT of facilities at Paoli in October 1997 is shown in this westward aerial view. The station is at the bottom; in the center of the photo are PAOLI Tower and the now-empty MU yards, and beyond are the substation and abandoned Car Shops.

Michael Smith/Aerial Views

TRIUMPH IN COLOR

PAOLI TOWER and substation are nicely framed by an inbound Silverliner and the platform canopy on 30 May 1998.

Chester D. Fuhrman

HERE we see PAOLI Tower again, this time with a pair of E44s returning from a helper assignment in April 1968.

TRIUMPH III

A STRING OF MP54s in PRR and PC schemes exemplify the merger transition outside the Paoli Car Shops on 8 September 1968.

THE WORK of maintaining the mainline SEPTA fleet is shared by the Overbrook facility (shown in Chapter 7) and this new shop at Frazer, built in 1996 and pictured here in a September 1997 aerial view. Overbrook services the Silverliners and this facility handles the AEM-7 powered push-pull trains, used during rush hours. The westward lead extends to the Trenton Cutoff (Conrail Dale Secondary) at Glen Loch.

Michael Smith/Aerial Views

TRIUMPH IN COLOR

A LONE Silverliner crosses the jumpover bridge after stopping at 52nd Street Station on its way west on the Schuylkill Branch in April 1968.

Chester D. Fuhrman

SILVERLINER No. 223 comprises Train No. 664 as it heads inbound across the concrete arch bridge from Manayunk on 18 January 1964.

Jim Brazel

A TRIO of RS-3s leads a train eastward over the Oakes Reach section of the Schuylkill Canal into Mont Clare in February 1966.

TRAIN TIME at the station in Pottstown in a ca. 1910 postcard scene finds a variety of horsedrawn equipment ready to do its duty

TRIUMPH IN COLOR

ON 15 MAY 1975, late in the Penn Central era, a quartet of black E44s moves a coal train southbound on the High Line, past the West Philadelphia Steam Plant.

Dave Hyer

IT'S NOW November 1988 and a Conrail lashup moves an ore train northward on the High Line, with sun reflecting off the windshield of the trailing unit.

Thomas Fuchs

A CONRAIL Geep works street trackage on Washington Avenue in South Philadelphia in May of 1994.

Andrew M. Wilson

ANOTHER Conrail operation in the street, this time on Delaware Avenue above Oregon Avenue, on 21 June 1998.

Andrew M. Wilson

CONRAIL Train XGW-48T enters Greenwich Yard at the location of former STADIUM Tower on 24 August 1991.

Jeremy Taylor

A PAIR of clean EMD six-axle power idles in Greenwich Yard, awaiting its assignment to a westbound string of hoppers in December 1993.

Andrew M. Wilson

TRIUMPH IN COLOR

ALL IS QUIET on Christmas Day 1998 as an assortment of Conrail powers sits in the snow near the yard tower.

Andrew M. Wilson

DINKIES No. 3 and 4, used to move hoppers at the Greenwich Point ore pier, sit idle on 24 November 1998.

Andrew M. Wilson

William J. Coxey

THE ORE UNLOADERS make an imposing scene silhouetted against the sky in March 1959, with a ship alongside the pier.

379

Andrew M. Wilson

A WESTBOUND Conrail freight makes its way from the ex-PRR Junction RR to ex-Reading trackage near Belmont Yard in August 1993.

William J. Coxey

HERE'S an interesting move – An MBM62T RPO (one of just four) and motorized combine move south from the Post Office on the River Line to ARSENAL Tower; then they will head north through the upper level of 30th Street to Suburban Station, where they will become the first two cars of Train No. 266, a New York MU local. This September 1958 shot is very near the end of MU RPO service in Philadelphia.

TRIUMPH IN COLOR

William J. Coxey

A BIT farther south GG1 No. 4989 heads Train No. 171, *The Colonial*, with a matched string of New Haven stainless steel equipment toward Washington, D.C. on a sunny day in September 1958.

William J. Coxey

AEM-7 No. 947 leads another matched set, this time Amfleet equipment in the Phase IV scheme, southbound past ARSENAL Tower on 1 October 1998.

TRIUMPH III

SPIRIT OF 76 — a pair of P42s heads Amtrak Train No. 630 northbound past CP ARSENAL on 1 October 1998.

A TRIO of outbound Silverliners heads toward Media on the R3 line, with the Philadelphia skyline in the background on the same day.

TRIUMPH IN COLOR

Andrew M. Wilson

HEADED SOUTH – A portent of the future as the Conrail business train leaves the Philadelphia skyline behind on 13 March 1999, most likely carrying Conrail and/or CSX/NS officials.

TRIUMPH III

HERE WE SEE the supreme headquarters, or lair if you were a competitor, of the World's greatest railroad. As Rome was to the Roman Republic and Empire, so was Philadelphia and Broad Street to a Railroad Empire beyond compare to any other. As with the Romans, PRR brought order, incredible accomplishment and magnificence with comparable coercion and brutality. PRR has been described as arrogant, obnoxious and ignorant with some justification. But it was also enormously successful and was literally the keystone in the industrial development of this nation. The reign of PRR was short by the standards of the Roman, but its legacy was as significant. We suspect that the nation will ultimately mourn its passing. *Sic transit gloria mundi.*

Chapter 9

Reflections

Disaster Incarnate

By Charles S. Roberts

When David M. LeVan, the last president of Conrail and ardent but lone voice in the wilderness, departed his post he rather laconically commented that the breakup of Conrail was "a mistake."

In *Triumph I* under the heading Prelude to Disaster we opined in some detail why that title was appropriate. (By the way, we also tried to enlist editorial opposition by a noted publication, without success.)

And in *Triumph II* as *Prelude to Disaster, Act Two* we updated the situation just as the breakup was being put into effect, hoping for the best but fearing the worst.

Now, one year into the breakup, we must confess that even we underestimated the extent of the looming catastrophe. Poor Cassandra. How frustrating her role must have been. Perhaps she too must have wondered if her audience had some kinks in their genetic spirals.

After all the press releases and assorted corporate flack float into the atmosphere, the immutable facts of transportation economics, arithmetic, past experience and financial facts of life remain starkly in place.

For example, the breakup would "enhance competition" and would be justified by grabbing enormous intermodal traffic from truck lines. *In fact, CSX and NS could not even hold the intermodal traffic enjoyed by Conrail because of service failures and congestion.* UPS, a very important railroad customer, first moved much of their traffic from NS to CSX only to revert to trucking for almost all of their movements. On one day in the Fall of 1999, sources say that CSX proudly announced that 26% of UPS trains were on time, a marked improvement over the previous day when only 22% were on time. The same day CSX has 89 "setbacks", trains without power. Very understandably, UPS was not amused by such "victories" and was caustic about the principle of "enhanced competition."

The litany of service collapses and congestion would fill many volumes and certainly no purpose would be served by listing them in this book. A few examples will suffice. In December 1999, a printer in Pennsylvania "served" by NS received only two of 170 cars of paper on time but were billed for 50 cars that were not theirs. "This approaches fraud," screamed the printer.

A desperately needed car of parts for an automobile assembly plant in Baltimore arrived in a nearby yard, but CSX could not find a way to deliver the car to the plant for days, forcing a shutdown and layoffs.

These examples are merely two of *thousands* of such horror stories. Of course, these problems were accompanied by a blizzard of press releases that go on to this moment. If you have read one, you have read them all. "Yes, we have a few problem areas but progress is being made and we will soon find the broad, sunlit uplands of nirvana."

Earnings of both railroads plummeted to the extent that questions were being raised as to the financial viability of both systems. Obviously, their stocks have sunk to new lows. Since there are only three sources of money (equity, debt and earnings) it is reasonable to wonder about the future. No rational person would buy their stock, they are borrowed to the hilt and earnings are reaching the vanishing point.

By the way, we have just read that Carl Icahn has signalled that he wishes to buy into CSX because he feels that CSX stock is undervalued. This gentleman has grown very rich by buying into situations and far be it from us to question his judgement or rationality. We would be delighted, of course, to sell him our books on this subject.

CSX has managed to get in the headlines in recent months. The FRA reported that their maintenance standards had declined to a dangerous level, with wide-gauge causing derailments including Amtrak's *Capitol Limited* at Connellsville PA on 30 January 2000. Shades of Penn Central.

And in April 2000 John W. Snow fired ex-Conrail executive Ronald J. Conway and serveral other ex-cons, as they became known. As nearly as we can discern, none of their replacements have any significant operating or marketing experience. More lawyers and bookkeepers. Mr. Snow himself has taken over the reins of management and promised dramatic improvement in 90 days.

Even STB Chairwoman Linda J. Morgan is wavering, wondering why the "benefits" of the Conrail "transaction" have not been realized.

NS has avoided some headlines, but the picture remains grim. They are now suffering the appellation "Prancing Pony" as congestion is relieved only by the loss of business. Several months ago there were unconfirmed rumors that they were having difficulty making their payroll.

Both railroads are being taunted by shippers that the old Conrail efficiently and effectively handled their shipments. Why can't CSX and NS? Another disquieting development is that some major chemical companies are informing the government that they are locating plants outside the US to get away from U.S. railroads. That captive and highly profitable chemical business may not be so captive after all.

We have, of course, been inundated by contacts from our readers who, in general, say that we predicted the future with precision. Our reply was and will always be that we are not happy to have been right.

The reason for our sadness is really quite simple. The best interests of this nation *require* a strong and viable railroad industry. One just has to look at the incredible congestion on our highways, with attendant pollution, to conclude that *we cannot go on this way.* Gridlock on our highways and airways are cancers on our society. Railroads are a solution for many of these problems. *As they built the nation, they can save it.*

Humpty Dumpty has had a great fall. Who will put Humpty together again?

4 July 2000

Tid Bits

By Charles S. Roberts

The student of railroad history must constantly remind himself of the fundamentals of transportation economics, tenets that reach back to the very early years.

Railroads must *increase the car miles* and *decrease the train miles.* When done to perfection, these principles produce economies unmatched by any other transportation form.

Railroads are very volume sensitive. Adding ten cars to a hundred car train does *not* increase cost by ten percent. While not completely cost-free, extra cars produce gravy revenue. To borrow from publishing/printing economics, once the *"nut"* is made the earnings are as close to printing money as one can get without running any risk of going to jail for counterfeiting.

Making the "nut" is the problem, because the economics in reverse are very painful.

And the great burden for railroads is terminal expense, on *both* ends. Cars must be gathered, formed into trains and then broken up on arrival ... time consuming and expensive. Out on the line of road the costs are so minimal that no other form of transportation can match railroad efficiency.

Why is double-stacking of containers so important? Half the tare, half the cars, half the slack and half the track space. The bugaboo, of course, is clearances.

Now let us wander a bit. The Penn Central collapse has been treated in this and may other books. An ex-PRR gentleman ordered one of our books and in the process stated "What did those New York Central people know about railroading!" To be fair, he later said "Just kidding, of course," but of course he was not. PRR and NYC were at war for so long that interlacing the management structure was doomed to discord and failure.

And on this subject, we want to put to rest an oft-repeated insinuation. Alfred E. Perlman, NYC's last president, was put out in the wilderness after the merger and religious differences were cited by many. This bothered us so much that, through sources, we interviewed a high-ranking NYC executive (retired) on this subject and the reply was unequivocal. Neither Perlman nor anyone else close to the actual events felt there was any merit to such assertions. History can lay a lot on PRR management, but anti-Semitism had nothing to do with it. Nothing.

In this and other books, we have taken more than a few shots at Philadelphia, including "Philadelphia Lawyers." Many years ago, we went up against a Philadelphia law factory named Duane, Morris and Hecksher. We were so impressed with their high ethical standards and competence that we later used them in another matter. And, yes, we did settle the first matter in the men's room.

Also, we should always remember that the Declaration of Independence and our glorious Constitution emanated from Philadelphia, to say nothing of PRR.

We characterize our House as journalist/historians with *no ties* to any of our subjects. We write and publish interpretative history, not sterile so-called "scholarly" history. We are completely independent and seek no "approvals" or endorsements other than from our readers and posterity. No public money, directly or indirectly, supports our activities.

And we are burdened in the search for truth because the vast majority of published sources are tainted by corporate sponsorhip.

There are a few shrill voices who find our "editorializing" on various subjects to be "grating."

Noted journalist Frank Miller, Jr., has stated that "The day you write to please everyone you are no longer in journalism. You are in Show Business." That some find our views to be "grating" is a measure of our success in our profession.

We have addressed a number of issues in our books, all related to the story being told. Will these comments change anything? We haven't the slightest idea.

But many books *have* changed things. A recent example. The heroine of true history authors is the late Barbara W. Tuchman. We worship at her feet to the extent that we insist anyone who wants to write for us must study her works and there will be an exam. In 1962 The Macmillan Company (New York) published her seminal work *The Guns of August*, detailing how Europe blundered into The Great War.

Several months ago we watched a television documentary on the Cuban Missile Crisis of 1962. People who were *present at the discussions* with President John F. Kennedy were interviewed. One of these gentlemen commented that Kennedy had just finished reading *Guns* and announced that he wanted to be sure that we did not blunder into nuclear war as in 1914. Did Tuchman ever think that her book would have any impact on current world history? Hardly. Yet it did.

On a lighter note, we cannot resist the following paraphrase. What is the difference between Jurassic Park and CSX/NS management? One is an amusement park run by dinosaurs. The other is a movie.

The Devil made us do it.

Ponderings

While completing this volume we have had time to review our decision to cover the Philadelphia Terminal Division separately from the Philadelphia Division (described in *Triumph II*). The magnitude of this volume serves as ample testimony to the validity of that decision. The complexity of the multitude of PRR terminals in Philadelphia alone is daunting, but because of the amount of material covering such diverse topics as the development of the yards and port facilities, the fascinating and at times bizarre interactions with the B&O and the Reading, and of course the commuter operations extending out to Chestnut Hill and the Main Line suburbs and even the problematic Schuylkill Branch, PRR's home city clearly warranted a separate volume.

The next – and unavoidable – decision was to omit coverage of the branch lines extending southward from the City and limit discussion of those off the Connecting RR to the Chestnut Hill Branch. The rest seem minor in comparison to the main traffic thoroughfares, although the former may be touched on in a subsequent volume on the Maryland Division.

Reflecting on this volume, we are struck by the saga of the multiple PRR station locations in Philadelphia and the forces that influenced them. Even with this historic insight, it still seems puzzling that it took the railroad nearly 100 years to determine the optimum placement of a world-class terminal. All three previous West Philadelphia stations (the 1864/67 depots, the Centennial station and particularly the 1903 station) were all commendable efforts, but they lacked a suitable track configuration and adequate capacity and support facilities to do the job. Broad Street Station suited the tenor of the times and served commuters reasonably well, but it was in the wrong place for efficient operations. *The combination of Suburban Station in Center City and 30th Street Station in West Philadelphia finally solved the problem of effectively serving both through and local trains and truly represents the long delayed triumph of PRR in Philadelphia.*

However, one still can't help but wonder what things would have looked like if Samuel Rea's original recommendation for a line from Kensington through Center City had come to fruition. With the construction of the Connecting Railway the die was cast for the through route – the City filled in around it and thus we will never know.

The other saga that stands out is the amazing struggle between PRR and just about everyone else involved – B&O, Reading, Jersey Central, even New York Central – for control of *the* north-south route through the City. That PRR prevailed and came to dominate is primarily because of the battles won at either end by John Edgar Thomson, and the vision and determination of A.J. Cassatt, aided and abetted by singular Reading-hater George Roberts, to win the subsequent ones in between (we will examine Cassatt's vision more closely in a later volume in the *Triumph* series on the New York Division). What made this titanic clash even more remarkable is the extent to which it was fomented by individuals, who personally led the battles to accomplish their goal. The battlefield is not a place for timid souls!

Finally, one can lament what has vanished of PRR throughout the system, including on the PT Division, but nowhere has PRR remained more in evidence than on the Main Line. Most of the infrastructure of this line – right-of-way, stations, towers, bridges, overhead catenary, etc. is still remarkably intact and functioning, and many of the stations are being restored to original condition or sensitively rehabilitated. May the triumph and legacy of PRR live on!

David W. Messer

Garth Wise Collection

ANOTHER PROPOSAL (see page 48) envisioned a dramatic high-rise tower facing Market Street, with upper and lower levels of West River Drive passing alongside. There is no indication of an upper-level suburban facility. This design never made it past the concept stage but it certainly would have attracted the eye had it come to fruition.

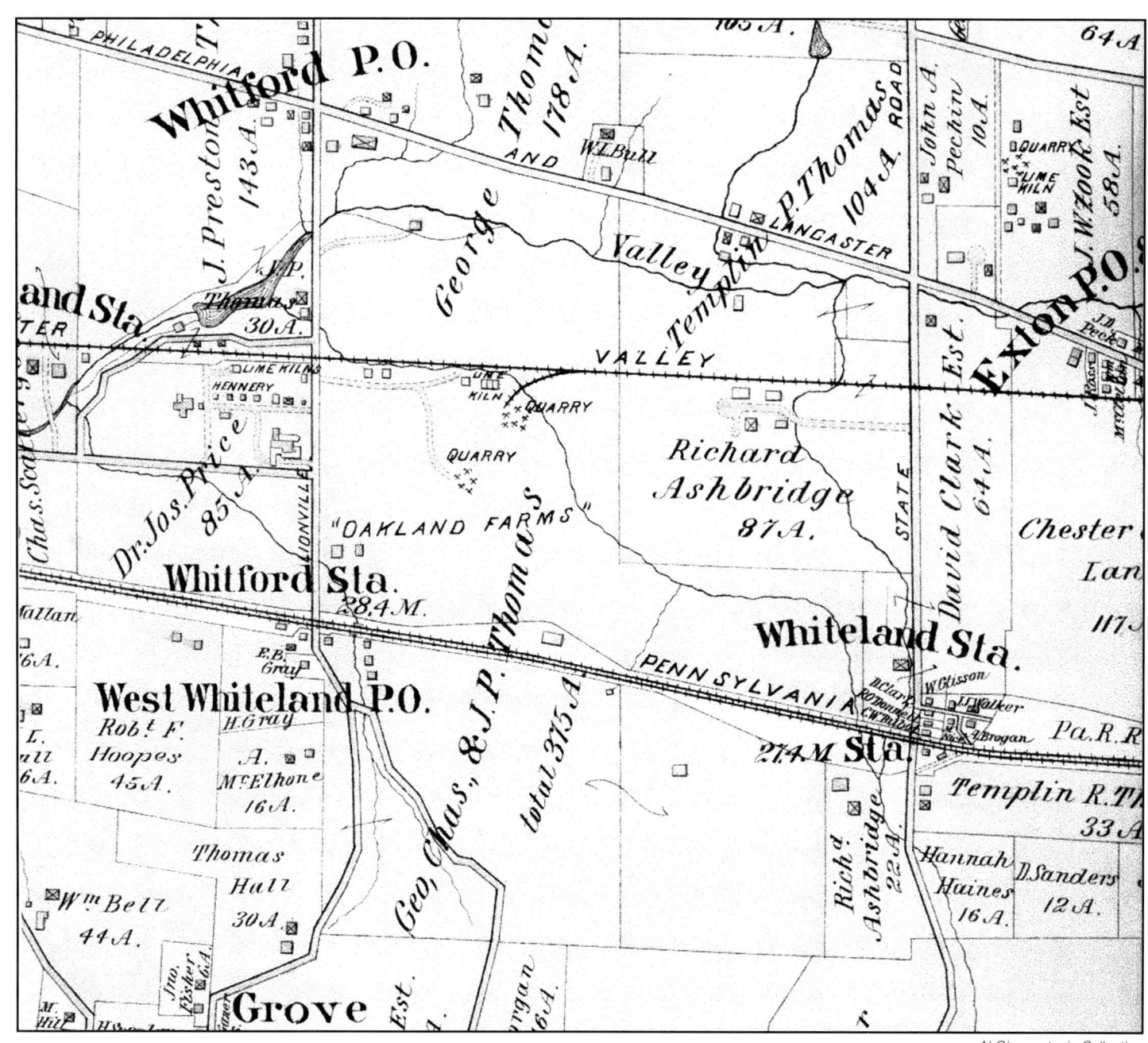

Al Giannantonio Collection

THIS IS WHITFORD, not Whiteland – We refer the reader to the series of photos on pages 65-6 of *Triumph II*, showing trains passing KD (not WD) Tower. Further research by two sharp-eyed Philadelphia-area historians has established that these photos were in fact taken at Whitford, one mile west of Whiteland. Our identification was based on the 1882 PRR List of Stations and Sidings, which puts KD Tower at Whiteland. However, the tower was evidently relocated at some point in its history (see the later map on page 78 of the same volume). The correct location was confirmed by matching the structures shown in the photo on page 66 (particularly the small coal dealership on the south side, also shown on page 70 in later years) with the 1897 Muehler Atlas map shown here. Also, we should note that the delightful Frontispiece photo in *Triumph II* is a view looking westward from the same location. Thanks to Dan DiAddezio and Al Giannantonio for their dedication and scholarship.

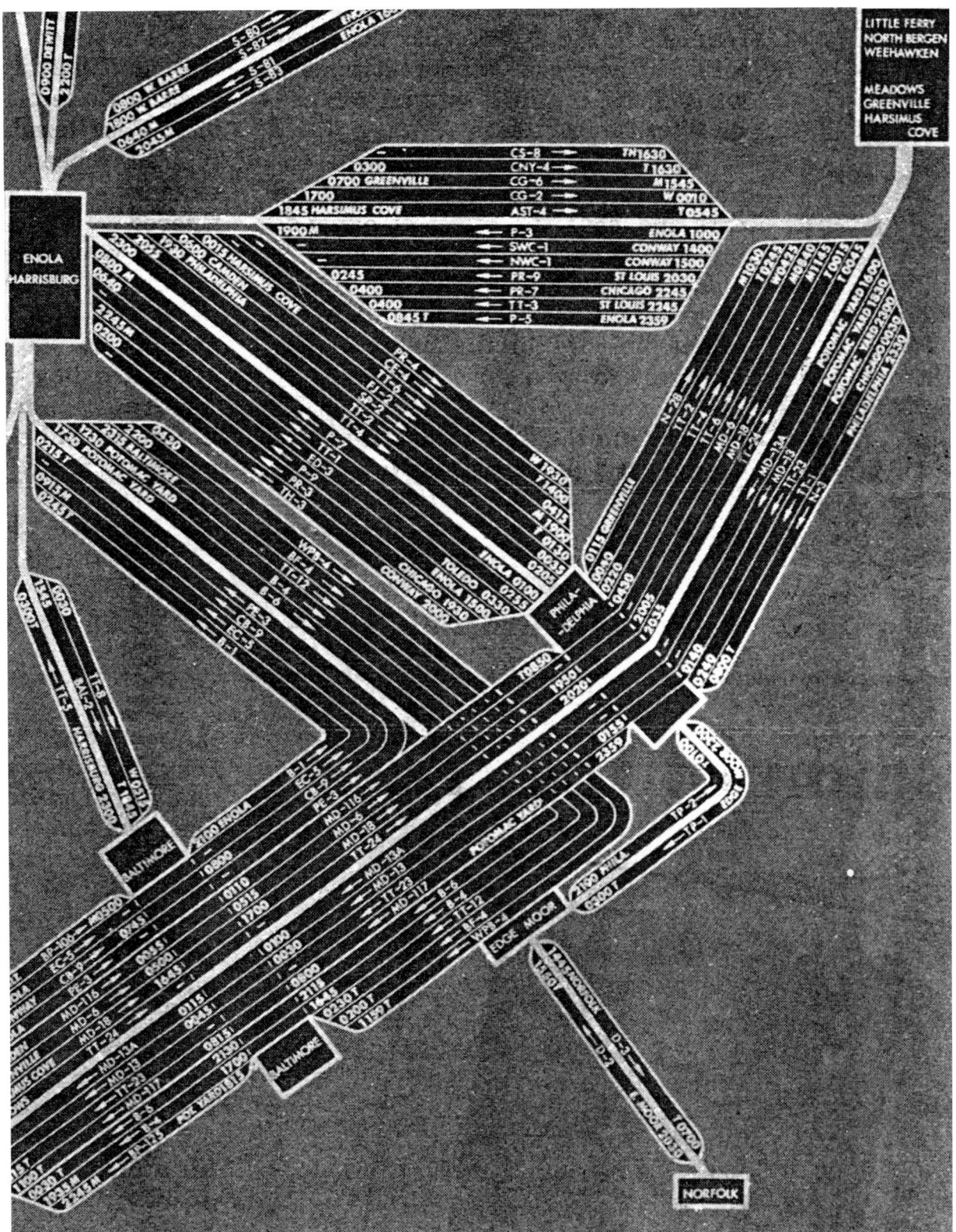

THE PHYSICAL VOLUME carried by PRR has always been awesome, even breathtaking, to every observer. Depicted here are just the symbol freight trains scheduled on 31 December 1968 in the greater Philadelphia area in, of course, the newborn Penn Central era. *Not* shown are passenger trains or mineral trains or extras. This illustration was taken from a 3 by 5 foot wall map which covered the entire Penn Central system and was prepared by Robert R. McPherson, supervisor of freight schedule planning in New York and an ex-NYC manager.

Acknowledgements

As always with an ongoing undertaking of this magnitude, there are many groups and individuals that we would like to thank for their invaluable contributions, both of images and information. Space does not permit acknowledging them all – indeed the identity of some of the long-ago photographers has forever been lost. But several individuals stand out for their contributions "above and beyond," answering repeated questions and even searching for more information or photos.

Special thanks to John Hepp, whose seminar presentation and subsequent thesis on PRR stations in Philadelphia before 30th Street more than any other document provided insight into the historic forces influencing station locations in the 19th Century. I am also indebted to Ted Xaras, a noted local historian and artist who not only harbors a veritable gold mine of early PRR photographic material but who was also willing to share his vast store of knowledge of PRR in Philadelphia, and William Coxey who provided black & white and color images as well as offered repeated and valuable insight into PRR operations in the City.

Proceeding alphabetically from there thanks to the following, who not only contributed material but also answered questions: Christopher Baer, Barbara Hall and Katie Newell, for their assistance in probing the extensive PRR records and photo archives in the Hagley Museum and Library – James Cassatt, Jr., (a distant relative of A.J.) for photos, operating information and continuing words of encouragement – Lois Donovan of the Historical Society of the Phoenixville Area who provided valuable information on the Phoenix Iron Company – Carolyn Fetterolf of the Spring-Ford Area Historical Society for her knowledge and assistance – Dave Kerns of the Pottstown Historical Society who provided valuable insight into the various iron and steel works in that borough – Dave Pfeiffer, who offered continued assistance at the National Archives – Mike Rabbitt who knows more than anyone about the Alan Wood Steel Company – Mike Sherbon who provided assistance with the extensive records in the Pennsylvania State Archives – Kurt Bell of the Railroad Museum of Pennsylvania for his assistance – Fred W. Schneider, III who provided numerous photos both black & white and color – Andrew Wilson, descendent of a PRR vice president, who provided Philadelphia photos and valuable information on George Roberts and the Schuylkill Division.

Finally, thanks to Charley Roberts of Barnard, Roberts for his continuing guidance, expertise and knowledge of railroads, railroad history, railroading and the ever-changing publishing business. Last but certainly not least to my loving wife, Jo-Ann, for her support, patience and understanding throughout this entire endeavor, particularly with the seemingly endless delays and personal financial hardship during the production of *Triumph II*.

Thanks also to the many other contributors who donated examples of their own photographic handiwork as well as other material to document PRR and its successors within the diverse and complex Philadelphia Terminal Division. Many of these individuals offered the hospitality of their home while I perused their collections, a few more than once. All the contributors are noted with each item.

In any case, we continue to hope that this ongoing endeavor will contribute to the knowledge and understanding of the triumph that was – and always will be - PRR.

David W. Messer

Appreciation and thanks also extends to those silent colleagues who contribute so much to the success of every book. Cherie Parkins of Cherie Parkins Designs for typography, page layout and scanning deserves lavish praise. Cherie is the daughter of the late Fran Weber of The Type House, a name familiar to many of our readers. Cherie is her mother's daughter in every sense of the word. And to Mike Goorevitz of MTG Associates for the splendid cover design. Bill Melton did an outstanding job on the "coloration" of the cover photograph. The entire crew of Walsworth Publishing Company, represented so ably by Jenny Shoemaker and Jan Maxwell, have again earned our plaudits. Thank you!

Charles S. Roberts

Bibliography

BOOKS AND REPORTS

Alexander, Edwin P., *The Pennsylvania Railroad – A Pictorial History*, Bonanza Books, New York, 1967.

Alexander, Edwin P., *On the Main Line – The Pennsylvania Railroad in the 19th Century*, Bramhall House, New York, 1971.

Ball, Don Jr., *The Pennsylvania Railroad – 1940s-1950s*, Elm Tree Books, Chester, VT, 1986.

Bowen, Eli, *The Pictorial Sketch-Book of Pennsylvania*, Willis P. Hazard, Philadelphia, 1852.

Brands, H.W., *T.R. – The Last Romantic*, Basic Books, New York, 1997.

Chancellor, Paul, *A History of Pottstown, Pennsylvania*, Historical Society of Pottstown, 1953.

Cupper, Dan (Editor), *The Pennsylvania Railroad – Its Place in History, 1846-1996*, Philadelphia Chapter, PRRT&HS, Wayne, PA, 1996.

Day, Sherman, *Historical Collections of the State of Pennsylvania*, Port Washington, NY, 1969 reprint of 1843 original.

Dredge, James, *The Pennsylvania Railroad – Its Origin, Construction and Management*, John Wiley & Sons, London and New York, 1879.

Daughen, Joseph R. and Binzen, Peter, *The Wreck of the Penn Central*, New American Library, New York, 1971.

Dubin, Arthur D., *Some Classic Trains*, Kalmbach Publishing Co., Milwaukee, 1964.

Harwood, Herbert H. Jr., *The Royal Blue Line*, Greenburg Publishing Co., Sykesville, MD, 1990.

Hepp, John H. IV, *Before 30th Street: A Century of Pennsylvania Railroad Passenger Terminals in Philadelphia, 1833-1933*, presented at the PRR Sesquicentennial Symposium, Railroad Museum of Pennsylvania, Strasburg, PA, October 11-13, 1996.

Highsmith, Carol M. and Holton, James L., *Reading Terminal and Market*, Chelsea Publications, Washington, D.C., 1994.

Holton, James L., *The Reading Railroad: History of a Coal Age Empire*, Volume I (1989), Volume II (1992), Garrigues House, Laurys Station, PA.

Jacobs, Timothy, *The History of The Pennsylvania Railroad*, Bonanza Books, Greenwich, CT, 1988.

McGonegal, Robert S., *Heart of the Pennsylvania Railroad*, Kalmbach Publishing Co., Milwaukee, 1996.

Messer, David W., *Triumph II – Philadelphia to Harrisburg 1828-1998*, Barnard, Roberts & Co., Baltimore, 1999

Roberts, Charles S., *Triumph I – Altoona to Pitcairn 1846-1997*, Barnard, Roberts & Co., Baltimore, 1997.

Roberts, Jeffrey P., *Railroads and the Downtown: Philadelphia 1830-1900*, in *The Divided Metropolis – Social and Spatial Dimensions of Philadelphia, 1800-1975*, Cutler, William W., III and Gillette, Howard, Ed., Greenwood Press, Westport, CT, 1980.

Schotter, H.W., *The Growth and Development of The Pennsylvania Railroad Company*, Allen, Lane & Scott, Philadelphia, 1927.

Staufer, Alvin F., *Pennsy Power I (1962), II (1968), III (1993)*, all by the author, Medina, OH.

Toll, Jean Barth and Schwager, Michael J. (Editors), *Montgomery County [PA] – The Second Hundred Years*, Montgomery County Federation of Historical Societies, 1983.

Ward, James A., *J. Edgar Thomson – Master of the Pennsylvania*, Greenwood Press, Westport, CT, 1980.

Weigley, Russell (Ed.), *Philadelphia – A 300 Year History*, W.W. Norton & Co, New York, 1982.

Wilson, William B., *History of the Pennsylvania Railroad Company*, 2 volumes, Henry T. Coates & Co., Philadelphia, 1899.

(unsigned), *Guide for the Pennsylvania Railroad*, T.K. and P.G. Collins (printers), Philadelphia, 1855.

PRR/PC/CONRAIL PUBLICATIONS AND RECORDS

Annual Reports, 1846-1968.

Burgess, George H. and Kennedy, Miles C. of Coverdale & Colpitts, Consulting Engineers, *Centennial History of the Pennsylvania Railroad Company, 1846-1946*, by the railroad, Philadelphia, 1949.

Collins, T.K. and P.G., *Director's View – 1855*, prepared for a stockholders and directors tour.

Coverdale & Colpitts, Consulting Engineers, *The Pennsylvania Railroad Company*, by the railroad and press of Allen, Lane and Scott, Philadelphia, ca. 1947.

Sipes, William B., *The Pennsylvania Railroad: Its Origin, Construction, Conditions and Connections*, by the railroad, Philadelphia, 1875.

Warner, Paul T., *Motive Power Development on the Pennsylvania Railroad System 1831-1924*, reprinted from the periodical "Baldwin Locomotives," probably by PRR, Philadelphia, 1924.

Watkins, John Elfreth, *History of the Pennsylvania Railroad Company 1846-1896*, 3 volumes, unpublished, ca. 1896.

Closing Broad Street Station, Pennsylvania Railroad, Eastern Region, Philadelphia Terminal Division, April 1952.

Employees Time Table No. 29, Pennsylvania Railroad System, Eastern Region – Philadelphia Terminal Division, April 25, 1937.

The Pennsylvania Railroad System at the Louisiana Purchase Exposition – Locomotive Tests and Exhibits, St. Louis, Missouri, 1904, by the Railroad, Philadelphia, 1905.

Various correspondence files, reports and memos (primarily PRR Engineering Dept.), as well as employee timetables and other operating publications.

PERIODICALS

The High Line, various issues 1990-1998, Philadelphia Chapter, PRRT&HS, and especially the following:

    Blardone, Charles Jr., *The Broad Street Station Fire of 1943*, Vol. 4, No. 1, Autumn 1983.

    Gross, Win, with Maguire, Rick, *Remembering Broad Tower*, Vol. 15, No. 1, March, 1996.

    Lynch, J.D. Jr., *A Brief History of "A" Tower*, Vol. 4, No. 1, Autumn 1983.

    Lynch, J.D. Jr., *The Chestnut Hill and Fort Washington Branches*, Issue No. 6, May 1982.

    Lynch, J.D. Jr., *The Proposed Darby Creek Low-Grade Freight Line – The Main Line From Overbrook to Paoli*, Vol.17, August 1999.

Mullen, Joseph G., *"A" Tower Operation*, Ibid.

Penrose, Robert L. *PRR Dispatcher – Part 1*, Vol. 10, No. 3, Spring 1990 and *Part II*, Vol. 10, No. 4, Summer 1990.

Penrose, Robert L. *The Frankford Change of Line*, Vol. 17, August 1999.

Underkofler, Allen P., *The Philadelphia Improvements – Part I*, Vol. 2, No. 2 and 3, May 1979, and *Part II*, Vol. 3, No. 1 and 2, September 1980.

Underkofler, Allen P., *46th Street Enginehouse*, Vol. 12, Nos. 2 and 3, Winter 1991/Spring 1992.

The Keystone, various issues 1990-1998, PRRT&HS.

National Railway Bulletin, Bruno, Malcolm L. and Purcell, Patrick E., *Schuylkill Valley – The Route of the Anthracite Express*, Vol. 46, No. 4, 1981.

Philadelphia Inquirer, various issues 1995-9.

Railway Age, various issues 1935-1944, and especially the following:

Howard, Neal D., *Philadelphia Improvements of the Pennsylvania Near Completion*, Vol. 97, No. 4, July 28, 1934.

The Railroad Gazette, Winery, S., *Improvements on the Pennsylvania Railroad*, Vol. XXXV, No. 13, March 27, 1903

Time Magazine, *The Pennsy's Predicament*, March 1948.

Trains Magazine, various issues, and especially the following:

Pennypacker, Bert, *The Grandest Railway Terminal in America*, December 1983.

Palmer, David, *Zoo Tower in Twilight*, March 1999.

MISCELLANEOUS

Baist's Atlas of the City of Philadelphia, G. Wm. Baist, Philadelphia, 1888.

Atlas of the City of Philadelphia, George W. and Walter S. Bromley, Philadelphia, 1910.

Atlas of Properties on the Mainline of the Pennsylvania Railroad, A.H. Meller & Co. Philadelphia, 1912.

Notes Regarding Certain Stations on the Main Line of the Pennsylvania Railroad, Mrs. Charles Carroll Suffren, Strafford, PA, January 2, 1949, Unpublished Manuscript in the Pennsylvania State Archives.

Reports from Her Majesty's Diplomatic and Consular Office Abroad on Subjects of Commercial and General Interest, Part IV- Pennsylvania Railroad, Harrison & Sons, London, August 1884.

Credit for certain material such as maps, track diagrams, photographs and specific sources are given throughout the volume.

Index

A (Tower) 32-4
Adamsdale 277
Alan Wood Steel Co. 228-31
Allen Lane 124, 358
ALLEN LANE 124
Amtrak 19, 340-1, 344-6
Anthracite 210-14, 279, 281-3
Anthracite Express 214, 256
AQ 124
Ardmore 177-8
Army-Navy Game 310-13, 362-3
ARSENAL 53, 311, 315, 326-7, 381-2, Rear Endpaper
Arsenal Bridge 288, 293-4, 333
Atterbury, W.W. 17, 71
Athensville 177
Auburn 276
AUSTIN(GK) 127

B (Tower) 34
Bala (Cynwyd) 216
Baltimore & Ohio RR 287, 295-6, 298-9, 307, 316-20, 330, 338
Barmouth 217
Belmont Branch 89, 315, 319, 380
Berwyn 199-200, 371-2
Bethlehem Steel 261
Betzwood 236-7
Bevan, David 343-4
Birdsboro 264-5
Bridesburg 154
Bridges 56-8, 64, 66, 92-3, 103-5, 112-116, 144-5, 215, 218-20, 237-8, 240-1, 250, 257, 262, 265-6, 269-71, 273-4, 276-7, 279-82, 288-90, 293-4, 375-6, Frontispiece
BRILL(FY) 315, 335
BROAD 53
Broad Street Station 13-18, 29-51, 54-5, 339, 384
Broadway Limited 112, 155, 165, 341, 360
BROOKE (P&R) 264
Bryn Mawr 162, 181-3, 364-5
BRYN MAWR(WH) 162, 183-4, 364-5
Bustleton Branch 146, 158
Butler St. Freighthouse 149

C (Tower) 57, 77
Carpenter 123
Cassatt, James 318-9
Centennial Exposition 12-3, 94-6, 196
Centennial Station 12-3, 15, 28, 73-4
Center City Commuter Connection 345, 347-9
Chelten Avenue 122

Chestnut Hill 126-8, 359
Chestnut Hill Branch 109-10, 118-27
Chinese Wall 16-7, 44-6, 56
Civil War Traffic 12, 316, 326
Connecting Railway 107-42
Conrail 344-5, 377-380, 383, 385-6
Conshohocken 227
Cresheim Junction 125
Cromby 251-2
Curve Reduction 140, 176, 199
CW 125
Cynwyd 217

D (Tower) 80
Darby Creek Line 100
Darkwater 282
Daylesford 201
Delair Bridge 144-5
Delaware Extension 284-313, 326
Delaware River RR & Bridge Co. 140, 144-5
Devault 250
Devon 197-8, 370
Douglassville 262

Eagle 195
Electrification 16, 110, 163-6, 214
Enginehouses 13, 73-5, 79-81, 97-9, 357

Fairhill Branch 137
Fairmount Park 94
Federal Street Yard 304, 307
Filbert Street Extension 13, 16-7, 44-6, 56, Frontispiece
FORD(FJ) 146, 152
Fort Washington Branch 110, 125, 128-9
Four-tracking 12, 163, 201
Frankford 153
Frankford Junction 140-2, 147-8, 361
FRANKLIN 235
Frazer Branch 248-50, 345
Furness, Frank 14, 338
FY 335

G (Tower) 80
Garrett, John 317-9
GD 131
General Wayne Inn 170
Germantown Junction 130
Gibbs & Hill 164, 6
Girard Avenue Bridge 245
Girard Point Branch 285-6
Girard Point Storage Co. 286, 296-7
GK 127

Gorman, Paul 343-4
Gowen, Franklin 317-8
Grain Depot 57, 77-8
Grays Ferry Branch 292, 319, 324-5, 332
Grays Ferry Yard 330-2
Great Fill 173, 175
Greenough, Allen 341-2
Greenwich (Point) 285-7, 298-301, 306, 309
Greenwich Yards 285-7, 303-4, 309-10, 352, 378-9
Griffen Gun 243

H (Tower) 84, 86
Hamburg 274
Haverford 179
Haws Avenue 236
HG 157
High Line 286-90, 292, 324-6, 351, 377
Hill Crest 129
HOLMES 146, 157-8, 363
Holmesburg Junction 156-8, 362-3

Iron and Steel Industry 210-1, 218, 224, 228-31, 242-7, 259-61, 267

Junction RR 11-2, 89, 291, 314-22

K (Tower) 87
Kensington 151
Kensington Branch 150-2
Kensington Viaduct 138

Leesport 273
Liberty Place 19, 352
Liddonfield 159

Main Line 160-207, 364-74
Manayunk 218-223, 375
Mantua Junction, Tower, Yard 62, 84-5, 90-1
Market East 345, 349
Market Street Bridge 56, Frontispiece
McClintic-Marshall Co. 260-1
McComb, Col. Henry 318-9
Merion 170-2, 364
Minersville Branch 213, 282-3
Mont Clare 238, 376
Morgan, J. P. 319
Morgan's Corner 188
Mt. Carbon 278-9
MP54's 164, 174, 186, 190, 207, 367-9, 374
MQ 173

Narberth 172-4
New Haven RR 342

395

Newkirk Viaduct 333
New York Central RR 317, 341-3
New York Junction 86-7
New York Subway (tunnel) 85-8
NJ Transit 351, 360
NORRIS 235
Norristown 232-6
Norristown Improvements 233-4, 236
Northeast Corridor 329, 340-1, 346
North Penn Junction 137
North Philadelphia 15, 110, 119, 130-6, 346, 350, 360
NORTH PHILADELPHIA 131, 146
NR 115

Oaks 238
Ontario Street Freighthouse 149
OV 201
Overbrook 167-9
OVERBROOK(OB) 161, 167-8
Overbrook Maintenance Facility 345, 350
Oxford Road Branch 137

Paoli 202-7, 346, 372-4
PAOLI (PA) 161, 205-6, 372-3
PARK 215
Parker Ford 255-6
Pencoyd 216
Pencoyd Branch 218
PENN 53, 69
Penn Center 18-9, 55, 342
Penn Central RR 19, 341-4
Perlman, Alfred 341-4
Philadelphia, Baltimore & Washington RR (PB&W) 22-3, 287, 292, 319-20, 332
Philadelphia & Columbia RR 20, 162-3
Philadelphia Improvements 16-8, 46-55
Philadelphia Port Facilities 285-7, 296-310
Philadelphia Rapid Transit Co. 54, 64-5
Philadelphia Stations (passenger) 9-69, 73-6
    Kensington (1834/40s - P&T, 1882-PRR) 151
    8th and Market (1850) 10, 25
    18th and Market (1853) 10-11, 25
    11th and Market (1843 - PW&B, 1853 - PRR) 11, 25
    Broad and Washington (1852 - PW&B) 336-7
    13th and Market (1853) 11, 25-7
    30th and Market (1864/7) 12, 27
    31st and Chestnut (1866 - WC&P)
    40th Street (1868) 85, 91
    52nd Street (1869/87/1903) 99-105
    32nd and Market (1876) 12, 15, 28, 73-4

    Broad Street (1881/93) 13-8, 29-51, 54-5
    Powelton Avenue (1882) 14-5, 80-1
    North Philadelphia (1901) 15, 110, 119, 130-6, 350, 360
    West Philadelphia (1903) 15, 59-61, 75
    Suburban (1930) 17, 46-7, 51-5, 353
30th Street (1933) 17-9, 64-9, 76, 353-5
Philadelphia Stations (freight)
    8th and Market (1850) 25
    13th and Market (1863) 11, 25-7
    31st and Market (1878) 59
    15th and Market (1881) 13, 31-2, 35
    52nd Street Transfer (1887) 96-8, 102
    17th and Market (1889) 14, 35
    30th and Market (1864) 27
    Broad and Washington (1876 - PW&B, 1881 - PRR) 337
    30th and Market (1889) 59-61
    Mantua (1883) 84
    North Philadelphia (1889/1903) 130, 136
    Ontario Street (1890) 149
    South Philadelphia Terminal (1928-9) 287, 304-5
    32nd and Chestnut (1929) 324-5
    Butler Street (1953) 149
Philadelphia & Trenton RR 20, 108-11, 143-59
Philadelphia, Wilmington & Baltimore RR (PW&B) 11, 20-2, 291, 294, 315-21, 330-1, 333, 336, 339
Philadelphia Zoo 85-6, 88-90
PHOENIX 247
Phoenix Bridge Co. 245
Phoenix Iron (& Steel) Co. 242-7
Phoenixville 241-8
Pittsburgh Subway (tunnel) 85-6
PN 247
Point Breeze Branch 286-7, 295
Port Clinton 276
Port Facilities 296-304, 306-10
Position Light Signals 164
Post Office 66-7, 325, 380
Pott, John, 281
Potts, John, 258
Pottstown 258-61, 376
Pottsville 280-2
Powelton Avenue Footbridge 80-2
Powelton Avenue Station 14-5, 80-1

Queen Lane 121

R (Tower) 191-2
Radnor 188-9, 367
Rea, Samuel 38-40, 347
Reading 267-72

Reading Iron Co. 267
Reading RR 15, 210-4, 223, 225-7, 233, 248-9, 251, 253, 258, 261, 263-4, 275-6, 283, 316-20, 345, 347-9
Reed Street Yard 307-8
Reeves Family 243-6
Roberts, George 70, 210, 216, 317-20
Rosemont 185

St. Asaph's 216
St. Clair Tunnel, 213, 282
St. Davids 190-1, 367
St. Martins 126, 359
Saunders, Stuart 342-4
Schuylkill Branch/Division 99-102, 208-83, 345, 375-6
Schuylkill Canal 210, 222, 232, 238-9, 253, 262-3, 266, 376
Schuylkill Haven 277
Schuylkill River 210-14, 251-4
Schuylkill River Branch 62, 286, 291
Schuylkill River Branch Extension 286
Schuylkill River Bridge 112-6
Schuylkill Valley Metro 346
SEPTA 186, 344-6, 349-50, 374
Shackamaxon Street Yard 308
Shawmont 224
Shoemakersville 273
Shops 73-5, 77-82, 98-9, 206-7, 374
SHORE 138-9, 146, 360
Silverliners 186, 207, 305
South Philadelphia Improvements 303-4
Southwark RR 321
Spring City 253-4
Spring Mill 226
STADIUM 310, 378
Staggers Act 345
Stockyards 73-5, 332-3
Stowe 261
Strafford 193, 196, 369-70
Suburban Station 17, 46-7, 51-5, 353
Symes, James 341-2
Swanson Street Branch 298-9, 304
SWEDE 235
SZ 196

Tacony 155
Tacony Branch 146
Thayer, Nathaniel 318
Thomson, John Edgar 11, 109, 317, 329
Towers 32-4, 53, 69, 84, 86, 90, 106, 131, 138-9, 146, 152, 167-8, 183, 196, 201, 205-6
Trenton Avenue Elevated 150
Trenton Cutoff 14, 129, 163, 231

TrucTrain 287, 341
Tulpehocken 122, 358

Upper Merion & Plymouth RR 228-31
Upsal 123
Upton 177, 188

VALLEY 215
Vanderbilt, W. H. 317-8, 343
Villanova 186-7, 366
VN 138-9

War Memorial 19, 68
Washington Avenue Branch 298-9, 303-4, 307, 315, 377

Wayne 192-4, 368
Wernwag, Louis 242
West Chester Branch 327-9, 332
West Chester & Philadelphia RR (WC&P) 291, 321, 323, 330
Westmoreland 120
West Philadelphia Elevated Branch 286-90, 292
West Philadelphia Office Building 17, 66
West Philadelphia Shops 73-5, 77-82
West Philadelphia Station (pass.) 15, 59-61, 75
West Philadelphia Yards 62, 72-6, 79-83
WH 183-4
White Hall 180-1
Whitemarsh 129

Wilson Brothers 13, 31, 78, 177, 181
Wissinoming 154
WO 259
WOODBINE 105
Woodland Cemetery 291, 329
Wynnefield 215
Wynnewood 175, 364

Yards 72-6, 79-86, 89-91, 96-102, 105-6, 130, 137, 140, 142-3, 147-8, 288, 291-2, 307-9, 324-6, 330-3, 355, 362, 378-9
Young, Robert 341

ZOO 53, 86, 88-90, 315, 346, 356, Rear Endpaper